Reader Comments

MW00775236

What People are Saying About the *Cherrypickers' Guide*

"The *Cherrypickers' Guide* is **the ultimate reference for variety collectors.** As a cataloger, I keep a copy of the book on my desk and refer to it constantly. When I travel to conventions, I never leave home without it."

Mark Borckardt
Numismatic researcher, Heritage Auctions

"I cannot imagine collecting U.S. coins without a copy of the *Cherrypickers' Guide* near at hand. In this latest volume, editor Ken Potter adds his expertise to the **rock-solid foundation** built by J.T. Stanton and Bill Fivaz."

Q. David Bowers
Chairman emeritus, Stack's Bowers Galleries
Numismatic director, Whitman Publishing, LLC
Research Editor, **A Guide Book of United States Coins**

"The *Cherrypickers' Guide* is **entertaining, educational, and useful in a thousand ways.**"

Kenneth Bressett
Past president, American Numismatic Association
Senior Editor, **A Guide Book of United States Coins**

"Numismatics should always be **a voyage of discovery, of learning new facts and having fun** in the process. I can think of no single, better resource for discovery, facts, and fun than the *Cherrypickers' Guide*. I still have a dog-eared copy of the first edition; when it was published, I predicted it would become a standard reference, running through edition after edition. And I was right."

Richard Doty
Senior Curator of Numismatics, the Smithsonian Institution
Author of **America's Money, America's Story**

"No numismatic reference grabs me the way the *Cherrypickers' Guide* does each and every time a new volume is published. I immediately devour the whole book as fast as I can. Now with Ken Potter as editor it should become even more popular. I love my numismatic library and this book is easily the most often used of them all!"

Mike Ellis
Governor, American Numismatic Association
Past president, CONECA

"**The launch pad for the die-variety revolution** was the landmark reference by Bill Fivaz and J.T. Stanton called the *Cherrypickers' Guide to Rare Die Varieties.* With this book the scene was set for an explosion in the way collectors collected. Previously it was just by date and mintmark. Now, it's by date, mintmark, and rare die variety."

Michael S. Fey
Author, **Top 100 Morgan Dollar Varieties**

"One of the great thrills of numismatics is to discover an unattributed rarity. The *Cherrypickers' Guide* provides the tools for anyone to make such a discovery. **A great book for beginners or advanced collectors!**"

Jeff Garrett
Numismatic author and coin dealer; governor, American Numismatic Association Valuations editor, **A Guide Book of United States Coins**

"The *Cherrypickers' Guide* helps identify that rare 'needle-in-a-haystack' variety with **easy-to-use attribution guides and excellent close-up images.** It's handy to carry, easy to navigate, and gives you the knowledge that was once available only to advanced collectors and specialists. One look at the price differential between common and rare varieties makes consulting the *Cherrypickers' Guide* before buying or selling a coin a no-brainer."

Ron Guth
President, PCGS CoinFacts
Coauthor, **100 Greatest U.S. Coins**

"The *Cherrypickers' Guide* continues to be **the standard bearer for popular variety collecting.** Professionally, I use it on an almost daily basis, and it's always within arm's reach."

David W. Lange
Research director, NGC
Author, **History of the United States Mint and Its Coinage**

"Fivaz and Stanton—they're the ones who **almost singlehandedly brought fun back to coin collecting,** along with, incidentally, a horde of new and enthusiastic collectors."

James Taylor
President, ANACS

"I wish I had an off-center cent for every time I referred a caller to check in the *Cherrypickers' Guide* for a die variety they just found. It's the best reference guide to the most important die varieties. The close-up photos make it easy for anyone—novice or advanced collector—to compare and identify their coins. The *Cherrypickers' Guide* is **an absolute must for your numismatic library.**"

Fred Weinberg
Numismatic researcher and Mint-error coin dealer
Coauthor, **100 Greatest U.S. Error Coins**

CHERRYPICKERS' GUIDE

to Rare Die Varieties of United States Coins

Fifth Edition • Volume II
Half Dimes Through Gold, Commemoratives, and Bullion Coinage

1888-O, Doubled-Die Obverse, Morgan Dollar

This dramatically doubled Morgan dollar is popularly known as the "Hot Lips" variety. In Mint State-60 grade, a normal 1888-O dollar is worth perhaps $50. The Hot Lips variety is worth $20,000!

Bill Fivaz · J.T. Stanton
edited by Ken Potter
forewords by Q. David Bowers and Kenneth Bressett

Whitman
Publishing, LLC
PUBLISHING SINCE 1934
www.whitman.com
Atlanta, Georgia

CHERRYPICKERS' GUIDE
to Rare Die Varieties of United States Coins
Fifth Edition • Volume II

© 2012 Whitman Publishing, LLC
3101 Clairmont Road · Suite G · Atlanta, GA 30329

The WCG™ grid used throughout this publication is patent pending. *The Cherrypickers' Guide* is a registered trademark of Whitman Publishing, LLC.

Correspondence concerning this book may be directed to the publisher, Attn: CPG, at the mailing address above.

ISBN: 0794832393
Printed in China

Disclaimer: Expert opinion should be sought in any significant numismatic purchase. This book is presented as a guide only. No warranty or representation of any kind is made concerning the completeness of the information presented. The authors and editor are professional numismatists who regularly buy, trade, and sometimes hold certain of the items discussed in this book.

Caveat: The price estimates given are subject to variation and differences of opinion. Before making a decision to buy or sell, consult the latest information. Past performance of the rare-coin market or any coin or series within that market is not necessarily an indication of future performance, as the future is unknown. Such factors as changing demand, popularity, grading interpretations, strength of the overall coin market, and economic conditions will continue to be influences.

Advertisements within this book: Whitman Publishing, LLC, does not endorse, warrant, or guarantee any of the products or services of its advertisers. All warranties and guarantees are the sole responsibility of the advertiser.

About the Cover: The central featured coin is the Proof 1961 Franklin half dollar with a doubled-die reverse (cataloged as FS-50-1961-801). This is a visually dramatic coin; you don't need a magnifying glass to see its strong doubling. Still, only a small number have come to light in the past few years, so readers are encouraged to search their 1961 Proof sets! A nice example can be worth $7,000 or more. The variety is popular enough to be listed in the *Guide Book of United States Coins* (the hobby's famous "Red Book"), and Rick Tomaska, in the *Guide Book of Franklin and Kennedy Half Dollars*, calls it "the king of 20th-century die varieties."

For a complete catalog of numismatic reference books, supplies, and storage products, visit Whitman Publishing online at www.Whitman.com, or scan the QR code shown on the inside front cover.

DEDICATION

Traditionally each volume of the *Cherrypickers' Guide* has included a dedication to an individual or group from the error-variety segment of the hobby community, for outstanding contributions to numismatics, especially from an educational standpoint. This entry, the fifth edition, volume II, is dedicated to numismatist, authenticator, author, and researcher Larry Briggs.

Well known among coin collectors, Larry has served the American Numismatic Association in numerous capacities, including as president of its Authentication Committee. He is particularly active in the study of Liberty Seated coinage, having served as vice president of the Liberty Seated Collectors Club, and frequently lectures on that coinage series. **Larry Briggs**

His dedication to the hobby includes life membership in the ANA, the American Numismatic Society, Florida United Numismatists, the John Reich Society, CONECA, and other groups; and regular membership in nearly a dozen other specialized and state coin clubs.

"I've been collecting, buying, and selling coins since I bought my first coin from the back page of a comic book," Larry says. "It was guaranteed to be at least 150 years old. It took me three weeks to save enough allowance for that fabulous $1.50 purchase. When the package arrived—an 1803 large cent—it was the most beautiful coin I'd ever seen. Today I can accept the fact that that large cent was, in fact, downright ugly. But it started a love affair with coins that has lasted well over 50 years."

A native of Ohio, Larry is a true Buckeyes fan, an avid fossil collector, and a student of archaeology and history. He served in the U.S. Air Force and worked for Ford Motor Company before launching his business, Larry Briggs Rare Coins, in 1978.

In addition to being a respected coin dealer (focusing on errors and varieties, Liberty Seated coinage, and early American coppers), Larry is the author, editor, or contributor to dozens of numismatic publications, including the *Guide Book of United States Coins* (the "Red Book"), the *Handbook of United States Coins* (the "Blue Book"), and of course the *Cherrypickers' Guide to Rare Die Varieties.*

Authors Bill Fivaz and J.T. Stanton, and editor Ken Potter, are pleased to dedicate this volume of the *Cherrypickers' Guide* to Larry Briggs. They join everyone at Whitman Publishing in thanking Larry for his long service to the numismatic community.

CONTENTS

FOREWORD

Time was when relatively few interesting die varieties were known to the coin-collecting fraternity. The *Guide Book of United States Coins* (the hobby's popular "Red Book," first issued in 1946) listed certain of these, after which ensuing editions listed more. Today the Red Book offers a few hundred, mostly devoted to early coinage issues. Examples include the 1794 copper cent with 94 five-pointed stars on the reverse, one of the most curious varieties of all time; and the cent of 1801 with the reverse having three errors—II and ITED instead of UNITED, one stem missing from the wreath, and the fraction expressed as the mathematically meaningless 1/000. A variety of 1800 silver dollar is called the AMERICAI, because of the extraneous I at the end of the word. Then we have various doubled-die coins, led by the famous 1955 doubled-die Lincoln cent, and joined by the 1916 doubled-die Buffalo nickel and others. With relatively few exceptions, these varieties listed in the Red Book are at once scarce and very expensive.

Q. David Bowers

As interesting as these Red Book–listed coins may be, they are only the tip of the iceberg!

A great change came to the hobby in 1963 when Frank G. Spadone published his *Major Variety and Error Guide*. This popular book was was, for lack of a better expression, for the "common man"—listing many varieties not found in the Red Book, but interesting to collect, and dating mainly from the modern era. Today, Spadone's pioneering work is little remembered, but it remains important as a foundation.

Enter Bill Fivaz and J.T. Stanton and their *Cherrypickers' Guide to Rare Die Varieties*. Greatly expanding the field of opportunity, the authors studied coins mainly from the 20th century and compiled a veritable encyclopedia of interesting repunchings, misaligned mintmarks, and the like. Armed with a copy of this book a collector, with magnifying glass in hand, could review a dealer's stock of seemingly ordinary Lincoln cents and find curious and interesting varieties—mintmarks misaligned or punched over each other, oddities in the lettering, and more. A very nice collection could be formed at modest cost, all the while offering the thrill of the chase.

Today the latest volume of the *Cherrypickers' Guide*, now with well-known expert Ken Potter building upon the work of Fivaz and Stanton, is the latest and most extensive passport to finding treasures. Coin conventions, shops, Internet listings, and even pocket change are the hunting field for varieties that in all instances are fascinating to own, and, in some cases, are very valuable. Recently a 1969-S doubled-die cent in Uncirculated grade was found, the third known, and the value was placed at more than $100,000! You might not find a coin that will enable you to tour the world in grand style for a year, but with the *Cherrypickers' Guide* the chances are very good that you will capture many different coin varieties and enjoy them all.

The treasure map is now in your hands. Good luck!

Q. David Bowers
Wolfeboro, New Hampshire

Since 1953, Q. David Bowers—the "Dean of American Numismatics"—has been active in the hobby as an award-winning author, coin dealer, auctioneer, and researcher. He is chairman emeritus of Stack's Bowers Galleries and numismatic director of Whitman Publishing, and serves as research editor of the Guide Book of United States Coins.

FOREWORD

Kenneth Bressett

There are many different ways to enjoy the hobby of numismatics. Nearly every collector has some uniquely personal motivation as to what is important or how to achieve their goals. The number of different coins available to hobbyists seems endless. The reasons for wanting to acquire, preserve, and classify these coins are equally numerous and complex.

For some collectors it is the thrill of the hunt, for others the pride of ownership or the satisfaction of completing a set or series. For most there is an underlying pleasure in knowing that acquiring a special coin was not only prudent but also profitable. Even the most altruistic collector takes pleasure in seeing that an investment of time and money has paid dividends.

When it comes to selecting coins to fit any collecting agenda, *saber es poder*—knowledge is power. Whatever your objectives are it is vitally important to know that each coin is genuine and to correctly interpret what you are seeing when you examine it. With that thought in mind, the *Cherrypickers' Guide* was written. This book is a gateway to understanding, classifying, and appreciating the many unusual—albeit sometimes minuscule—varieties of United States coins that are often misunderstood or ignored by a vast majority of collectors.

What originally began as a basic listing of valuable varieties that might be disregarded by the casual or traditional collector has, in the latest expanded volume of this book, morphed into a new sphere of specialization that is of interest to thousands of collectors. Taking a more careful look at *all* coins is no longer something reserved for specialists, but a necessity for anyone interested in learning about how coins are made, what can go wrong in the minting process, and why some seemingly unimportant variations can make a difference of hundreds of dollars in value.

Selecting which varieties belong in a specialized book like this is no easy task. Some of the pieces listed here are included to illustrate abnormal coins even though they have little or no premium value. Most listings, however, show which varieties have a numismatic premium that might otherwise go unnoticed by the casual observer. Learning to identify the kinds of variations that are included in this catalog will arm even the most novice hobbyist with a knowledge of what to look for in discovering similar valuable varieties and perhaps open a whole new world of collectible coins.

We are fortunate to have this extensive listing by some of the country's leading experts to guide us through this exciting field of collecting. People frequently asked why certain of these coins are not listed in the *Guide Book of United States Coins* (the "Red Book"). Or why some are there while others are not. The reason is there would never be enough room to include them all in the Red Book, and thus this specialized catalog has been produced. I am sure you will find it entertaining, educational, and useful in a thousand ways.

Kenneth Bressett
Colorado Springs, Colorado

Kenneth Bressett, longtime editor of the best-selling Guide Book of United States Coins *(the "Red Book"), has been active in numismatics since the 1940s. His accomplishments—research, writing, and serving in hobby organizations, including as president of the American Numismatic Association—have earned him nearly every important award in the hobby.*

PREFACE

Numismatist Bill Fivaz, by mid-1989, was well known for his curious habit of searching collections and dealers' inventories for neat coin varieties. Around June of that year, J. Woodside of Scotsman Coins in St. Louis, Missouri, suggested to Bill that he should write a book telling other collectors about his interest. Bill called a friend and fellow variety enthusiast, printer J.T. Stanton, to talk about the idea, and they agreed that such a reference was needed by the hobby community.

Bill and J.T. were very experienced in numismatics, but both were novices when it came to publishing—and certainly not prepared for the monumental project they were about to undertake. Their first thought was to include about 100 of the most significant coinage varieties—the ones that any collector would certainly want. Those 100 varieties quickly grew into more than 160. With that, the two collectors worked out a format for the book, and the first *Cherrypickers' Guide* blossomed.

J.T. was well established in the printing business, so he handled the book's production. The U.S. Postal Service was kept busy as copy was shuttled back and forth between Bill, in Dunwoody, Georgia, and J.T., 275 miles away in Savannah. They sent the final laid-out pages to press in November 1989, hoping to have the book printed, bound, and ready for distribution in time for the Florida United Numismatists (FUN) convention the first weekend of January 1990. On his way to that show in Tampa, J.T. stopped by the bindery in Jacksonville, Florida. His plan was to pick up about 500 copies—a sufficient quantity for the show, they felt, not quite sure how well the book would be received and how brisk its sales would be.

When they left Tampa that Sunday, they had sold all 500 copies, and had a backlog of orders for more to be shipped and mailed as soon as possible.

That first edition of the *Cherrypickers' Guide* was a great learning experience for Bill and J.T. both. They didn't expect to sell the entire initial print run of 3,000 copies, and actually felt lucky when they sold out in less than 10 months. Before long, they planned a second edition, with more listings and the addition of retail values, along with other improvements. Thanks to coverage in the numismatic press and word-of-mouth publicity among variety enthusiasts, excitement grew for the second edition. Dealers and wholesalers wanted the book to offer to their customers. The new edition's print run of 5,000 copies sold out in about six months.

Bill and J.T. were very pleased with the hobby's acceptance of the *Cherrypickers' Guide*—and the fact that grading services were using the Fivaz-Stanton (FS) attribution numbers on their slabs. (To the best of the authors' knowledge, ANACS was the first to recognize a coin with a Fivaz-Stanton designation.) It seemed that Bill and J.T. had luckily stumbled onto a book with the right topic at the right time.

The second edition was made in both regular and spiral-bound formats. "The *Cherrypickers' Guide* might well have been the first mainstream numismatic book to be offered with the spiral or coil binding," says Stanton. This format is perfect for collectors: they can lay the book open to a particular variety without struggling to keep the book flat, leaving their hands free to hold a coin and magnifying glass.

For the third edition, the entire print run was published in the spiral format.

When it was time for that third edition, the authors had a big hurdle to overcome: J.T. simply didn't have time to handle the production. So they set out to find a willing publisher. Several were contacted, and several were interested, with Bowers and Merena being the authors' ultimate choice. They worked to provide the hobby community what would become their best effort yet. The third edition featured about five times as many varieties as the first; it went to six printings and more than 28,000 copies before the fourth edition finally came out.

Since J.T. was in the business of printing (and by this time some publishing), he and Bill asked famous numismatist Q. David Bowers (a principal of Bowers and Merena) if they could produce the fourth edition themselves. Being the gentleman everyone knows, Bowers immediately agreed—if that's what they wanted, that's what he wanted.

The fourth edition became by far the duo's largest effort to that date, so large in fact that it had to be divided into two volumes to accommodate the spiral binding. Volume I included half cents through nickels. Volume II (published by Whitman Publishing in 2006) picked up with half dimes and bigger denominations. The division was a natural one. Volume I contained all minor coinage, and there are a lot of people who collect only cents and nickels. Volume II included other popular series comprising silver half dimes through dollars (including Bust and Liberty Seated series), federal gold coinage, and commemoratives.

The fifth edition, volume I, carried on the *Cherrypickers'* tradition, with updated market information, new varieties, a new appendix on the minting process, and other improvements.

Now, with the fifth edition, volume II, Bill Fivaz and J.T. Stanton—while remaining involved in the book's production—have passed the torch to a new editor. Ken Potter is well known in the hobby as a coin dealer, a published researcher, and the consummate die-variety specialist. His finger is constantly on the pulse of the variety-collecting segment of numismatics. Thanks to Ken's coordination and management, this latest volume of the *Cherrypickers' Guide* includes dozens of upgraded photographs, more than 100 new listings, updated content, and even a whole new section on silver, gold, and platinum bullion-coin varieties. Ken has brought together a team of pricing experts and analysts to provide the most accurate market pricing on the coins listed. The book is 32 pages longer than the fourth edition's volume II, and it features nearly 800 unique varieties—about five times the coverage of the first edition published twenty-some years ago.

"The *Cherrypickers' Guide* proves that there are times when someone can get lucky, and tackle the right subject at the right time," Bill and J.T. have said. "We've enjoyed the experience of creating the book, and hope our readers have learned a lot from the contributions of all the people who have made it possible—those who have provided varieties and information, and who have made other contributions, including values, rarity data, and other vital details."

The *Cherrypickers' Guide* is nearing its 25th anniversary. If collector enthusiasm is any gauge, it will continue to serve the hobby well beyond.

J.T. Stanton, CONECA past president Mike Ellis, and Bill Fivaz pose with the *Cherrypickers' Guide* at the American Numismatic Association's summer show, Denver, Colorado, 2006.

CREDITS AND ACKNOWLEDGMENTS

Bill Fivaz and J.T. Stanton are the authors of the *Cherrypickers' Guide*—and now Ken Potter has joined the team as the book's editor—but the backbone of the book is the contributions of hundreds of coin collectors, dealers, and specialists over the years. Without those very important people offering new listings, detailed descriptions, rarity information, market values (updated on a constant basis), and detailed knowledge of a variety or series, the *Cherrypickers' Guide* would not have become the popular and indispensable reference that it is today.

Special thanks begins with **Larry Briggs**—for generously sharing his knowledge of new varieties, for offering coins for study and photography, for weighing in with a real-world look at the market, and for moving the book forward in a thousand other ways.

James Wiles, who oversees CONECA's 20th- and 21st-century die-variety files and has authored many books on the subject, contributed countless hours gathering images, taking photographs, and providing technical information for this volume. He shared valuable advice throughout the manuscript's preparation, and reviewed page proofs up to press time.

David W. Lange is the author of many important numismatic books including the *Guide Book of Modern United States Proof Coin Sets* and *History of the United States Mint and Its Coinage.* As the research director at NGC, Dave examines thousands of die varieties every year. He supplies photographs of many new discoveries, and is always happy to share his knowledge with the hobby community.

Rick Snow is another numismatist who gives of his time and talents. Rick is the author of numerous standard references (including Whitman's *Guide Book of Flying Eagle and Indian Head Cents*), and has studied in depth the famous Extra Leaf varieties of the 2004 Wisconsin quarter dollar. He generously shares his expertise.

Richard Bateson, author of *Richard's Roosevelt Dime Review—The Silver Years,* loaned his entire collection of Roosevelt dimes, along with a number of other denominations, to editor Ken Potter for photography.

Brett Parrish provided his expertise in the area of Franklin half dollars, sharing many coins (including RPMs and new doubled dies) for photography along with rarity rating for the "Bugs Bunny" varieties.

Timothy A. Clough provided a number of *Cherrypickers' Guide*–caliber Kennedy half-dollar varieties for photography and offered a number of tweaks for that section of the book.

Larry Nienaber also significantly improved the Kennedy half dollar section by sharing his knowledge and resources.

Michael S. Fey, Ash Harrison, Jeff Oxman, and **John Roberts,** recognized as experts in the Morgan and Peace dollar series, contributed their specialized knowledge to this volume. Fey created a census of the top grades for each VAM variety listed.

Rob Ezerman, of the Ike Group, contributed an enormous amount of information on Eisenhower dollars.

Accurate and timely analysis of pricing in the coin market is very important to hobbyists. We're fortunate to rely on the expertise of seasoned dealers—among them **Jack Beymer, Larry Briggs, Ash Harrison, Dick Osburn,** and **Rick Snow**—in helping in the compilation of values given in this volume of the *Cherrypickers' Guide.*

John Wexler, author of dozens of books on varieties and often referred to as the "Grandfather of Doubled Dies," spent countless hours digging through his archive of images and shooting new photos for this volume.

There are numerous other collectors, dealers, and specialists who have contributed since the first edition of the *Cherrypickers' Guide.* We wish to thank all those variety enthusiasts who are willing to share their coins, photographs, knowledge, and experience. Those who have contributed to this and previous volumes are noted here. If we have missed anyone it is with our most sincere apologies.

Bill Affanato	Bill Bugert	Rick DeSanctis	Robert Griffiths
Leonard Albrecht	B. Buholtz	Daniel Dodge	Linda Hagopian
Roger Alexander	Vincent Burke	J.T. Donahue	Richard Hana
Brian Alford	Ty Buxton	David Druzisky	Joe Haney
Brian Allen	Cameo Coin	Justin Duane	Rob Hanks Jr.
Matt Allman	Gallery	Elliott Durann	Lloyd Hanson*
Gary Alt	David J. Camire	Edgewood Coin Co.	B.D. Harding
ANACS	Will Camp	Brian Edwards	Linda Harp
Walter Anderson	Terry Campbell*	Harry Ellis*	Ash Harrison
Guy Araby	Donald Cantrell	Mike Ellis	Tom Hart
Richard Austin	Rick Carpenter	Larry Emard	Donald Hauser
Chuck Avery	Jennifer Casazza	Bill Erdokos	James W. Hay
Saverio Barbieri	Charles Cataldo Jr.	Richard Evans	Dennis Heard
Richard Bateson	Ken Chylinski	Rob Ezerman	Doug Heisler
Frank Baumann	Nicholas Ciancio	Michael "Skip"	Richard Helbig
Joe Beaupied	Ted Clark*	Fazzari	John Hemphill
Ed Becker	Clem Clement	Joe Feld	Alan Herbert
Roger Beckner	Mark Clewell	Ron Fern	Ronald Hickman
Steve Bernatowicz	Tim Clough	Michael Fey	Lee Hiemke
Jack Beymer	Blaine Coffey	Gerald Fishman	Doug Hill
David Biglow	*Coin World*	Jason Fishman	Ken Hill
Dick Bland	Lou Coles	Ed Fletcher	Mike Holstein
Al Blythe*	Frank Colletti	Kevin Flynn	ICG
Cliff Bolling	CONECA	Gerry Fortin	The Ike Group
Don Bonser	Jim Conrad*	Geoffrey Fults	Adrian Jellinek
John Bordner	Edward Cook	Paul Funaiole	Jim Jones
Q. David Bowers	Bert Corkhill	Bill Gase	Martin Jordan
Charlie Boyd*	José Cortez	Paul Geiserbach	Matt Juppo
Mike Bozovich	Billy Crawford	Ray Gelewski	Mike Jurek
Dan Brady	David Crawford	Jack Gorby*	Carl Kanoff
Jym Braun	Whaden Curtis	Don Gordon*	Gary Kelly
Kenneth Bressett	Charles Daughtrey	Rudy Gos	Jerry Kennison
Larry Briggs	Dave's DCW Col-	Mike Gourley	Jonathan Kern
David Brody	lection	Peter Goyos	Jeff Kierstead
Robert Bruce	Ray Davis	Jane Gray	Derry King
Gene Bruder	Lee Day	David Greenfelder	Joe Kirchgessner
Mike Bruggeman	Tom DeLorey	Brian Greer	Keith Klopfenstein*
Paul Bucerel	George Derwart	Bob Grellman	Robert Knauss

* deceased

Gerald Kochel
Bud Kolanda
Martin Krashoc
James Kropp
Harold Kuykendall
L&C Coins
Jim Lafferty
Rick Lajoie
David W. Lange
Frank Leone
Akio Li
Fred Lindsey
Don Lommler
Mark Lowers
Carl R. Loyd
Lee Lydston
Lee Maples
Aimee McCabe
Steve McCabe
Mark McWherter
Roy Maines
Ross Manning
Arnold Margolis
J.P. Martin
Kip Mecum
R.A. Medina
Tom Mendonca
Anthony Mesaros
Michael Mesaros
Michael Michel
Ed Miller
Joe Miller
John Miller
Tom Miller
Ward Miller
Warren Mills
Mike Mizak
MMNS
Michael Morris
David Moss
Wali Motorwalla
Allan C. Murphy
Dan Murray
BJ Neff

NGC
Gene Nichols
Neil Niederman
P. Nilson
John Nogosek
Charlie Nowack
Numismatic News
Numismedia.com
Jim O'Donnell*
Old Pueblo Coin
   Exchange
Dick Osborne
Lynn Ourso
Jeff Oxman
Dick Painter
Mike Paradis
Brett Parrish
Dennis Paulsen
George Pauwells
Richard Pawley
Daniel Pazsint
PCGS
PCI
Ben Peters
Karen Peterson*
Larry Philbrick*
Bob Piazza
Chris Pilliod
Denny Polly
Ron Pope
Ken Potter
Colleen Prebish
Andrew Prechtl*
Al Raddi
Brian Raines
Wayne Rattray
RCNH
Roger Reiner
Paul Reitmeir
Doug Riley
Mike Ringo
Joe Rizdy
John Roberts
Emory Robinson

Rogers' Coins
Del Romines
Lee Roschen
Gary Rosner
P. Scott Rubin
Tony Russo
Bob Ryan
Rick Rybicki
Jerry Sajbel
Steve Santangelo
Charles Schaefer
George Schaetzle
Steve Schmidt
Terry Searcy
SEGS
Mark Serafine
Gary Shaffstall
Blaise Sidor
Rich Sisti
Sue Sisti
E.O. Smith
Jim Smith
Les Leroy Smith
Ruben Smith
Richard Snow
Art Snyder
Terry Souder
Max Spiegel
Howard Spindel
Jeff Stahl
John Starr
Larry Steve
Suzanne Stewart
Bob Stimax
Tom Stott
Jim Stoutjesdyk
Eric Striegel
Dave Stutzman
Andrew Suchan
Kevin Swan
Norm Talbert*
Sol Taylor
David Thacker
Dave Thomas

Jeff Thomas
Carson Torpey
Lee Tucker
Andy Turnbull
Leroy Van Allen
Marilyn Van Allen
John L. Veach
Michael Volz
Gary Wagnon
Dan Walker
Mike Wallace
J.R. Walters
Jonathan Warren
Troy Watkins
Richard Watts
Val Webb
David Welch
John Wells
Dave Welsh
Michael Werda
Vic West
John Wexler
Paul Wheeler
Bill White
Bob White
C.C. Whitaker
John Whitworth
James Wiles
Dave Wilson
Al Windholtz
Chuck Wishon
Tim Wissert
Andy Wong
Jay Woodside
Hank Woods
C.L. Wyatt
Jerry Wysong
Vicken Yegparian
Dan Zaporra
Frank M. Zapushek
Anthony Zito

* deceased

HOW TO USE THIS BOOK

As do most technical reference books (especially those involving numismatics), the *Cherrypickers' Guide* frequently uses abbreviations, acronyms, and numbering systems to identify and attribute its listings as clearly as possible. Most experienced collectors will recognize and understand the format used herein. However, novices will find this section very helpful.

SYMBOLS USED IN THIS BOOK

PC The *Pocket Change* symbol indicates a variety that may reasonably be expected to be found in circulation today.

Pocket Change varieties typically are cents dated after 1959, Jefferson nickels (other than silver wartime issues), dimes and quarters minted after 1964, half dollars minted after 1970, and some circulation-strike modern dollars.

RB The *Red Book* symbol indicates a variety that is listed in the most recent edition of R.S. Yeoman's *Guide Book of United States Coins* (popularly known as the "Red Book"), the best-selling annual price guide of U.S. coins.

YN The *Young Numismatists* symbol indicates a variety that young and/or emerging collectors might want to focus on. Many of these fall into the Pocket Change category as well.

In most cases, coins marked with the YN symbol are varieties of coins that are very inexpensive when found in their "normal" format, either in Mint State or high circulated grades. They usually can be sold for significant premiums through private sale or through auctions (such as those held periodically by CONECA). Finding these varieties can help finance the collection of a numismatist with modest funds.

ABBREVIATIONS USED IN THIS BOOK

DDO	doubled-die obverse	PUP	Pick-Up Point (*see text*)
DDR	doubled-die reverse	R	rarity
I	Interest Factor	RPD	repunched date
L	Liquidity Factor	RPM	repunched mintmark
LD	Large Date	SD	Small Date
MPD	misplaced date	SMS	Special Mint Set
n/a	not available	TDO	tripled-die obverse
NA	No Arrows	TDR	tripled-die reverse
ND	No Drapery	URS	Universal Rarity Scale
N/L	not listed	WA	With Arrows
OMM	over mintmark	WD	With Drapery
PF	Proof		

PICK-UP POINTS (PUPS)

A variety's *Pick-Up Point* is its area most prone to exhibit whatever characteristic(s) makes the variety unique. In most cases, this will be the date, the mintmark, or legends. Other PUPs include denticles, stars, designer's initials, and various design elements.

Variety Value and Normal Value

Throughout the guide we offer values for varieties in several grades of preservation. (For more information on grading, refer to the *Official American Numismatic Association Grading Standards for United States Coins* and *Grading Coins by Photographs: An Action Guide for the Collector and Investor.*) Sources for the values of varieties include:

- actual sales (retail or auction) reported to us, with the most recent sales bearing the most weight;
- our assessments comparing one variety to another similar in rarity, collectibility, interest, and other factors; and
- recommendation by those who specialize in particular series or denominations.

Also included in this volume are fair-market values for each variety's *normal*-version coin. These values are derived from the *Guide Book of United States Coins* (the "Red Book") and the Professional Edition Red Book, 3rd edition. They reflect actual retail sales from some of the most respected dealers across the country. These "normal coin" values provide an easy comparison for the amount or percentage of premium each variety can command.

As with any price guide, the values listed should be used strictly as a reference. Although great pains are taken to ensure as much accuracy as possible, values can and do change, especially among varieties that trade frequently.

Factors Affecting Value

Always keep in mind the two major factors affecting the value of any item: supply and demand. That advice has never been proven wrong. If 10 people want a particular variety and only 6 examples are available, the value will be far greater than a similar variety desired by 10 people with 20 examples available.

With numismatic varieties especially, add to those two factors a very important third: *eye appeal!* As a general rule (there may be very few exceptions), the more visually dramatic a variety, the greater its value. For instance, compare two different repunched dates, with similar rarity and in similar grade, on two 1868 Shield nickels— one with a wide degree of separation and one with a very close separation. The variety with the wide separation will always command a greater price.

Values are subject to change whenever a variety becomes more readily available or more desirable. Variety values certainly change with the normal fluctuations of the numismatic market. Remember that, generally speaking, the higher the numismatic value of a particular coin, the lower the premium associated with its varieties. For example, a nice doubled die on an Uncirculated Liberty Head $20 gold coin will (generally) command little, if any, premium for the knowledgeable collector.

A variety's die state (or stage) can also play an important part in pricing. Earlier die states that show sharper doubling than later die states (where the doubling may be subdued or nearly gone) typically sell for higher prices. Exceptions exist where a later die state may actually be stronger, or other variations to the die may create greater demand, but as a general rule, the earlier the die state, the more the coin is worth to a specialist.

Values for Actively Traded Varieties

Some of the varieties listed in the *Cherrypickers' Guide* are also noted in other hobby price guides that are updated on a regular basis. The values for these varieties, such as the 1955 Doubled-Die Lincoln cent, fluctuate quite often as a result of market trends. In these instances, we highly recommend that you refer to other *current* price guides to obtain an up-to-date value for the variety. Values for these varieties are included in the *Cherrypickers' Guide* for reference only. Collectors and dealers can compare the prices noted with current prices and use the difference as a guide for possibly adjusting other similar varieties.

THE FIVAZ-STANTON (FS) NUMBERING SYSTEM

The Fivaz-Stanton (FS) numbering system dramatically changed in the fourth edition, volume II (published in 2006).

In the older system, adding new listings was problematic as additional decimal places were required in many instances. Furthermore, an attribution number such as FS-05-003.752, or even FS-10c-0.008 was very complicated, and not within the normal thought processes of most collectors. The older system simply left no room for additions. The current system allows for additions to the listings on an ongoing basis, and *without any limitation!*

Reading the Fivaz-Stanton Number

With the Fivaz-Stanton numbering system, the complete listing number includes

- the **denomination,** followed by
- the **date** and **mintmark** (if there is a mintmark), and finally
- the sequential **"identifier" number.**

The identifiers essentially denote the type of variety, and/or the location of its point of interest. This number is usually three digits, but can be four digits.

A four-digit identifier is used for dates that include two or more major types. For instance, a date variety on an 1867 With Rays Shield nickel might be FS-05-1867-301, yet a date variety on an 1867 No Rays Shield nickel might be FS-05-1867-1301. There are a few instances when there are three or more distinctive types, such as the 1864 Indian Head cent (copper-nickel, bronze No L, and bronze With L). In these cases the first type will be three digits, with the second and third types will be four digits, such as 1301 and 2301.

With two major types, such as the 1867 With Rays and 1867 No Rays nickels, the With Rays varieties would have three digits, such as 301. The No Rays varieties would have four digits, such as 1301. The 1 at the beginning of the No Rays varieties differentiates the second type from the first.

There is one major exception in the identifier number system. The Morgan and Peace dollar series use their Van Allen–Mallis (VAM) numbers (when available) as the identifier. This is more convenient for VAM enthusiasts and for the grading services. For instance, with an 1878 VAM-44, the FS number is FS-S1-1878-044.

Most third-party grading services will gladly change an existing slab with the old FS number for a new slab with the newer FS numbering system. A fee for this service can be expected, but it will usually be lower than a normal submission.

Identifiers for Fivaz-Stanton Numbers

The following are the identifiers for the Fivaz-Stanton numbers and their related meanings:

101–299	obverse doubled die and/or obverse die variety
301–399	obverse date variety
401–499	obverse variety, miscellaneous
501–699	mintmark variety
701–799	miscellaneous variety
801–899	reverse doubled die
901–999	reverse variety, miscellaneous

Note: As mentioned, Morgan and Peace dollar varieties have Van Allen–Mallis (VAM) numbers as the primary number sequence of their identifiers.

Old Fivaz-Stanton Numbers Included in the Listings

For this volume some old FS numbers are included as a cross-reference. The new FS number is primary, and the old FS number (when available) is secondary, in parentheses.

Abbreviations for Denominations

HC	half cent	S1	silver dollar
LC	large cent	T1	trade dollar
01	small cent	C1	clad dollar / golden dollar
02	two-cent piece	G1	gold dollar
3S	three-cent piece (silver)	G2.5	$2.50 gold piece
3N	three-cent piece (nickel)	G5	$5 gold piece
05	nickel five-cent piece	G10	$10 gold piece
H10	half dime	G20	$20 gold piece
10	dime	C50	commemorative half dollar
20	twenty-cent piece	P25	$25 platinum piece
25	quarter dollar	P100	$100 platinum piece
50	half dollar	SE	$1 Silver Eagle

RARITY FACTOR

The rarity factors used in the *Cherrypickers' Guide* are based upon the Universal Rarity Scale developed by Q. David Bowers. This is the only rarity scale available that is reasonably accurate for die varieties of the late-19th and 20th centuries. Following you will find a background of the older Sheldon rarity scale, and details of Bowers's Universal Rarity Scale.

The Sheldon Scale

For many years, the only method of reasonably identifying rarity was with the use of the Sheldon scale, designed by numismatic author Dr. William H. Sheldon to identify the rarity of large-cent varieties. Put to that use, the Sheldon scale worked very well, as most varieties ranged from scarce to very rare. It was further adapted for use with grading and rarity of many other coin series and denominations, as it was the only common scale in existence. However, it was not quite appropriate for most series, most varieties, or most errors.

The Sheldon scale was simply a progression of eight levels into which the populations of all large-cent varieties were to fall. Each level was prefaced with the letter R, for Rarity:

R-1 common

R-2 not so common

R-3 scarce

R-4 very scarce (est. 76–200 pieces in existence)

R-5 rare (31–75 pieces)

R-6 very rare (13–30 pieces)

R-7 extremely rare (4–12 pieces)

R-8 unique, or nearly so (1–3 pieces)

Numismatic writers adopted this scale to represent coins that were considered scarce or rare. However, as one can imagine, the scale is not appropriate for many coins, especially those of the late 19th and 20th centuries, with their high mintages. For instance, using this scale, the 1955 Doubled-Die Lincoln cent would be considered "common" or "not so common." Yet we know it is in fact scarce or rare.

Bowers's Universal Rarity Scale (URS)

Clearly, another scale was needed by the hobby community for indicating rarity of all coins. Leave it to numismatic historian Q. David Bowers to recognize the need and develop a method that could be used for any series, and any rarity. (In fact, it can be used not only for coins, but for virtually anything whose rarity, scarcity, or availability is important.) Bowers developed the Universal Rarity Scale (URS), which, as its name implies, is universal for any coin or item. He outlined this scale in the June 1992 issue of *The Numismatist*. It has been adopted by many writers and catalogers and is used throughout the *Cherrypickers' Guide*.

The URS is simple and reasonable in its mathematical progression:

URS-0	none	URS-12	1,001 to 2,000
URS-1	1; unique	URS-13	2,001–4,000
URS-2	2	URS-14	4,001–8,000
URS-3	3 or 4	URS-15	8,001–16,000
URS-4	5–8	URS-16	16,001–32,000
URS-5	9–16	URS-17	32,001–65,000
URS-6	17–32	URS-18	65,001–125,000
URS-7	33–64	URS-19	125,001–250,000
URS-8	65–125	URS-20	250,001–500,000
URS-9	126–250	URS-21	500,001–1,000,000
URS-10	251–500	URS-22	1,000,001–2,000,000
URS-11	501–1,000	(etc.)	

When using rarity numbers with coins, there are a couple important factors to remember:

1. **Rarity generally differs from one grade to another.** If a coin is listed as URS-13 (2,001 to 4,000 known) it might be relatively common. However, if there are only two pieces known in grades above About Uncirculated, it would be a true rarity (URS-2) in MS-63. Such is the case with the 1888-O Morgan dollar, Hot Lips variety. These are fairly common in Very Good and Fine, but virtually unknown above About Uncirculated. Such a coin is often referred to as a *condition rarity*.

2. **Rarity and value are not always as closely related as one might expect.** If there are 10 known examples of a particular variety, but only seven or eight collectors are interested in it, the coin would certainly be rare, but because of a relatively low Interest Factor (low demand), it would not command much of a premium. Conversely, there could be 10,000 pieces known of a variety, but if 20,000 collectors are interested in obtaining one, the premium over the normal value of the coin would be much greater, due to the high Interest Factor (high demand). This brings us back to the age-old law of supply and demand.

INTEREST FACTOR

Interest Factor is a term we use to indicate just how much demand a particular coin or variety has.

- A variety with a very high Interest Factor is in high demand, with several thousands of collectors desiring it.
- A medium Interest Factor may indicate that the variety is desired by hundreds or a few thousand people.
- A low Interest Factor might indicate that the coin is sought by just a handful of collectors.

In this guide, we rate each variety's Interest Factor as follows:

I-5   very high interest (most general collectors interested)

I-4   high interest (most variety collectors interested)

I-3   moderate interest (most series collectors interested)

I-2   minimal interest (some collectors interested)

I-1   very low interest (only very specialized collectors interested)

The Interest Factor, combined with the rarity, helps to determine the value of a variety or error. However, eye appeal is also a very important factor and must be considered in the final evaluation. A critical part of eye appeal for a variety or error is the relative strength or visibility of its defining characteristic—how easily can it be seen?

As a variety receives more publicity within the numismatic press, its Interest Factor might rise as demand increases. This can cause the price or value to increase without any change in the estimated quantity available.

LIQUIDITY FACTOR

The Liquidity Factor indicates how quickly or how easily a coin or variety *should* sell at auction, given normal market conditions.

- A coin with a high Liquidity Factor would be expected to sell right away, generally commanding full or inflated values.
- A coin with a low Liquidity Factor would not normally sell very easily or quickly, and then usually at a discount from suggested values.

Hot or highly active market conditions can inflate the Liquidity Factor of any coin, with a cold market having the opposite effect.

Our Liquidity Factor scale is as follows:

L-5   will sell easily, and often above listed value

L-4   will usually sell quickly at listed value (for variety enthusiasts)

L-3   will often sell in a reasonable time period, often to specialists

L-2   might sell in time, maybe at a discounted price

L-1   might sell provided the right buyer is available, but at a discount

OTHER NUMBERS AND ABBREVIATIONS

Identification numbers and abbreviations appear more frequently in the study of mint errors (and especially die varieties) than within the regular segment of the hobby. Some are easy methods of precisely identifying different varieties. Others are used to describe rarity, or even a certain class or type of variety. The important fact is with the use of these numbers, most specialists will know right away exactly which variety is being discussed. At the very least, a dealer or collector can consult a reference and find the corresponding number along with photos or detailed descriptions, which can easily and accurately identify a certain variety.

Most of these identification systems are simply numbers listed after the date and denomination. Some are more complex identification listings and include letters or symbols to further identify the variety or error.

RPM and OMM Listing Numbers

These are the original RPM (repunched mintmark) and OMM (over mintmark) listing numbers compiled by CONECA (Combined Organizations of Numismatic Error Collectors of America). You will notice most RPMs and OMMs are identified simply, such as 1949-D/S 5c, OMM-001. These numbers indicate that the coin is a 1949-D nickel, with an over mintmark (D Over S), and is over mintmark #1. This indicates that it was the first OMM listed for that particular date by John Wexler and Tom Miller when they originally began to catalog these varieties in the early 1980s. This cataloging system soon became the *RPM Book*, published in 1982.

Just because a variety is listed as #1 in no way should suggest it is the strongest, the most desirable, or the most valuable (although this is often the case).

Other publications listing all known varieties for a series will normally include newer listings for that series. These newer listings are being cataloged by Dr. James Wiles for CONECA.

Doubled-Die-Listing Numbers

As with the RPMs and OMMs, doubled dies are also assigned numbers that correspond to the listing numbers in CONECA's files. This numbering system was originally developed by Alan Herbert and John Wexler. These numbers can be confusing to the beginner, but they have a very logical and important sequence for serious collectors, so a brief explanation is included herewith.

There are eight basic classes of doubled dies. These classes generally have little to do with the strength of the doubling. Rather, they indicate how the particular doubling occurred. (Because of the complexity, the "how" of the doubling is not covered in this general overview.) To collectors, the strength of a doubling is generally more important than how it came about.

For example, there is a Lincoln cent listed as 1971-S PF 1c 1-O-II. These numbers indicate that the coin is a 1971-S Proof cent, listed as die #1, with the doubling on the obverse, and it is a Class II doubled die. As with the RPMs, if the coin is listed as die #1, it does not necessarily mean that it is the strongest doubled die for that date, only the first one listed. In this instance, die #2 for the 1971-S Proof cent is actually stronger, more valuable, and certainly in greater demand.

The sequence for these doubled-die listing numbers will always be the same. Following the date of the coin will be the indication of a Proof (if it is a Proof), then the denomination, the die number (indicated by Arabic numerals), an O or R signifying the doubled die is on the obverse or reverse, and finally the class of doubled die (indicated by Roman numerals). There are some doubled dies that were made as a result of a combination of more than one class of doubled die, such as 1971-S PF 1c 2-O-II+V-CW. The CW at the end indicates the spread of the doubling (from the Class V) is in a clockwise direction. Class I and Class V doubled dies use this CW or CCW direction indicator, meaning either a clockwise or counterclockwise spread. There are also cases in which a coin will have a doubled die on the obverse *and* reverse, such as 1963 25c 7-O-II+1-R-I. As mentioned above, these identification numbers should become easy to understand.

A more detailed description of each doubled die, by class, is published in *The Lincoln Cent Doubled Die*, by John Wexler, a book highly recommended for all variety enthusiasts. Although published in 1984, it is still a valuable source of information. These classes are also included in the *Cherrypickers' Guide* (third edition, and volume I of the fourth and fifth editions).

OTHER IDENTIFICATION NUMBERS

Other numbers are used from time to time in this book to indicate how a variety is cataloged in another reference book. The list below might not be comprehensive, as new books and reference works are being produced constantly.

Breen	*Walter Breen's Complete Encyclopedia of U.S. and Colonial Coins*
FS (Fivaz-Stanton)	*The Cherrypickers' Guide*
Greer	Brian Greer, *Complete Guide to Liberty Seated Dimes*
L	David Lawrence's books on Barber coinage (as mentioned in the text)

VAM (Van Allen–Mallis)   *Comprehensive Catalog and Encyclopedia of
Morgan and Peace Dollars*

WB (Wiley-Bugert)   *Complete Guide to Liberty Seated Half Dollars*

AVERAGE DIE LIFE

This chart indicates the average number of strikes that each obverse and reverse die
for current coin designs is expected to produce. These figures are simply averages and
expectations for circulation strikes. Dies can and do last longer, or may be retired from
service earlier due to damage.

Damage can and does occur early in the life of a die. Depending on the severity of the
damage, the die may be repaired, or (often) will be retired early. Retirement can also
occur if an abnormality—such as doubling or another inaccuracy—is discovered on a die.
The following list shows the average number of strikes for each type and denomination:

Lincoln cent	1,400,000
Jefferson nickel	200,000 (This figure is for the 2006 Monticello design.)
Roosevelt dime	300,000 (At the time of publication, Denver was averaging about 400,000; Philadelphia, about 230,000.)
Washington quarter	752,000
statehood quarter	275,000
Kennedy half dollar	160,000
Sacagawea dollar	250,000

According to a U.S. Mint official (as reported to the authors in May 2006), a coin's
redesign will negatively affect the expected life of a die by some 30 to 50 percent. The
average will improve slightly over time, as technicians analyze problems from the preceding year and "tweak" dies to address cracking issues. Once a new design is in operation for three to five years, Mint personnel will have improved die life to its maximum.

The new Presidential dollar coins are expected to have an average die life of
150,000 to 200,000. This die life can't be predicted definitely until the Mint has more
experience with the design.

CHANGES TO THIS VOLUME OF
THE *CHERRYPICKERS' GUIDE*

We have introduced two significant cataloging changes in the fifth edition, volume II.

Treatment of New Variety Listings

For most new listings, we do not include values, rarity ratings, or Interest or Liquidity
factors. The reasoning is simple. The very act of listing a variety in the *Cherrypickers'
Guide*—even if specialists have known of its existence for years—can increase its
market value to double its pre-listing value (or even greater), purely because it has
been elevated to the status of a published CPG variety. We cannot predict the fluctu-
ating value of new listings, so initially we will mark them as *n/a*. Regarding Interest
factors: If estimated too low, an Interest factor can become self-fulfilling; some

cherrypickers collect only those varieties with medium or high Interest factors. For new listings, we will monitor post-publication interest within the hobby community and base our conclusions on the activity we see over the coming months. Rarity, too, has proven to be a moving target immediately following publication of a new listing; when a variety is first included in the *Cherrypickers' Guide*, thousands of collectors who might never have taken the time to look for it will start their search. Some "rare" varieties have become more common soon after publication, as collectors learned of their existence; others have continued to be quite elusive. For now, we will not include a rarity estimate for new listings, but will monitor market activity and discoveries following publication.

Removal of Low-Interest and Debunked Varieties

The second significant change in this volume: Certain varieties have proven over time to be of low collector interest, and we have slated these for future removal from the coin-by-coin listings in order to make room for other, more important, varieties. They will remain *Cherrypickers' Guide* varieties (as opposed to being "delisted," as such); for example, they will continue to be cross-referenced and summarized in Appendix I. (An exception would be varieties debunked as counterfeit or which later research revealed to be erroneous classifications. These will be delisted entirely.)

Capped Bust Half Dimes, 1829–1837

Bust coinage varieties may be slightly different from what many of us are accustomed to encountering in late-19th-century and later coinage. During the Bust era the die-making process was somewhat different from that of later years.

Often a template and punches were used to place many of the design elements, letters, and numbers into the working die, rather than the hub (as was used for later coinage). Therefore, it is not uncommon to see slight differences in positioning of these elements. In some cases individual letter or number punches were used, which can account for one or more letters or numbers appearing over another.

One of the most active and educational specialty clubs in the United States is the John Reich Collectors Society. Bust half dimes, dimes, quarters, half dollars, and dollars are all within the focus of this excellent group.

At the time of this publication, membership is $25 annually. However, it is always suggested to write first, as dues and other requirements can change. Take a tip from us—membership in any numismatic specialty club is always highly educational and worth the modest cost of membership.

The JRCS has a fabulous web site, http://logan.com/jrcs, with a membership application, club details, and educational information. Contact the society at

John Reich Collectors Society
Attn: Stephen A. Crain
P.O. Box 1680
Windham, ME 04062

1829 FS-H10-1829-301

VARIETY: Repunched Date
PUP: 9 of date
URS-2 · I-1 · L-3

Description: The repunching is evident on the 9.
Comments: This variety was previously listed as an overdate. It is now considered a repunched date. (Note: Because of its low Interest Factor, this variety will be removed from this chapter in the next edition of this volume, to make room for more popularly collected pieces. The Fivaz-Stanton number will be retained for this variety and it will remain in the cross-references at the back of the book.)

1834, 3 Over Inverted 3 FS-H10-1834-301 (1/2-10c-000.3)

VARIETY: Repunched Date **VALENTINE-5; BREEN-2997**
PUP: 3 of date
URS-6 · I-2 · L-3

Description: The 3 of the date was first punched into the die in an inverted position, then corrected without any attempt to remove the initial punching.
Comments: Although this variety has been known for some time, collector interest only started to grow about 1997.

	VG-8	F-12	VF-20	EF-40	AU-50	MS-63	MS-65
VARIETY	$65	$83	$120	$180	$275	$925	$3,000
NORMAL	60	75	110	165	250	850	2,850

1836   FS-H10-1836-301

VARIETY: Repunched Date   **BREEN-3003**
PUP: Date   *"BLUNDERED DATE" VARIETY*
NEW LISTING

 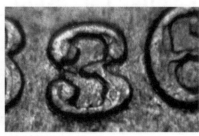

Description: The date shows a repunched 3 over an inverted 3.

Comments: Interest should grow for this variety as it has for the 1834 half dime with blundered date.

	VG-8	F-12	VF-20	EF-40	AU-50	MS-63	MS-65
VARIETY	n/a	n/a	n/a	n/a	n/a	n/a	n/a
NORMAL	$60	$75	$110	$165	$250	$850	$2,850

The Cherrypickers' Guide HELPFUL HINTS

Remember, if you can't see the characteristics of a coin clearly, you'll likely miss the important one. Don't take a chance. Always use a good, triplet magnifier (7x or 10x). The added expense will be more than offset by just one nice find. There are additional magnifying suggestions in appendix C.

Liberty Seated Half Dimes, 1837–1873

To quote the late Al Blythe, a good friend and specialist in these coins, "The Liberty Seated half dime series is rich in varieties, overdates, repunched dates, and blundered dies. This provides a fertile ground for collectors who enjoy this facet of numismatics." Truer words could not be spoken.

Typically, specialists who collect any one of the Liberty Seated denominations will collect them all. The design is arguably one of the most interesting in United States numismatics. In addition, there were numerous changes during the many years the design was in use.

Liberty Seated half dimes contain numerous varieties, including some that are considered very rare by specialists. In addition, a large percentage of the varieties in the series are in great demand, and are almost always easy to sell.

For those seriously interested in the series, we strongly recommend membership in the Liberty Seated Collectors Club, one of the best specialized clubs in numismatics. *The Gobrecht Journal,* the official publication of the club, is issued three times annually. This extensive newsletter is loaded with excellent educational articles. The club also has a web site at www.lsccweb.org. At the time of publication, membership dues were $20 per year. For membership information, contact

Liberty Seated Collectors Club
Leonard Augsburger, Secretary-Treasurer
P.O. Box 6114
Vernon Hills, IL 60061
E-mail: leonard_augsburger@hotmail.com

1838 — FS-H10-1838-901

VARIETY: Rusted Reverse Die
PUP: Reverse around AMERICA
URS-4 · I-4 · L-4

Description: Rough, pebbly appearance on the reverse.
Comments: Generally speaking, evidence of rust on working dies is very rare. Only a very few examples are known to exist for some reverse dies. Very little information is available for this variety. Its value is subjective at this point. Collectors of Liberty Seated coinage consider this one of the more desirable varieties.

	G-4	VG-8	F-12	VF-20	EF-40	AU-50	MS-60
VARIETY	$22	$25	$33	$43	$90	$190	$310
NORMAL	18	21	28	35	75	160	260

1839-O — FS-H10-1839o-501

VARIETY: Reverse of 1838
PUP: Mintmark
URS G/VG-6, F/VF-6, EF/AU-7, MS-UNKNOWN

BREEN-3414; VALENTINE-1

Large O mintmark of 1838 | Normal O, used on majority of 1839 mintage

Description: This variety has the large O mintmark on the reverse (type of 1838).
Comments: According to Al Blythe, eight were reported in the LSCC Variety Survey. Although this is apparently a very rare variety, surely a few more survive just waiting to be found. Early-die-state, high-grade specimens also show a repunched 9.

	G-4	VG-8	F-12	VF-20	EF-40	AU-50	MS-60
VARIETY	n/a	n/a	n/a	n/a	n/a	n/a	n/a
NORMAL	$22	$23	$29	$38	$80	$170	$525

5

1840-O, No Drapery — FS-H10-1840o-901 (000.5)

VARIETY: Transitional Reverse — **VALENTINE-6**
PUP: Reverse letters, buds, and leaf clusters by DIME
URS-6 · I-5 · L-5

Description: This rare transitional variety exhibits large letters and open or split buds on the reverse die, along with a small O mintmark. The key diagnostic of the variety is three-leaf clusters on either side of the word DIME, while the common reverse has four-leaf clusters.

Comments: The Open Buds reverse was intended for use from 1841 through 1853.

	G-4	VG-8	F-12	VF-20	EF-40	AU-50	MS-60
VARIETY	$100	$150	$225	$400	$800	$1,250	n/a
NORMAL	20	23	30	40	80	235	$725

1842-O — FS-H10-1842o-301

VARIETY: Repunched Date
PUP: Date
URS-4 · I-1 · L-3

Description: Very slight doubling is evident on the 1, 8, and 2 of the date.

Comments: (Note: Because of its low Interest Factor, this variety will be removed from this chapter in the next edition of this volume, to make room for more popularly collected pieces. The Fivaz-Stanton number will be retained for this variety and it will remain in the cross-references at the back of the book.)

1843 — FS-H10-1843-301 (000.06)

VARIETY: Repunched Date   VALENTINE-6A
PUP: Date
URS-8 · I-4 · L-4

Description: A very nice repunched date, most evident with secondary numerals 1, 8, and 4 south of the primary date.

Comments: High-grade examples are always in demand. This is a well-known RPD, and very popular among Liberty Seated specialists.

	G-4	VG-8	F-12	VF-20	EF-40	AU-50	MS-60	MS-63
VARIETY	$20	$28	$38	$55	$90	$185	$250	$375
NORMAL	16	20	27	35	75	160	210	325

1844 — FS-H10-1844-301 (000.063)

VARIETY: Repunched Date   VALENTINE-3C
PUP: Date
URS-7 · I-4 · L-4

Description: This is a wonderful RPD, with secondary images evident north and south of the primary 1 and 8, and secondary images evident south on the first 4. Overlapping images are also evident on the last 4 of the date.

Comments: This variety is always popular among Liberty Seated specialists.

	G-4	VG-8	F-12	VF-20	EF-40	AU-50	MS-60	MS-63
VARIETY	$23	$30	$40	$60	$110	$190	$300	$600
NORMAL	16	20	27	35	75	160	210	325

1845 FS-H10-1845-301 (000.65)

VARIETY: Repunched Date
PUP: Date
URS-2 · I-5 · L-5

Description: This variety exhibits an 8 and a 4 clearly protruding from the rock above the date.

Comments: Discovered in 1997 by Bill Fivaz, this should be considered very rare due to the length of time it remained unknown. Very few are known to date!

	G-4	VG-8	F-12	VF-20	EF-40	AU-50	MS-60	MS-63
VARIETY	n/a	n/a	n/a	n/a	n/a	n/a	n/a	n/a
NORMAL	$16	$20	$27	$35	$75	$160	$210	$325

1845 FS-H10-1845-302 (000.66)

VARIETY: Repunched Date   **VALENTINE-5**
PUP: Date
URS-7 · I-5 · L-5

Description: All four digits of the date are repunched, with the secondary image slightly northwest of the primary date.

Comments: This variety is a well-known repunched date; it is in high demand by Liberty Seated specialists.

	VG-8	F-12	VF-20	EF-40	AU-50	MS-60	MS-63
VARIETY	$27	$45	$70	$100	$185	$300	$450
NORMAL	20	27	35	75	160	210	325

1848   FS-H10-1848-301 (001)

VARIETY: Large Date   **VALENTINE-1A**
PUP: Date
URS-11 · I-5 · L-5

Description: The digits of the date are much larger than normal. It is very obvious a 4-digit logotype punch intended for a dime was used. The digits protrude well into the rock. A secondary 8 is evident between the 4 and second 8.

Comments: Beware of coins listed as the large date that are not! The "Normal" values listed are for the Medium Date.

	VG-8	F-12	VF-20	EF-40	AU-50	MS-60	MS-63
VARIETY	$40	$70	$100	$175	$360	$485	$950
NORMAL	20	27	35	75	160	210	325

1848   FS-H10-1848-302 (001.3)

VARIETY: Overdate
PUP: Date
URS-6 · I-4 · L-4

Description: Many specialists believe this to be a tripled overdate, 8/7/6. Further study may prove this to be a normal RPD as the "spike" believed to be that of the 7 appears very much like a portion of an underlying 8, partially polished off.

Comments: The lower portion of a repunched 4 is evident left of the primary 4. The "Normal" values listed are for the Medium Date.

	VG-8	F-12	VF-20	EF-40	AU-50	MS-60	MS-63
VARIETY	$35	$50	$75	$150	$300	$400	$700
NORMAL	20	27	35	75	160	210	325

1849, 9 Over 8 — FS-H10-1849-301 (001.5)

VARIETY: Overdate
PUP: Date
URS-8 · I-5 · L-4

VALENTINE-1

Description: The 4 of the date is at least triple punched, with one secondary 4 south and one east of the primary 4. There is also a secondary numeral east of the lower portion of the 9, which some specialists believe may be an 8. Some believe it to be an inverted 6 (improbable), and still others believe it to be a 9.

Comments: Coauthor J.T. Stanton believes the image below the 9 is that of an 8.

	VG-8	F-12	VF-20	EF-40	AU-50	MS-60	MS-63
VARIETY	$35	$50	$75	$110	$265	$550	$1,100
NORMAL	22	28	40	75	150	235	520

1849, 9 Over 8 — FS-H10-1849-302 (001.55)

VARIETY: Overdate
PUP: Date
URS-7 · I-5 · L-5

VALENTINE-2

 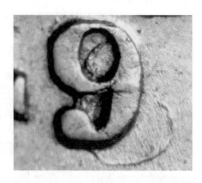

Description: Long described and listed as a 9/6 overdate, it is quite evident this is actually a 9/8. The underlying digit exhibits an inward curve midway up on the left side, indicative of an 8. A 6 would have a relatively straight left side.

Comments: This is a very popular variety among Liberty Seated specialists.

	VG-8	F-12	VF-20	EF-40	AU-50	MS-60	MS-63
VARIETY	$40	$65	$105	$190	$315	$600	$1,250
NORMAL	22	28	40	75	150	235	520

1853, Arrows
FS-H10-1853-301 (001.8)

VARIETY: Misplaced Date
PUP: Date
URS-5 · I-4 · L-4

Description: The lower portions of numerals 8, 5, and 3 are visible protruding from the lower portion of the rock above the primary date. Al Blythe says that remains of a 2 can be seen behind the upper portion of the primary 3.

Comments: Certainly a nice MPD; this may prove to be an overdate.

	VG-8	F-12	VF-20	EF-40	AU-50	MS-60	MS-63
VARIETY	n/a	n/a	n/a	n/a	n/a	n/a	n/a
NORMAL	$22	$24	$35	$65	$130	$210	$310

1853, Arrows
FS-H10-1853-401

VARIETY: Dot Below 5 of Date
PUP: 5 of date
NEW LISTING

VALENTINE-1

Description: On this variety a dot appears to have been intentionally placed below the 5 of the date.

Comments: The location of the dot indicates that it may have been placed during die engraving to help align the date; if so, it was inadvertently left on the die instead of ground or polished away.

	VG-8	F-12	VF-20	EF-40	AU-50	MS-60	MS-63
VARIETY	n/a	n/a	n/a	n/a	n/a	n/a	n/a
NORMAL	$22	$24	$35	$65	$130	$210	$310

1855

Variety: Doubled-Die Obverse, Clashed Dies   **Valentine-7**
PUP: Lower skirt
New Listing

Obverse clash marks   Reverse clash marks

Description: Shows strong doubling on the lower edges of Miss Liberty's skirt; perhaps the shield, too.

	VG-8	F-12	VF-20	EF-40	AU-50	MS-60	MS-63
Variety	n/a	n/a	n/a	n/a	n/a	n/a	n/a
Normal	$22	$24	$35	$65	$130	$210	$300

1856

Variety: Misplaced Date
PUP: Rock above date
URS-6 · I-4 · L-4

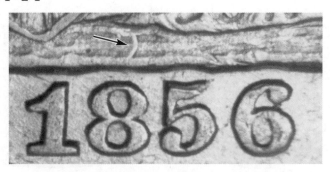

Description: A portion of an 8 is quite evident in the rock just above the primary 8.

Comments: This is one of the many nice varieties discovered by Joe Miller.

	VG-8	F-12	VF-20	EF-40	AU-50	MS-60	MS-63
Variety	$30	$50	$75	$100	$160	$215	$370
Normal	22	25	35	65	130	185	320

1858
FS-H10-1858-301 (002)

VARIETY: Repunched Date
BREEN-3090
PUP: Date
URS-10 · I-5 · L-5

Description: The date was first punched into the die very high, then corrected and punched in the normal location. The original high-date punch remains very evident within the upper portions of the primary date.

Comments: This is considered one of the rarest and most desirable Liberty Seated half dime varieties.

	VG-8	F-12	VF-20	EF-40	AU-50	MS-60	MS-63
VARIETY	$60	$85	$165	$225	$375	$550	$950
NORMAL	22	25	35	55	95	185	320

1858
FS-H10-1858-302 (003)

VARIETY: Date Over Inverted Date
BREEN-3091
PUP: Date
URS-8 · I-5 · L-5

Description: The first date punch was punched into the die in an inverted orientation, then corrected. The bases of the secondary digits are visible above the primary digits.

Comments: Although one of the most well-known varieties of the series, and very spectacular, this can still be cherrypicked at times. This variety is very rare, and more difficult to locate than the 1858 repunched date.

	VG-8	F-12	VF-20	EF-40	AU-50	MS-60	MS-63
VARIETY	$65	$90	$175	$240	$400	$625	$1,200
NORMAL	22	25	35	55	95	185	320

1861, 1 Over 0 — FS-H10-1861-301 (003.6)

VARIETY: Overdate
PUP: Date
URS-9 · I-5 · L-5

VALENTINE-5

Description: An 1860 date was first punched into the die, after which an 1861 date was punched into the die over the 0.

Comments: This is one of the top five varieties for the series, with more demand than supply. Some specialists feel this is not an overdate.

	VG-8	F-12	VF-20	EF-40	AU-50	MS-60	MS-63
VARIETY	$40	$50	$90	$190	$340	$535	$875
NORMAL	20	25	30	50	80	160	225

1865-S — FS-H10-1865S-301 (003.8)

VARIETY: Repunched Date
PUP: Date
URS-6 · I-4 · L-3

VALENTINE-1

Description: The RPD is evident with a secondary 5 south of the primary 5, and secondary 1 and 6 north of those numbers.

Comments: Due to the scarcity of the date, this variety may prove to be a large percentage of the existing population. It was incorrectly listed as FS-H10-1865-301 in the fourth edition, volume II.

	VG-8	F-12	VF-20	EF-40	AU-50	MS-60	MS-63
VARIETY	n/a	n/a	n/a	n/a	n/a	n/a	n/a
NORMAL	$340	$425	$550	$675	$750	$850	$1,200

1871   FS-H10-1871-301 (003.9)

VARIETY: Misplaced Date
PUP: Rock
URS-5 · I-1 · L-3

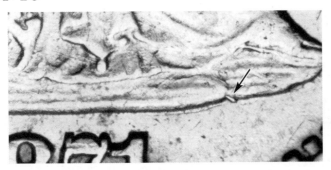

Description: A spike, which is likely the base of a 1, is evident protruding from the base of the rock, above and right of the last 1.

Comments: This is a somewhat recent discovery. (Note: Because of its low Interest Factor, this variety will be removed from this chapter in the next edition of this volume, to make room for more popularly collected pieces. The Fivaz-Stanton number will be retained for this variety and it will remain in the cross-references at the back of the book.)

1872   FS-H10-1872-101 (004)

VARIETY: Doubled-Die Obverse   **VALENTINE-6**
PUP: AMERICA
URS-8 · I-5 · L-5

Description: Doubling is evident on UNITED STATES OF AMERICA and on most elements of Miss Liberty. AMERICA is the strongest point.

Comments: This is one of the more popular varieties of the series.

	VG-8	F-12	VF-20	EF-40	AU-50	MS-60	MS-63
VARIETY	$35	$50	$75	$160	$225	$450	$700
NORMAL	20	25	30	45	80	150	250

1872-S, Mintmark Below Bow   FS-H10-1872S-301 (005)

VARIETY: Misplaced Date   **VALENTINE-4 AND/OR -6; BREEN-3136**
PUP: Skirt
URS-5 · I-3 · L-2

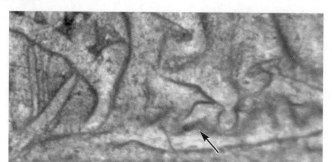

Description: The top of a numeral is evident in the skirt just below and right of the Y in LIBERTY. This has been reported as being a 7, but most certainly is a 1. There is doubling in the date.

Comments: This is a somewhat recent discovery whose Interest and Liquidity factors may increase.

	VG-8	F-12	VF-20	EF-40	AU-50	MS-60	MS-63
VARIETY	$28	$33	$38	$55	$90	$175	$325
NORMAL	20	25	30	45	80	150	275

1872-S, Mintmark Below Bow   FS-H10-1872S-302

VARIETY: Misplaced Date   **VALENTINE-5**
PUP: Left of and below pendant
NEW LISTING

Mintmark location

Description: Apparent misplaced numerals appear to the left of the pendant and below the skirt on the rock. The variety is controversial among specialists, who disagree as to whether these are misplaced numerals or die gouges.

Comments: This variety appears to be rare.

	VG-8	F-12	VF-20	EF-40	AU-50	MS-60	MS-63
VARIETY	n/a	n/a	n/a	n/a	n/a	n/a	n/a
NORMAL	$20	$25	$30	$45	$80	$150	$275

Capped Bust Dimes, 1809–1837

Bust coinage varieties may be slightly different from what many of us are accustomed to encountering in late-19th-century and later coinage. During the Capped Bust era the die-making process was somewhat different from that of later years.

Often a template and punches were used to place many of the design elements, letters, and numbers into the working die, rather than the hub (as was used for later coinage). Therefore, it is not uncommon to see slight differences in positioning of these elements. In some cases individual letter or number punches were used, which can account for one letter or number appearing over another.

One of the most active and educational specialty clubs in the United States is the John Reich Collectors Society. Capped Bust half dimes, dimes, quarters, half dollars, and dollars are all within the focus of this excellent group.

At the time of this publication, membership is $25 annually. However, it is always suggested to write first, as dues and other requirements can change. Take a tip from us—membership in any numismatic specialty club is always highly educational and well worth the modest cost of membership.

The JRCS has a fabulous web site, http://logan.com/jrcs, with a membership application, club details, and educational information. Contact the society at

John Reich Collectors Society
Attn: Stephen A. Crain
P.O. Box 1680
Windham, ME 04062

1829

FS-10-1829-301 (10c-001)

VARIETY: Curl-Base 2
PUP: 2 of date
URS-4 · I-5 · L-5

BREEN-3188

Description: The base of a typical 2 for this date is flat with a slight serif. This rare variety exhibits a wavy or "curled" base on the 2. Only one working die had this curled base 2, and it was obviously used for a short press run.

Comments: Almost all specimens are low grade, i.e., Fine or below. A small number are known in VF. Demand is very high for any grade and the coin sells virtually immediately when offered.

	G-4	VG-8	F-12	VF-20	EF-40	AU-50	AU-55
VARIETY	$4,500	$6,500	$8,500	n/a	n/a	n/a	n/a
NORMAL	30	40	45	$80	$300	$425	$550

1829

FS-10-1829-901 (10c-002)

VARIETY: Small Over Large 10 C
PUP: Denomination 10 C
URS-7 · I-5 · L-5

BREEN-3187

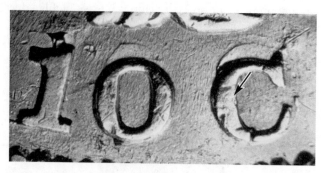

Description: The denomination, 10 C, on the reverse die was punched first with a large 10 C, then again with a smaller 10 C. The large 10 C is clearly evident north of the primary small 10 C.

Comments: Although this variety has been known for some time, interest in it has increased since 1997.

	G-4	VG-8	F-12	VF-20	EF-40	AU-50	MS-60	MS-63
VARIETY	$36	$50	$55	$95	$350	$500	$1,100	$2,200
NORMAL	30	40	45	80	300	425	850	1,600

1830, 30 Over 29

FS-10-1830-301 (10c-003)

VARIETY: Overdate
PUP: Date
URS-8 · I-3 · L-3

BREEN-3194

Description: Portions of the underlying 2 and 9 are evident behind the 3 and 0 in the date. The tail of the 2 is evident to the right of the lower curve of the 3. The very top of the 9 is evident above the 0. Surface doubling from the initial 1829 punch is also evident on the 8.

Comments: There are three or four known dies of this overdate. All are similar and command similar prices. When this variety was first publicized in *Scott's Comprehensive Catalogue and Encyclopedia of U.S. Coins*, in 1971, it was considered exceedingly rare.

	VG-8	F-12	VF-20	EF-40	AU-50	MS-60	MS-63
VARIETY	$65	$125	$175	$425	$750	$1,350	$3,900
NORMAL	40	45	80	250	425	850	1,600

THE CHERRYPICKERS' GUIDE **HELPFUL HINTS**

Be sure to read and re-read the appendix on die doubling.

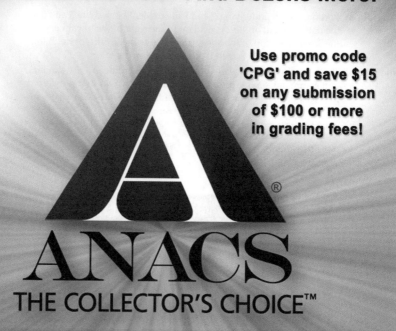

Liberty Seated Dimes, 1837–1891

Liberty Seated dimes are a paradise for variety enthusiasts. Significant varieties are known and can be found for virtually every date and mint. From minor repunched mintmarks to major doubled dies, and even major design changes, the varieties are abundant.

Virtually all of the varieties within the series are in high demand by the large number of Liberty Seated specialists. In general, values for the varieties have been increasing at an even faster rate than for the normal coins. An eagle-eyed cherrypicker can easily earn a significant income by picking the varieties that go unnoticed by most non-specialist dealers.

For those seriously interested in the series, we strongly recommend membership in the Liberty Seated Collectors Club (LSCC), one of the best specialty clubs in numismatics. The club issues its official publication, the Gobrecht Journal, three times each year. This information-packed newsletter is loaded with excellent educational articles.

The club has an outstanding web site at www.lsccweb.org. As of this writing, the annual dues are $20—a bargain, considering the amount of information available. If you join the LSCC, you will be connecting with the most serious and knowledgeable collectors and dealers in the hobby. For more information, contact

Liberty Seated Collectors Club
Leonard Augsburger, Secretary-Treasurer
P.O. Box 6114
Vernon Hills, IL 60061
E-mail: leonard_augsburger@hotmail.com

1838, Small Stars
FS-10-1838-801 (Small Stars)

VARIETY: Doubled-Die Reverse
PUP: Bow on reverse
URS-20 · I-3 · L-3

GREER: IDENTIFIED

Description: Doubling is evident on the D of DIME, the bow, and lower portions of the wreath. All of this date and type exhibit the DDR.

Comments: The same reverse die was used for a few of the 1838, Large Stars variety.

	G-4	VG-8	F-12	VF-20	EF-40	AU-50	MS-60
VARIETY	$22	$26	$30	$40	$120	$250	$350
NORMAL	22	26	30	40	120	250	350

1838, Large Stars
FS-10-1838-802

VARIETY: Doubled-Die Reverse
PUP: D of DIME
URS-7 · I-4 · L-4

GREER-101

Description: The same die was used for the 1838, Small Stars DDR. Doubling is evident on the D of DIME, the bow, and lower portions of the wreath.

Comments: The value is for the doubled die, as it is for the Small Stars issue.

	G-4	VG-8	F-12	VF-20	EF-40	AU-50	MS-60
VARIETY	$27	$32	$40	$55	$150	$280	$385
NORMAL	22	26	30	40	120	250	350

1839-O
FS-10-1839o-501 (003.28)

VARIETY: Repunched Mintmark
PUP: Mintmark
URS-7 · I-4 · L-4

GREER-102

Description: On the Large O variety, the secondary O mintmark is evident southeast of the primary O. This O mintmark variety has a very slight tilt to the right.

Comments: This very strong RPM is listed as Greer-102.

	G-4	VG-8	F-12	VF-20	EF-40	AU-50	MS-60
VARIETY	$30	$35	$50	$55	$150	$325	$750
NORMAL	24	30	40	45	135	275	450

1841-O
FS-10-1841o-901 (003.3)

VARIETY: Transitional Reverse (Small O Reverse)
PUP: Reverse, buds and leaf by U of UNITED
URS-3 · I-5 · L-5

GREER-102

Description: This die pair was struck with a reverse die that was to have been discontinued in 1840, but continued to see limited use into 1841. Note the closed buds and the second leaf from the left in the group of four to the left of the bow knot. The leaf on the Closed Bud reverse reaches only halfway across the bottom of the U of UNITED.

Comments: This is a very rare and important variety in this series. It has the Small O mintmark. (Compare it to the next listing.)

	G-4	VG-8	F-12	VF-20	EF-40	AU-50	MS-60
VARIETY	$650	$1,100	$1,750	$2,850	$6,250	n/a	n/a
NORMAL	25	30	35	50	85	$225	$900

1841-O

FS-10-1841o-902 (003.3)

VARIETY: Transitional Reverse (Large O Reverse)   GREER-102
PUP: Reverse, buds and leaf by U of UNITED
URS-6 · I-5 · L-5

Description: This die pair was struck with a reverse die that was to have been discontinued in 1840, but continued to see limited use into 1841. Note the closed buds and the second leaf from the left in the group of four to the left of the bow knot. The leaf on the Closed Bud reverse reaches only halfway across the bottom of the U of UNITED.

Comments: This is a very rare and important variety in this series. It has the large, or Normal O, mintmark. (Compare it to the preceding listing.)

	G-4	VG-8	F-12	VF-20	EF-40	AU-50	MS-60
VARIETY	$400	$600	$1,350	$2,450	$5,250	n/a	n/a
NORMAL	25	30	35	50	85	$225	$900

1843

FS-10-1843-301

VARIETY: Repunched Date   GREER-101
PUP: Date
URS-7 · I-3 · L-3

Description: This is a nice repunched date, with a secondary 1 and 8 evident north, and a secondary 4 and 3 evident northeast of the primary numerals.

Comments: This is a vivid repunched date.

	G-4	VG-8	F-12	VF-20	EF-40	AU-50	MS-60
VARIETY	$25	$30	$35	$43	$90	$215	$450
NORMAL	20	25	30	35	50	125	400

1853, Arrows — FS-10-1853-301

VARIETY: Repunched Date — **GREER-103**
PUP: Date
URS-6 · I-3 · L-3

Description: The secondary image is evident on all four digits, to the east.

Comments: This is the most evident RPD for this date and the 1853–1855 type. This variety was incorrectly listed as FS-10-1853-130 in the fourth edition, volume II.

	VG-8	F-12	VF-20	EF-40	AU-50	AU-55	MS-60
VARIETY	n/a	n/a	n/a	n/a	n/a	n/a	n/a
NORMAL	$15	$20	$30	$50	$175	$200	$300

1856, Small Date — FS-10-1856-101

VARIETY: Doubled-Die Obverse — **GREER-101**
PUP: Shield
URS-5 · I-4 · L-4

Description: Doubling is evident with a close spread on the right side and top of the shield, on the banner across the shield, and as a doubled pole.

Comments: This doubled die is difficult to notice on lower-grade pieces. There is also a Proof doubled die that is very similar, but commands little or no premium.

	VG-8	F-12	VF-20	EF-40	AU-50	MS-60
VARIETY	$25	$30	$40	$65	$150	$350
NORMAL	15	20	30	50	130	300

1856-O

VARIETY: Repunched Date
PUP: Date
URS-6 · I-3 · L-3

GREER-101

Description: This is one of the stronger repunched dates in the series, and can be located in lower grades.

Comments: This obverse is paired with a die exhibiting the Large O mintmark.

	VG-8	F-12	VF-20	EF-40	AU-50	MS-60
VARIETY	$23	$40	$65	$110	$290	$850
NORMAL	15	25	35	65	250	800

1872

VARIETY: Doubled-Die Obverse
PUP: Shield, lower robe

Description: Doubling is evident on the shield, the banner across shield, the lower folds of the robe, and the lower edges of the rock.

Comments: This photo was used in error in the previous edition. It is actually a photo of a half dime.

1872

FS-10-1872-301

VARIETY: Repunched Date

GREER-101

PUP: Date

URS-9 · I-3 · L-2

Description: The weaker secondary date is visible south and west of the primary date. Most evident is the upper loop of the secondary 2 within the loop of the primary 2.

Comments: This variety is somewhat common.

	VG-8	F-12	VF-20	EF-40	AU-50	MS-60
VARIETY	$25	$50	$75	$100	$125	$225
NORMAL	15	25	30	40	90	175

1872

FS-10-1872-302

VARIETY: Misplaced Date

GREER-104

PUP: Outer curve of 2 in rock

NEW LISTING

 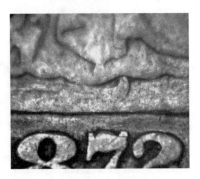

Description: The outer curve of a 2 shows in the rock above the 7 of the date.

Comments: This is one of the nicer misplaced dates known.

	VG-8	F-12	VF-20	EF-40	AU-50	MS-60
VARIETY	n/a	n/a	n/a	n/a	n/a	n/a
NORMAL	$15	$25	$30	$40	$90	$175

1872

VARIETY: Doubled-Die Reverse
PUP: Entire reverse
URS-3 · I-5 · L-5

GREER: N/L

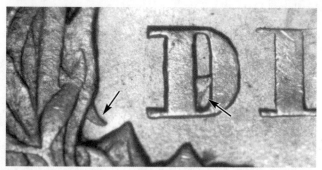

Description: The first hubbing was almost totally obliterated by the second, which was rotated about 170° from the first. The key indicators are inside the opening of the D and the center arm of the E of ONE. The tip of the weaker lower-left leaf is evident above the primary E of ONE. Other elements are also clearly visible.

Comments: This is one of the most dramatic doubled dies ever discovered. Lee Day reported this variety to J.T. Stanton in 1997, and Tom DeLorey confirmed that the variety is a doubled die.

	VG-8	F-12	VF-20	EF-40	AU-50	MS-60
VARIETY	$50	$75	$150	$250	$375	$800
NORMAL	15	25	30	40	90	175

1873, Closed 3 — FS-10-1873-301 (003.6)

VARIETY: Repunched Date   **GREER-101**
PUP: Date
URS-6 · I-3 · L-3

Description: This strong repunched date shows secondary digits west of the primary digits.
Comments: This variety is still very scarce.

	VG-8	F-12	VF-20	EF-40	AU-50	MS-60
VARIETY	$25	$50	$75	$175	$275	$500
NORMAL	15	22	25	40	90	150

1873, Arrows — FS-10-1873-101

VARIETY: Doubled-Die Obverse   **GREER-101**
PUP: Shield
URS-4 · I-5 · L-5

RB

Description: This is an extremely rare doubled die. Doubling is evident on the shield and on the banner across the shield.
Comments: Although well known for decades, very few specimens have been reported. The highest-graded example known is an AU. This variety was incorrectly listed as FS-10-1873-2101 in the fourth edition, volume II.

	VG-8	F-12	VF-20	EF-40	AU-50	MS-60
VARIETY	$575	$900	$1,450	$3,000	$4,500	n/a
NORMAL	20	26	55	140	300	$550

1875　　　　　　　　　　　　　　　　　　FS-10-1875-301

VARIETY: Misplaced Date　　　　　　　　　　　　**GREER-104**
PUP: Denticles below date
URS-6 · I-3 · L-3

Description: The top of a 1 is clearly evident protruding from the denticles below the date.

Comments: Chris Pilliod discovered this variety in January 1991.

	VG-8	F-12	VF-20	EF-40	AU-50	MS-60
VARIETY	$25	$35	$50	$75	$100	$200
NORMAL	15	20	22	30	80	150

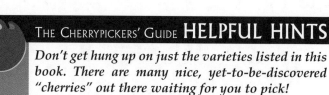

THE CHERRYPICKERS' GUIDE HELPFUL HINTS

Don't get hung up on just the varieties listed in this book. There are many nice, yet-to-be-discovered "cherries" out there waiting for you to pick!

1876-CC

VARIETY: Doubled-Die Obverse
PUP: OF AMERICA
URS-6 · I-4 · L-4

GREER-101A

FS-101 Level CC

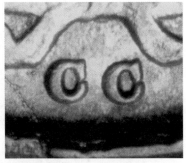

FS-102 Right C High

FS-103 Right C Low (rarest)

Description: Doubling with a very strong spread is evident on OF AMERICA. Doubling is also visible on the lower folds of the gown and on the lower portion of the rock.

Comments: Value depends upon the reverse die pairing. The doubled-die obverse shown here has been paired with three different reverse dies. FS-101 has a level CC mintmark; FS-102 has the second C high; FS-103 has the second C low. Values are for the most common pairing.

	VG-8	F-12	VF-20	EF-40	AU-50	MS-60
VARIETY	$25	$40	$75	$125	$250	$450
NORMAL	18	24	38	65	100	230

1876-CC · FS-10-1876CC-301 (003.7)

VARIETY: Misplaced Date
PUP: Gown by shield
URS-4 · I-3 · L-3

GREER-104

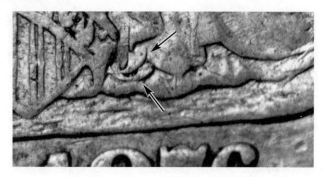

Description: The bases of two 6's are evident in the gown by the shield, overlapping one another.

Comments: This variety shows another very massive misplaced date.

	VG-8	F-12	VF-20	EF-40	AU-50	MS-60
VARIETY	$40	$65	$95	$150	$275	$475
NORMAL	18	24	38	65	100	230

1876-CC · FS-10-1876CC-901 (005)

VARIETY: Type II Reverse
PUP: Reverse ribbon
URS-7 · I-4 · L-4

GREER: LISTED

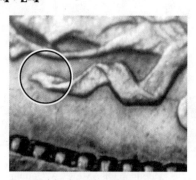
Type II (single-point ribbon end)

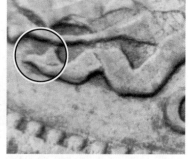
Type I (split ribbon end)

Description: This scarce Type II reverse exhibits a single point to the left ribbon end; the common Type I reverse exhibits a split of the left ribbon end.

Comments: This has become a highly collectible variety.

	VG-8	F-12	VF-20	EF-40	AU-50	MS-60
VARIETY	$50	$100	$150	$225	$350	$500
NORMAL	18	24	38	65	100	230

1876-S
FS-10-1876S-301

VARIETY: Repunched Date
PUP: 18 of date
NEW LISTING

FORTIN-122

Description: Repunching is strongly apparent on the 18 of the date and possibly
a bit on the lower 7.

Comments: This variety was recently listed by Gerry Fortin as F-122.

	VG-8	F-12	VF-20	EF-40	AU-50	MS-60
VARIETY	n/a	n/a	n/a	n/a	n/a	n/a
NORMAL	$18	$20	$25	$40	$80	$150

1877-CC
FS-10-1877CC-301

VARIETY: Overdate
PUP: Date
NEW LISTING

FORTIN-108

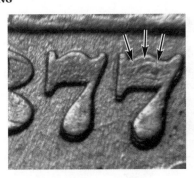

Description: Surface doubling of the upper curve of a 6 is apparent on the horizontal bar of the
second 7. Also visible are a 1/1 and doubling and tripling of the lower 7s.

Comments: This variety was recently listed by Gerry Fortin, who found that this obverse die is
paired with two different reverse dies. The first die pairing is listed by Fortin as F-107.
Both F-107 and F-108 feature a diagonal die gouge that runs through the shield. The
gouge is diagnostic for this variety. Compare this to the 1877/6 Liberty Seated half dollar.

	VG-8	F-12	VF-20	EF-40	AU-50	MS-60
VARIETY	n/a	n/a	n/a	n/a	n/a	n/a
NORMAL	$22	$24	$38	$65	$100	$230

1887-S
FS-10-1887S-501

VARIETY: Repunched Mintmark
PUP: Mintmark
URS-3 · I-3 · L-3

GREER: N/L

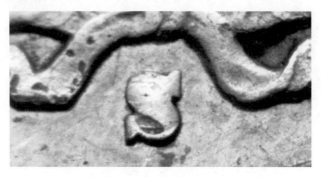

Description: The secondary S is evident within the lower loop of the primary S.

Comments: This does not appear to match the photos of CONECA RPM-2, which is also listed as Greer-102.

	VG-8	F-12	VF-20	EF-40	AU-50	MS-60
VARIETY	$25	$35	$50	$75	$125	$225
NORMAL	15	20	25	35	80	150

1888-S
FS-10-1888S-501

VARIETY: Repunched Mintmark
PUP: Mintmark
URS-7 · I-3 · L-3

GREER-101

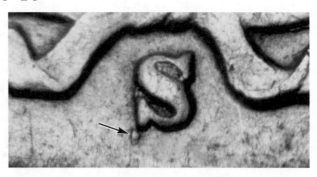

Description: The secondary S is evident just below the primary S, showing only the lower serif. The left curve of the secondary S is also visible in the lower opening of the primary S.

Comments: Greer lists this variety as very scarce.

	VG-8	F-12	VF-20	EF-40	AU-50	MS-60
VARIETY	$25	$35	$50	$75	$125	$325
NORMAL	15	20	25	35	100	250

1889 FS-10-1889-801 (005.3)

VARIETY: Doubled-Die Reverse, Repunched Date
PUP: Left wreath on reverse; 1 of date
URS-11 · I-3 · L-3

GREER-101;
CONECA: DDR-001

Description: The doubling is evident on the wreath between 7 o'clock and 11 o'clock. The date is repunched.

Comments: The doubling is also evident on the O and D of ONE DIME. This is designated by CONECA (in its 1994 U.S. Doubled Die Master Listing) as Stage-A, with a Repunched Date that shows as an underlying 18 north of the primary 18. This is the same reverse doubled die listed for FS-801, which is presumably the same as CONECA's Stage-B with normal obverse.

	VG-8	F-12	VF-20	EF-40	AU-50	MS-60
VARIETY	$25	$30	$38	$53	$120	$245
NORMAL	15	20	25	35	80	150

1890 FS-10-1890-301 (005.5)

VARIETY: Misplaced Date
PUP: Gown by shield
URS-11 · I-3 · L-3

GREER-101

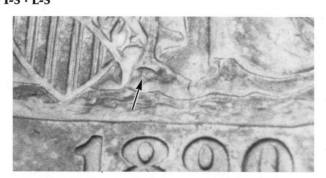

Description: The top of a digit—probably a 9—is evident in the gown just right of the banner across the shield.

Comments: This is another wildly misplaced date.

	VG-8	F-12	VF-20	EF-40	AU-50	MS-60
VARIETY	$25	$35	$50	$75	$125	$250
NORMAL	15	20	25	35	80	150

1890 FS-10-1890-302 (005.6)

VARIETY: Misplaced Date   **GREER-102**
PUP: Gown by shield
URS-6 · I-3 · L-3

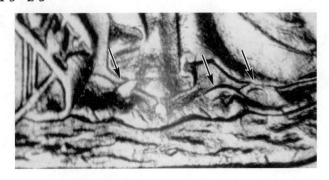

Description: The tops of several digits are evident in the gown.
Comments: This is a wildly misplaced date.

	VG-8	F-12	VF-20	EF-40	AU-50	MS-60
VARIETY	$25	$35	$50	$75	$125	$250
NORMAL	15	20	25	35	80	150

1890-S FS-10-1890S-501

VARIETY: Repunched Mintmark   **GREER-101; CONECA: RPM-001**
PUP: Mintmark
URS-7 · I-3 · L-3

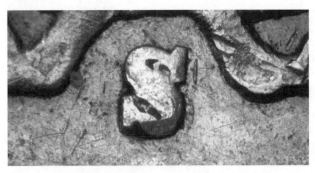

Description: The primary S mintmark, larger and centered over the initial smaller S, is evident within and to the right of the upper loop of the primary S.
Comments: This is a very tough variety to locate in any grade.

	VG-8	F-12	VF-20	EF-40	AU-50	MS-60
VARIETY	$30	$55	$80	$115	$250	$450
NORMAL	20	25	55	85	150	350

1890-S
FS-10-1890S-502 (006)

VARIETY: Repunched Mintmark
PUP: Mintmark
URS-7 · I-3 · L-3

GREER-102; CONECA: RPM-001; AWASH-3

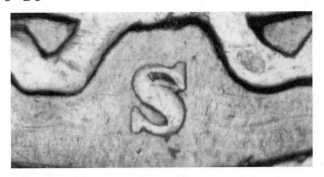

Description: The primary S mintmark, larger and centered over the initial smaller S, is evident within the upper loop of the primary S.

Comments: This is a very tough variety to locate in any grade. (Note: This variety was incorrectly listed as FS-10-1890S-501 in the fourth edition, volume II.)

	VG-8	F-12	VF-20	EF-40	AU-50	MS-60
VARIETY	$30	$55	$80	$115	$250	$450
NORMAL	20	25	55	85	150	350

1891
FS-10-1891-301

VARIETY: Misplaced Date
PUP: Denticles below date
URS-6 · I-3 · L-3

GREER-101

Description: The top of a digit—most likely an 8—is evident in the denticles below the 8 and 9 in the date.

Comments: The misplaced date is very evident even in lower grades.

	VG-8	F-12	VF-20	EF-40	AU-50	MS-60
VARIETY	$25	$35	$50	$75	$100	$200
NORMAL	15	20	25	35	80	150

1891-O
FS-10-1891o-501 (005.6)

VARIETY: Repunched Mintmark
PUP: Mintmark
URS-8 · I-3 · L-3

GREER-101; CONECA: RPM-002

Description: The primary mintmark was punched over a previously punched horizontal O.

Comments: Though very rare, this has always been a very popular variety.

	VG-8	F-12	VF-20	EF-40	AU-50	MS-60
VARIETY	$40	$75	$125	$200	$300	$450
NORMAL	15	20	30	60	110	200

1891-S
FS-10-1891S-501 (007)

VARIETY: Repunched Mintmark
PUP: Mintmark
URS-9 · I-3 · L-3

GREER-101; CONECA: RPM-001; AWASH-5

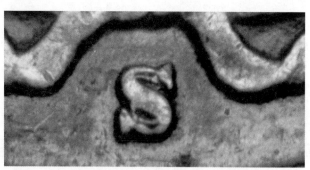

Description: As on the 1890 coin, the larger primary S mintmark (known as the medium S) was punched squarely over the smaller initial S, and is evident within both loops of the primary S.

Comments: This is another extremely popular variety.

	VG-8	F-12	VF-20	EF-40	AU-50	MS-60
VARIETY	$30	$40	$75	$110	$200	$350
NORMAL	15	20	25	35	80	175

Barber or Liberty Head Dimes, 1892–1916

Only a limited number of varieties in the Barber series were reported when the third edition of the *Cherrypickers' Guide* went to press. Furthermore, some varieties were known but were not included in that edition. Since that time a significant number of new varieties have been reported, and there are undoubtedly many varieties yet to be discovered. Therefore, we encourage close inspection of all Barber coins.

To obtain more knowledge of Barber coins in general and Barber varieties in particular, we suggest membership in the Barber Coin Collectors' Society. Annual dues are $15. For more information, contact

BCCS
Eileen Ribar
2053 Edith Place
Merrick, NY 11566
E-mail: bccs@BarberCoins.org

The society's quarterly publication, the *Journal,* contains educational information on all denominations of the Barber design. The web site address is www.barbercoins.org. Visitors to the site can find educational articles; membership information; and general information concerning the Barber design, the three Barber silver series, and Liberty Head nickels.

1892   FS-10-1892-301 (10c-008.3)

VARIETY: Repunched Date   **LAWRENCE: N/L**
PUP: Date
URS-3 · I-3 · L-3

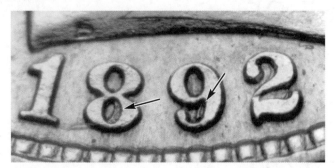

Description: The secondary digits 8, 9, and 2 are visible left of the primary numbers. Although this variety is extremely similar to Lawrence 102 (Breen 3472), the difference is discernible by comparing the alignment of the 8 and 9 with the denticles below the date.

Comments: This specimen is different from the better-known RPD as indicated above, and should be considered rarer because few examples have been reported.

	F-12	VF-20	EF-40	AU-50	AU-55	MS-60	MS-63
VARIETY	$30	$40	$65	$100	$125	$150	$250
NORMAL	18	25	30	75	90	125	200

1892   FS-10-1892-302 (10c-008.4)

VARIETY: Repunched Date   **LAWRENCE-102**
PUP: Date
URS-4 · I-3 · L-3

Description: This RPD is evident with secondary numbers left of the primary numbers on the 8, 9, and 2. Additional doubling is visible south of the 2.

Comments: As with many repunched dates of the series, value is subjective.

	F-12	VF-20	EF-40	AU-50	AU-55	MS-60	MS-63
VARIETY	$30	$40	$65	$100	$125	$150	$250
NORMAL	18	25	30	75	90	125	200

1892-O
FS-10-1892o-301 (10c-008.5)

VARIETY: Repunched Date
PUP: Date
URS-4 · I-3 · L-2

LAWRENCE-101

Description: This is another somewhat typical RPD, with secondary digits visible west of the primary digits. The secondary 2 is weaker than the other numbers.

Comments: This is a fairly well known variety.

	F-12	VF-20	EF-40	AU-50	AU-55	MS-60	MS-63
VARIETY	$40	$60	$85	$105	$140	$200	$340
NORMAL	35	50	75	95	110	165	290

1893-S
FS-10-1893S-501 (10c-009)

VARIETY: Repunched Mintmark
PUP: Mintmark
URS-6 · I-3 · L-3

LAWRENCE-101; CONECA: RPM-001

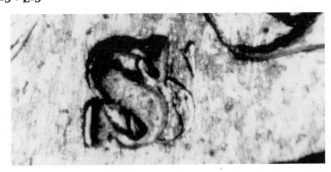

Description: The secondary S is evident east of the primary S.

Comments: This is a well-known RPM among variety and Barber specialists. There are two other interesting repunched mintmarks known for this date. We would like to examine them for photos! Strike doubling is evident to the left of the primary S.

	F-12	VF-20	EF-40	AU-50	AU-55	MS-60	MS-63
VARIETY	$48	$73	$98	$170	$210	$335	$750
NORMAL	37	60	85	140	175	290	675

1895-S   FS-10-1895S-301 (10c-009.2)

VARIETY: Repunched Date
PUP: Date
URS-5 · I-3 · L-2

LAWRENCE-101

Description: The secondary 9 and 5 are evident north of the primary numbers.
Comments: To the best of our knowledge, this RPD is rather scarce.

	F-12	VF-20	EF-40	AU-50	AU-55	MS-60
VARIETY	$150	$215	$265	$335	$385	$600
NORMAL	135	190	240	310	335	500

1896   FS-10-1896-301 (10c-009.3)

VARIETY: Repunched Date
PUP: Date
URS-5 · I-3 · L-2

LAWRENCE: N/L

Description: A secondary 8, 9, and 6 are evident south of the primary digits. The secondary 8 is primarily visible within the lower loop of the primary 8.
Comments: This is a very attractive RPD!

	VG-8	F-12	VF-20	EF-40	AU-50	AU-55	MS-60
VARIETY	$30	$60	$85	$115	$135	$150	$190
NORMAL	22	50	75	100	120	140	175

1897 — FS-10-1897-301

VARIETY: Repunched Date
PUP: Date
URS-6 · I-3 · L-2

LAWRENCE-101

Description: The secondary digits of the date are evident west of the primary digits.

Comments: This is one of the most dramatic RPDs of the series.

	VG-8	F-12	VF-20	EF-40	AU-50	AU-55	MS-60
VARIETY	$20.00	$35	$55	$70	$95	$115	$165
NORMAL	3.50	8	15	30	70	85	135

1897 — FS-10-1897-302 (10c-009.51)

VARIETY: Repunched Date
PUP: Date
URS-6 · I-2 · L-2

LAWRENCE: N/L

Description: Like the FS-301, this variety shows the secondary digits west of the primary, but they are slightly different and somewhat less evident.

Comments: Demand for this variety is moderate.

	VG-8	F-12	VF-20	EF-40	AU-50	AU-55	MS-60
VARIETY	$20.00	$35	$55	$70	$95	$115	$165
NORMAL	3.50	8	15	30	70	85	135

1897 FS-10-1897-303

VARIETY: Repunched Date   **LAWRENCE: N/L**
PUP: Date
NEW LISTING

Description: A bold underlying 8 is visible to the south of the primary 8, and a bit of an underlying 7 shows at the upper right corner of the 7.

Comments: This is one of the nicest RPDs for the date.

	VG-8	F-12	VF-20	EF-40	AU-50	AU-55	MS-60
VARIETY	n/a	n/a	n/a	n/a	n/a	n/a	n/a
NORMAL	$3.50	$8	$15	$30	$70	$85	$135

1899-O FS-10-1899o-301 (10c-009.83)

VARIETY: Repunched Date   **LAWRENCE: N/L**
PUP: Date
URS-6 · I-3 · L-2

Description: The loop of a secondary 9 is visible within the loop of the last 9.

Comments: This variety is most evident on higher-grade specimens.

	F-12	VF-20	EF-40	AU-50	AU-55	MS-60
VARIETY	$80	$115	$165	$245	$310	$475
NORMAL	65	95	140	225	285	400

1899-O

FS-10-1899o-501 (10c-009.8)

VARIETY: Repunched Mintmark
PUP: Mintmark
URS-7 · I-3 · L-2

LAWRENCE-103; CONECA: RPM-001

Description: The secondary mintmark is evident west of the primary. The upper portion of the left side of the secondary O apparently was polished away.

Comments: This is a very well known variety!

	F-12	VF-20	EF-40	AU-50	AU-55	MS-60
VARIETY	$90	$150	$190	$250	$325	$500
NORMAL	65	95	140	225	285	400

1901-O

FS-10-1901o-501 (10c-010)

VARIETY: Repunched Mintmark
PUP: Mintmark
URS-4 · I-3 · L-3

LAWRENCE-103; CONECA: RPM-001

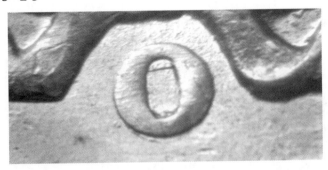

Description: This variety is commonly referred to as an O over horizontal O. The mintmark was punched into the die horizontally and later corrected.

Comments: Another one of the many O over horizontal O RPMs known on U.S. coins.

	F-12	VF-20	EF-40	AU-50	AU-55	MS-60
VARIETY	$50	$75	$125	$235	$290	$550
NORMAL	16	28	65	180	230	400

1903   FS-10-1903-301 (10c-010.025)

VARIETY: Repunched Date
PUP: Date
URS-2 · I-3 · L-2

LAWRENCE: N/L

Description: Secondary digits are visible west of the primary digits, with the 1 and 0 being the most prominent.

Comments: The image at the lower left of the 0 is likely a small die chip. A higher-grade specimen is necessary for further study.

	VG-8	F-12	VF-20	EF-40	AU-50	AU-55	MS-60
VARIETY	$20	$35	$55.00	$70	$95	$115	$165
NORMAL	4	5	7.50	25	70	80	110

1903-O   FS-10-1903o-301

VARIETY: Repunched Date
PUP: Date
URS-5 · I-3 · L-2

LAWRENCE: N/L

DESCRIPTION: A secondary 3 is evident west of the primary 3.

COMMENTS: Although some collectors believe this to be a 3 over 2, the detail of this early die state clearly shows a 3 over 3.

	VG-8	F-12	VF-20	EF-40	AU-50	AU-55	MS-60
VARIETY	$25	$40	$60	$75	$120	$135	$300
NORMAL	5	14	25	50	110	125	275

1906

FS-10-1906-301 (10c-010.085)

LAWRENCE-103

VARIETY: Repunched Date
PUP: Date
URS-8 · I-3 · L-2

Description: The last two digits of the date are repunched, with the secondary digits evident west of the primary digits. The secondary 0 in this photo does not show well.

Comments: Because of low liquidity, expect only higher-grade specimens to sell easily.

	VG-8	F-12	VF-20	EF-40	AU-50	AU-55	MS-60
VARIETY	$10	$15	$25	$40	$75	$90	$125
NORMAL	3	4	7	22	70	80	110

1906-D

FS-10-1906D-301 (10c-010.088)

LAWRENCE: N/L

VARIETY: Repunched Date, Repunched Mintmark
PUP: Date, mintmark
URS-4 · I-2 · L-3

Description: Several secondary numbers are evident in various directions. A secondary 1 is visible west of the primary, a secondary 9 slightly north, a barely evident secondary 0 far south, and a secondary 6 west within the loop of the primary 6. The secondary D mintmark is evident east of the primary D.

Comments: This is an interesting RPD/RPM combination.

	VG-8	F-12	VF-20	EF-40	AU-50	AU-55	MS-60
VARIETY	$12	$18	$28	$40	$90	$125	$185
NORMAL	5	8	15	35	80	90	165

1906-D

FS-10-1906D-302 (10c-010.089)

VARIETY: Repunched Date, Repunched Mintmark
PUP: Date, mintmark
URS-4 · I-2 · L-3

LAWRENCE: N/L

 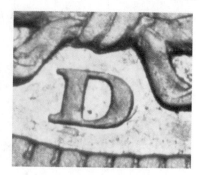

Description: This variety is similar to the previous listing, but differs in several aspects. The secondary date digits are visible very slightly south on all digits. The lower right side of the secondary D mintmark is evident east and slightly north of the primary D.

Comments: Like the previous coin, this is an interesting RPD/RPM combination.

	VG-8	F-12	VF-20	EF-40	AU-50	AU-55	MS-60
VARIETY	$12	$18	$28	$40	$90	$125	$185
NORMAL	5	8	15	35	80	90	165

1906-D

FS-10-1906D-303 (10c-010.089)

VARIETY: Repunched Date, Misplaced Date
PUP: Date, mintmark
URS-1 · I-4 · L-3

LAWRENCE: N/L

Description: This very interesting variety features a repunched date showing a secondary 9 within the loop of the primary 9, a secondary 0 far south but barely evident within the lower portion of the primary 0, and a secondary 6 within the loop of the primary 6. The most remarkable features of this variety, though, are the numerous date digits protruding from the denticles below the primary date. We've counted as many as nine digits in the denticles.

Comments: To date no other specimens have been reported to us.

	VG-8	F-12	VF-20	EF-40	AU-50	AU-55	MS-60
VARIETY	n/a	n/a	n/a	n/a	n/a	n/a	n/a
NORMAL	$5	$8	$15	$35	$80	$90	$165

1906-O

FS-10-1906o-301

VARIETY: Repunched Date, Misplaced Date
PUP: Date
URS-3 · I-3 · L-2

LAWRENCE: N/L

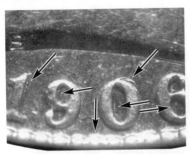 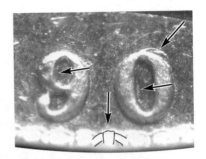

Description: All four digits are repunched, with the secondary 1 and 9 east, the secondary 0 northeast, and the secondary 6 evident within the loop of the primary 6. Another digit, possibly a 0, is visible within the denticles between the 9 and the 0.

Comments: Auction data are unknown for this variety.

	VG-8	F-12	VF-20	EF-40	AU-50	AU-55	MS-60
VARIETY	n/a	n/a	n/a	n/a	n/a	n/a	n/a
NORMAL	$14	$45	$75	$95	$130	$150	200

1906-S

FS-10-1906S-301

VARIETY: Repunched Date, Repunched Mintmark
PUP: Date, mintmark
URS-4 · I-3 · L-3

LAWRENCE: N/L

Description: A secondary digit is evident within the lower loop of the 9 and within the upper loop of the 6. The earlier die states show a secondary S north of the primary S, indicating that there may have been more than one repunched S.

Comments: This is certainly a variety worth searching for.

	VG-8	F-12	VF-20	EF-40	AU-50	AU-55	MS-60
VARIETY	$10	$20	$32	$55	$125	$155	$300
NORMAL	6	13	25	45	110	135	275

1907
FS-10-1907-301

VARIETY: Repunched Date

LAWRENCE-103

PUP: Date

URS-4 · I-3 · L-3

Description: This very interesting repunched date shows secondary images north of the primary 1 and 9.

Comments: This is one of the more attractive RPDs in the series.

	VG-8	F-12	VF-20	EF-40	AU-50	AU-55	MS-60
VARIETY	$20	$30	$40	$60	$80	$115	$165
NORMAL	3	4	7	22	70	80	110

1907-D
FS-10-1907D-301

VARIETY: Repunched Date

LAWRENCE-101

PUP: Date

URS-5 · I-2 · L-2

Description: Secondary images are visible within the lower loop of the 9 and below the tail of the 7.

Comments: This variety can be located with some searching.

	VG-8	F-12	VF-20	EF-40	AU-50	AU-55	MS-60
VARIETY	$20	$30	$40	$60	$125	$160	$300
NORMAL	4	9	18	45	110	135	275

1907-O

FS-10-1907o-501

VARIETY: Repunched Mintmark
PUP: Mintmark
URS-6 · I-3 · L-3

LAWRENCE: N/L

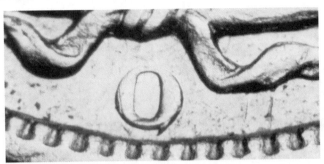

Description: The weaker O mintmark is evident south of the primary mintmark.
Comments: This is a very collectible variety!

	VG-8	F-12	VF-20	EF-40	AU-50	AU-55	MS-60
VARIETY	$25	$45	$65	$90	$125	$150	$225
NORMAL	7	30	45	70	110	135	210

1908

FS-10-1908-301

VARIETY: Repunched Date
PUP: Date
URS-6 · I-3 · L-3

LAWRENCE-101

Description: This is a fairly well known repunched date, with secondary images evident south on the 9, 0, and 8.
Comments: This is another nice RPD for the series.

	VG-8	F-12	VF-20	EF-40	AU-50	AU-55	MS-60
VARIETY	$30	$60	$110	$135	$160	$200	$250
NORMAL	3	4	7	22	75	85	110

1908   FS-10-1908-302

VARIETY: Repunched Date
PUP: Date
URS-7 · I-3 · L-3

LAWRENCE: N/L

Description: A secondary 0 is clearly evident inside the lower left portion of the 0. There is also a secondary image of some type within the upper loop of the 8.

Comments: This is one of the more attractive RPDs in the series.

	VG-8	F-12	VF-20	EF-40	AU-50	AU-55	MS-60
VARIETY	$30	$60	$110	$135	$160	$200	$250
NORMAL	3	4	7	22	75	85	110

1908   FS-10-1908-303

VARIETY: Repunched Date
PUP: Date
URS-5 · I-2 · L-2

LAWRENCE: N/L

Description: This is a nice repunched date, with multiple secondary images evident on all four digits southeast of the primary digits.

Comments: There may be as many as four complete dates punched into this die.

	VG-8	F-12	VF-20	EF-40	AU-50	AU-55	MS-60
VARIETY	$30	$60	$110	$135	$165	$210	$260
NORMAL	3	4	7	22	75	85	110

1908-D

FS-10-1908D-301 (10c-010.220)

VARIETY: Repunched Date
PUP: Mintmark
URS-4 · I-2 · L-3

LAWRENCE: N/L

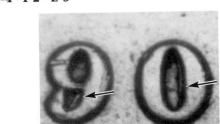 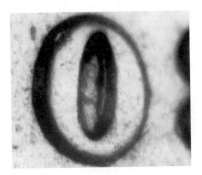

Description: This is a variety considered by some to be an overdate. A secondary image, which may be a low 0, is evident within the lower loop of the 0. Secondary images are also evident within the lower loop of the 9 and within the 8.

Comments: Another interesting variety in this series.

	VG-8	F-12	VF-20	EF-40	AU-50	AU-55	MS-60
VARIETY	$25	$45	$65	$80	$115	$165	$215
NORMAL	3	6	10	28	75	90	130

1908-D

FS-10-1908D-302 (10c-010.210)

VARIETY: Repunched Date
PUP: Date
URS-3 · I-3 · L-3

LAWRENCE: N/L

Description: Secondary digits are evident within the 0 and the 8, south of the primary digits.

Comments: Please let us know if you locate other specimens!

	VG-8	F-12	VF-20	EF-40	AU-50	AU-55	MS-60
VARIETY	$20	$30	$40	$55	$80	$115	$165
NORMAL	3	6	10	28	75	90	130

1908-D
FS-10-1908D-303 (10c-010.200)

VARIETY: Overdate
PUP: Date
URS-7 · I-3 · L-3

LAWRENCE-104

Description: This is a very attractive overdate with multiple punchings. Secondary digits are evident within the 9, the 0, and the 8.

Comments: This is another very collectible overdate.

	VG-8	F-12	VF-20	EF-40	AU-50	AU-55	MS-60
VARIETY	$20	$30	$40	$55	$90	$165	$330
NORMAL	3	6	10	28	75	90	130

1908-D
FS-10-1908D-304 (10c-010.225)

VARIETY: Repunched Date
PUP: Date
URS-7 · I-3 · L-3

LAWRENCE-105

Description: The top of a 0 is evident within the loop of the 0.

Comments: This is a very dramatic variety.

	VG-8	F-12	VF-20	EF-40	AU-50	AU-55	MS-60
VARIETY	$20	$30	$40	$55	$80	$115	$165
NORMAL	3	6	10	28	75	90	130

1908-D
FS-10-1908D-305 (10c-010.230)

VARIETY: Repunched Date
PUP: Date
URS-6 · I-3 · L-3

LAWRENCE-101

Description: This RPD shows evidence of multiple date punches, particularly within the opening of the 0 and within both loops of the 8. Very little repunching is evident on the 1.

Comments: This RPD may be difficult to detect in low grades.

	VG-8	F-12	VF-20	EF-40	AU-50	AU-55	MS-60
VARIETY	$20	$30	$40	$55	$80	$115	$165
NORMAL	3	6	10	28	75	90	130

1908-D
FS-10-1908D-306 (10c-010.235)

VARIETY: Repunched Date
PUP: Date
URS-6 · I-3 · L-3

LAWRENCE: N/L

Description: The initial date was punched too low and then corrected. Secondary images are evident within the 0 and within both loops of the 8.

Comments: This variety may be difficult to determine in lower grades.

	VG-8	F-12	VF-20	EF-40	AU-50	AU-55	MS-60
VARIETY	$20	$30	$40	$55	$115	$165	$285
NORMAL	3	6	10	28	75	90	130

1908-D

FS-10-1908D-307 (10c-010.240)

VARIETY: Repunched Date
PUP: Date
URS-3 · I-3 · L-3

LAWRENCE: N/L

Description: On this particular specimen, the only visible evidence of a repunched date is the protruding 1 below the primary 1. This is the only known 1908-D with a strong repunched 1.

Comments: We really need to see a higher-grade specimen.

	VG-8	F-12	VF-20	EF-40	AU-50	AU-55	MS-60
VARIETY	$20	$30	$40	$55	$115	$165	$285
NORMAL	3	6	10	28	75	90	130

1908-O

FS-10-1908o-301 (10c-010.250)

VARIETY: Repunched Date
PUP: Date area, above-right of the 8
URS-2 · I-4 · L-5

LAWRENCE: N/L

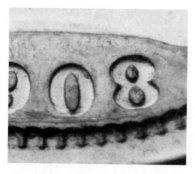 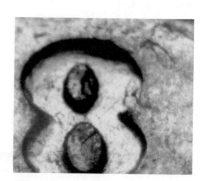

Description: This is a very dramatic repunched date, with remnants of an underlying 8 evident above and far right of the primary 8. There is evidence that other numbers were repunched as well.

Comments: We need to see a higher-grade specimen of this variety!

	VG-8	F-12	VF-20	EF-40	AU-50	AU-55	MS-60
VARIETY	$40	$60	$75	$115	$190	$255	$380
NORMAL	12	45	65	95	150	185	300

1908-O

FS-10-1908o-302 (10c-010.260)

VARIETY: Repunched Date
PUP: Date
URS-6 · I-3 · L-3

LAWRENCE: N/L

 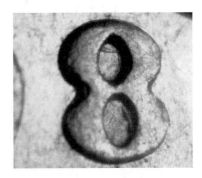

Description: Secondary images are evident within the loops of the 8. Remnants of other underlying numbers can be seen within the 9 and the 0.

Comments: These variations may be difficult to detect in low grades.

	VG-8	F-12	VF-20	EF-40	AU-50	AU-55	MS-60
VARIETY	$30	$50	$75	$100	$170	$215	$340
NORMAL	12	45	65	95	150	185	300

1912-S

FS-10-1912S-101 (10c-010.250)

VARIETY: Doubled-Die Obverse
PUP: UNITED
URS-3 · I-1 · L-4

LAWRENCE: N/L

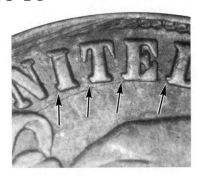 

Description: The doubling is evident on all lettering of UNITED STATES OF AMERICA, most notably on UNITED.

Comments: (Note: Because of its low Interest Factor, this variety will be removed from this chapter in the next edition of this volume, to make room for more popularly collected pieces. The Fivaz-Stanton number will be retained for this variety and it will remain in the cross-references at the back of the book.)

Mercury Dimes, 1916–1945

Mercury dimes are one of the most widely collected series of the 20th century. Both the artistic design and the fact that the coins were still in circulation during the collecting boom of the 1950s have served to intensify collector interest. Unlike Jefferson nickels, Roosevelt dimes, or Lincoln cents, this series has relatively few varieties. Several of them, however, are quite dramatic and in very high demand. Serious collectors are obviously interested in the scarce and rare dates, but also among those specimens are some well-struck coins that exhibit "full split bands" on the reverse.

The most remarkable and well-known varieties are certainly the overdates of 1942 and 1942-D, though other significant varieties do exist. The 1945-D, D Over Horizontal D, and the 1945-S, S Over Horizontal S, are highly prized finds. Other varieties include repunched mintmarks, doubled dies, and a very likely S Over D variety from 1945.

As of this publication date there are no clubs devoted strictly to the study of the Mercury dime. However, for those interested primarily in the varieties within the series, we suggest membership in CONECA, the national error and variety club. Each issue of their bi-monthly publication, the *ErrorScope,* contains articles on errors and varieties of all types, and even from other countries. For adults, annual dues are $25 (for bulk mailing; contact the Membership Coordinator for current First Class or international rates). For Young Numismatists (under age 18), dues are $7.50 (online membership only, which includes digital access to *ErrorScope*) or $17.50 (online membership plus hard-copy subscription to *ErrorScope*). An application can be obtained online at www.conecaonline.org, or from Rachel Irish at the following address:

CONECA
Rachel Irish
101 W. Prairie #323
Hayden, ID 83835
E-mail: MRirish5@roadrunner.com

1928-S

FS-10-1928S-501 (10c-010.26)

VARIETY: Large S Mintmark
PUP: Mintmark
URS-5 · I-4 · L-4

CONECA: MMS-003

Common Small S

Scarce Large S

Description: The mintmark on this variety is relatively large, with two distinct serifs.

Comments: This variety has proven quite rare in Mint State. The normal or "small" mintmark is the typical size for the era. About 80% of the coins of this date are the Small S variety.

	VF-20	EF-40	AU-50	MS-60	MS-63
VARIETY	$13	$45	$90	$210	$360
NORMAL	6	16	45	140	275

1929-S

FS-10-1929S-101 (10c-010.3)

VARIETY: Doubled-Die Obverse
PUP: Date, IN GOD WE TRUST
URS-4 · I-3 · L-2

CONECA: DDO-001

Description: This doubled die is evident with moderate doubling on the date and IN GOD WE TRUST.

Comments: This variety has not attracted a lot of interest. We would like to see a higher-grade example with a strong strike on the date.

	VF-20	EF-40	AU-50	MS-60	MS-63
VARIETY	$28	$40	$55	$80	$140
NORMAL	5	10	20	30	45

1931-D

FS-10-1931D-101

VARIETY: Doubled-Die Obverse, Doubled-Die Reverse   **CONECA: DDO-001**
PUP: Date
URS-3 · I-2 · L-2

Description: Light doubling is evident on the date, and very light doubling on the leaves by OF on the reverse.

Comments: This variety was first listed in the fourth edition, volume II.

	VF-20	EF-40	AU-50	MS-60	MS-63
VARIETY	$50	$60	$85	$135	$190
NORMAL	20	35	60	85	140

1931-S

FS-10-1931S-101

VARIETY: Doubled-Die Obverse   **CONECA: DDO-001**
PUP: Date
URS-4 · I-2 · L-3

Description: This is a moderate doubled die, with the doubling evident on the date and IN GOD WE TRUST.

Comments: This is one of the few doubled dies known in the Mercury dime series.

	VF-20	EF-40	AU-50	MS-60	MS-63
VARIETY	$23	$38	$65	$135	$190
NORMAL	10	16	45	75	150

1934-D

FS-10-1934D-501

VARIETY: Repunched Mintmark
PUP: Mintmark
NEW LISTING

CONECA: RPM-001

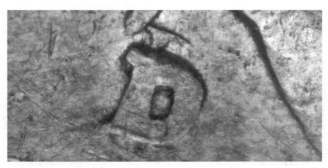

Description: A secondary D shows wide and to the north of the primary D; the secondary D touches an olive leaf, which is the probable cause for the correction.

Comments: Some feel this is a Large D Over Small D, but there is no conclusive evidence to support this; nor is it listed by CONECA as such. No matter—it is a great RPM that we would like to photograph in a higher grade.

	VF-20	EF-40	AU-50	MS-60	MS-63
VARIETY	n/a	n/a	n/a	n/a	n/a
NORMAL	$3	$8	$12	$19	$60

1935-S

FS-10-1935S-501 (10c-010.5)

VARIETY: Repunched Mintmark
PUP: Mintmark
URS-9 · I-3 · L-3

CONECA: RPM-001

Description: The secondary S is evident south of the primary S.

Comments: On the specimen examined, strike doubling was also evident on the north side of the primary mintmark.

	VF-20	EF-40	AU-50	MS-60	MS-63
VARIETY	$20.00	$30	$40.00	$65	$95
NORMAL	2.75	5	7.50	11	30

1936 FS-10-1936-101 (10c-010.5)

VARIETY: Doubled-Die Obverse   **CONECA: DDO-001**
PUP: Date, IN GOD WE TRUST
URS-9 · I-3 · L-3

Description: Moderate doubling is evident on IN GOD WE TRUST and the date. Lesser doubling is also visible on LIBERTY.

Comments: This is one of the stronger doubled dies known for this series.

	VF-20	EF-40	AU-50	AU-55	MS-60	MS-63	MS-65
VARIETY	$17.00	$25.00	$33	$40.00	$55	$110	$175
NORMAL	2.50	3.50	6	7.50	9	18	30

1936-S FS-10-1936S-110

VARIETY: Possible Overdate   **CONECA: N/L**
PUP: Date
URS-1 · I-4 · L-5

Description: The secondary image of a 2 is evident beneath the 3 of the date. Most evident is the flat portion of the base of the underlying 2. Remains of what may be a secondary 9 are evident to the left of the primary 9. Many die polish marks are also evident throughout the surface of the obverse. No doubling is evident on other elements.

Comments: Many specialists disagree as to whether this is an overdate. The length of time between the striking of the last 1929-dated coins and this 1936 coin would seem to eliminate the possibility of a 2 underlying the 3. However, examination has matched the shapes on the image under the 3 to that of the 2 on 1929-dated dimes. Stranger things have happened. Keep in mind that 1936 was during the Great Depression, when Mint personnel wanted to save money whenever possible. No auction data exist to determine current values.

	EF-40	AU-50	AU-55	MS-60	MS-63	MS-65
VARIETY	n/a	n/a	n/a	n/a	n/a	n/a
NORMAL	$3.50	$6	$9	$14	$30	$35

1937

Variety: Doubled-Die Obverse
PUP: IN GOD WE TRUST
URS-8 · I-1 · L-2

CONECA: DDO-001

Description: A very close spread is evident on IN GOD WE TRUST, the date, and designer's initials.

Comments: This variety exhibits somewhat minor doubling. (Note: Because of its low Interest Factor, this variety will be removed from this chapter in the next edition of this volume, to make room for more popularly collected pieces. The Fivaz-Stanton number will be retained for this variety and it will remain in the cross-references at the back of the book.)

1937-S

Variety: Doubled-Die Obverse
PUP: Date, IN GOD WE TRUST
URS-4 · I-3 · L-3

CONECA: DDO-001

Description: Doubling is evident on the date, IN GOD WE TRUST, and the designer's initials.

Comments: This variety attracts premiums of about 45% to 65% of the normal coin's value.

	EF-40	AU-50	AU-55	MS-60	MS-63	MS-65
Variety	$8.00	$11	$16	$30	$45	$75
Normal	3.50	6	9	14	30	40

1939   FS-10-1939-101

VARIETY: Doubled-Die Obverse   **CONECA: DDO-001**
PUP: Date
URS-6 · I-2 · L-2

Description: Light doubling is evident on the date, and IN GOD WE TRUST.

Comments: This variety can be located with a little searching.

	EF-40	AU-50	AU-55	MS-60	MS-63	MS-65
VARIETY	n/a	n/a	n/a	n/a	n/a	n/a
NORMAL	$3	$6	$8	$10	$12	$25

1939-D   FS-10-1939D-501

VARIETY: Repunched Mintmark   **CONECA: RPM-001**
PUP: Mintmark
URS-4 · I-3 · L-3

Description: The secondary D is evident south of the primary D.

Comments: RPMs in the Mercury dime series are highly collectible.

	EF-40	AU-50	AU-55	MS-60	MS-63	MS-65
VARIETY	$11.00	$16	$22	$30	$50	$75
NORMAL	3.25	6	8	10	12	28

1940-S

FS-10-1940S-501

VARIETY: Repunched Mintmark
PUP: Mintmark
URS-5 · I-3 · L-3

CONECA: RPM-001

Description: This S/S/S/S quadruple-punched mintmark is evident with secondary images west, and several split serifs.

Comments: This is a very nice RPM—the nicest for the date, and one of the nicest seen so far in the series.

	EF-40	AU-50	AU-55	MS-60	MS-63	MS-65
VARIETY	$20.00	$40	$50	$65	$75	$100
NORMAL	3.25	6	8	11	15	35

1940-S

FS-10-1940S-901

VARIETY: Doubled-Die Obverse, Doubled-Die Reverse
PUP: Date on obverse, ES of STATES on reverse
NEW LISTING

CONECA: DDO-002, DDR-001;
WEXLER: WDDO-001, WDDR-001

Description: Doubling on the obverse is evident on the date, designer's initials, and motto. On the reverse, a spread toward the center shows on STATES OF, the top of the fasces, the upper leaves, and the top right branches.

Comments: This is another of the many nice doubled dies on the Mercury dime series. We would like to see an example fully struck-up on the date.

	EF-40	AU-50	AU-55	MS-60	MS-63	MS-65
VARIETY	n/a	n/a	n/a	n/a	n/a	n/a
NORMAL	$3.25	$6	$8	$11	$15	$35

1941 — FS-10-1941-101

VARIETY: Doubled-Die Obverse
PUP: TRUST
URS-4 · I-3 · L-3

CONECA: DDO-002

Description: Strong doubling is evident on the RUS of TRUST. Other doubling is evident on the nose, the truncation of the bust, and the base of the 1 on the date. Strong die polish is also evident through the S and T.

Comments: This variety commands strong premiums over the normal coin's value.

	EF-40	AU-50	AU-55	MS-60	MS-63	MS-65
VARIETY	$18.00	$30	$45	$60	$85	$145
NORMAL	3.25	4	5	6	12	30

1941-D — FS-10-1941D-101

VARIETY: Doubled-Die Obverse, Doubled-Die Reverse
PUP: Date, IN GOD WE TRUST
URS-6 · I-4 · L-2

CONECA: DDO-001, DDR-001

Description: The doubling is most evident on IN GOD WE TRUST, the date, and OF AMERICA.

Comments: Having a doubled die on both obverse and reverse is somewhat unusual and increases interest in this variety. We would like to see an uncirculated earlier die state with full strike.

	EF-40	AU-50	AU-55	MS-60	MS-63	MS-65
VARIETY	$17.00	$22	$28	$33	$65	$95
NORMAL	3.25	4	5	6	12	25

1941-S

VARIETY: Repunched Mintmark
PUP: Mintmark
URS-5 · I-3 · L-3

CONECA: RPM-001

Description: The secondary S is evident north of the primary S.

Comments: RPMs in this series are highly collectible. This is not a large S over small S mintmark.

	EF-40	AU-50	AU-55	MS-60	MS-63	MS-65
VARIETY	$25.00	$35	$45	$60	$90	$135
NORMAL	3.25	4	5	6	12	30

1941-S

VARIETY: Repunched Mintmark
PUP: Mintmark
URS-3 · I-3 · L-3

CONECA: RPM-005

Description: A slightly tilted secondary S is evident east.

Comments: This is another very nice RPM for the Mercury dime series.

	EF-40	AU-50	AU-55	MS-60	MS-63	MS-65
VARIETY	$9.00	$12	$17	$22	$27	$55
NORMAL	3.25	4	5	6	12	30

1941-S
FS-10-1941S-511

VARIETY: Large S Mintmark
PUP: Mintmark
URS-7 · I-5 · L-5

CONECA: MMS-004

Common Small S

Scarce Large S

Description: The upper serif points downward and the lower serif is rounded, like the bell of a trumpet.

Comments: This is the "trumpet tail" S, which is rare for this date. The Large S variety has long been overlooked by collectors, but has gained popularity in recent years. There are several dies known for the Large S dime, including one that is repunched.

	EF-40	AU-50	AU-55	MS-60	MS-63	MS-65
VARIETY	$30.00	$65	$90	$120	$165	$325
NORMAL	3.25	4	5	6	12	30

1941-S
FS-10-1941S-801

VARIETY: Doubled-Die Reverse
PUP: E PLURIBUS UNUM
URS-4 · I-1 · L-1

CONECA: DDR-001

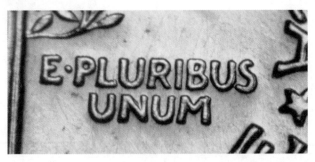

Description: Very light doubling is evident on E PLURIBUS UNUM, on the right side of DIME, and on AMERICA.

Comments: Lacking strong doubling, this variety will probably be tough to sell for much profit. (Note: Because of its low Interest Factor, this variety will be removed from this chapter in the next edition of this volume, to make room for more popularly collected pieces. The Fivaz-Stanton number will be retained for this variety and it will remain in the cross-references at the back of the book.)

1942, 42 Over 41 — FS-10-1942-101 (010.7)

VARIETY: Doubled-Die Obverse, Overdate
PUP: Date
URS-4 · I-5 · L-5

CONECA: DDO-001

Description: The doubling is evident as the 42 over 41 overdate, and slightly evident on IN GOD WE TRUST.

Comments: The values for this variety will fluctuate. Be sure to check current price guides.

	EF-40	AU-50	AU-55	MS-60	MS-63	MS-65
VARIETY	$800.00	$1,100	$1,250	$2,450	$4,300	$15,000
NORMAL	3.25	4	5	6	12	30

1942-D, 42 Over 41 — FS-10-1942D-101 (010.8)

VARIETY: Doubled-Die Obverse, Overdate, Repunched Mintmark
PUP: Date
URS-4 · I-5 · L-5

CONECA: DDO-001, RPM-004

Description: Doubling is evident as the 42 over 41 overdate, slightly evident on IN GOD WE TRUST, and as a D over D slanted west.

Comments: The values for this variety will fluctuate. Be sure to check current price guides.

	EF-40	AU-50	AU-55	MS-60	MS-63	MS-65
VARIETY	$750	$1,150	$1,325	$2,550	$4,500	$9,000
NORMAL	3	4	5	6	12	30

1942-D

FS-10-1942D-501

VARIETY: Repunched Mintmark
PUP: Mintmark
URS-6 · I-3 · L-3

CONECA: RPM-005

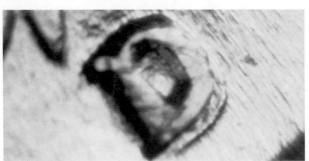

Description: The repunched mintmark is southeast of the primary D, making this another very evident D over D RPM.

Comments: This variety commands strong premiums, especially in lower grades.

	EF-40	AU-50	AU-55	MS-60	MS-63	MS-65
VARIETY	$8	$10	$15	$20	$25	$50
NORMAL	3	4	5	6	12	30

1942-S

FS-10-1942S-501

VARIETY: Inverted Mintmark
PUP: Mintmark
URS-5

WEXLER: WIMM-001;
POTTER: VCR-001, IMM-001

Normal S

Description: The mintmark on this variety is inverted.

Comments: Just a handful of these have been reported in spite of the variety's being well publicized in recent years. At first glance this mintmark style seems virtually symmetrical. However, it's characterized by a more oval center within the upper loop of the S—a diagnostic normally found at the lower loop of this mintmark style—and the serifs are angled slightly different from each other. These characteristics make it possible to conclusively attribute the variety as an Inverted S on high-grade / early-die-state specimens. This variety is not recognized by CONECA.

	EF-40	AU-50	AU-55	MS-60	MS-63	MS-65
VARIETY	n/a	n/a	n/a	n/a	n/a	n/a
NORMAL	$2.50	$4	$5	$7.50	$20	$35

1943-S
FS-10-1943S-501

VARIETY: Repunched Mintmark
PUP: Mintmark
URS-5 · I-3 · L-3

CONECA: RPM-001

Description: This is an S/S/S/S, with secondary mintmarks visible north, northeast, and southwest of the primary S.

Comments: This may be the nicest RPM for this date.

	EF-40	AU-50	AU-55	MS-60	MS-63	MS-65
VARIETY	$8	$10	$15	$20	$25	$50
NORMAL	3	4	5	7	16	30

1943-S
FS-10-1943S-511

VARIETY: Trumpet Tail Mintmark
PUP: Mintmark
URS-3 · I-4 · L-4

CONECA: MMS-004

Description: The top serif of the Trumpet-Tail S points downward, with the lower serif rounded, much like the bell of a trumpet.

Comments: This variety is considerably rarer than the 1941-S Large S, and is extremely rare in Mint State. Specimens with full bands command a significant premium.

	EF-40	AU-50	AU-55	MS-60	MS-63	MS-65
VARIETY	$65	$85	$115	$150	$215	$375
NORMAL	3	4	5	7	16	30

1944-D · FS-10-1944D-501

VARIETY: Repunched Mintmark   **CONECA: RPM-003**
PUP: Mintmark
URS-5 · I-3 · L-3

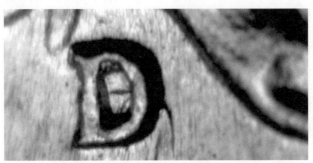

Description: The secondary D is evident southeast of the primary D.
Comments: This is a very nice D over D variety.

	EF-40	AU-50	AU-55	MS-60	MS-63	MS-65
VARIETY	$8	$10	$15	$20.00	$25	$50
NORMAL	3	4	5	6.50	15	30

1945 · FS-10-1945-901

VARIETY: Doubled-Die Obverse   **CONECA: DDO-002**
PUP: Date
NEW LISTING

Description: A rather nice spread can be seen on the date. More doubling
might be evident on earlier die stages. The coin shown here
is in late die state.

Comments: This is a rather new find, suggesting that there are many nice
varieties out there still waiting to be discovered. At least two
other rather decent DDOs are known for this date.

	EF-40	AU-50	AU-55	MS-60	MS-63	MS-65
VARIETY	n/a	n/a	n/a	n/a	n/a	n/a
NORMAL	$2.50	$4	$5	$6	$12	$28

1945-D
FS-10-1945D-501

VARIETY: Repunched Mintmark
PUP: Mintmark
URS-5 · I-3 · L-3

CONECA: RPM-001

Description: The secondary D is evident northeast of the primary D.

Comments: This variety commands strong premiums, especially in the lower grades.

	EF-40	AU-50	AU-55	MS-60	MS-63	MS-65
VARIETY	$8	$10	$15	$20	$25	$50
NORMAL	3	4	5	6	12	30

1945-D
FS-10-1945D-506 (010.95)

VARIETY: Repunched Mintmark
PUP: Mintmark
URS-4 · I-5 · L-5

CONECA: RPM-006

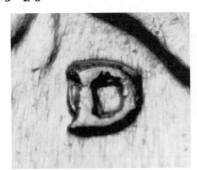 

Description: The first D mintmark was punched into the die horizontally and then corrected.

Comments: This discovery was made in the late 1990s.

	EF-40	AU-50	AU-55	MS-60	MS-63	MS-65
VARIETY	$200	$325	$375	$450	$575	$850
NORMAL	3	4	5	6	12	30

1945-S

FS-10-1945S-503 (011)

VARIETY: Repunched Mintmark

CONECA: RPM-003

PUP: Mintmark

URS-5 · I-5 · L-5

Description: The first S mintmark was punched into the die horizontally and then corrected.

Comments: This variety was discovered prior to the previous 1945-D, D Over Horizontal D, and is considered very rare.

	EF-40	AU-50	AU-55	MS-60	MS-63	MS-65
VARIETY	$200	$325	$375	$450	$600	$950
NORMAL	3	4	5	6	12	30

1945-S

FS-10-1945S-511

VARIETY: Possible Over Mintmark

CONECA: N/L

PUP: Mintmark

URS-2 · I-1 · L-4

Description: The primary S mintmark is evident; however, what may be an underlying D is evident within the upper and lower loops of the S.

Comments: The discovery and examination of a higher-grade example may determine whether this variety shows die cracks or, in fact, an underlying D. (Note: Because of its low Interest Factor, this variety will be removed from this chapter in the next edition of this volume, to make room for more popularly collected pieces. The Fivaz-Stanton number will be retained for this variety and it will remain in the cross-references at the back of the book.)

1945-S

VARIETY: Micro S Mintmark

CONECA: MMS-007

PUP: Mintmark

URS-10 · I-5 · L-4

Common Knob Tail S

Scarce Micro S

Description: The S is significantly smaller than the normal S punches.

Comments: This variety has the only mintmark punch of this type and size known to have been used during the 1940s.

	EF-40	AU-50	AU-55	MS-60	MS-63	MS-65
VARIETY	$6	$10	$15	$25	$40	$85
NORMAL	3	4	5	6	12	30

THE CHERRYPICKERS' GUIDE HELPFUL HINTS

If you can't discern a variety with a 7x loupe, it probably isn't significant.

Roosevelt Dimes, 1946 to Date

As of our publication date, there are no clubs devoted strictly to the study of the Roosevelt dime. However, with the rapidly growing interest in this series, a Roosevelt dime club is sure to be formed soon. This series is widely collected, both as a series and for varieties. And if you're interested in varieties, this is certainly an area that can hold a pot of gold.

Varieties include visually attractive doubled dies, repunched mintmarks, over mintmarks, and even missing mintmarks. In fact, the CONECA Die Variety Master Listing shows hundreds each of doubled dies and repunched mintmarks for this series. Some of the most attractive and desirable doubled dies include a 1950-D reverse, several 1960 Proof obverses, and 1968-S Proof obverse. The over mintmarks include a 1947-S, S Over D; and 1950-D, D Over S. Also included are a really attractive and scarce 1953-D Over Horizontal D; a 1959-D, D Over Inverted D; and a 1962-D, D Over Horizontal D. The majority of the most valuable varieties in the series are illustrated in this section.

Repunched mintmarks are abundant, and RPM collectors are growing constantly. Together, with the numerous RPMs appearing, and the growth of collectors, RPMs in this and other series are becoming more popular—and valuable!

For those interested primarily in the varieties within the series, we would suggest membership in CONECA, the national error and variety club. Each issue of their bi-monthly publication, the *ErrorScope*, contains articles on errors and varieties of all type, and even from other countries. For adults, annual dues are $25 (for bulk mailing; contact the Membership Coordinator for current First Class or international rates). For Young Numismatists (under age 18), dues are $7.50 (online membership only, which includes digital access to *ErrorScope*) or $17.50 (online membership plus hard-copy subscription to *ErrorScope*). An application can be obtained online at www.conecaonline.org, or from Rachel Irish at the following address:

CONECA
Rachel Irish
101 W. Prairie #323
Hayden, ID 83835
E-mail: MRirish5@roadrunner.com

1946 — FS-10-1946-101

VARIETY: Doubled-Die Obverse, Doubled-Die Reverse
PUP: Date, LIBERTY, ONE DIME
URS-3 · I-3 · L-3

CONECA: DDO-004, DDR-003

Description: Strong doubling is evident on all obverse lettering, on the date, and on the designer's initials. Doubling on the reverse is evident on OF AMERICA, ONE DIME, UNUM, and the dot to the right of UNUM.

Comments: This is one of the more popular varieties of the 1946 dime.

	EF-40	AU-50	MS-60	MS-63	MS-65	MS-66
VARIETY	n/a	$15	$20.00	$30.00	$60	$160
NORMAL		3	3.25	3.50	12	28

1946 — FS-10-1946-102

VARIETY: Doubled-Die Obverse, Doubled-Die Reverse
PUP: Date, IN GOD WE TRUST, LIBERTY, designer's initials
URS-2 · I-4 · L-4

CONECA: DDO-004, DDR-004

Description: This is the same obverse die as the previous listing, but with a different doubled-die reverse.

	EF-40	AU-50	MS-60	MS-63	MS-65	MS-66
VARIETY	n/a	$15	$20.00	$30.00	$60	$160
NORMAL		3	3.25	3.50	12	28

1946 — FS-10-1946-103

VARIETY: Doubled-Die Obverse, Doubled-Die Reverse
PUP: IN GOD WE TRUST, date
URS-3 · I-3 · L-3

CONECA: DDO-026, DDR-009

Description: Strong doubling is evident on LIBERTY, the motto, the date, and the designer's initials.

Comments: Several other doubled dies for this date are somewhat similar to this one.

	EF-40	AU-50	MS-60	MS-63	MS-65	MS-66
VARIETY	n/a	$30	$55.00	$110.00	$175	$275
NORMAL		3	3.25	3.50	12	28

1946 — FS-10-1946-104

VARIETY: Doubled-Die Obverse
PUP: Date, IN GOD WE TRUST, LIBERTY, designer's initials
URS-4 · I-3 · L-3

CONECA: DDO-008

Description: Strong doubling is evident on IN GOD WE TRUST, the date, and the designer's initials. A medium counterclockwise spread is evident on LIBERTY.

Comments: Like most of the 1946 varieties, this one commands healthy premiums.

	EF-40	AU-50	MS-60	MS-63	MS-65	MS-66
VARIETY	n/a	$30	$60.00	$125.00	$200	$350
NORMAL		3	3.25	3.50	12	28

1946

VARIETY: Doubled-Die Reverse
CONECA: DDR-006
PUP: UNITED
URS-1 · I-3 · L-3

Description: Strong doubling is evident on UNITED, the olive branches, and the leaves.
Comments: A strong die crack is evident through the T of STATES and the oak leaf.

	EF-40	AU-50	MS-60	MS-63	MS-65	MS-66
VARIETY	n/a	$20	$50.00	$75.00	$125	$200
NORMAL		3	3.25	3.50	12	28

1946

VARIETY: Doubled-Die Reverse
CONECA: DDR-007
PUP: Olive stem
URS-2 · I-3 · L-3

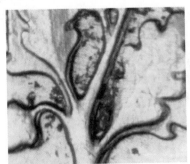

Description: Very strong doubling is evident on the olive stem, branches, and leaves; with very close doubling visible on UNUM.
Comments: This variety is unusual in that the very strong doubling is evident only in this area.

	EF-40	AU-50	MS-60	MS-63	MS-65	MS-66
VARIETY	n/a	$30	$60.00	$125.00	$200	$350
NORMAL		3	3.25	3.50	12	28

1946-D
FS-10-1946D-501

VARIETY: Repunched Mintmark
PUP: Mintmark
URS-3 · I-3 · L-3

CONECA: RPM-025

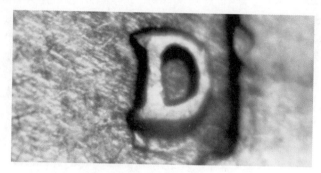

Description: A strong RPM is evident south.
Comments: This RPM has recently been listed by CONECA.

	EF-40	AU-50	MS-60	MS-63	MS-65	MS-66
VARIETY	n/a	$10	$19.00	$23.00	$33	$45
NORMAL		3	3.25	3.50	14	30

1946-D
FS-10-1946D-502

VARIETY: Repunched Mintmark
PUP: Mintmark
URS-3 · I-3 · L-3

CONECA: RPM-015

Description: A secondary D is evident north of the primary D mintmark.
Comments: This RPM was not listed in the RPM book by Tom Miller and John Wexler.

	EF-40	AU-50	MS-60	MS-63	MS-65	MS-66
VARIETY	n/a	$10	$19.00	$23.00	$33	$45
NORMAL		3	3.25	3.50	14	30

1946-D

FS-10-1946D-503

VARIETY: Repunched Mintmark
PUP: Mintmark
URS-3 · I-3 · L-3

CONECA: UNKNOWN

Description: This variety has a very strong RPM with the secondary D south of the primary D.

Comments: This RPM may be CONECA RPM-011, -017, or -018, but further study is needed.

	EF-40	AU-50	MS-60	MS-63	MS-65	MS-66
VARIETY	n/a	$10	$19.00	$23.00	$33	$45
NORMAL		3	3.25	3.50	14	30

1946-S

FS-10-1946S-501

VARIETY: Repunched Mintmark, Doubled-Die Reverse
PUP: Mintmark
URS-5 · I-4 · L-3

CONECA: RPM-001, DDR-001

Description: The doubled die is most evident on AMERICA, the right branch, the leaves, UNUM, and DIME. The RPM is quadrupled, with the remnants of three secondary S mintmarks north of the primary.

Comments: Most of the value for this variety is for the significant RPM. Note that the mintmark photo in the previous edition was incorrect.

	EF-40	AU-50	MS-60	MS-63	MS-65	MS-66
VARIETY	n/a	$15	$27.00	$33.00	$55	$80
NORMAL		3	3.25	4.50	20	32

1946-S

FS-10-1946S-502 (011.6)

VARIETY: Repunched Mintmark, Doubled-Die Reverse
PUP: Mintmark, UNITED STATES
URS-6 · I-3 · L-3

**CONECA: RPM-002,
DDR-002**

Description: The secondary mintmark is evident southeast of the primary S. Doubling is most noticeable on UNITED STATES and E PLURIBUS.

Comments: As with the previous listing, most of the value is for the RPM.

	EF-40	AU-50	MS-60	MS-63	MS-65	MS-66
VARIETY	n/a	$15	$27.00	$33.00	$55	$80
NORMAL		3	3.25	4.50	20	32

1946-S

FS-10-1946S-503

VARIETY: Repunched Mintmark
PUP: Mintmark
URS-3 · I-3 · L-3

CONECA: RPM-013

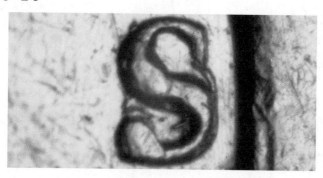

Description: This is a very strong RPM—actually, a triple-punched mintmark—with both secondary images evident north of the primary S.

Comments: This variety has been recently confirmed by CONECA as RPM-013.

	AU-50	MS-60	MS-63	MS-65	MS-66
VARIETY	$12	$23.00	$30.00	$50	$70
NORMAL	3	3.25	4.50	20	32

1946-S

VARIETY: Sans Serif Mintmark
PUP: Mintmark
URS-2 · I-5 · L-5

CONECA: MMS-003

Description: The mintmark on this one die is the sans serif type, i.e., without serifs.

Comments: Until the discovery of this piece, the sans serif S mintmark was only known on 1947-dated dimes. Any other finds should be considered extremely rare. The only known Mint State specimen of this variety sold for $750 in 2007.

	MS-60	MS-63	MS-65	MS-66
VARIETY	n/a	n/a	n/a	n/a
NORMAL		$4.50	$20	$32

1947

VARIETY: Doubled-Die Obverse
PUP: Mintmark
URS-3 · I-3 · L-3

CONECA: DDO-002

Description: Very strong doubling is evident on the date, the motto, the designer's initials, and LIBERTY.

Comments: This is a very strong DDO, especially when compared to others of the series. This variety was illustrated in *Cherrypickers' News*, number 13.

	EF-40	AU-50	MS-60	MS-63	MS-65	MS-66
VARIETY	$30	$45	$70	$140	$300	n/a
NORMAL		3	4	6	12	$24

1947-D

VARIETY: Doubled-Die Obverse
PUP: Date
NEW LISTING

CONECA: DDO-003

Description: Strong doubling is evident on the date and the designer's initials. There is extreme thickening of IN GOD WE TRUST that would probably show strong separation lines on earlier die states.

Comments: We'd like to see an early die state of this variety.

	EF-40	AU-50	MS-60	MS-63	MS-65	MS-66
VARIETY	n/a	n/a	n/a	n/a	n/a	n/a
NORMAL	$2.25	$3	$4	$6.50	$12	$27

1947-D

VARIETY: Doubled-Die Obverse
PUP: LIBERTY
NEW LISTING

CONECA: DDO-001

Description: The strongest doubling on this variety is evident on LIBERTY. It is also evident to a greater or lesser degree on IN GOD WE TRUST and a bit on the date. An earlier die state would undoubtedly show more.

Comments: We would like to see an early die state of this variety.

	EF-40	AU-50	MS-60	MS-63	MS-65	MS-66
VARIETY	n/a	n/a	n/a	n/a	n/a	n/a
NORMAL	$2.25	$3	$4	$6.50	$12	$27

1947-S

FS-10-1947S-501

VARIETY: Repunched Mintmark
PUP: Mintmark
URS-6 · I-4 · L-4

CONECA: OMM-001

Description: The S mintmark was punched over a D mintmark. Remnants of the initial D mintmark are evident only across the opening of the lower loop, and slightly right of the lower loop.

Comments: This variety and the next are very similar; however, number 501 is the sans serif S mintmark, and number 502 is the "Trumpet-Tail" S mintmark.

	EF-40	AU-50	MS-60	MS-63	MS-65	MS-66
VARIETY	$30	$40	$45	$50	$160	$375
NORMAL		3	4	6	12	30

1947-S

FS-10-1947S-502

VARIETY: Repunched Mintmark
PUP: Mintmark
URS-6 · I-4 · L-4

CONECA: OMM-002

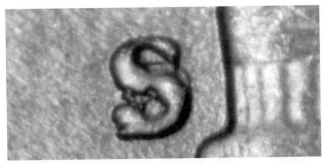

Description: The S mintmark was punched over a D mintmark. Remnants of the initial D mintmark are evident within the upper loop of the S, and across the opening of the lower loop.

Comments: This variety and the previous are very similar; however, number 501 is the sans serif S mintmark, and number 502 is the "Trumpet-Tail" S mintmark.

	EF-40	AU-50	MS-60	MS-63	MS-65	MS-66
VARIETY		$40	$45	$50	$160	$375
NORMAL		3	4	6	12	30

1947-S

FS-10-1947S-503

VARIETY: Repunched Mintmark
PUP: Mintmark
URS-7 · I-3 · L-3

CONECA: RPM-002

Description: The secondary S is evident protruding north of the primary S.

Comments: There are several nice RPMs for 1946 and 1947, in both D- and S-mintmark coins.

	EF-40	AU-50	MS-60	MS-63	MS-65	MS-66
VARIETY		$10	$15	$25	$60	$130
NORMAL		3	4	6	12	30

1947-S

FS-10-1947S-504

VARIETY: Repunched Mintmark
PUP: Mintmark
URS-8 · I-3 · L-3

CONECA: RPM-004

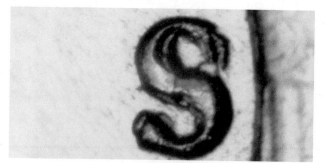

Description: The secondary S is somewhat centered under the primary S, with a rotation clockwise, showing right of the primary upper loop and left of the primary second loop.

Comments: CONECA has six RPMs listed for the 1947-S dime. There are probably others. Try to locate them all!

	EF-40	AU-50	MS-60	MS-63	MS-65	MS-66
VARIETY		$6	$10	$15	$35	$50
NORMAL		3	4	6	12	30

1947-S

FS-10-1947S-801 (013.5)

VARIETY: Doubled-Die Reverse
PUP: E PLURIBUS UNUM
URS-5 · I-3 · L-3

CONECA: DDR-001

Description: The very strong doubling is evident on all reverse lettering, on E PLURIBUS UNUM, on almost all leaves and branches, and especially on the flame.

Comments: On the few specimens we have examined, there is a spike protruding from the top of the R in PLURIBUS. Early die state specimens should command a higher premium.

	EF-40	AU-50	MS-60	MS-63	MS-65	MS-66
VARIETY	$10	$20	$35	$45	$90	$150
NORMAL		3	4	6	12	30

1948

FS-10-1948-801

VARIETY: Doubled-Die Reverse
PUP: UNITED STATES OF AMERICA, flame
URS-4 · I-3 · L-3

CONECA: DDR-001

Description: Strong doubling is evident on all outer letters, on the flame tips, and slightly on the branches and leaves.

Comments: This variety is not well known, but is a very nice doubled-die reverse.

	EF-40	AU-50	MS-60	MS-63	MS-65	MS-66
VARIETY	$10	$20	$35.00	$45	$90	$150
NORMAL		3	3.50	4	12	30

1948-S
FS-10-1948S-501

VARIETY: Repunched Mintmark
PUP: Mintmark
NEW LISTING

CONECA: RPM-001

Description: An underlying S appears south of the mintmark.
Comments: This is one of the more dramatic RPMs for the series.

	EF-40	AU-50	MS-60	MS-63	MS-65	MS-66
VARIETY	n/a	n/a	n/a	n/a	n/a	n/a
NORMAL	$2.50	$3	$4	$5.50	$12	$32

1950, Proof
FS-10-1950-801

VARIETY: Doubled-Die Reverse
PUP: AMERICA
URS-5 · I-2 · L-2

CONECA: DDR-001

Description: Moderate doubling is evident on UNUM, DIME, and OF AMERICA.
Comments: Although on a Proof specimen, this may be difficult to sell.

	PF-63	PF-65	PF-66
VARIETY	$25	$60	$90
NORMAL	20	50	65

1950-D

FS-10-1950D-501

VARIETY: Repunched Mintmark
PUP: Mintmark
URS-1 · I-5 · L-5

CONECA: N/L

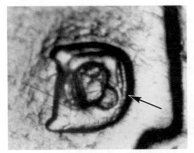 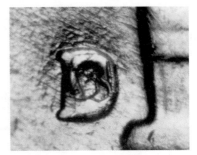

Description: The diagonal stroke of the initially punched S mintmark is visible within the opening of the primary D mintmark. The lower curve of the S is evident on the lower right curve of the D.

Comments: It is remarkable that this variety escaped notice for so long. One would think the late discovery would be a clear indication of rarity. Because there is some question as to whether this might actually be die damage instead of a variety, we would like to see another example to confirm.

	EF-40	AU-50	MS-60	MS-63	MS-65	MS-66
VARIETY	n/a	n/a	n/a	n/a	n/a	n/a
NORMAL	$2.50	$3	$4	$6	$12	$28

1950-D

FS-10-1950D-801 (014)

VARIETY: Doubled-Die Reverse
PUP: E PLURIBUS UNUM
URS-8 · I-4 · L-4

CONECA: DDR-001

Description: Strong doubling is evident on E PLURIBUS UNUM, the lower portions of the oak and olive branches, and the lower left portion of the torch.

Comments: This variety has been known for a long time, but is still very much in demand.

	EF-40	AU-50	MS-60	MS-63	MS-65	MS-66
VARIETY	$40.00	$50	$75	$235	$365	$550
NORMAL	2.50	3	4	6	12	28

1950-S

VARIETY: Repunched Mintmark
PUP: Mintmark
URS-7 · I-4 · L-4

CONECA: RPM-005

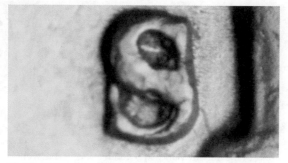

Description: The S mintmark is punched squarely over a previously punched S.

Comments: This variety was previously listed as an overmintmark (S/D). CONECA now lists it as S Over Inverted S, indicating that the line enclosing the lower loop is that of the long upper serif on an inverted S, and the authors are inclined to agree.

	EF-40	AU-50	MS-60	MS-63	MS-65	MS-66
VARIETY	$25	$50	$65	$125	$300	n/a
NORMAL	5	8	16	36	42	$75

1951-D

VARIETY: Repunched Mintmark
PUP: Mintmark
NEW LISTING

CONECA: RPM-001

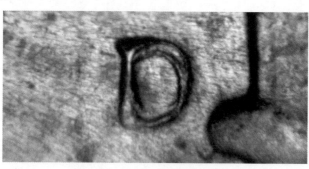

Description: An underlying D appears north of the mintmark.

Comments: This is one of the more dramatic RPMs for the series.

	EF-40	AU-50	MS-60	MS-63	MS-65	MS-66
VARIETY	n/a	n/a	n/a	n/a	n/a	n/a
NORMAL	$2.25	$2.50	$3	$3.25	$10	$28

1952-S

VARIETY: Repunched Mintmark
PUP: Mintmark
NEW LISTING

CONECA: RPM-001

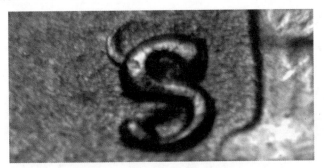

Description: An underlying S appears north of the mintmark.
Comments: This is one of the more dramatic RPMs for the series.

	EF-40	AU-50	MS-60	MS-63	MS-65	MS-66
VARIETY	n/a	n/a	n/a	n/a	n/a	n/a
NORMAL	$2.25	$3.50	$5	$8	$12	$35

1953-D

VARIETY: Repunched Mintmark
PUP: Mintmark
URS-4 · I-4 · L-4

CONECA: RPM-003

Description: The first D mintmark was punched horizontally, with the primary mintmark punched in the correct (vertical) orientation. The variety can easily be identified by the upper serif of the underlying D, which appears as a spike protruding from the upper part of the curve.
Comments: This variety is a relatively new discovery.

	EF-40	AU-50	MS-60	MS-63	MS-65	MS-66
VARIETY	$9	$15	$35.00	$55.00	$80	$125
NORMAL		3	3.25	3.50	8	20

1953-S

VARIETY: Repunched Mintmark
PUP: Mintmark
NEW LISTING

CONECA: RPM-002

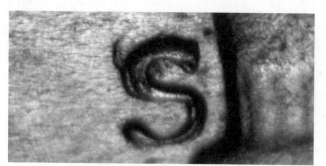

Description: An underlying S appears north of the mintmark.

Comments: This is one of the more dramatic RPMs for the series. Earlier die states show more of the upper curve.

	EF-40	AU-50	MS-60	MS-63	MS-65	MS-66
VARIETY	n/a	n/a	n/a	n/a	n/a	n/a
NORMAL	$2.25	$2.50	$2.75	$3	$8	$25

1954, Proof

VARIETY: Doubled-Die Obverse
PUP: Date
URS-6 · I-3 · L-3

CONECA: DDO-001

Description: The doubling is evident as extreme extra thickness on all obverse lettering, especially on the 9 and 4 of the date.

Comments: This variety can be easily detected by the die chip at the base of the 4.

	PF-63	PF-65	PF-66
VARIETY	$25	$40	$70
NORMAL	15	18	25

1954 — FS-10-1954-801

VARIETY: Doubled-Die Reverse
PUP: Right side of torch base and oak stem
URS-1 · I-4 · L-5

CONECA: DDR-002

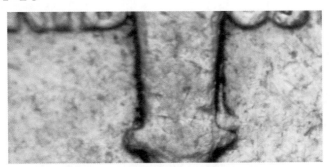

Description: The doubling is evident at the bottom of the torch and on the oak stem, rotated slightly in a counterclockwise direction.

Comments: This is a very exciting variety. Further study and improved photographs will require a higher-grade specimen.

	EF-40	AU-50	MS-60	MS-63	MS-65	MS-66
VARIETY	n/a	n/a	n/a	n/a	n/a	n/a
NORMAL		$3	$3.25	$3.50	$8	$20

1954-S — FS-10-1954S-501

VARIETY: Repunched Mintmark
PUP: Mintmark
URS-5 · I-3 · L-3

CONECA: RPM-001

Description: Secondary S mintmarks are evident northwest of the primary S, and very slightly south of the primary S.

Comments: RPMs in this series are comparatively marketable.

	EF-40	AU-50	MS-60	MS-63	MS-65	MS-66
VARIETY	n/a	$15	$20.00	$30.00	$48	$150
NORMAL		3	3.25	3.50	8	15

1954-S FS-10-1954S-901

VARIETY: Missing Designer's Initials · **BREEN-3736**
PUP: Below bust, to left of date
NEW LISTING

Description: John Sinnock's initials are missing from their normal location below the bust to the left of the date.

Comments: Breen says this was discovered in September 1983. The motto and other areas are weak due to extreme die wear and abrasion.

	AU-50	MS-60	MS-63	MS-65	MS-66
VARIETY	n/a	n/a	n/a	n/a	n/a
NORMAL	$2.50	$2.75	$3	$8	$15

1956, Proof FS-10-1956-101

VARIETY: Doubled-Die Obverse · **CONECA: DDO-002**
PUP: IN GOD WE TRUST, date
URS-7 · I-2 · L-3

Description: Extreme extra thickness, typical of the Class VI doubled dies, is evident on IN GOD WE TRUST, LIBERTY, the date, and designer's initials.

Comments: To date not much interest has been shown, but it certainly is worth looking for.

	PF-63	PF-65	PF-66
VARIETY	$20	$35	$50
NORMAL	6	8	10

1959-D
FS-10-1959D-501

VARIETY: Repunched Mintmark
PUP: Mintmark
URS-4 · I-4 · L-5

CONECA: RPM-002

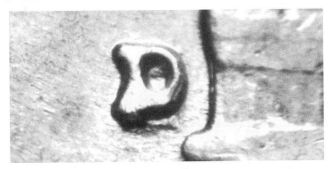

Description: The D mintmark was punched into the die inverted, then punched with the D correct.

Comments: This is a somewhat difficult variety to locate. (Note: This variety was incorrectly listed as FS-10-1959D-511 in the fourth edition, volume II.)

	EF-40	AU-50	MS-60	MS-63	MS-65	MS-66
VARIETY	n/a	$20.00	$25.00	$35.00	$60	$120
NORMAL	$2.25	2.50	2.75	3.00	7	14

1959-D
FS-10-1959D-502

VARIETY: Repunched Mintmark
PUP: Mintmark
URS-4 · I-3 · L-3

CONECA: RPM-004

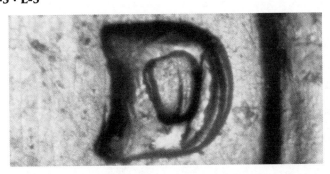

Description: This RPM exhibits a secondary curve west evident within the primary loop, and portions of the secondary vertical to the left of the primary.

Comments: The primary D exhibits strike doubling on the right.

	EF-40	AU-50	MS-60	MS-63	MS-65	MS-66
VARIETY	n/a	$10.00	$15.00	$20	$30	$40
NORMAL	$2.25	2.50	2.75	3	7	14

1959-D
FS-10-1959D-503

VARIETY: Repunched Mintmark
PUP: Mintmark
URS-4 · I-3 · L-3

CONECA: RPM-003

Description: Portions of a secondary D mintmark are evident west of the primary D, most noticeably the lower serif of the weaker D left of the primary D.

Comments: This is one of many recently listed Roosevelt dime RPMs.

	EF-40	AU-50	MS-60	MS-63	MS-65	MS-66
VARIETY	n/a	$10.00	$15.00	$20	$30	$40
NORMAL	$2.25	2.50	2.75	3	7	14

1959-D
FS-10-1959D-504

VARIETY: Repunched Mintmark
PUP: Mintmark
NEW LISTING

CONECA: RPM-001

Description: A very strong underlying D appears north of the mintmark.

Comments: This is one of the strongest RPMs known for the Roosevelt dime.

	EF-40	AU-50	MS-60	MS-63	MS-65	MS-66
VARIETY	n/a	n/a	n/a	n/a	n/a	n/a
NORMAL	$2.25	$2.50	$2.75	$3	$7	$14

1960, Proof FS-10-1960-101

VARIETY: Doubled-Die Obverse
PUP: TRUST
NEW LISTING

CONECA: DDO-001

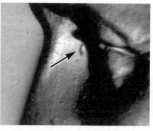

Die gouge at eye is diagnostic on all stages.

Description: Doubling is strongly evident on IN GOD WE TRUST, moderately so on LIB of LIBERTY, the designer's initials, and the date.

Comments: This variety is easily confused with FS-104; see the comparison of doubling on the I of IN at that entry. Early die states of this coin show doubling on the date while it is virtually absent on later die states.

	PF-63	PF-65	PF-66	PF-67
VARIETY	n/a	n/a	n/a	n/a
NORMAL		$4	$10	$18

1960, Proof FS-10-1960-102a

VARIETY: Doubled-Die Obverse, Early Die State
PUP: Date, IN GOD WE TRUST
URS-5 · I-4 · L-4

CONECA: DDO-005

Description: Extremely strong doubling is evident on all obverse lettering and on the date.

Comments: Because it has been well known for many years, this variety may be difficult to cherry-pick! The early die state is somewhat rarer than the late die state. The specimen shown is early- to mid-die state.

	PF-63	PF-65	PF-66	PF-67
VARIETY	$65	$125	$165	$275
NORMAL		4	10	18

1960, Proof
FS-10-1960-102b

VARIETY: Doubled-Die Obverse, Late Die State
PUP: Date, IN GOD WE TRUST
URS-9 · I-1 OR 2 · L-1 OR 2

CONECA: DDO-005

Description: Extremely strong doubling is evident on all obverse lettering and on the date. The late die state specimens exhibit a very weak date.

Comments: Values are for late die state specimens and are usually lower than for the early die state specimens. Note that much of the 19 of the date has been polished away. Intermediate states exist between the extremes shown here and in the preceding listing.

	PF-63	PF-65	PF-66	PF-67
VARIETY	$50	$110	$140	$225
NORMAL		4	10	18

1960, Proof
FS-10-1960-103

VARIETY: Doubled-Die Obverse
PUP: Designer's initials, TRUST
NEW LISTING

CONECA: DDO-004

Description: Medium to strong doubling is evident on IN GOD WE TRUST, the designer's initials, and the date.

Comments: This variety is not very well known, and thus is extremely underrated.

	PF-63	PF-65	PF-66	PF-67
VARIETY	n/a	n/a	n/a	n/a
NORMAL		$4	$10	$18

1960, Proof | FS-10-1960-104

VARIETY: Doubled-Die Obverse
PUP: TRUST
NEW LISTING

CONECA: DDO-007

FS-10-1960-104   FS-10-1960-101

Description: Medium to strong doubling is evident on IN GOD WE TRUST, LIBERTY, and the designer's initials; slight doubling can been seen on the upper part of the date.

Comments: This is not a very well known variety; consequently, it is extremely underrated. The specimen shown here also exhibits a slight bit of strike doubling below the hub doubling. The variety is easily confused with FS-101, but note the difference in the doubling on the I of IN, which is stronger on FS-104.

	PF-63	PF-65	PF-66	PF-67
VARIETY	n/a	n/a	n/a	n/a
NORMAL		$4	$10	$18

1960, Proof | FS-10-1960-105

VARIETY: Doubled-Die Obverse
PUP: TRUST
NEW LISTING

CONECA: DDO-008

Description: Doubling is evident on IN GOD WE TRUST and the designer's initials, as well as slightly on the date. Very nice surface doubling can be seen on TRUST, and tripling even shows in some areas.

Comments: This is one of several 1960 Proof dime varieties that is quite underrated because it is not yet well known.

	PF-63	PF-65	PF-66	PF-67
VARIETY	n/a	n/a	n/a	n/a
NORMAL		$4	$10	$18

1960, Proof | FS-10-1960-801

VARIETY: Doubled-Die Reverse
PUP: UNITED
URS-4 · I-3 · L-2

CONECA: DDR-001

Description: Moderate doubling is evident on all reverse lettering, with the strongest spread on UNITED, ONE, and E PLU.

Comments: Relatively few specimens of this variety have been reported to date.

	PF-63	PF-65	PF-66
VARIETY	$30.00	$45	$90
NORMAL	3.75	4	10

1960-D | FS-10-1960D-501

VARIETY: Repunched Mintmark
PUP: Mintmark
URS-5 · I-3 · L-3

CONECA: RPM-003

Description: This RPM is evidenced by two secondary vertical lines within the opening of the main D, and a spike right of the primary D.

Comments: This is one of many recently listed Roosevelt dime RPMs.

	EF-40	AU-50	MS-60	MS-63	MS-65	MS-66
VARIETY	n/a	$10	$15.00	$20.00	$30	$40
NORMAL		3	3.25	3.50	6	15

1961-D

FS-10-1961D-801

VARIETY: Doubled-Die Reverse
PUP: UNITED
URS-5 · I-3 · L-2

CONECA: DDR-001

Description: Moderate doubling is evident on UNITED, and ONE DIME, with a lighter spread on STATES OF AMERICA and E PLURIBUS UNUM.

Comments: Relatively few specimens have been reported to date.

	EF-40	AU-50	MS-60	MS-63	MS-65	MS-66
VARIETY	n/a	$10	$15.00	$20.00	$30	$50
NORMAL		3	3.25	3.50	6	12

1962-D

FS-10-1962D-501

VARIETY: Repunched Mintmark
PUP: Mintmark
URS-4 · I-5 · L-5

CONECA: RPM-005

Description: The D was punched into the die horizontally first, then corrected.

Comments: This is a relatively new discovery; few specimens have been reported.

	EF-40	AU-50	MS-60	MS-63	MS-65	MS-66
VARIETY	$20	$25	$35.00	$50.00	$75	$115
NORMAL		3	3.25	3.50	6	12

1963 · FS-10-1963-101

VARIETY: Doubled-Die Obverse
PUP: Date
URS-5 · I-3 · L-2

CONECA: DDO-001
"FORKED-TAIL" VARIETY

Description: The doubling is evident on the date, LIBERTY, and IN GOD WE TRUST.
Comments: This variety can be found in Mint sets. Referred to as the "forked-tail" variety.

	EF-40	AU-50	MS-60	MS-63	MS-65	MS-66
VARIETY	n/a	$11	$17.00	$22.00	$35	$60
NORMAL		3	3.25	3.50	6	12

1963, Proof · FS-10-1963-801 (017)

VARIETY: Doubled-Die Reverse
PUP: UNITED
URS-7 · I-3 · L-3

CONECA: DDR-007

Description: The doubling is evident with a strong spread on UNITED, and to a lesser degree, on STATES OF AMERICA, E PLURIBUS UNUM, the leaves, and ONE DIME.
Comments: Collectors are advised to check all early-1960s Proof sets for die varieties.

	PF-63	PF-65	PF-66
VARIETY	$35.00	$50	$85
NORMAL	3.75	4	8

1963, Proof — FS-10-1963-802 (017.5)

VARIETY: Doubled-Die Reverse
PUP: UNITED, ONE DIME
URS-9 · I-3 · L-3

CONECA: DDR-009

Description: Very strong doubling is evident on all lettering, but strongest on UNITED and ONE DIME.

Comments: This is likely the most impressive reverse doubled die for the date in Proof.

	PF-63	PF-65	PF-66
VARIETY	$70.00	$90	$160
NORMAL	3.75	4	8

1963, Proof — FS-10-1963-803 (018)

VARIETY: Doubled-Die Reverse
PUP: UNITED STATES
URS-6 · I-3 · L-3

CONECA: DDR-012

Description: The doubling is evident on UNITED STATES, and E PLU, with weaker doubling visible on OF AMERICA, ONE DIME, and other elements.

Comments: There are 21 different doubled dies listed by CONECA for the 1963 Roosevelt reverse. Eighteen of those are on Proof coinage.

	PF-63	PF-65	PF-66
VARIETY	$45.00	$90	$150
NORMAL	3.75	4	8

1963, Proof
FS-10-1963-804

VARIETY: Doubled-Die Reverse
CONECA: DDR-004
PUP: UNITED
URS-6 · I-3 · L-3

Description: The doubling is very strong on UNITED, with split serifs on most other reverse letters.

Comments: This variety is somewhat similar to FS-10-1963-801 (017).

	PF-63	PF-65	PF-66
VARIETY	$35.00	$50	$70
NORMAL	3.75	4	8

1963
FS-10-1963-805

VARIETY: Doubled-Die Reverse
CONECA: DDR-014
PUP: UNITED
URS-6 · I-3 · L-2

Description: Doubling is evident on UNITED, E PLURIBUS, the olive branch, and the stem. Lesser doubling is also visible on ONE DIME.

Comments: Reminder—this is not a Proof coin!

	EF-40	AU-50	MS-60	MS-63	MS-65	MS-66
VARIETY	n/a	$15	$25.00	$35.00	$55	$80
NORMAL		3	3.25	3.50	6	12

1963-D
FS-10-1963D-801

VARIETY: Doubled-Die Reverse
PUP: AMERICA
URS-5 · I-3 · L-3

CONECA: DDR-001

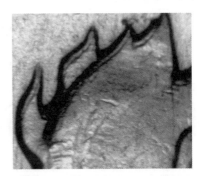

Description: Doubling is evident on all reverse lettering, with the most evident doubling on AMERICA and the top of the flame.

Comments: Most Mint State specimens will be MS-63 or lower.

	EF-40	AU-50	MS-60	MS-63	MS-65	MS-66
VARIETY	n/a	$25	$60.00	$120.00	$200	$275
NORMAL		3	3.25	3.50	6	12

1964, Proof
FS-10-1964-101 (018.4)

VARIETY: Doubled-Die Obverse
PUP: IN GOD WE TRUST, LIBERTY
URS-3 · I-4 · L-4

CONECA: DDO-005

Description: Strong doubling is evident on IN GOD WE TRUST, LIBERTY, and on the designer's initials.

Comments: There are at least four weaker obverse doubled dies for 1964 Proof dimes.

	PF-63	PF-65	PF-66
VARIETY	$350.00	$550	$750
NORMAL	3.75	4	8

1964

VARIETY: Doubled-Die Reverse
PUP: DIME, AMERICA
URS-4 · I-3 · L-3

CONECA: DDR-006

Description: The doubling is evident on all reverse lettering, oak stems and leaves, and the flame. Doubling is strongest on DIME and AMERICA.

Comments: This variety and the next are similar, but the doubling is in different directions.

	EF-40	AU-50	MS-60	MS-63	MS-65	MS-66
VARIETY	$50	$75	$100.00	$175.00	$250	$375
NORMAL		3	3.25	3.50	6	12

1964

VARIETY: Doubled-Die Reverse
PUP: DIME, AMERICA
URS-4 · I-3 · L-3

CONECA: DDR-008

Description: The doubling is evident on all reverse lettering, oak stems, and the flame. Doubling is strongest on AMERICA.

Comments: Compare the direction of the doubling with that of the previous listing.

	EF-40	AU-50	MS-60	MS-63	MS-65	MS-66
VARIETY	$20	$30	$40.00	$50.00	$75	$100
NORMAL		3	3.25	3.50	6	12

1964-D

FS-10-1964D-501

VARIETY: Repunched Mintmark
PUP: Mintmark
URS-5 · I-3 · L-3

CONECA: RPM-003

Description: The secondary mintmark is visible with a wide spread toward the northeast. The left upright and lower right curve of the weaker D are evident.

Comments: Specimens above MS-65 are rare.

	EF-40	AU-50	MS-60	MS-63	MS-65	MS-66
VARIETY	n/a	$7	$10.00	$15.00	$25	$35
NORMAL		3	3.25	3.50	6	12

1964-D

FS-10-1964D-502 (018.7)

VARIETY: Misplaced Mintmark
PUP: Mintmark—torch area
URS-3 · I-4 · L-5

CONECA: RPM-006

Description: A trace of a secondary mintmark is evident protruding from the left side of the torch.

Comments: This variety was discovered in 1996 by Joe Miller, and is one of the most dramatic RPMs ever found!

	EF-40	AU-50	MS-60	MS-63	MS-65	MS-66
VARIETY	$25	$50	$75.00	$125.00	$250	$400
NORMAL		3	3.25	3.50	6	12

1964-D

FS-10-1964D-503

VARIETY: Repunched Mintmark
PUP: Mintmark
URS-4 · I-3 · L-3

CONECA: RPM-004

Description: The secondary mintmark is visible south of the primary, but is somewhat weak. The lower serif on the secondary D is most prominent.

Comments: This is a relatively new discovery.

	EF-40	AU-50	MS-60	MS-63	MS-65	MS-66
VARIETY	n/a	$7	$10.00	$15.00	$25	$35
NORMAL		3	3.25	3.50	6	12

1964-D

FS-10-1964D-504

VARIETY: Repunched Mintmark
PUP: Mintmark
URS-4 · I-3 · L-3

CONECA: UNKNOWN

Description: The secondary D is visible south of the primary, but is very weak. Only the left upright and a small portion of the right lower curve of the secondary D are evident.

Comments: This is a relatively new discovery.

	EF-40	AU-50	MS-60	MS-63	MS-65	MS-66
VARIETY	n/a	$7	$10.00	$15.00	$25	$35
NORMAL		3	3.25	3.50	6	12

1964-D

VARIETY: Repunched Mintmark
PUP: Mintmark
URS-4 · I-3 · L-3

CONECA: UNKNOWN

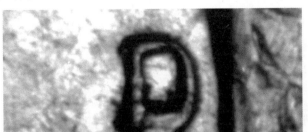

Description: This RPM is very similar to FS-503, yet the underlying mintmark on FS-505 is positioned just slightly further left than on FS-503.

Comments: This variety is also a relatively new discovery.

	EF-40	AU-50	MS-60	MS-63	MS-65	MS-66
VARIETY	n/a	$7	$10.00	$15.00	$25	$35
NORMAL		3	3.25	3.50	6	12

1964-D

VARIETY: Repunched Mintmark
PUP: Mintmark
URS-4 · I-3 · L-3

CONECA: RPM-009

Description: The secondary D is evident south of the primary D. The most evident portion of the underlying D is the lower serif.

Comments: This is another relatively new discovery.

	EF-40	AU-50	MS-60	MS-63	MS-65	MS-66
VARIETY	n/a	$7	$10.00	$15.00	$25	$35
NORMAL		3	3.25	3.50	6	12

1964-D

VARIETY: Doubled-Die Reverse
PUP: UNITED STATES OF AMERICA, ONE DIME
URS-5 · I-3 · L-3

CONECA: DDR-001

Description: Doubling is evident on all reverse lettering, the top of the flame, and the tips of the leaves on higher-grade specimens.

Comments: Specimens above MS-65 are rare.

	EF-40	AU-50	MS-60	MS-63	MS-65	MS-66
VARIETY	$35	$55	$75.00	$100.00	$250	$500
NORMAL		3	3.25	3.50	6	12

1964-D

VARIETY: Doubled-Die Reverse
PUP: ONE, E PLU
URS-6 · I-3 · L-3

CONECA: DDR-003

Description: The doubling is most evident on ONE DIME, UNITED, E PLU, and the oak stems. Lesser doubling is visible on RIBUS UNUM and AMERICA.

Comments: This variety may be undervalued.

	EF-40	AU-50	MS-60	MS-63	MS-65	MS-66
VARIETY	$35	$55	$75.00	$100.00	$150	$250
NORMAL		3	3.25	3.50	6	12

1964-D
FS-10-1964D-803

VARIETY: Doubled-Die Reverse
PUP: AMERICA, ONE DIME

CONECA: N/L

Comments: We believe this was a misattributed FS-801. It will be removed from the next edition of this volume.

1967
FS-10-1967-101 (019)

VARIETY: Doubled-Die Obverse
PUP: IN GOD WE TRUST
URS-3 · I-4 · L-5

CONECA: DDO-001

PC

YN

Description: Doubling is evident on IN GOD WE TRUST, the date, and the designer's initials.
Comments: Although it has been known for years, this remains a very rare doubled die.

	EF-40	AU-50	MS-60	MS-63	MS-65	MS-66
VARIETY	$75	$100	$150	$250	$400	$575
NORMAL					1	

1968 — FS-10-1968-101

VARIETY: Doubled-Die Obverse
PUP: LIBERTY
URS-5 · I-3 · L-2

CONECA: DDO-001

Description: The doubling is evident on LIBERTY, IN GOD WE TRUST, the date, and the designer's initials.

Comments: Discovered by James Wiles, this variety can be found in some Mint sets.

	EF-40	AU-50	MS-60	MS-63	MS-65	MS-66
VARIETY	$20	$30	$50	$65	$85	$175
NORMAL					1	

1968-S, Proof — FS-10-1968S-101 (020)

VARIETY: Doubled-Die Obverse
PUP: LIBERTY
URS-3 · I-4 · L-4

CONECA: DDO-002

Description: The doubling is evident on LIBERTY and IN GOD WE TRUST, and slightly on the date.

Comments: Although it has been known for years, this remains a very rare variety.

	PF-63	PF-65	PF-66
VARIETY	$90	$125.00	$150
NORMAL	1	1.50	4

1968-S, Proof
FS-10-1968S-102 (020.2)

VARIETY: Doubled-Die Obverse
PUP: IN GOD WE TRUST, date
URS-3 · I-4 · L-4

CONECA: DDO-008

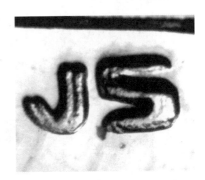

Description: There is moderate doubling on IN GOD WE TRUST, the designer's initials, and the date, with a light spread on LIBERTY.

Comments: This is also a very rare variety.

	PF-63	PF-65	PF-66
VARIETY	$90	$125.00	$150
NORMAL	1	1.50	4

1968, Proof, No S
FS-10-1968S-501

VARIETY: Missing Mintmark
PUP: Mintmark area near date
URS-5 · I-5 · L-5

CONECA: MMO-001

Description: The S mintmark was inadvertently omitted from the die.

Comments: The defective die was probably discovered before the end of the die's life. This is a popular variety with high liquidity. Consult the most current pricing resources. Other S-Mint dimes lacking the mintmark were minted in 1970, 1975, 1983, and 1990.

	PF-63	PF-65	PF-66	PF-67
VARIETY	$10,500	$12,000.00	$14,500	$18,500
NORMAL	1	1.50	4	6

1968-S, Proof
FS-10-1968S-502

VARIETY: Repunched Mintmark
CONECA: RPM-001
PUP: Mintmark
URS-4 · I-3 · L-3

Description: The secondary mintmark is very close to and west of the primary S.

Comments: The obverse is also a very minor doubled die, but that does not increase the coin's value.

	PF-63	PF-65	PF-66
VARIETY	$10	$15.00	$50
NORMAL	1	1.50	4

1968-S, Proof
FS-10-1968S-801 (020.3)

VARIETY: Doubled-Die Reverse
CONECA: DDR-001
PUP: UNITED, DIME
URS-4 · I-3 · L-3

Description: The doubling is evident on UNITED STATES, ONE DIME, and E PLURIBUS UNUM. Weaker doubling is evident on AMERICA and on the olive stems.

Comments: This variety is considered very rare.

	PF-63	PF-65	PF-66
VARIETY	$45	$65.00	$250
NORMAL	1	1.50	4

1968-S, Proof
FS-10-1968S-802

VARIETY: Doubled-Die Reverse
PUP: UNITED
URS-2 · I-3 · L-2

CONECA: DDR-004

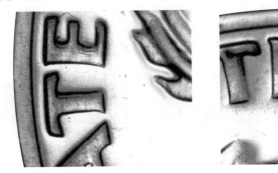

Description: Moderate doubling is clear on UNITED STATES OF AMERICA, but lesser doubling is visible on ONE DIME.

Comments: This variety may be difficult to find.

	PF-63	PF-65	PF-66
VARIETY	n/a	n/a	n/a
NORMAL	$1	$1.50	$4

1969-D
FS-10-1969D-501 (020.4)

VARIETY: Repunched Mintmark
PUP: Mintmark
URS-5 · I-3 · L-3

CONECA: RPM-001

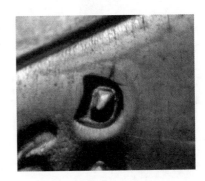

Description: This RPM has a very wide spread to the northeast.

Comments: Look in those Mint sets for this variety!

	EF-40	AU-50	MS-60	MS-63	MS-65	MS-66
VARIETY	n/a	n/a	$30	$40	$75	$150
NORMAL					1	

1969, 1970, 1970-D   FS-10-1969-901, -1970-901, -1970D-901

VARIETY: Reverse of 1968
PUP: Flames of torch
NEW LISTING

CONECA: RDV-002

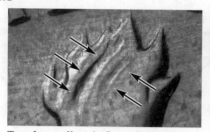

Two deep valleys in flame, high relief

Light valley in flame, low relief (the common circulation-strike design style)

Description: Two deep valleys appear in the flame, which is struck in high relief.

Comments: Made public just months before press time, these are not very well known. The reverse on these dimes was first used for the 1968 Proofs, on which both RDV-002 and RDV-001 are common. Largely restricted to Proof dimes for the next three years, the design appears on just a few 1969, 1970, and 1970-D circulation strikes, and so far seems to be rare. After 1970 this reverse became the standard for all Roosevelt dimes from all mints through 1980.

	EF-40	AU-50	MS-60	MS-63	MS-65	MS-66
VARIETY	n/a	n/a	n/a	n/a	n/a	n/a
NORMAL					$1	

THE CHERRYPICKERS' GUIDE **HELPFUL HINTS**

The varieties listed in this book are only the tip of the iceberg. Even more are yet to be discovered. Always examine closely any coin you obtain. You may soon discover that one great variety wanted by every collector in the hobby! And let us know when you do.

1970

VARIETY: Doubled-Die Reverse
PUP: UNITED STATES OF AMERICA
URS-3 · I-4 · L-5

CONECA: DDR-001

Description: Doubling is evident on all reverse lettering, especially on UNITED STATES OF AMERICA, with slightly weaker doubling on ONE DIME.

Comments: This variety is extremely rare.

	EF-40	AU-50	MS-60	MS-63	MS-65	MS-66
VARIETY	$25	$75	$150	$225	$300	$650
NORMAL					1	

1970-D

VARIETY: Doubled-Die Reverse
PUP: AMERICA
URS-8 · I-3 · L-2

CONECA: DDR-001

PC

Description: Doubling is evident on UNITED STATES OF AMERICA, the flame, the tops of the oak leaves, and very slightly on UNUM.

Comments: This is one of three different reverse doubled dies known that have been found in Mint sets.

	EF-40	AU-50	MS-60	MS-63	MS-65	MS-66
VARIETY	$6	$10	$15	$23	$50	$75
NORMAL					1	

1970-D

FS-10-1970D-802

VARIETY: Doubled-Die Reverse
PUP: UNITED STATES OF AMERICA
URS-7 · I-3 · L-2

CONECA: DDR-004

Description: Moderate doubling is evident on all reverse lettering, the flame, and the tops of the oak leaves.

Comments: This is arguably the nicest of all the 1970-D reverse doubled dies. This variety can also be found in Mint sets.

	EF-40	AU-50	MS-60	MS-63	MS-65	MS-66
VARIETY	$10	$15	$20	$25	$65	$90
NORMAL					1	

1975-S, Proof

FS-10-1975S-501

VARIETY: Repunched Mintmark
PUP: Mintmark
URS-6 · I-3 · L-3

CONECA: RPM-001

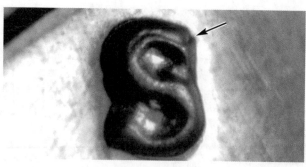

Description: The secondary mintmark north is very close, visible at the top of the S.

Comments: There are at least two different RPMs for this date and mint.

	PF-63	PF-65	PF-66
VARIETY	$10	$15	$40
NORMAL	1	2	4

1982, No P FS-10-1982-501 (021)

VARIETY: Missing Mintmark, Strong Strike
PUP: Mintmark area
URS-10 · I-4 · L-4

CONECA: MMO-001

Description: The mintmark (P) was omitted from this working die. The strike ranges from strong to weak. The strongest strikes are far more valuable and in demand than the weaker ones.

Comments: Compare the strong strike here with the weak strike in the next listing.

	AU-50	MS-60	MS-63	MS-65	MS-66
VARIETY	$75	$110	$135	$225	$300
NORMAL				7	

1982, No P FS-10-1982-502

VARIETY: Missing Mintmark, Weak Strike
PUP: Mintmark area
URS-11 · I-2 · L-2

CONECA: MMO-001

Description: The mintmark (P) was omitted from this working die. This is a weak strike, which is less interesting and commands far less value than the previous listing.

Comments: This weak strike is listed here so that collectors will be able to make comparisons and offer values for the weak-strike version. Some specimens that are not as strong as our "Strong Strike" are of significantly greater strength than illustrated here. They should command a premium over the weakest strike but not as high as for the strongest (shown in the previous listing).

	AU-50	MS-60	MS-63	MS-65	MS-66
VARIETY	$25	$30	$45	$80	$100
NORMAL				7	

1983-D

FS-10-1983D-501

VARIETY: Repunched Mintmark
PUP: Mintmark
URS-5 · I-3 · L-3

CONECA: RPM-001

Description: A secondary D is visible protruding from the primary D. Only a small portion of the left upright bar of the underlying D is visible.

Comments: This is one of the latest-dated RPMs for the series!

	EF-40	AU-50	MS-60	MS-63	MS-65	MS-66
VARIETY	$10	$15	$20	$25	$50.00	$75
NORMAL					1.50	

1985-P–1987-P

No FS#

Questionable Varieties

We have included the next three listings for several reasons. These varieties do catch the eye of many collectors, both novice and seasoned. Some variety enthusiasts believe them to be misplaced-mintmark varieties; however, while all three varieties show an image that appears to be a misplaced mintmark, in our opinion there is simply not enough evidence to classify them conclusively. We do not intend to state categorically that they are not misplaced mintmarks; we simply can't state for sure they are. We have not assigned an FS number to them.

All the specimens we have seen come from very late die states, as evidenced by the "orange-peel" effect clearly visible on the coins' surfaces. We have not seen any of these in an earlier die state.

The inclusion of these varieties will provide a reference for understanding or describing the variety. Additionally, the novice collector will recognize that there are still questions about their validity.

1985-P–1987-P (continued)   No FS#

VARIETY: Possible Misplaced Mintmark   **CONECA: N/L**
PUP: Area on neck and field
URS-N/A · I-2 · L-2

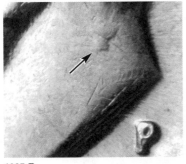
1985-P

1985-P (close-up)

1986-P

1986-P (close-up)

1987-P

1987-P (close-up)

Description: For the 1985-P, a faint image, which some enthusiasts believe is a misplaced P mintmark, is visible on the neck just below the hairline. For the 1986-P, a faint image, which some enthusiasts believe is a misplaced P mintmark, is visible in the field just right of the primary mintmark. For the 1987-P, a faint image, which some enthusiasts feel is a misplaced P mintmark, is visible in the field by the neck on an even level with the lower ear.

Comments: These varieties are questionable. Please read the commentary on the preceding page.

	MS-63	MS-65	MS-66
VARIETY	n/a	n/a	n/a
NORMAL		$1.25	

121

2004-D

FS-10-2004D-701

VARIETY: Curved Image
PUP: Ear
URS-2 · I-4 · L-4

CONECA: N/L

PC

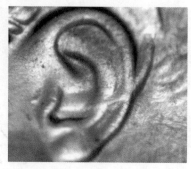

Description: There is a circular image overlapping the ear.

Comments: An employee of the Denver Mint may have added the circular image to the die deliberately. The size and shape of this added image are very similar to those known on the reverse of the two different 2004 Wisconsin D-Mint quarters, also featured in this volume. There is some unconfirmed evidence that this might be a doubled die.

	MS-63	MS-65	MS-66
VARIETY	$100	$150.00	$200
NORMAL		0.75	

THE CHERRYPICKERS' GUIDE HELPFUL HINTS

Check the coins already in your collection. In many cases, collectors will find a variety they had no idea they had. In some cases, these unfound varieties can be quite valuable. This first happened to J.T. Stanton back in 1982, and it can happen to you!

Twenty-Cent Pieces, 1875–1878

This abbreviated denomination was produced for circulation only in 1875 and 1876, but Proof coinage was also struck in 1877 and 1878. Mintages were low for the circulation coinage, meaning very few production dies were used. As a result, the varieties that do exist are relatively common. In fact, misplaced dates for the 1875-S in this series are far more common than the date without the misplaced date.

For those seriously interested in the series, we strongly recommend membership in the Liberty Seated Collectors Club (LSCC), which we believe to be one of the very best specialty clubs in numismatics. The club issues its official publication, the *Gobrecht Journal,* three times each year. This impressive newsletter is loaded with excellent educational articles. The club also has a web site at www.lsccweb.org. At the time of publication, membership dues were $20 per year. For membership information, contact

Liberty Seated Collectors Club
Leonard Augsburger, Secretary-Treasurer
P.O. Box 6114
Vernon Hills, IL 60061
E-mail: leonard_augsburger@hotmail.com

1875-S FS-20-1875S-301

VARIETY: Misplaced Date, Repunched Mintmark
PUP: Denticles below date
URS-14 · I-3 · L-2

Description: The top of a digit, likely an 8, is visible in the denticles below the primary 8.

Comments: Don't expect a premium on this variety or the next. This date without an MPD is actually scarcer than one with the digits in the denticles.

	VG-8	F-12	VF-20	EF-40	AU-50	MS-60	MS-63
VARIETY	$120	$150	$175	$250	$375	$600	$1,300
NORMAL	120	150	175	250	375	600	1,300

1875-S FS-20-1875S-302

VARIETY: Misplaced Date, Repunched Mintmark   **CONECA: RPM-001**
PUP: Denticles below date, mintmark
URS-14 · I-3 · L-2

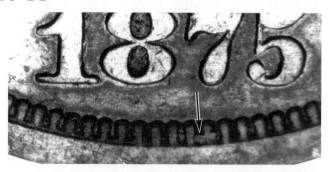

Description: The top of a digit, likely a 5, is visible in the denticles below the primary 7. The S mintmark is repunched, with the secondary S evident and tilted.

Comments: Don't expect a premium on this variety or the previous. This date without an MPD is actually scarcer than one with the digits in the denticles.

	VG-8	F-12	VF-20	EF-40	AU-50	MS-60	MS-63
VARIETY	$120	$150	$175	$250	$375	$600	$1,300
NORMAL	120	150	175	250	375	600	1,300

Capped Bust Quarters, 1815–1838

Capped Bust coinage varieties may be slightly different from what many of us are accustomed to encountering in late-19th-century and later coinage. During the Bust era the die-making process was somewhat different from that of later years.

Often a matrix and punches were used to place many of the design elements, letters, and numbers into the working die, rather than the hub (as was used for later coinage). Therefore, it is not uncommon to see slight differences in positioning of these elements. In some cases individual letter or number punches were used, which can account for one letter or number appearing over another.

Membership in a specialty club is always informative and well worth the relatively modest cost. The John Reich Collectors Society, which focuses on Capped Bust half dimes, dimes, quarters, halves, and dollars, is one of the most active and educational clubs in the United States.

The JRCS has a fabulous web site, http://logan.com/jrcs, with a membership application, club details, and educational information. Contact the society at

John Reich Collectors Society
Attn: Stephen A. Crain
P.O. Box 1680
Windham, ME 04062

1831, Large Letters FS-25-1831-301

VARIETY: Repunched Date   **BREEN-3919**
PUP: Numeral 1's in date
URS-7 · I-3 · L-3

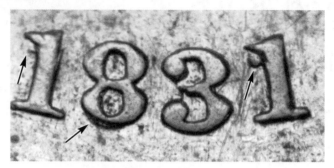

Description: A large-date logo punch was used over a small-date logo punch. The 1's and the 8 are clearly repunched.

Comments: This variety brings a small premium over the normal coin.

	VF-20	EF-40	AU-50	MS-60	MS-63
VARIETY	$175	$520	$925	$1,435	$5,000
NORMAL	150	450	800	1,250	4,500

1833 FS-25-1833-901

VARIETY: Die Doubling   **BREEN-3924**
PUP: OF AMERICA on reverse
URS-8 · I-3 · L-3

Description: The letters OF and AM on the reverse have been widely repunched.

Comments: This variety can be found with a little looking! Perhaps three out of every five 1833 Capped Bust quarters are of this variety.

	VF-20	EF-40	AU-50	MS-60	MS-63
VARIETY	$200	$475	$925	$1,600	$5,500
NORMAL	200	475	925	1,600	5,500

1834, O Over F

VARIETY: Die Doubling
PUP: OF AMERICA on reverse
URS-4 · I-4 · L-3

BREEN: N/L

Description: Very similar to the previous listing, the OF is widely repunched with the letters connected at the top, and the first A in AMERICA is also re-engraved. Other identifying characteristics: no period after C in denotation; 5 and C are farther apart.

Comments: This is a rare variety, especially if very sharp. Too little information is available to value this variety. This may be from the same reverse die as the 1833; more research is needed.

	VF-20	EF-40	AU-50	MS-60	MS-63
VARIETY	n/a	n/a	n/a	n/a	n/a
NORMAL	$150	$450	$800	$1,250	$4,300

THE CHERRYPICKERS' GUIDE HELPFUL HINTS

Please read the information in the front of this book. It sets the tone for the material that follows and makes it easier to interpret the information for each listing.

Liberty Seated Quarters, 1838–1891

Liberty Seated quarters are a paradise for variety enthusiasts. Significant varieties are known and can be found for virtually every date and mint. From minor repunched mintmarks to major doubled dies, and even major design changes, the varieties are abundant

Virtually all of the varieties within the series are in high demand by the large number of Liberty Seated specialists. In general, values for the varieties have been increasing at an even faster rate than for the normal coins. An eagle-eyed cherrypicker can easily earn a significant income by picking the varieties that go unnoticed by most dealers.

For those seriously interested in the series, we strongly recommend membership in the Liberty Seated Collectors Club (LSCC), which we believe to be one of the very best specialty clubs in numismatics. The club issues its official publication, the *Gobrecht Journal,* three times each year. This award-winning newsletter is loaded with excellent educational articles.

The club has an outstanding web site at www.lsccweb.org. As of this writing, the annual dues are $20—a bargain, considering the amount of information available. If you join the LSCC, you will be connecting with some of the most serious and knowledgeable collectors and dealers in the hobby. For more information, contact

Liberty Seated Collectors Club
Leonard Augsburger, Secretary-Treasurer
P.O. Box 6114
Vernon Hills, IL 60061
E-mail: leonard_augsburger@hotmail.com

1840-O, With Drapery

FS-25-1840o-501

VARIETY: Large O Mintmark
PUP: Mintmark
URS-7 · I-3 · L-3

BRIGGS: REV A

Description: The O mintmark punch used on this reverse die is about 25% larger than the others of this date and type.

Comments: There are two known reverse dies, with one showing doubled denticles.

	F-12	VF-20	EF-40	AU-50	MS-60	MS-63
VARIETY	$1,400	$2,500	$3,750	$4,850	$9,000	n/a
NORMAL	75	110	210	500	1,200	$3,500

1841-O, With Drapery

FS-25-1841o-101 (001)

VARIETY: Doubled-Die Obverse
PUP: Shield
URS-7 · I-3 · L-3

BRIGGS: OBV 2

Description: Doubling is evident on the shield, ribbon, rock, and lower gown.

Comments: The first three stars on the left show major doubling.

	F-12	VF-20	EF-40	AU-50	MS-60	MS-63
VARIETY	$80	$100	$200	$400	$950	$2,250
NORMAL	60	80	175	320	800	1,800

1843-O   FS-25-1843o-301

VARIETY: Repunched Date   **BRIGGS: OBV 2**
PUP: Date
URS-8 · I-1 · L-3

Description: The secondary digits are evident north of the primary 1 and 8.

Comments: The crossbar of the 4 is doubled on higher-grade specimens. (Note: Because of its low Interest Factor, this variety will be removed from this chapter in the next edition of this volume, to make room for more popularly collected pieces. The Fivaz-Stanton number will be retained for this variety and it will remain in the cross-references at the back of the book.)

1843-O   FS-25-1843o-501 (001.5)

VARIETY: Large O Mintmark   **BRIGGS: REV F**
PUP: Mintmark
URS-8 · I-3 · L-3

Description: The O mintmark was probably intended for a half dollar die.

Comments: Notice the pits in the die evident on the reverse, by the mintmark.

	F-12	VF-20	EF-40	AU-50	MS-60	MS-63
VARIETY	$600	$850	$1,600	$3,000	n/a	n/a
NORMAL	60	125	250	800	$2,500	$6,000

1845   FS-25-1845-301

VARIETY: Repunched Date   **BRIGGS: OBV 3**
PUP: Date
URS-6 · I-3 · L-3

Description: The primary 5 was punched over a smaller secondary 5, evident north.

Comments: A secondary 8 and 4 can be seen north on higher-grade specimens. These digits also appear smaller, supporting our theory that the initial date punch was likely intended for a half dime or dime.

	F-12	VF-20	EF-40	AU-50	MS-60	MS-63
VARIETY	$80	$145	$240	$375	$600	$1,325
NORMAL	35	45	80	160	550	1,200

1847   FS-25-1847-301 (002.3)

VARIETY: Misplaced Date   **BRIGGS: OBV 3**
PUP: Rock area above 8 of date
URS-8 · I-3 · L-3

Description: The lower portion of an 8 is evident protruding from the rock above the primary 8.

Comments: Remember to look in the rock and gown on all Liberty Seated coins for misplaced digits.

	F-12	VF-20	EF-40	AU-50	MS-60	MS-63
VARIETY	$55	$80	$115	$225	$800	$1,600
NORMAL	35	45	80	200	750	1,500

1847

FS-25-1847-801 (002)

VARIETY: Doubled-Die Reverse, Repunched Date
PUP: UNITED STATES
URS-9 · I-3 · L-3

BRIGGS: OBV 2, REV A

Description: This variety is most valuable for the doubled-die reverse, which is evident on UNITED STATES OF AMERICA and QUAR. DOL., the olive leaves, the eagle's left talon and eye, and the horizontal shield lines. The RPD is evident with a secondary 7 left of the primary 7.

Comments: Although somewhat strong, the RPD is not as important as the DDR.

	F-12	VF-20	EF-40	AU-50	MS-60	MS-63
VARIETY	$125	$225	$400	$650	$1,250	n/a
NORMAL	35	45	80	200	750	$1,500

1850

FS-25-1850-301

VARIETY: Misplaced Digit
PUP: Denticles below date
URS-11 · I-3 · L-3

BRIGGS: OBV 1

Description: The lower base of a 1 is evident protruding from the denticles.

Comments: This variety may be found with a bit of searching.

	F-12	VF-20	EF-40	AU-50	MS-60	MS-63
VARIETY	$125	$200	$350	$500	$1,500	n/a
NORMAL	65	95	175	240	900	$2,300

1853, No Arrows

VARIETY: Repunched Date
PUP: Date
URS-7 · I-3 · L-3

BRIGGS: OBV 1

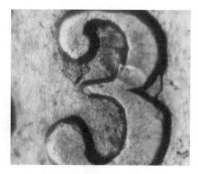

Description: This RPD is evident with the secondary 5 and 3 south of the primary digits.

Comments: At one time, this variety was erroneously attributed as a 53 Over 2 overdate. This is the only die known for 1853 that lacks the arrows and rays.

	F-12	VF-20	EF-40	AU-50	MS-60
VARIETY	$750	$1,000	$1,600	$3,000	$4,500
NORMAL	600	800	1,450	2,100	3,600

1853, Arrows and Rays

VARIETY: Overdate
PUP: Date and right arrow shaft
URS-6 · I-4 · L-4

BRIGGS: OBV 1

Description: The 3 of the date is punched over a 4. Also evident are the repunched 8 and 5, with the weaker images slightly north and west. The right arrow shaft is also doubled north of the primary.

Comments: On well worn or late-die-state specimens, the doubling of the arrow shaft may be the only evidence of the overdate. This is the only quarter-dollar date known to be punched over the *following* year!

	F-12	VF-20	EF-40	AU-50	MS-60	MS-63
VARIETY	$150	$250	$450	$800	$2,000	$3,500
NORMAL	35	55	175	300	950	2,200

1853-O, Arrows and Rays   FS-25-1853o-501

VARIETY: Repunched Mintmark   **BRIGGS: N/L**
PUP: Mintmark
URS-4 · I-4 · L-4

Description: A relatively new discovery, the first O mintmark punch entered the die horizontally, with a subsequent punch in the correct orientation. The horizontal O is evident within the opening of the primary O and can also be seen right of the primary O.

Comments: This variety commands a fair premium.

	F-12	VF-20	EF-40	AU-50	MS-60	MS-63
VARIETY	$75	$150	$400	$1,250	$4,000	n/a
NORMAL	60	75	250	1,100	3,500	$9,500

1854-O, Arrows   FS-25-1854o-501 (004)

VARIETY: Huge O Variety   **BRIGGS: REV A**
PUP: Mintmark
URS-7 · I-4 · L-4

Description: This particular O mintmark is very large, extremely thick on left side, and most irregular. This suggests that the O may have been carved into the die by hand.

Comments: There are other characteristics unique to this reverse die. Only one example has been reported in Mint State.

	VG-8	F-12	VF-20	EF-40	AU-50	AU-55	MS-60	MS-63
VARIETY	$1,100	$1,875	$3,250	$5,700	$8,500	$9,850	n/a	n/a
NORMAL	30	40	55	115	250	550	$1,000	$2,200

1856   FS-25-1856-301

VARIETY: Misplaced Date   **BRIGGS: N/L**
PUP: Robe right of Y of LIBERTY
URS-3 · I-3 · L-3

Description: The top left and bottom of a 1 is evident in the gown immediately right of the Y of LIBERTY. The top curve of a 6 is visible protruding from the rock below the foot (not shown)

Comments: Although the true rarity of this variety is not yet known, it must be assumed to be extremely rare. Market values have yet to be established.

	F-12	VF-20	EF-40	AU-50	MS-60	MS-63
VARIETY	n/a	n/a	n/a	n/a	n/a	n/a
NORMAL	$35	$45	$75	$160	$325	$600

1856-S, S Over Small S   FS-25-1856S-501 (005)

VARIETY: Repunched Mintmark   **BRIGGS: REV E; CONECA: RPM-001**
PUP: Mintmark
URS-4 · I-3 · L-3

Description: A larger S mintmark is punched over a much smaller S mintmark. The smaller S mintmark was probably intended for a half dime.

Comments: This is one of the more desirable mintmark varieties in the Liberty Seated series.

	F-12	VF-20	EF-40	AU-50
VARIETY	$1,150	$1,500	$2,000	$3,000
NORMAL	100	200	500	2,000

1857 FS-25-1857-401

VARIETY: Die Gouge
PUP: Miss Liberty's fingers   *"SMOKING LIBERTY" VARIETY*
NEW LISTING

Description: On FS-401, a die gouge creates the appearance that Liberty is holding a cigar or cigarette. The variety is affectionately referred to by specialists who are aware of it as "Smoking Liberty."

Comments: Saverio Barbieri amassed a small hoard of 28 pieces of this variety over a period of eight years (starting in 2000). In 2009, he had Dominion Grading Service grade 26 of them, attribute them as "Smoking Liberty," and designate them as being from the "Barbieri Cache."

	F-12	VF-20	EF-40	AU-50	MS-60	MS-63
VARIETY	n/a	n/a	\n/a	n/a	n/a	n/a
NORMAL	$35	$45	$75	$160	325	600

1857 FS-25-1857-901 (006)

VARIETY: Multidenomenational Clash   **BRIGGS: REV F**
PUP: Reverse by eagle's neck
URS-6 · I-4 · L-4

Description: The reverse of this 1857 Large Date quarter clashed with the reverse die of an 1857 Flying Eagle cent. Images of the FE cent reverse die are easily seen on either side of the eagle's neck, within the shield, and below the eagle's left (viewer's right) wing.

Comments: Refer also to the 1857 Flying Eagle cent with muled clashed dies, in the *Cherrypickers' Guide*, fifth edition, volume I.

	F-12	VF-20	EF-40	AU-50	MS-60	MS-63
VARIETY	$175	$375	$850	$2,100	n/a	n/a
NORMAL	35	45	75	160	$325	$600

1857-O
FS-25-1857o-301 (006.2)

VARIETY: Misplaced Digit
PUP: Denticles below date
URS-3 · I-3 · L-3

BRIGGS: N/L

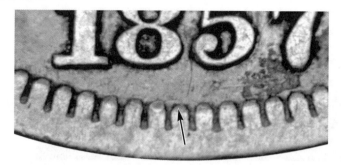

Description: The upper portion of an 8 is evident protruding from the denticles below the right side of the primary 8.

Comments: This coin from Larry Briggs was discovered after the publication of his book on Liberty Seated quarters.

	F-12	VF-20	EF-40	AU-50	MS-60
VARIETY	$65	$80	$150	$400	$1,200
NORMAL	50	60	125	300	1,100

1872
FS-25-1872-301

VARIETY: Repunched Date
PUP: Date
URS-3 · I-3 · L-3

BRIGGS: N/L

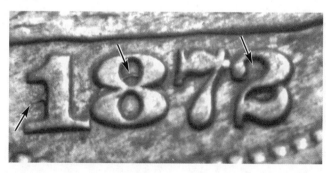

Description: The digits are repunched, with the secondary images south of the primary. On the coin examined, the secondary 7 is not noticeable, but the 1, 8, and 2 are all dramatic.

Comments: This is another variety discovered after the publication of *Comprehensive Encyclopedia of United States Liberty Seated Quarters* by Larry Briggs.

	F-12	VF-20	EF-40	AU-50	MS-60
VARIETY	$100	$160	$265	$400	$800
NORMAL	60	115	160	225	600

1875   FS-25-1875-301 (006.75)

VARIETY: Misplaced Date   **BRIGGS: N/L**
PUP: Denticles below date
URS-3 · I-3 · L-3

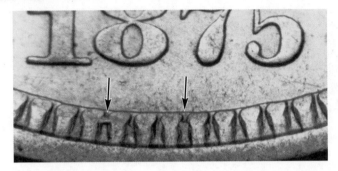

Description: The upper portion of an 8 and a 7 can be seen within the denticles below the primary date.

Comments: This is another variety discovered after the publication of the Briggs encyclopedia.

	F-12	VF-20	EF-40	AU-50	MS-60	MS-63
VARIETY	$50	$75	$110	$250	$350	$650
NORMAL	35	45	65	160	275	550

1876   FS-25-1876-301

VARIETY: Misplaced Date   **BRIGGS: N/L**
PUP: Denticles below date
URS-3 · I-2 · L-2

Description: The upper portion of a 6 can be seen within the denticles below the primary 6.

Comments: This variety was discovered after the publication of the Briggs encyclopedia.

	F-12	VF-20	EF-40	AU-50	MS-60	MS-63
VARIETY	$50	$75	$110	$250	$350	$650
NORMAL	35	45	65	160	275	550

1876

FS-25-1876-302 (006.8)

VARIETY: Repunched Date
PUP: Date
URS-3 · I-4 · L-4

BRIGGS: N/L

Description: The "flag" of a secondary 1 is evident south and west of the primary 1, and a third 1 is south and west of the primary 8.

Comments: This variety, too, was discovered after the publication of the Briggs encyclopedia.

	F-12	VF-20	EF-40	AU-50	MS-60	MS-63
VARIETY	$75	$150	$225	$300	$450	$750
NORMAL	35	45	65	160	275	550

1876

FS-25-1876-303 (006.85)

VARIETY: Misplaced Date
PUP: Rock above date
URS-3 · I-3 · L-3

BRIGGS: N/L

Description: The base of a number (likely a 6) is evident protruding from the rock above the date, between the 8 and the 7.

Comments: Always check the rock and skirt on Liberty Seated coins.

	F-12	VF-20	EF-40	AU-50	MS-60	MS-63
VARIETY	$50	$75	$110	$250	$350	$650
NORMAL	35	45	65	160	275	550

1876

FS-25-1876-304

VARIETY: Repunched Date
PUP: Date
URS-5 · I-3 · L-3

BRIGGS: OBV 6

Description: Repunching is evident as a triple punched 6, seen within the loop of the 6, and very slightly north on the base of the 1.

Comments: Always check all elements on all Liberty Seated coins.

	F-12	VF-20	EF-40	AU-50	MS-60	MS-63
VARIETY	$75	$150	$225	$300	$450	$750
NORMAL	35	45	65	160	275	550

1876

FS-25-1876-305

VARIETY: Misplaced Date
PUP: Denticles below date
URS-5 · I-3 · L-3

BRIGGS: OBV 2

Description: The tops of a 1 and an 8 are evident in the denticles below the date.

Comments: Always check the denticles on Liberty Seated coins.

	F-12	VF-20	EF-40	AU-50	MS-60	MS-63
VARIETY	$50	$75	$110	$250	$350	$650
NORMAL	35	45	65	160	275	550

1876-S   FS-25-1876S-301

VARIETY: Misplaced Date   **BRIGGS: N/L**
PUP: Denticles below date
URS-5 · I-3 · L-3

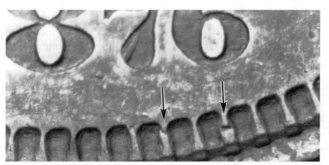

Description: The tops of a 7 and a 6 can be seen in the denticles below the date.
Comments: The reverse type is unknown, but is probably Type 2.

	F-12	VF-20	EF-40	AU-50	MS-60	MS-63
VARIETY	$50	$75	$110	$250	$350	$650
NORMAL	35	45	65	160	275	550

1876-S   FS-25-1876S-302

VARIETY: Misplaced Date   **BRIGGS: N/L**
PUP: Denticles below date
URS-5 · I-3 · L-3

Description: The tops of two 8's are evident below the primary 8.
Comments: The reverse type is unknown, but is probably Type 2.

	F-12	VF-20	EF-40	AU-50	MS-60	MS-63
VARIETY	$50	$75	$110	$250	$350	$650
NORMAL	35	45	65	160	275	550

1876-CC   FS-25-1876CC-301

VARIETY: Repunched Date   **BRIGGS:** N/L
PUP: Date
URS-3 · I-3 · L-3

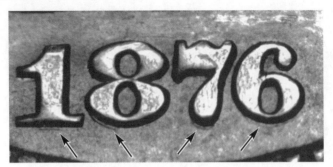

Description: Secondary digits for the 1, 8, and 7 are evident south of the primary
digits. The secondary digits are very close to the primary.

Comments: The reverse type is unknown, but is probably Type 2.

	F-12	VF-20	EF-40	AU-50	MS-60	MS-63
VARIETY	$85	$95	$130	$235	$525	$1,050
NORMAL	75	85	120	225	500	1,000

1877-CC   FS-25-1877CC-301

VARIETY: Repunched Date   **BRIGGS:** OBV 2
PUP: Date
URS-7 · I-3 · L-3

 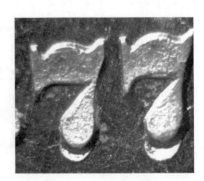

Description: The two 7's of the date are strongly repunched south.

Comments: A second, very similar RPD is also known for this date.

	F-12	VF-20	EF-40	AU-50	MS-60	MS-63
VARIETY	$80	$90	$125	$230	$485	$775
NORMAL	75	85	120	220	475	750

1877-S, S Over Horizontal S

FS-25-1877S-501

VARIETY: Repunched Mintmark
PUP: Mintmark
URS-6 · I-4 · L-4

BRIGGS: REV D; CONECA: RPM-001

Description: The initial S mintmark was punched into the die horizontally, then corrected with an upright S mintmark.

Comments: This is one of the most collectible mintmark varieties in the series, of longstanding fame—cherrypicked back to the 1950s.

	F-12	VF-20	EF-40	AU-50	MS-60	MS-63
VARIETY	$90	$185	$275	$375	$625	$1,450
NORMAL	35	45	65	160	275	550

1891

FS-25-1891-301

VARIETY: Misplaced Date
PUP: Denticles below the date
URS-7 · I-3 · L-3

BRIGGS: OBV 7

Description: The tops of an 8 and 9 are very evident protruding from the denticles below the primary date.

Comments: This is one of the more evident MPDs in this series.

	F-12	VF-20	EF-40	AU-50	MS-60	MS-63
VARIETY	$75	$150	$250	$350	$475	$750
NORMAL	35	45	65	160	260	550

Barber or Liberty Head Quarters, 1892–1916

The three series of the Barber design have long been neglected when one considers the typical varieties, such as doubled dies, repunched mintmarks, overdates, and the like. For many collectors, the Barber quarter series has been somewhat of an afterthought when searching for nice varieties. But all that is changing now that many new varieties are discovered and reported, and some of the known varieties are becoming more popular. We encourage close inspection of all Barber coins.

Only a limited number of varieties in the Barber quarter series were known when the fourth edition of the *Cherrypickers' Guide* went to press. In this volume of the *Cherrypickers' Guide* we have included more than a dozen varieties that are rapidly gaining in popularity. Compared to the four listings in the third edition, one can easily see the increased interest. More varieties will certainly be included in the sixth edition. New listings are also included for the Barber dimes and Barber half dollars. Be sure to check those sections for other new listings.

To obtain more knowledge on Barber coins in general, and Barber varieties in particular, we suggest membership in the Barber Coin Collectors Society. Annual dues are $15. You may make contact through

Eileen Ribar
2053 Edith Place
Merrick, NY 11566
E-mail: emcrib@optonline.net

Their quarterly publication, the *Journal*, contains educational information on all denominations of the Barber design. The society also has a web site at www.barbercoins.org. Visitors to the site can find educational articles; membership information; and general information concerning the Barber design, the three Barber series, and Liberty Head nickels.

Reverse Types of 1892

VARIETY: Reverse Types

1892, Type 1 reverse   1892, Type 2 reverse

Description: There are two varieties of the 1892 Barber quarter reverse design, distinguished by the position of the eagle's wing tip relative to the E in UNITED. On Type 1, the wing covers only half of the E. On Type 2, the wing covers most of the E.

Comments: Coins of Type 1 are somewhat scarcer than those of Type 2; however, the market has yet to make a significant distinction in pricing.

1892   FS-25-1892-101 (007.7)

VARIETY: Doubled-Die Obverse   **LAWRENCE-104**
PUP: Motto
URS-8 · I-2 · L-2

Description: Doubling is very evident on IN GOD WE TRUST.

Comments: This variety commands modest premiums. It is on the Type 2 reverse.

	VG-8	F-12	VF-20	EF-40	AU-50	MS-60	MS-63
VARIETY	$12	$29	$50	$83	$135	$240	$475
NORMAL	10	26	45	75	125	225	425

1892
FS-25-1892-301

VARIETY: Repunched Date, Tripled-Die Obverse
PUP: Date, Motto
URS-4 · I-1 · L-2

LAWRENCE: N/L

Description: The repunched date is most evident below the primary 8. The TDO is a very close spread, mostly visible on TRUST.

Comments: The tripled obverse die is relatively minor and it fades with just a little circulation (or a weak strike); therefore, most of the value is for the repunched date. (Note: Because of its low Interest Factor, this variety will be removed from this chapter in the next edition of this volume, to make room for more popularly collected pieces. The Fivaz-Stanton number will be retained for this variety and it will remain in the cross-references at the back of the book.)

1892
FS-25-1892-801

VARIETY: Tripled-Die Reverse
PUP: Reverse lettering
URS-7 · I-1 · L-3

LAWRENCE-105

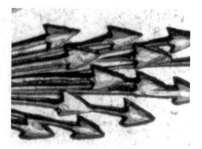

Description: Tripling is evident on all outer lettering, with doubling visible on several stars, the ribbon ends, and the arrows.

Comments: Two different die states are known. Later states appear with chips evident on the upper loops of the first and last S of STATES. Die chips are common. This is on the Type 2 reverse. (Note: Because of its low Interest Factor, this variety will be removed from this chapter in the next edition of this volume, to make room for more popularly collected pieces. The Fivaz-Stanton number will be retained for this variety and it will remain in the cross-references at the back of the book.)

1892-O

VARIETY: Doubled-Die Obverse
PUP: Motto
URS-8 · I-3 · L-3

LAWRENCE-103

Description: Doubling is very evident on IN GOD WE TRUST and the ribbon ends.
Comments: The reverse is a minor DDR. It is the Type 2 reverse.

	VG-8	F-12	VF-20	EF-40	AU-50	MS-60	MS-63
VARIETY	$25	$55	$90	$135	$225	$340	$550
NORMAL	20	45	60	95	160	300	500

1892-O

VARIETY: Repunched Date
PUP: Date
URS-9 · I-3 · L-3

LAWRENCE-102

Description: Secondary digits are visible south on all numbers, but most noticeable on the 2 of the date.
Comments: This variety will bring a modest premium. This is a Type 2 reverse. This variety was erroneously listed as FS-501 in the fourth edition.

	VG-8	F-12	VF-20	EF-40	AU-50	MS-60	MS-63
VARIETY	$25	$55	$90	$135	$225	$340	$550
NORMAL	20	45	60	95	160	300	500

1892-O, Covered E Reverse   FS-25-1892o-901

VARIETY: Clashed Dies
PUP: Profile
NEW LISTING

Description: This variety displays a strong clashed-die obverse and reverse. Stars transferred from the reverse die and jutting prominently from Liberty's neck is the most dramatic aspect of this coin. Other obverse and reverse clash marks are evident.

Comments: This appears to be a very recent find.

	VG-8	F-12	VF-20	EF-40	AU-50	MS-60	MS-63
VARIETY	n/a	n/a	n/a	n/a	n/a	n/a	n/a
NORMAL	$20	$45	$60	$95	$160	$300	$500

1892-S   FS-25-1892S-501

VARIETY: Repunched Mintmark   **LAWRENCE-101; CONECA: RPM-001**
PUP: Mintmark
URS-7 · I-3 · L-3

Description: The secondary S is evident northwest of the primary S.

Comments: This is a very evident and popular RPM. The reverse is Type 1.

	VG-8	F-12	VF-20	EF-40	AU-50	MS-60	MS-63
VARIETY	$65	$95	$145	$250	$375	$600	$1,150
NORMAL	50	80	130	200	300	500	1,000

1899
FS-25-1899-901

VARIETY: Doubled-Die Reverse **WEXLER: WDDR-001**
PUP: Profile
NEW LISTING

Description: Very strong doubling is visible on the word DOLLAR, the arrows clutched in the eagle's claws, and the eagle's leg.

Comments: A higher grade would probably show more doubling.

	VG-8	F-12	VF-20	EF-40	AU-50	MS-60	MS-63
VARIETY	n/a	n/a	n/a	n/a	n/a	n/a	n/a
NORMAL	$10	$26	$45	$75	$125	$225	$450

1902-O
FS-25-1902o-301

VARIETY: Misplaced Date **LAWRENCE: N/L**
PUP: Denticles below date
URS-4 · I-2 · L-2

Description: The top of a digit (likely a 0) can be seen in the denticles below the primary 0 of the date.

Comments: This is one of the few listed MPDs for the Barber quarter series.

	VG-8	F-12	VF-20	EF-40	AU-50	MS-60	MS-63
VARIETY	$25	$65	$100	$170	$250	$525	$1,450
NORMAL	16	50	85	140	225	475	1,400

1907-D

VARIETY: Repunched Date, Doubled-Die Obverse
PUP: Date
URS-4 · I-3 · L-3

LAWRENCE-102

Description: Secondary digits are evident south on all four digits, most noticeable on the 9, 0, and 7. Minor doubling is evident on the first two stars on left and ribbon ends.

Comments: Keep an eye out for this variety.

	VG-8	F-12	VF-20	EF-40	AU-50	MS-60	MS-63
VARIETY	$25	$50	$75	$100	$200	$325	$850
NORMAL	10	26	48	80	175	250	750

1907-S

VARIETY: Repunched Mintmark
PUP: Mintmark
URS-7 · I-3 · L-3

LAWRENCE-102; CONECA: N/L

Description: This RPM is evident on the notched serifs on the S. The secondary S is rotated slightly.

Comments: There are at least two other RPMs known for this date.

	VG-8	F-12	VF-20	EF-40	AU-50	MS-60	MS-63
VARIETY	$25	$55	$90	$175	$350	$550	$1,000
NORMAL	18	45	70	140	280	475	900

1908-D
FS-25-1908D-301

VARIETY: Misplaced Date
PUP: Denticles below the date
URS-4 · I-2 · L-2

LAWRENCE: N/L

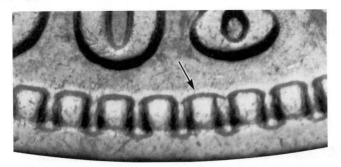

Description: The top of a digit (likely a 0) is visible in the denticles below the space between the 0 and 8.

Comments: Very few MPDs are listed in this series.

	VG-8	F-12	VF-20	EF-40	AU-50	MS-60	MS-63
VARIETY	$20	$35	$60	$95	$150	$260	$480
NORMAL	10	26	45	75	125	225	425

1914-D
FS-25-1914D-101 (007.99)

VARIETY: Doubled-Die Obverse
PUP: Motto
URS-5 · I-3 · L-3

LAWRENCE-102

Description: Doubling is evident on all obverse lettering, ribbon ends, and stars.

Comments: This is a very nice doubled die, and still findable!

	VG-8	F-12	VF-20	EF-40	AU-50	MS-60	MS-63
VARIETY	$25	$50	$75	$100	$200	$265	$480
NORMAL	10	26	45	75	125	225	425

1916-D

FS-25-1916D-501 (008)

VARIETY: Repunched Mintmark
PUP: Mintmark
URS-8 · I-4 · L-4

LAWRENCE-102; CONECA: RPM-002

Description: The secondary D mintmark is evident within the opening of the primary mintmark. We believe this is a large D over a small D; others feel it is just a D over D.

Comments: There are at least three other RPMs known for the date. All command a small premium.

	VG-8	F-12	VF-20	EF-40	AU-50	MS-60	MS-63
VARIETY	$11	$28	$50	$80	$135	$235	$450
NORMAL	10	26	45	75	125	225	425

Standing Liberty Quarters, 1916–1930

For some unknown reason, there are very few varieties in the Standing Liberty quarter series. In this volume, we have included only the varieties of which we are certain. Obviously, the most dramatic variety in the series is the 1918-S, 8 Over 7, which is a very rare variety, especially in high grade.

As we have mentioned elsewhere in the text, major varieties for the 20th century seem to occur during wartime years, and the monster overdate of 1918 is a good example. One obvious reason, which is very well known, is the U.S. government will do anything and everything possible to conserve metal for use with ammunition and equipment. This could possibly explain the use of overdated dies for production during these times.

More information about varieties in the series can be obtained from the CONECA web site. CONECA is the national error/variety club devoted to the study of numismatic errors and varieties. James Wiles is the primary attributor of 20th-century die varieties for the organization. Dr. Wiles maintains a complete list of all varieties listed in the CONECA register. This list is available to Internet users.

If you're interested in learning as much as possible about errors and varieties, we highly suggest membership in CONECA. For adults, annual dues are $25 (for bulk mailing; contact the Membership Coordinator for current First Class or international rates). For Young Numismatists (under age 18), dues are $7.50 (online membership only, which includes digital access to *ErrorScope*) or $17.50 (online membership plus hard-copy subscription to *ErrorScope*). An application can be obtained online at www.conecaonline.org, or from Rachel Irish at the following address:

CONECA
Rachel Irish
101 W. Prairie #323
Hayden, ID 83835
E-mail: MRirish5@roadrunner.com

1917-D, Type 1

FS-25-1917D-801

VARIETY: Doubled-Die Reverse   **CONECA: DDR-001; WEXLER: WDDR-001**
PUP: Letters of motto
NEW LISTING

Description: A strong spread to the east shows on E PLURIBUS UNUM, MER of AMERICA, the lower left wing feathers, and some inner feather details on the right wing.

Comments: Very few doubled dies are known among this series, and this is a nice one!

	VG-8	F-12	VF-20	EF-40	AU-50	MS-60	MS-63	MS-65
VARIETY	n/a	n/a	n/a	n/a	n/a	n/a	n/a	n/a
NORMAL	$60	$90	$125	$200	$250	$325	$450	$900

1918-S, 8 Over 7

FS-25-1918S-101 (008.5)

VARIETY: Overdate, Doubled-Die Obverse   **BREEN-4235; CONECA: DDO-001**
PUP: Date
URS-11 · I-5 · L-5

Description: This clear overdate, 1918/7, was caused by using two different dated hubs when the die was made. Because of the boldness of the 7, this variety can be confirmed easily in low grades.

Comments: This variety is extremely rare in high grades. We recommend authentication because fraudulent alterations do exist. Genuine specimens have a small die chip above the pedestal, just to the left of the lowest star on the right.

	VG-8	F-12	VF-20	EF-40	AU-50	MS-60	MS-63	MS-65
VARIETY	$2,200	$3,600	$5,000	$8,000	$13,000	$19,000	$32,500	$75,000
NORMAL	22	35	45	60	120	210	310	1,300

1920
FS-25-1920-401

VARIETY: Double-Clashed Obverse Die
PUP: Inverted doubled E in drapery
NEW LISTING

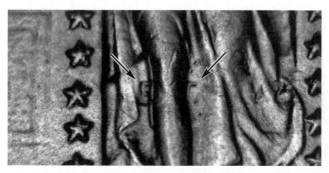

Description: The obverse shows typical elements of a strong clashed die. An inverted and doubled E of E PLURIBUS is evident protruding from the viewer's left of Liberty's right leg at the knee, while an inverted L shows on the opposite side of her knee. A weak star is visible left of Liberty's head.

Comments: A single-clash is also known for this date and listed as Knauss: K-0077.

	VG-8	F-12	VF-20	EF-40	AU-50	MS-60	MS-63	MS-65
VARIETY	n/a	n/a	n/a	n/a	n/a	n/a	n/a	n/a
NORMAL	$20	$30	$35	$55	$100	$175	$250	$600

1920-S
FS-25-1920S-401

VARIETY: Clashed Obverse Die
PUP: Inverted doubled E in drapery
NEW LISTING

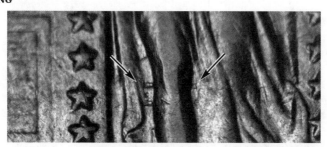

Description: The obverse shows typical elements of a strong clashed die. An inverted and doubled E of E PLURIBUS is evident protruding from the viewer's left of Liberty's right leg at the knee, while an inverted L shows on the opposite side of her knee.

Comments: A single-clash is also known for this date and listed as Knauss: K-0078. Clashes involving an inverted E and L are known for almost every date and mintmark for the series. The only dates for which they are not yet known are 1916, 1919-D, 1920-D, 1924-D, and 1929-D.

	VG-8	F-12	VF-20	EF-40	AU-50	MS-60	MS-63	MS-65
VARIETY	n/a	n/a	n/a	n/a	n/a	n/a	n/a	n/a
NORMAL	$25	$35	$50	$65	$140	$270	$775	$2,200

1928-S   FS-25-1928S-501

VARIETY: Inverted Mintmark   **BREEN: N/L**
PUP: Mintmark
URS-3 · I-3 · L-3

Description: An inverted S mintmark was clearly punched into the die.

Comments: Inverted S-mintmark varieties are rapidly gaining in popularity.

	VG-8	F-12	VF-20	EF-40	AU-50	MS-60	MS-63
VARIETY	$275.00	$400.00	n/a	n/a	n/a	n/a	n/a
NORMAL	7.75	8.50	$22	$40	$90	$160	$250

1928-S   FS-25-1928S-502

VARIETY: Repunched Mintmark   **BREEN-4259; CONECA: RPM-001**
PUP: Mintmark
URS-3 · I-3 · L-3

Description: The primary S is punched over a slightly east and tilted S.

Comments: This variety may be CONECA RPM-001.

	VG-8	F-12	VF-20	EF-40	AU-50	MS-60	MS-63
VARIETY	$35.00	$50.00	$75	$100	$200	$300	$450
NORMAL	7.75	8.50	22	40	90	160	250

1929-S

VARIETY: Clashed Obverse Die
PUP: Right of Liberty's right leg
URS-3 · I-3 · L-3

BREEN: N/L

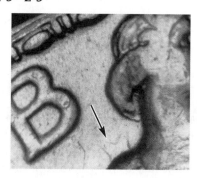 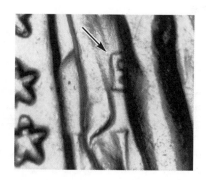

Description: This obverse die shows typical elements of a strong clashed die. An inverted E of PLURIBUS is evident protruding from the viewer's left of Liberty's right leg. The letter I of AMERICA is also evident below this B. Stars are visible left of Liberty's head.

Comments: This is becoming a popular variety! Note that clash marks may be found in several coins in this series.

	VG-8	F-12	VF-20	EF-40	AU-50	MS-60	MS-63
VARIETY	$14.00	$19.00	$23	$50	$115	$175	$290
NORMAL	7.75	8.50	17	35	80	150	240

1930-S

VARIETY: Likely Repunched Mintmark
PUP: Mintmark
URS-3 · I-1 · L-3

BREEN: N/L

Description: The S mintmark appears to be punched over another S mintmark, but other possible explanations exist. This is definitely not the common shearing seen on many mintmarks. In all likelihood, this is a small S over a larger S.

Comments: We would like to examine a higher-grade specimen! (Because there is some doubt as to whether this variety is genuine, it will be removed from the next edition of this volume. The Fivaz-Stanton number will be retained for this now.)

Washington Quarters, 1932 to Date

Collectors of Washington quarter varieties are as avid as any group of variety specialists, and very serious in their quest for the most popular and rare specimens. They will actively compete for a hard-to-find variety.

When the first edition of the *Cherrypickers' Guide* was published in 1989, this series was one of the "sleepers" for variety specialists. At that time, many of the better varieties were known only to a few collectors, so the pickings were relatively easy. However, since about 1990, the series has become increasingly more popular, making the searches much more challenging.

Interesting and rare varieties in the Washington quarter series include some spectacular doubled dies, significant repunched mintmarks, over mintmarks, and master die alterations. One of the few known totally separated, repunched mintmarks, the 1940-D and D, is still considered one of the most elusive varieties. A couple of other very significant misplaced mintmarks have also been found in this series.

Very few reference books specializing in this series contain significant details of varieties. The most complete work is that of James Wiles, former president of the Combined Organizations of Numismatic Error Collectors of America (CONECA).

The varieties listed in this volume of the *Cherrypickers' Guide* are generally considered the best of the best. However, some of the lesser varieties are also included so that our Young Numismatists (YNs) and other novice enthusiasts can find some of the many nice varieties known in the series.

If you're interested in learning as much as possible about errors and varieties, we highly suggest membership in CONECA. For adults, annual dues are $25 (for bulk mailing; contact the Membership Coordinator for current First Class or international rates). For Young Numismatists (under age 18), dues are $7.50 (online membership only, which includes digital access to *ErrorScope*) or $17.50 (online membership plus hard-copy subscription to *ErrorScope*). An application can be obtained online at www.conecaonline.org, or from Rachel Irish at the following address:

CONECA
Rachel Irish
101 W. Prairie #323
Hayden, ID 83835
E-mail: MRirish5@roadrunner.com

MAJOR DESIGN ALTERATIONS
FOR WASHINGTON QUARTERS

Washington quarter specialist José Cortez, one of only a handful of people who have studied this series extensively, graciously provided this research. Not only has he shared this important information, he has also contributed several varieties for inclusion in this volume. His experience and guidance have been invaluable in the development of this section, including in its valuations.

In 1932 the U.S. Mint began production of the George Washington quarter dollar. Initially intended to commemorate the 200th anniversary of the president's birth, its popularity was the basis for the Mint's decision to retain the design for regular coin production from that date forward.

Between 1932 and 1964 there were three major obverse design alterations, and three reverse design alterations—all relatively minor, but all significant in the minds of collectors.

The Obverse Design Alterations

Oddly, all three obverse design alterations occurred in 1934. Initial production began with the obverse design as adopted in 1932, now referred to as the Light Motto. The letters of the motto are very weak and mushy, and become progressively lighter from the rim to the portrait. The letters of the word WE are often so light that it is difficult to discern them clearly from the field in macro photos.

In an effort to enhance the motto, the Mint designed a new master hub with what is now referred to as the Heavy Motto variety. This alteration had a much bolder motto than the first effort. It is easily identified by viewing the center stroke of the W in WE, which rises above the two outer strokes. This motto was used from 1936 forward on Proof and circulation-strike coinage. Philadelphia and Denver also used this variety in 1934.

In the same year (1934), another master hub was used, also with a bolder motto, but with the center stroke of the W in WE below the two outer strokes. This design, referred to as the Medium Motto, was used at Philadelphia and Denver in 1934 and 1935, and at San Francisco in 1935. Therefore, 1935 is the only year that the Medium Motto variety was used at all three mints. It was also the last year this variety was used, as the Heavy Motto variety was adopted permanently in 1936.

The Reverse Design Alterations

The reverse design changes began in 1936 with production of the first Proof coins of the series. The design alteration, or rather *enhancement,* produced a bolder view of the eagle's tail feathers, the leaves, and the arrows. The alteration also resulted in wider separation between the E and S of STATES. This design is referred to as the Type B reverse for the series. This design was intended for use on Proof issues from 1936 to 1964, and 1968 to 1972.

The Type B reverse also exists on regular circulation-strike issues for Philadelphia from 1956 to 1964. All are considered scarce to very scarce. Mint sets of 1957, 1959, and 1960 are known with Type B reverse quarters.

Another reverse alteration began to be used with the introduction of the new copper-nickel clad series in 1965. This variety became known as the Type C reverse. Close examination shows that it is a bolder version of the Type A reverse. It differs from the Type A in that the leaves are bolder and more distinct. The leaf above the first L in DOLLAR is very distinct and almost touches the L. The leaf that disappeared in front of the bundle of arrow tips on the Type A reverse is now very bold and comes to a noticeable point at the tip of the top arrow. The tail feathers are bolder, showing lines in the center of the feathers that are more distinct.

Although adopted for use on clad issues beginning with coins dated 1965, one Type C reverse die was mistakenly punched with a D mintmark and sent to the Denver Mint. This was actually used to produce silver quarters dated 1964. These 1964-D quarters with the Type C reverse are considered very scarce.

There has been speculation over the years that there may be Denver-minted Washington quarters with the Type B reverse from 1956 to 1964; however, none have yet been confirmed.

The only year in which all three reverse types are known to have been used is 1964. This became possible when the lone Type C die bearing the D mintmark was sent to Denver for production of 1964 circulation-strike coins.

Reverse Hub Comparisons

Distinguishing among the different reverse hubs of the Washington quarter is relatively easy once one has the opportunity to compare the differences. In the following pages we illustrate photos of the key areas of the three hubs, side by side.

TYPE A REVERSE (CONECA: RDV-001)

On the Type A reverse, the tip of the leaf is pointed and ends below the topmost arrow tips; the design overall is in lower relief.

The Type A reverse is known on all circulation strikes, from all mints, from 1932 through 1964, as well as on Proofs from 1936. All are common.

Type B Reverse (CONECA: RDV-002)

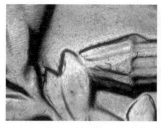

On the Type B reverse, the tip of the leaf is pointed, extending above the topmost arrow tip, and angles slightly to the left at the top. The overall design is in higher relief.

The Type B reverse is known on some Philadelphia circulation strikes from 1956 through 1964, and on Proofs from 1937 through 1942 and from 1950 through 1964. The 1956 Type B reverse is the scarcest of the nine dates.

Type C Reverse (CONECA: RDV-003)

On the Type C reverse, the N in UNUM has a very slight spur at the top of the right-hand stroke, and the tail feathers are stronger than they are on the previous two types, with center lines in each.

The Type C reverse is known on 1964-D, 1965, and 1967 strikes. The 1964-D and the 1967 are scarce to rare.

Type D Reverse (CONECA: RDV-004)

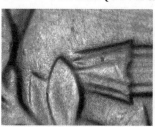

On the Type D reverse, the tip of the leaf is pointed and ends below the topmost arrow tip. There is no spur at the top of the right-hand stroke of the N in UNUM.

The Type D reverse is found on all of the following, and all are common: Philadelphia, 1965 through 1968; Denver, 1968 and 1969; and Special Mint Set coins of 1965 through 1967.

TYPE E REVERSE (CONECA: RDV-005)

On the Type E reverse, the tip of the leaf is pointed and ends below the topmost arrow tip. There is no doubling on the Q in QUARTER.

The Type E reverse is found on all of the following: Philadelphia, 1965 through 1968; Denver, 1968 and 1969; Special Mint Set coins of 1965 through 1967; and San Francisco, 1968. Of these, the 1968-S is extremely rare.

TYPE F REVERSE (CONECA: RDV-006)

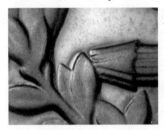 

On the Type F reverse, the tip of the leaf is pointed and ends below the topmost arrow tip. The Q in QUARTER displays master-die doubling.

The Type F reverse is found on all of the following: Philadelphia, 1967 through 1972; Denver, 1968 through 1972; and San Francisco, 1968. The 1968-S is rare.

TYPE G REVERSE (CONECA: RDV-007)

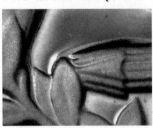 

On the Type G reverse, the tip of the leaf is rounded and rests slightly below the topmost arrow tips. Doubling is evident on the Q in QUARTER.

The Type G reverse is found on the 1968-S, 1969-D, 1970, and 1970-D, and all are common.

TYPE H REVERSE (CONECA: RDV-008)

Very similar to the Type B reverse, the Type H reverse shows the leaf pointed and extending above the topmost arrow tips; and the overall design is in high relief.

The Type H reverse is found on all of the following: Denver, 1969 through 1972; and San Francisco, 1968 through 1972. The 1969-D is rare, while the 1970-D, 1971-D, and 1972-D are very rare.

SEE THE CHARTS ON PAGES 203 AND 204 FOR INDIVIDUAL VALUATIONS OF THE SCARCE TO RARE VARIETIES.

1932   FS-25-1932-101

VARIETY: Doubled-Die Obverse   **CONECA: DDO-001**
PUP: Earlobe
URS-4 · I-3 · L-3

 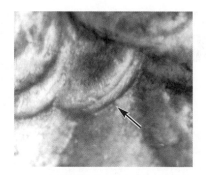

Description: The doubling is evident as a doubled earlobe, with additional doubling visible on the nostril and the back of the queue.

Comments: Previous editions of this guide indicated that the reverse contained a minor doubled die, which was inaccurate.

	VF-20	EF-40	AU-50	MS-60	MS-63	MS-65
VARIETY	$30	$60	$110	$175	$450	$775
NORMAL	10	11	15	25	50	425

1934   FS-25-1934-101

VARIETY: Doubled-Die Obverse   **CONECA: DDO-001**
PUP: IN GOD WE TRUST
URS-10 · I-4 · L-4

Description: Very strong doubling is evident on the motto, LIBERTY, and the date. This is a Medium Motto variety. (See FS-25-1934-402.)

Comments: This obverse, one of the strongest and most popular of all Washington quarter varieties, can also be found matched with a significant Class VI reversed doubled die (CONECA DDR-001) that is overshadowed by the DDO and largely ignored by mainstream buyers.

	VF-20	EF-40	AU-50	MS-60	MS-63	MS-65
VARIETY	$165	$225	$450	$900	$2,000	$4,250
NORMAL	8	10	15	30	50	150

1934   FS-25-1934-401

VARIETY: Light Motto   **BREEN-4270; CONECA: ODV-001**
PUP: IN GOD WE TRUST
URS-13 · I-3 · L-4

Description: Notice the considerable weakness in the letters of the motto. In addition, the center point of the W is pointed.

Comments: Of the three primary 1934 obverse hubs, this is the one that will command a premium.

	VF-20	EF-40	AU-50	AU-55	MS-60	MS-63	MS-65
VARIETY	$13	$18	$27	$40	$65	$100	$320
NORMAL	8	10	15	20	30	50	120

1934   FS-25-1934-402

VARIETY: Medium Motto   **BREEN-4271; CONECA: ODV-002**
PUP: IN GOD WE TRUST
URS-22 · I-2 · L-1

Description: The motto is more pronounced than the Light Motto. The center point of the W is somewhat squared off, not pointed like on the Light Motto.

Comments: This is the most common of the three primary 1934 obverse designs and is shown here for informational purposes only.

	VF-20	EF-40	AU-50	AU-55	MS-60	MS-63	MS-65
VARIETY	$8	$10	$15	$20	$30	$50	$120
NORMAL	8	10	15	20	30	50	120

1934   FS-25-1934-403

VARIETY: Heavy Motto   **BREEN-4272; CONECA: ODV-003**
PUP: IN GOD WE TRUST
URS-21 · I-2 · L-1

Description: The motto has very thick letters. The center point of the W is pointed and rises slightly above the other letters.

Comments: This variety is shown here for informational purposes only.

	VF-20	EF-40	AU-50	AU-55	MS-60	MS-63	MS-65
VARIETY	$8	$10	$15	$20	$30	$50	$120
NORMAL	8	10	15	20	30	50	120

1934-D

VARIETY: Mintmark of 1932
PUP: Mintmark
URS-3 · I-3 · L-4

BREEN: N/L; CONECA: MMS-001

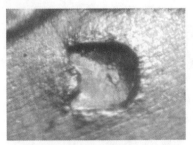

Small D (Rare) Type of 1932   Normal D (Common) Type of 1934

Description: The D mintmark is smaller than the common D of 1934.

Comments: This is the D mintmark of 1932, and is likely the result of a single die left over from that year. This is a rare variety by any standard. According to James Wiles, it comes mated with ODV-002 and 003.

	VF-20	EF-40	AU-50	AU-55	MS-60	MS-63	MS-65
VARIETY	n/a	n/a	n/a	n/a	n/a	n/a	n/a
NORMAL	$12	$25	$85	$125	$250	$350	$1,500

1935

VARIETY: Doubled-Die Obverse
PUP: IN GOD WE TRUST
URS-4 · I-2 · L-2

CONECA: DDO-001

Description: Doubling is evident on the motto and on the L of LIBERTY.

Comments: We would very much like to examine a higher-grade specimen.

	VF-20	EF-40	AU-50	AU-55	MS-60	MS-63	MS-65
VARIETY	$13.00	$15.00	$25	$35	$50	$65	$175
NORMAL	7.75	8.50	10	15	22	35	95

1936   FS-25-1936-101 (011)

VARIETY: Doubled-Die Obverse   **CONECA: DDO-001**
PUP: IN GOD WE TRUST
URS-4 · I-4 · L-5

Description: Very strong doubling is evident on the motto, LIBERTY, and the date.

Comments: This very rare variety is always in high demand.

	EF-40	AU-50	AU-55	MS-60	MS-63	MS-65
VARIETY	$200.00	$275	$350	$450	$700	n/a
NORMAL	7.75	10	15	25	35	$90

1937   FS-25-1937-101 (012)

VARIETY: Doubled-Die Obverse   **CONECA: DDO-001**
PUP: IN GOD WE TRUST
URS-4 · I-5 · L-5

Description: Very strong doubling is evident on the motto, LIBERTY, the date, and the end of the ribbons.

Comments: This variety is considered one of the most important in the series.

	VF-20	EF-40	AU-50	AU-55	MS-60	MS-63	MS-65
VARIETY	$225	$425.00	$950	$1,500	$2,500	$3,900	$7,500
NORMAL		7.75	18	20	25	35	90

1939-D
FS-25-1939D-501 (012.3)

VARIETY: Over Mintmark
PUP: Mintmark
URS-2 · I-3 · L-4

CONECA: N/L

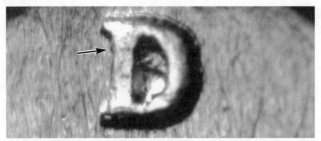

Description: This particular reverse die illustrates a D mintmark punched over an S mintmark. The center curve of the S is clearly evident within the opening of the D, and the left-most upper curve of the S is evident immediately left of the upright of the D.

Comments: There is a coin listed as FS-12.3 by Flynn and Wexler in their book *Over Mintmarks and Hot Repunched Mintmarks.* That coin is shown as being a refuted over mintmark, but is not the same die as listed here. More study is needed.

	EF-40	AU-50	AU-55	MS-60	MS-63	MS-65
VARIETY	$50	$65	$75	$100	$125	$250
NORMAL	11	20	28	40	50	100

1939-S
FS-25-1939S-101

VARIETY: Doubled-Die Obverse
PUP: IN GOD WE TRUST
URS-7 · I-2 · L-2

CONECA: DDO-001

Description: Doubling is evident on the motto, LIBERTY, and the date.

Comments: This is an interesting but minor variety.

	VF-20	EF-40	AU-50	AU-55	MS-60	MS-63	MS-65
VARIETY	$15	$25	$65	$75	$95	$130	$315
NORMAL		20	60	70	90	125	290

1940-D

FS-25-1940D-101

VARIETY: Doubled-Die Obverse
PUP: IN GOD WE TRUST
URS-6 · I-3 · L-4

CONECA: DDO-001

Description: Strong doubling is evident on the motto, and lesser doubling is visible on LIBERTY and the date.

Comments: This is a very attractive doubled die!

	VF-20	EF-40	AU-50	AU-55	MS-60	MS-63	MS-65
VARIETY	$50	$75	$100	$125	$150	$225	$350
NORMAL		24	65	85	120	165	300

1940-D

FS-25-1940D-501 (012.4)

VARIETY: Repunched Mintmark
PUP: Mintmark
URS-3 · I-5 · L-5

CONECA: RPM-002

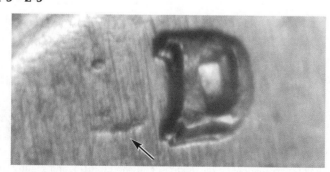

Description: This highly unusual repunched mintmark shows a secondary D totally separated and west of the primary D.

Comments: This is one of about 10 known repunched mintmarks that are totally separated. Discovered by Lee Hiemke, this is a very rare variety and is in very high demand.

	EF-40	AU-50	AU-55	MS-60	MS-63	MS-65
VARIETY	$75	$125	$165	$210	$290	$525
NORMAL	24	65	85	120	165	300

1941 FS-25-1941-101 (012.7)

VARIETY: Doubled-Die Obverse
PUP: IN GOD WE TRUST
URS-7 · I-2 · L-2

CONECA: DDO-003

Description: The doubling is most evident on GOD WE and the UST of TRUST.

Comments: The doubling is very obvious.

	EF-40	AU-50	MS-60	MS-63	MS-65
VARIETY	$20.00	$40.00	$60.00	$85	$130
NORMAL	7.75	8.25	8.50	14	43

1941 FS-25-1941-102 (012.9)

VARIETY: Doubled-Die Obverse
PUP: IN GOD WE TRUST
URS-7 · I-3 · L-3

CONECA: DDO-006

Description: Doubling is very evident on the motto, slightly on LIBERTY, and slightly west on the date.

Comments: There are several other 1941 obverse doubled dies. The two illustrated here are those in highest demand.

	EF-40	AU-50	MS-60	MS-63	MS-65
VARIETY	$35.00	$45.00	$60.00	$85	$130
NORMAL	7.75	8.25	8.50	14	43

1941　　　　　　　　　　　　　　　　　　　　　FS-25-1941-103

VARIETY: Doubled-Die Obverse　　　　**CONECA: DDO-004; WEXLER: WDDO-002**
PUP: IN GOD WE TRUST, date
NEW LISTING

Description: A strong Class II spread toward the center shows on IN GOD WE TRUST, the date, LIBERTY, and Washington's queue.

Comments: Of the many 1941 doubled-die obverses for this date, this is one of the better ones.

	EF-40	AU-50	MS-60	MS-63	MS-65
VARIETY	n/a	n/a	n/a	n/a	n/a
NORMAL	$7.75	$8.25	$8.50	$14	$43

1941　　　　　　　　　　　　　　　　　　　　FS-25-1941-801 (013)

VARIETY: Doubled-Die Reverse　　　　　　　**CONECA: DDR-004**
PUP: Eagle's beak
URS-5 · I-3 · L-4

YN

Description: Doubling is evident on the eagle's beak, doubled south. Other doubling is also visible on portions of QUARTER DOLLAR.

Comments: CONECA lists at least 15 other reverse doubled dies for 1941-(P) that are somewhat similar to this variety. All command a nice premium. It is suggested to have any similar variety accurately attributed.

	EF-40	AU-50	MS-60	MS-63	MS-65
VARIETY	$30.00	$40.00	$50.00	$65	$85
NORMAL	7.75	8.25	8.50	14	43

1941-D   FS-25-1941D-101

VARIETY: Doubled-Die Obverse
PUP: IN GOD WE TRUST, date
NEW LISTING

BREEN-4309; CONECA: DDO-001

Description: Doubling is evident on portions of IN GOD WE TRUST and, lightly, in the 41 of the date.

Comments: Known for many years, this variety has always been popular with specialists. It should see even greater interest now that it is in the *Cherrypickers' Guide*.

	EF-40	AU-50	MS-60	MS-63	MS-65
VARIETY	n/a	n/a	n/a	n/a	n/a
NORMAL	$7	$13	$32	$55	$70

1941-D   FS-25-1941D-801

VARIETY: Doubled-Die Reverse
PUP: Reverse lettering
URS-7 · I-3 · L-4

CONECA: DDR-001

Description: The doubling is most evident on STATES OF AMERICA, with a light spread on the D of UNITED and the AR of DOLLAR.

Comments: This reverse doubled die is considered rare and in demand by Washington variety enthusiasts.

	EF-40	AU-50	MS-60	MS-63	MS-65
VARIETY	$30.00	$40	$70	$110	$150
NORMAL	7.75	13	32	55	70

1941-S

Variety: Large S Mintmark
PUP: Mintmark
URS-7 · I-5 · L-5

CONECA: MMS-002

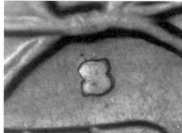

Normal, Small S   Scarce Large S

Description: The S mintmark on a very few 1941-S coins exhibits the large S, or "Trumpet-Tail" style mintmark. Compare to the normal or small S mintmark. Some of the Large S varieties have a filled upper loop.

Comments: There are 10 known reverse dies with this large S mintmark. One Large S die has the same style S as on the Large S nickels, with a triangular lower serif (see photo below).

	EF-40	AU-50	MS-60	MS-63	MS-65
VARIETY	$25.00	$35	$55	$125	$325
NORMAL	7.75	11	28	55	70

1941-S

Variety: Large S Mintmark
PUP: Mintmark
URS-5 · I-5 · L-5

CONECA: MMS-002

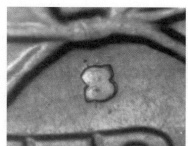
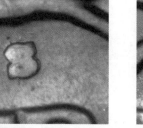

Normal, Small S   Large Triangular Serif S

Description: This Large S mintmark, with triangular lower serif, is the same Large S as found on scarce 1941-S Large S nickels.

Comments: Only one reverse die is known as of this writing. This is a very difficult variety to find.

	EF-40	AU-50	MS-60	MS-63	MS-65
VARIETY	$25.00	$45	$60	$125	$350
NORMAL	7.75	11	28	55	70

1942 — FS-25-1942-101

VARIETY: Doubled-Die Obverse   **CONECA: DDO-003**
PUP: IN GOD WE TRUST
URS-5 · I-3 · L-4

Description: Doubling is evident on the lower portions of the motto. Secondary images are especially evident on GOD and TRUST.

Comments: Other obverse doubled dies are known for this date, but all are less evident.

	EF-40	AU-50	MS-60	MS-63	MS-65
VARIETY	$20.00	$40	$50.00	$65	$160
NORMAL	7.50	8	8.25	10	35

1942 — FS-25-1942-801 (014)

VARIETY: Doubled-Die Reverse   **CONECA: DDR-002**
PUP: Reverse lettering
URS-6 · I-4 · L-5

YN

Description: Clockwise doubling is extremely strong on UNITED STATES OF AMERICA, with lesser doubling, although evident, on QUARTER DOLLAR.

Comments: Be careful not to confuse this variety with the next one.

	EF-40	AU-50	MS-60	MS-63	MS-65
VARIETY	$115.00	$185	$275.00	$385	n/a
NORMAL	7.50	8	8.25	10	$35

1942

VARIETY: Doubled-Die Reverse
PUP: Reverse lettering
URS-7 · I-4 · L-5

CONECA: DDR-005

Description: This is one of the strongest reverse doubled dies known for the Washington series. The doubling is evident on all reverse lettering, with a clockwise spread.

Comments: This variety is extremely rare in high grade!

	EF-40	AU-50	MS-60	MS-63	MS-65
VARIETY	$95.00	$185	$275.00	$385	n/a
NORMAL	7.50	8	8.25	10	$35

1942

VARIETY: Doubled-Die Reverse
PUP: Eagle's beak
URS-6 · I-3 · L-4

CONECA: DDR-006

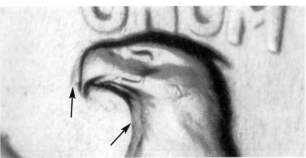

Description: The doubling on this variety can be seen on the eagle's right side (viewer's left), and is most evident as a strongly doubled lower beak and neck.

Comments: This is a very attractive and elusive variety.

	EF-40	AU-50	MS-60	MS-63	MS-65
VARIETY	$75.00	$100	$150.00	$225	$350
NORMAL	7.50	8	8.25	10	35

1942-D

FS-25-1942D-101 (015)

VARIETY: Doubled-Die Obverse
PUP: IN GOD WE TRUST, LIBERTY
URS-5 · I-5 · L-5

CONECA: DDO-001

Description: Doubling is evident, with a very strong spread, on LIBERTY, the date, and the motto. This is one of the most popular Washington quarter varieties.

Comments: If you can locate a high-grade example, you will have no trouble selling it.

	EF-40	AU-50	MS-60	MS-63	MS-65
VARIETY	$350.00	$850	$1,700	$3,250	$5,250
NORMAL	7.50	10	17	20	40

1942-D

FS-25-1942D-801 (016)

VARIETY: Doubled-Die Reverse
PUP: Eagle's beak, branch
URS-5 · I-5 · L-5

CONECA: DDR-001

Description: The doubling on this variety is most prominent on the eagle's beak, the arrows, and the branch above the mintmark.

Comments: This is another of the most popular Washington varieties.

	EF-40	AU-50	MS-60	MS-63	MS-65
VARIETY	$225.00	$385	$750	$1,250	$2,250
NORMAL	7.50	10	17	20	40

1943

FS-25-1943-101 (16.5)

VARIETY: Doubled-Die Obverse
PUP: IN GOD WE TRUST
URS-7 · I-2 · L-2

CONECA: DDO-005

Description: The doubling is very strong northwest on the motto, and to a lesser degree on LIBERTY.

Comments: This variety was discovered by Glenn Jeong.

	EF-40	AU-50	MS-60	MS-63	MS-65
VARIETY	$85.00	$140	$225.00	$325	$550
NORMAL	7.50	8	8.25	10	35

1943

FS-25-1943-102

VARIETY: Doubled-Die Obverse
PUP: LIBERTY
URS-3 · I-3 · L-3

CONECA: DDO-006

Description: Doubling is very strong on LIBERTY, with lesser doubling on the date and the motto.

Comments: This variety is very popular among Washington specialists.

	EF-40	AU-50	MS-60	MS-63	MS-65
VARIETY	$75.00	$125	$200.00	$300	$500
NORMAL	7.50	8	8.25	10	35

1943

VARIETY: Doubled-Die Obverse
CONECA: DDO-011
PUP: IN GOD WE TRUST
URS-2 · I-5 · L-5

Description: This very strong doubled die was discovered about 1993 or 1994 by Eric Striegel. The doubling is very strong on the motto, LIBERTY, and the date, and appears very similar to the popular and well-known 1943-S.

Comments: Any grade would likely sell in a heartbeat! On March 20, 2011, a PCGS AU-53 white specimen sold for $3,900 in a public auction.

	EF-40	AU-50	MS-60	MS-63	MS-65
VARIETY	$600.00	$1,000	$2,000.00	$3,900	$5,750
NORMAL	7.50	8	8.25	10	35

1943-D

VARIETY: Doubled-Die Obverse
CONECA: DDO-004
PUP: Ear
URS-3 · I-3 · L-3

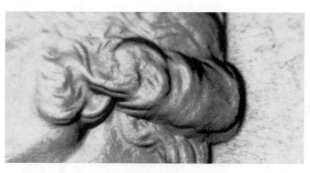

Description: The doubling is evident on the chin, ear, hair curls, and queue.

Comments: This is a most interesting variety.

	EF-40	AU-50	MS-60	MS-63	MS-65
VARIETY	$35	$50	$75	$150	$275
NORMAL	8	15	28	39	50

1943-S

VARIETY: Doubled-Die Obverse
PUP: IN GOD WE TRUST, LIBERTY
URS-9 · I-5 · L-5

CONECA: DDO-001

Description: Very strong doubling is evident on the motto, LIBERTY, the designer's initials, and the date.

Comments: This dramatic doubled die has long been known to collectors. Values for this variety are generally firm, but do change with market conditions and demand fluctuations.

	EF-40	AU-50	MS-60	MS-63	MS-65
VARIETY	$190	$350	$600	$975	$2,250
NORMAL	9	13	26	42	50

1943-S

VARIETY: Die Deformation
PUP: Washington's throat
NEW LISTING

"GOITER" VARIETY

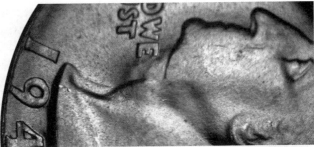

Description: Severe deterioration of the obverse die occurred due to unknown causes. Washington's mouth and chin are flat and lack definition; the area below his jaw is sunken while the area of field in front of his Adam's apple is buckled upward.

Comments: This variety has been known for decades, but it is apparently rare, as few have surfaced. It is affectionately referred to as the "Goiter" variety by old-time collectors.

	EF-40	AU-50	MS-60	MS-63	MS-65
VARIETY	n/a	n/a	n/a	n/a	n/a
NORMAL	$9	$13	$26	$42	$50

1943-S   FS-25-1943S-501

VARIETY: Trumpet-Tail S   **CONECA: MMS-002**
PUP: Mintmark
URS-5 · I-4 · L-5

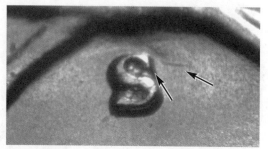

Trumpet Tail

Description: The upper serif is pointed downward, not up and down as on the Large S varieties common to this date.

Comments: This variety is infinitely rarer than the 1941-S Trumpet Tail. A handful of specimens in AU or higher are known. Some experts feel that the difference between this S mintmark and the normal one is more a matter of punch strength than actual size.

	EF-40	AU-50	MS-60	MS-63	MS-65
VARIETY	$50	$80	$140	$350	$625
NORMAL	9	13	26	42	50

1943-S   FS-25-1943S-502

VARIETY: Medium S Mintmark   **CONECA: N/L**
PUP: Mintmark
URS-4 · I-4 · L-4

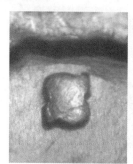 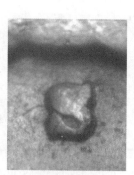 

Filled medium mintmark	Partial filled medium mintmark	Large S (common) medium mintmark

Description: This variety exhibits a slightly smaller medium S mintmark. Shown for comparison is the Large S (common).

Comments: This variety was unknown for this date until recently.

	EF-40	AU-50	MS-60	MS-63	MS-65
VARIETY	n/a	n/a	n/a	n/a	n/a
NORMAL	$9	$13	$26	$42	$50

1943-S

VARIETY: Repunched Mintmark
PUP: Mintmark
URS-4 · I-3 · L-4

CONECA: RPM-002

Description: A secondary S mintmark is evident south of the primary
S on the Large S variety.

Comments: The filled primary S mintmark is common for this date.

	EF-40	AU-50	MS-60	MS-63	MS-65
VARIETY	$30	$35	$75	$125	$175
NORMAL	9	13	26	42	50

1943-S

VARIETY: Repunched Mintmark
PUP: Mintmark
URS-5 · I-1 · L-4

CONECA: RPM-004

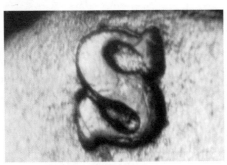

Description: A secondary S mintmark is visible south of the primary S.
The lower left knob of that secondary S is barely visible
south of the primary.

Comments: (Note: Because of its low Interest Factor, this variety will be
removed from this chapter in the next edition of this volume,
to make room for more popularly collected pieces. The Fivaz-
Stanton number will be retained for this variety and it will
remain in the cross-references at the back of the book.)

1944 — FS-25-1944-101

VARIETY: Doubled-Die Obverse
PUP: IN GOD WE TRUST
URS-7 · I-2 · L-3

CONECA: DDO-006

Description: Doubling is evident south on the motto IN GOD WE TRUST, with a medium spread, and somewhat evident on LIBERTY.

Comments: All 1944 quarters are from a doubled master die (nose, earlobe). There are several similar doubled dies for this date. Keep searching!

	EF-40	AU-50	MS-60	MS-63	MS-65
VARIETY	$20.00	$25	$35.00	$50	$95
NORMAL	7.50	8	8.25	10	35

1944-D — FS-25-1944D-101

VARIETY: Doubled-Die Obverse
PUP: LIBERTY
URS-8 · I-3 · L-3

CONECA: DDO-002

Description: Doubling is most evident on ERTY of LIBERTY, and slightly on the date and the designer's initials.

Comments: This is another of the many doubled dies known for this series.

	EF-40	AU-50	MS-60	MS-63	MS-65
VARIETY	$10.00	$15	$30	$55	$75
NORMAL	7.75	10	17	20	40

1944-S

VARIETY: Doubled-Die Obverse
PUP: IN GOD WE TRUST
URS-19 · I-2 · L-2

CONECA: DDO-001

Description: Doubling is evident south on the motto, and slightly on LIBERTY, the date, and the designer's initials.

Comments: This variety, although very evident, is relatively easy to find with enough looking.

	EF-40	AU-50	MS-60	MS-63	MS-65
VARIETY	$10.00	$15	$25	$30	$55
NORMAL	7.75	10	14	20	35

1945

VARIETY: Doubled-Die Obverse
PUP: IN GOD WE TRUST
URS-7 · I-2 · L-2

CONECA: DDO-001

Description: Doubling is most evident slightly northwest on the motto, on LIBERTY, and on the date.

Comments: This variety is tough to locate in high grade.

	EF-40	AU-50	MS-60	MS-63	MS-65
VARIETY	$40.00	$50	$80.00	$125	$200
NORMAL	7.50	8	8.25	10	35

1945-S
FS-25-1945S-101

VARIETY: Tripled-Die Obverse
PUP: IN GOD WE TRUST
URS-6 · I-2 · L-3

CONECA: DDO-002

Description: Doubling is most evident on IN GOD WE TRUST, and slightly on the date and LIBERTY. Tripling is evident on the designer's initials.

Comments: This variety has proven to be very elusive!

	EF-40	AU-50	MS-60	MS-63	MS-65
VARIETY	$15.00	$20	$30	$40	$60
NORMAL	7.50	8	9	14	35

1945-S
FS-25-1945S-102

VARIETY: Doubled-Die Obverse
PUP: IN GOD WE TRUST
URS-5 · I-3 · L-4

CONECA: DDO-004

Description: Extreme extra thickness is evident on the motto, with doubling also evident on LIBERTY.

Comments: This is another very tough variety to locate.

	EF-40	AU-50	MS-60	MS-63	MS-65
VARIETY	$20.00	$30	$50	$75	$175
NORMAL	7.50	8	9	14	35

1946
FS-25-1946-101

VARIETY: Doubled-Die Obverse
PUP: LIBERTY, 4 of date, and E
URS N/A

CONECA: DDO-002

Description: This variety displays a strong spread on the date, IN GOD WE TRUST, LIBERTY, the ribbon, and the designer's initials.

Comments: This variety's photo was incorrect in the *Cherrypickers' Guide,* fourth edition. (Note: Because of its low Interest Factor, this variety will be removed from this chapter in the next edition of this volume, to make room for more popularly collected pieces. The Fivaz-Stanton number will be retained for this variety and it will remain in the cross-references at the back of the book.)

1946
FS-25-1946-801 (018.2)

VARIETY: Doubled-Die Reverse
PUP: IN GOD WE TRUST
URS-4 · I-2 · L-2

CONECA: DDR-002

Description: The doubling is most evident on E PLURIBUS UNUM, STATES OF, and IN GOD WE TRUST; it is slightly visible on AMERICA. There is a very minor DDO paired with this reverse die, listed as CONECA DDO-008.

Comments: This is yet another variety that may be very difficult to locate in high grade.

	EF-40	AU-50	MS-60	MS-63	MS-65
VARIETY	$20.00	$25	$35.00	$50	$75
NORMAL	7.50	8	8.25	10	40

1946-D
FS-25-1946D-501

VARIETY: Repunched Mintmark
PUP: Mintmark
URS-2 · I-3 · L-3

CONECA: N/L

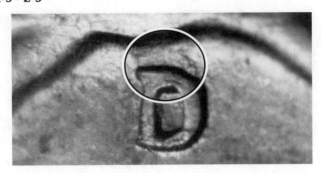

Description: The secondary D is weak but evident north of the primary D, and touching the branch above.

Comments: This RPM is not currently listed by CONECA.

	EF-40	AU-50	MS-60	MS-63	MS-65
VARIETY	$10.00	$15	$25.00	$50	$140
NORMAL	7.50	8	8.25	12	40

1946-S
FS-25-1946S-501

VARIETY: Repunched Mintmark
PUP: Mintmark
URS-7 · I-3 · L-3

CONECA: RPM-002

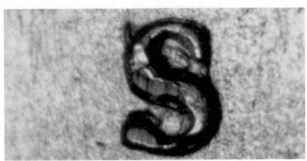

Description: A secondary S is evident north of and within the primary mintmark.

Comments: This RPM is in fairly high demand.

	EF-40	AU-50	MS-60	MS-63	MS-65
VARIETY	$10.00	$15	$23.00	$30	$60
NORMAL	7.50	8	8.25	12	40

1947 — FS-25-1947-101

VARIETY: Doubled-Die Obverse
PUP: LIBERTY
URS-3 · I-3 · L-3

CONECA: DDO-001

Description: Doubling is evident mainly on LIBERTY, with an extremely weak spread on the date, the designer's initials, and the motto IN GOD WE TRUST.

Comments: To date this is a very rare variety!

	EF-40	AU-50	MS-60	MS-63	MS-65
VARIETY	$25.00	$50	$75	$100	$150
NORMAL	7.50	8	12	20	45

1947-S — FS-25-1947S-501

VARIETY: Repunched Mintmark
PUP: Mintmark
URS-5 · I-3 · L-3

CONECA: RPM-001

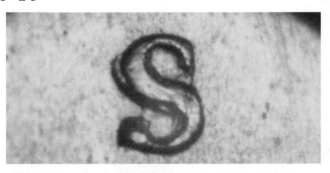

Description: The weaker S is evident west of the primary S. The most prominent portion of the underlying S is the upper left loop, protruding left of the primary.

Comments: This is a highly collectible RPM.

	EF-40	AU-50	MS-60	MS-63	MS-65
VARIETY	$15.00	$20	$25	$35	$90
NORMAL	7.50	8	10	15	35

1947-S

FS-25-1947S-502

VARIETY: Repunched Mintmark
PUP: Mintmark
URS-2 · I-4 · L-4

CONECA: RPM-002

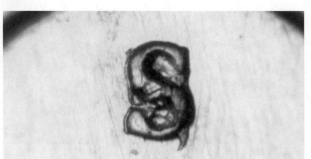

Description: The secondary S is evident south of the primary S. There is also a third S mintmark protruding from the upper left loop of the primary S mintmark.

Comments: This is an outstanding RPM in earlier die states (as shown here). Later die states show less doubling.

	EF-40	AU-50	MS-60	MS-63	MS-65
VARIETY	$15.00	$20	$25	$50	$110
NORMAL	7.50	8	10	15	35

1948-S

FS-25-1948S-501 (018.4)

VARIETY: Repunched Mintmark
PUP: Mintmark
URS-2 · I-4 · L-4

CONECA: RPM-002

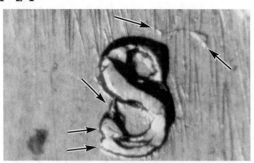

Description: The tops of two different S mintmarks are visible north of the primary, and a total of at least three are evident within the lower loop of the primary. It seems there are four different mintmark punches on this die.

Comments: This is one of the most dramatic repunched mintmarks in the entire series.

	EF-40	AU-50	MS-60	MS-63	MS-65
VARIETY	$15.00	$20	$25.00	$40	$150
NORMAL	7.50	8	8.25	14	45

1949-D · FS-25-1949D-501

VARIETY: Repunched Mintmark
PUP: Mintmark
URS-2 · I-4 · L-4

CONECA: N/L

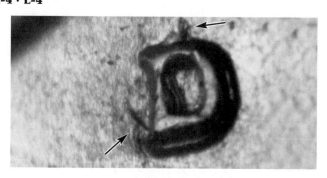

Description: This very interesting RPM shows what appears to be a secondary D northeast of the primary, and another west of the primary. The image west may be the remains of either an inverted D or a horizontal D. Further study may prove the image west as one way or the other.

Comments: This variety may actually be a die gouge; it needs more study.

	EF-40	AU-50	MS-60	MS-63	MS-65
VARIETY	$10.00	$20	$30	$48	$80
NORMAL	7.50	9	16	38	50

1949-D · FS-25-1949D-601 (018.8)

VARIETY: Over Mintmark
PUP: Mintmark
URS-2 · I-4 · L-4

CONECA: RPM-003

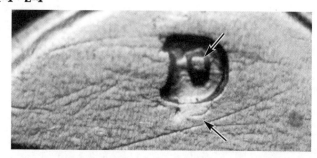

Description: The remnants of a secondary mintmark are evident south of the primary D. Some specialists believe this to be a D/D and not a D/S. However, it is still the opinion of the authors that the underlying mintmark is an S, as evidenced by the curvature of the lower bar on the underlying image. Additionally, the overall width of the underlying image appears too narrow to be that of a D.

Comments: The coin illustrated above is obviously a later die state. Questions about the underlying mintmark may be answered definitively if an earlier die state is discovered.

	EF-40	AU-50	MS-60	MS-63	MS-65
VARIETY	n/a	n/a	n/a	n/a	n/a
NORMAL	$7.50	$9	$16	$38	$50

1950

VARIETY: Doubled-Die Reverse
PUP: Eagle's beak
URS-10 · I-3 · L-2

CONECA: DDR-001

Description: Doubling is most evident on the eagle's beak, the lower-left wing edges, and the leaves and stems on the left side.

Comments: An early-die-state specimen will command higher values.

	EF-40	AU-50	MS-60	MS-63	MS-65
VARIETY	$15.00	$22	$30	$40	$65
NORMAL	7.50	8	9	10	35

1950-D

VARIETY: Repunched Mintmark
PUP: Mintmark
URS-6 · I-3 · L-3

CONECA: RPM-002

Description: The secondary mintmark is evident north of the primary D.

Comments: This variety is one of the more attractive RPMs for the date.

	EF-40	AU-50	MS-60	MS-63	MS-65
VARIETY	$15.00	$20	$25.00	$35	$50
NORMAL	7.50	8	8.25	11	35

1950-D

FS-25-1950D-801 (020)

VARIETY: Doubled-Die Reverse
PUP: Eagle's talons
URS-9 · I-2 · L-2

CONECA: DDR-001

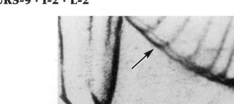

Description: Doubling is evident on the eagle's talons, the arrow points, and the feathers on the legs.

Comments: Discovered by Del Romines, this variety can be found with some searching.

	EF-40	AU-50	MS-60	MS-63	MS-65
VARIETY	$20.00	$35	$45.00	$55	$130
NORMAL	7.50	8	8.25	11	35

1950-D

FS-25-1950D-802

VARIETY: Doubled-Die Reverse
PUP: Reverse lettering
URS-5 · I-2 · L-2

CONECA: DDR-002

Description: As with all Class VI doubled dies, this variety exhibits the typical extra thickness on all reverse lettering. This extra thickness is especially strong on UNITED and QUARTER DOLLAR, where some separation in the letters may be evident.

Comments: For a Class VI, most of which aren't much to get excited about, this is a strong variety and worth hunting for.

	EF-40	AU-50	MS-60	MS-63	MS-65
VARIETY	$15.00	$25	$35.00	$50	$85
NORMAL	7.50	8	8.25	11	35

1950-D, D Over S FS-25-1950D-601 (021)

VARIETY: Over Mintmark **CONECA: OMM-001**
PUP: Mintmark
URS-9 · I-5 · L-5

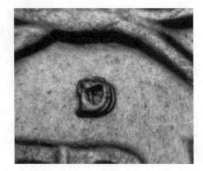

Description: The upper left curve of the underlying S is evident west and north of the D.

Comments: Most specimens exhibit strike doubling on the D, and have brilliant surfaces.

	EF-40	AU-50	MS-60	MS-63	MS-65
VARIETY	$140.00	$180	$400.00	$750	$3,400
NORMAL	7.50	8	8.25	11	35

1950-S FS-25-1950S-801

VARIETY: Doubled-Die Reverse **CONECA: N/L**
PUP: Arrows
URS-4 · I-2 · L-2

Description: Doubling is visible on the lower arrows and on some of the lower leaves.

Comments: The large leaf at the arrow tips appears to indicate a Type B over Type A reverse, as the tip points distinctly to the left. This variety may be DDR-001, 003, or 004 (004 is shown). Although a relatively minor doubled die, it is featured as an example of some of the varieties that are still to be found!

	EF-40	AU-50	MS-60	MS-63	MS-65
VARIETY	$15.00	$20.00	$25	$35	$50
NORMAL	7.75	8.50	12	16	45

1950-S
FS-25-1950S-501

VARIETY: Repunched Mintmark
PUP: Mintmark
URS-7 · I-3 · L-3

CONECA: RPM-001

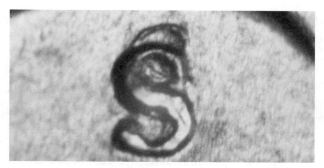

Description: The weaker S mintmark is evident wide north of the primary S.
Comments: This is considered a very wide repunching on a mintmark.

	EF-40	AU-50	MS-60	MS-63	MS-65
VARIETY	$10.00	$15.00	$20	$30	$50
NORMAL	7.75	8.50	12	16	45

1950-S, S Over D
FS-25-1950S-601 (022)

VARIETY: Over Mintmark
PUP: Mintmark
URS-9 · I-5 · L-5

CONECA: OMM-001

Description: The underlying D mintmark is clearly visible beneath the primary S.
Comments: Certainly one of the most popular Washington varieties. Most Uncirculated specimens have a frosty luster, compared to the brilliant surfaces on most Uncirculated 1950-D, D/S quarters.

	EF-40	AU-50	MS-60	MS-63	MS-65
VARIETY	$200.00	$300.00	$500	$1,050	$1,750
NORMAL	7.75	8.50	12	16	45

1951-D

FS-25-1951D-101

VARIETY: Doubled-Die Obverse
PUP: LIBERTY
URS-5 · I-3 · L-3

CONECA: DDO-002

Description: The doubling is most evident on LIBERTY, and on IN GOD WE TRUST.

Comments: This is a most underrated doubled die.

	EF-40	AU-50	MS-60	MS-63	MS-65
VARIETY	$35.00	$45	$60.00	$75	$95
NORMAL	7.50	8	8.25	11	35

1951-D

FS-25-1951D-501

VARIETY: Repunched Mintmark
PUP: Mintmark
NEW LISTING

CONECA: RPM-004

Description: A relatively strong secondary mintmark can be seen to the south of the primary D.

Comments: This variety is thought by some to be a D/S. It is a D/D.

	EF-40	AU-50	MS-60	MS-63	MS-65
VARIETY	n/a	n/a	n/a	n/a	n/a
NORMAL	$6.50	$7	$7.50	$11	$35

1952, Proof
FS-25-1952-901

VARIETY: Engraving Error (?)
PUP: Eagle's breast
URS-9 · I-3 · L-3

CONECA: N/L
"SUPERBIRD" VARIETY

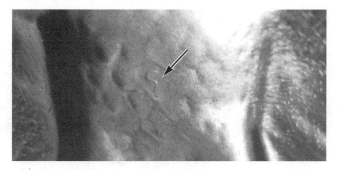

Description: There is an unusual S-shaped mark on the breast of the eagle. The cause of this mark is unknown.

Comments: The nickname for this well-known variety is, suitably, "Superbird"! This variety is featured in the Professional Edition Red Book.

	PF-63	PF-65	PF-66
VARIETY	$90	$145	$175
NORMAL	35	45	70

1952, Proof
FS-25-1952-902

VARIETY: Hand-Engraved Tail Feathers, "Superbird"
PUP: Tail feathers, eagle's breast
NEW LISTING

CONECA: DDO-004,
RED-001
"SUPERBIRD" VARIETY

Description: This is a later die state of the so-called "Superbird" variety. At this stage, part of the lower loop of the S is worn or polished away, and the tail-feather details have been strengthened by hand engraving. It is far scarcer than the earlier die states with only the "Superbird" feature.

Comments: This coin is popular among hobbyists for the "Superbird" feature. Few specialists actually realize that the late die state displays enhanced wing feathers, which in itself is probably more interesting than the S on the eagle's breast. The obverse of this coin is a minor doubled die. Two other Washington quarter dates, 1953 and 1957-D, are known with hand-engraved feathers.

	PF-63	PF-65	PF-66
VARIETY	n/a	n/a	n/a
NORMAL	$35	$45	$70

1952-D
FS-25-1952D-101

VARIETY: Doubled-Die Obverse
PUP: LIBERTY
URS-4 · I-2 · L-2

CONECA: DDO-001

Description: Moderate doubling is evident on the date, the motto, and LIBERTY.

Comments: This variety can still be located with a little searching.

	EF-40	AU-50	MS-60	MS-63	MS-65
VARIETY	$50.00	$75	$100.00	$175	$275
NORMAL	7.50	8	8.25	11	40

1952-D
FS-25-1952D-501

VARIETY: Huge Mintmark
PUP: Mintmark
URS-1 · I-3 · L-4

CONECA: MMS-004

Huge D   Medium D   Small D

Description: A medium and small D are shown for comparison.

Comments: The huge D mintmark is considered very rare, with very few specimens known to the authors as of publication. The size of this D mintmark is unknown on any other U.S. coin.

	EF-40	AU-50	MS-60	MS-63	MS-65
VARIETY	$100.00	$125	$175.00	$350	$700
NORMAL	7.50	8	8.25	11	40

1952-S

FS-25-1952S-501

Variety: Repunched Mintmark
PUP: Mintmark
URS-7 · I-3 · L-3

CONECA: RPM-001

Description: This is a triple-punched mintmark, with a secondary S evident north of the primary, and another overlapping the primary.

Comments: RPMs in the Washington quarter series are becoming highly collectible.

	EF-40	AU-50	MS-60	MS-63	MS-65
Variety	$12.00	$15.00	$23	$35	$50
Normal	7.50	8.50	13	25	45

1952-S

FS-25-1952S-502

Variety: Repunched Mintmark
PUP: Mintmark
URS-4 · I-3 · L-3

CONECA: RPM-002

Description: The secondary mintmark is evident north of the primary.

Comments: New RPMs in the Washington quarter series are being reported every year!

	EF-40	AU-50	MS-60	MS-63	MS-65
Variety	$12.00	$15.00	$20	$30	$50
Normal	7.50	8.50	13	25	45

1953, Proof — FS-25-1953-101 (022.1)

VARIETY: Doubled-Die Obverse
PUP: IN GOD WE TRUST
URS-9 · I-3 · L-3

CONECA: DDO-001

Description: Doubling is evident on all obverse lettering, very strongly so on the motto, date, and designer's initials.

Comments: This is a fairly well known variety, but it can still be cherrypicked!

	PF-63	PF-65	PF-66
VARIETY	$75	$150	$250
NORMAL	35	50	60

1953, Proof — FS-25-1953-901

VARIETY: Re-engraved Tail Feathers
PUP: Tail feathers
NEW LISTING

CONECA: RED-001

Normal tail feathers on a 1953 Proof quarter

Description: Many of the tail-feather details were polished away, resulting in the removal of the incuse separation lines between the feathers. The design was then strengthened by the cutting in of crude tail-feather outlines that are raised. The lower edges of the feathers were also strengthened in the same manner.

Comments: This variety appears to be rare, as very few have surfaced. Two other Washington quarter dates, 1952 (Proof) and 1957-D, are known with hand-engraved tail-feather outlines.

	PF-63	PF-65	PF-66
VARIETY	n/a	n/a	n/a
NORMAL	$35	$50	$60

1953-D
FS-25-1953D-801 (022.2)

Variety: Doubled-Die Reverse
CONECA: DDR-001
PUP: UNITED STATES OF AMERICA
URS-6 · I-3 · L-3

Description: Doubling is evident on all reverse lettering, strongest on UNITED STATES OF AMERICA, and weaker on QUARTER DOLLAR.

Comments: This variety is one of the strongest reverse doubled dies in the series. (Note: This variety was wrongly listed as FS-25-1953D-101 in the fourth edition, volume II.)

	EF-40	AU-50	MS-60	MS-63	MS-65
VARIETY	$35.00	$55	$75.00	$125	$200
NORMAL	7.50	8	8.25	10	40

1953-D
FS-25-1953D-501

Variety: Repunched Mintmark (Inverted)
CONECA: RPM-001
PUP: Mintmark
URS-3 · I-5 · L-5

 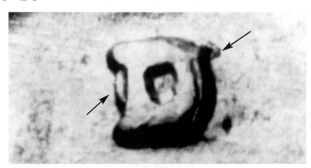

Description: The primary D mintmark is punched over what is believed to be an inverted mintmark. Further study may determine the underlying D to be horizontal, but the current photos lean more toward the inverted orientation.

Comments: This is an extremely popular variety.

	EF-40	AU-50	MS-60	MS-63	MS-65
VARIETY	$30.00	$40	$75.00	$150	$225
NORMAL	7.50	8	8.25	10	40

1953-D   FS-25-1953D-601 (022.3)

VARIETY: Over Mintmark   **CONECA: OMM-001**
PUP: Mintmark
URS-3 · I-5 · L-4

 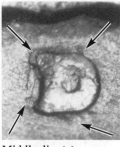 

| Early die state | Middle die state | Late die state |

Description: Multiple mintmark punches produced this fascinating variety, creating a D/D/D/S/S over mintmark. Some specialists consider only one underlying S, but these photos clearly show at least two S mintmark punches.

Comments: This variety is not very well known, but can be found with some searching. The values shown are for the early die state. The late die stage (illustrated above) is often overlooked, and not as saleable.

	EF-40	AU-50	MS-60	MS-63	MS-65
VARIETY	$30.00	$40	$65.00	$125	$225
NORMAL	7.50	8	8.25	10	40

1956, Proof   FS-25-1956-701

VARIETY: Reverse Die Gouge   **CONECA: N/L**
PUP: Reverse under talons
URS-2 · I-3 · L-3

Description: A very unusual die gouge is evident on the arrows below the eagle's right talons. Another die scratch is evident under the eagle's left talons.

Comments: The causes of these gouges are unknown, but they are extremely interesting.

	PF-63	PF-65	PF-66
VARIETY	$12	$25	$40
NORMAL	12	15	25

1956–1964, Type B Reverses

Variety: Type B Reverse
PUP: Eagle's tail feathers, STATES
URS-4 · I-3 · L-4

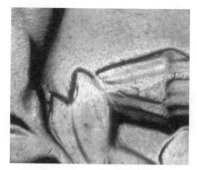

Description: As discussed in the introduction to the section on Washington quarters, they are known with at least eight different reverse varieties. The Type B reverses and their valuations are listed here. The Type B reverse is characterized by a pointed tip to the leaf nearest the arrow points; by the fact that this leaf tip extends above the topmost arrow tips; and by the fact that the design overall is in higher relief. This reverse style is known on all Philadelphia circulation strikes from 1956 through 1964 (which are listed here), as well as on Proofs from 1937 through 1942 and from 1950 through 1964.

1956, FS-25-1956-901 (CONECA: RDV-002)

	AU-50	MS-60	MS-63	MS-65
Variety	$25.00	$35.00	$75	$200
Normal	7.50	8.50	12	22

1957, FS-25-1957-901 (CONECA: RDV-002)

	AU-50	MS-60	MS-63	MS-65
Variety	$25.00	$35.00	$45	$75
Normal	7.50	8.50	9	30

1958, FS-25-1958-901 (CONECA: RDV-002)

	AU-50	MS-60	MS-63	MS-65
Variety	$25.00	$33	$65.00	$125
Normal	7.50	8	8.25	20

1959, FS-25-1959-901 (CONECA: RDV-002)

	AU-50	MS-60	MS-63	MS-65
Variety	$35.00	$60	$125.00	$225
Normal	7.50	8	8.25	25

1960, FS-25-1960-901 (CONECA: RDV-002)

	AU-50	MS-60	MS-63	MS-65
Variety	$30.00	$55	$115.00	$225
Normal	7.50	8	8.25	20

Charts continued on next page

1961, FS-25-1961-901 (CONECA: RDV-002)

	MS-60	MS-63	MS-65
VARIETY	$50.00	$75.00	$160
NORMAL	7.75	8.25	15

1962, FS-25-1962-901 (CONECA: RDV-002)

	MS-60	MS-63	MS-65
VARIETY	$20.00	$25.00	$95
NORMAL	7.75	8.25	15

1963, FS-25-1963-901 (CONECA: RDV-002)

	MS-60	MS-63	MS-65
VARIETY	$75.00	$150.00	$250
NORMAL	7.75	8.25	15

1964, FS-25-1964-901 (CONECA: RDV-002)

	AU-55	MS-60	MS-63	MS-65	MS-66
VARIETY	$25.00	$30.00	$45	$80.00	$150
NORMAL	7.25	7.50	8	8.50	15

1956-D   FS-25-1956D-501 (022.4)

VARIETY: Repunched Mintmark (Inverted)   **CONECA: RPM-001**
PUP: Mintmark
URS-7 · I-4 · L-4

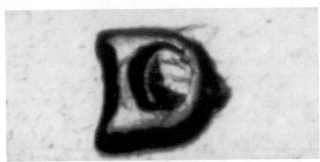

Description: The initial mintmark was punched into the die inverted, and then the second (primary) mintmark was punched correctly, creating this variety.

Comments: This is a very interesting and popular variety.

	AU-50	MS-60	MS-63	MS-65
VARIETY	$20.00	$30.00	$50	$150
NORMAL	7.50	8.50	10	30

1957-D

FS-25-1957D-501

VARIETY: Repunched Mintmark (Master Die)
PUP: Separate D above stem of olive branch
NEW LISTING

Description: An apparent D mintmark shows above the left olive branch.

Comments: This particular mark is known on several different reverse dies, suggesting the original might have been intended to be a working die, blundered, set aside, and then mistakenly used as a master die (which in turn was used to make a working hub with which several working dies were created). Most specialists accept this as a "Master Die RPM" while others believe it to be a form of hub damage. Some specialists attempt to own one from each die. Note that the doubling on the primary D below the wreath is strike doubling—not an RPM.

	AU-50	MS-60	MS-63	MS-65
VARIETY	n/a	n/a	n/a	n/a
NORMAL	$7	$7.50	$9	$25

1957-D

FS-25-1957D-901

VARIETY: Re-engraved Tail Feathers
PUP: Tail feathers
NEW LISTING

CONECA: RED-001

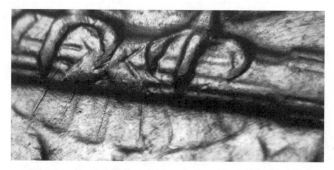

Description: Many of the tail-feather details were polished or abraded away; the design was then strengthened by the cutting in of crude tail-feather outlines.

Comments: Two other Washington quarter dates, 1952 and 1953 (both Proofs), are known with hand-engraved tail-feather outlines.

	AU-50	MS-60	MS-63	MS-65
VARIETY	n/a	n/a	n/a	n/a
NORMAL	$7	$7.50	$9	$25

1959, Proof

VARIETY: Doubled-Die Obverse
CONECA: DDO-004
PUP: IN GOD WE TRUST
URS-5 · I-3 · L-3

Description: Doubling is dramatic on all obverse lettering, especially on IN GOD WE TRUST.

Comments: There are at least five different obverse doubled dies for the 1959 Proofs, but this is by far the nicest.

	PF-63	PF-65	PF-66
VARIETY	$35	$70	$100
NORMAL	11	12	25

1959-D

VARIETY: Repunched Mintmark
CONECA: RPM-001
PUP: Mintmark
URS-4 · I-3 · L-3

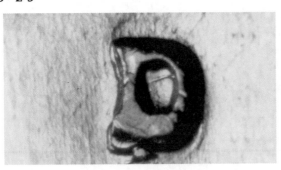

Description: Secondary D mintmarks are evident north and southeast of the primary D.

Comments: This RPM is relatively new, and can likely be found with a little searching.

	AU-50	MS-60	MS-63	MS-65
VARIETY	$11.00	$17	$33.00	$48
NORMAL	7.50	8	8.25	35

1960, Proof

FS-25-1960-801

VARIETY: Doubled-Die Reverse
PUP: QUARTER DOLLAR
URS-5 · I-3 · L-3

CONECA: DDR-002

Description: The doubling on this variety is evident on all reverse lettering, and many of the other design elements. A strong spread is evident on the eagle's wings, the leaf stems, and especially QUARTER DOLLAR.

Comments: This is one of the strongest Proof reverse doubled dies in the Washington series.

	PF-63	PF-65	PF-66
VARIETY	$45	$100	$160
NORMAL	11	12	20

1961, Proof

FS-25-1961-101

VARIETY: Doubled-Die Obverse
PUP: IN GOD WE TRUST
URS-5 · I-2 · L-2

CONECA: DDO-001

Description: Moderate doubling is evident on the date, the designer's initials, and the motto.

Comments: There are several other obverse doubled dies for the 1961 Proof.

	PF-60	PF-63	PF-65
VARIETY	$20	$25	$65
NORMAL	10	11	12

1961-D   FS-25-1961D-501

VARIETY: Repunched Mintmark   **CONECA: RPM-005**
PUP: Mintmark
URS-4 · I-3 · L-3

Description: The secondary D is evident north of the primary D.

Comments: This is a fairly strong RPM for the Washington quarter series.

	MS-60	MS-63	MS-65
VARIETY	$10.00	$15.00	$35
NORMAL	7.75	8.25	15

1961-D   FS-25-1961D-502

VARIETY: Repunched Mintmark   **CONECA: RPM-004**
PUP: Mintmark
URS-3 · I-3 · L-3

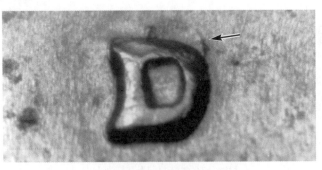

Description: The secondary D is evident north of the primary D.

Comments: This listing is clearly different from the previous one.

	MS-60	MS-63	MS-65
VARIETY	$10.00	$15.00	$35
NORMAL	7.75	8.25	15

1962

VARIETY: Doubled-Die Obverse
PUP: IN GOD WE TRUST
URS-4 · I-4 · L-4

CONECA: DDO-004

 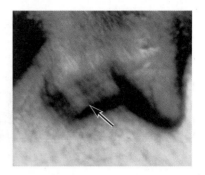

Description: The extra thickness on all lettering is typical of the Class VI doubled die. However, close examination will show four separate hubbings, especially on the R of TRUST and the end of the ribbon.

Comments: This is an extremely strong Class VI variety.

	MS-63	MS-65	MS-66
VARIETY	$75	$95	$150
NORMAL	10	12	20

1962-D

VARIETY: Repunched Mintmark
PUP: Mintmark
URS-3 · I-3 · L-3

CONECA: RPM-003

Description: Remnants of a secondary D mintmark are evident northeast of the primary D. The vertical of the secondary D is protruding from the upper right portion of the primary D.

Comments: An earlier die state of this RPM would be a great find!

	MS-60	MS-63	MS-65
VARIETY	$12.00	$18.00	$30
NORMAL	7.75	8.25	15

1963 — FS-25-1963-101 (023)

VARIETY: Doubled-Die Obverse
PUP: IN GOD WE TRUST
URS-10 · I-3 · L-2

CONECA: DDO-001

Description: Doubling is evident on all obverse lettering and the date.
Comments: This variety can be found in Mint sets, if any remain. This has been a known packaged variety for several years.

	MS-60	MS-63	MS-65
VARIETY	$25.00	$45.00	$70
NORMAL	7.75	8.25	15

1963 — FS-25-1963-102

VARIETY: Doubled-Die Obverse, Doubled-Die Reverse
PUP: IN GOD WE TRUST, AMERICA
URS-6 · I-3 · L-3

CONECA: DDO-007, DDR-001

  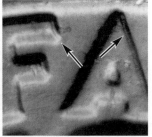

Description: The obverse doubling is the same as FS-101. The reverse is doubled on all lettering around the rim.
Comments: This variety can also be found in Mint sets.

	MS-60	MS-63	MS-65
VARIETY	$60.00	$90.00	$200
NORMAL	7.75	8.25	15

1963
FS-25-1963-103

VARIETY: Doubled-Die Obverse
PUP: Date
URS-4 · I-3 · L-3

CONECA: DDO-005

Description: The doubling is most evident on the 6 and 3 of the date. The secondary 6 is clear to the right of the loop of the primary 6.

Comments: This is one of the more interesting doubled dies for this date.

	MS-60	MS-63	MS-65
VARIETY	$25.00	$40.00	$65
NORMAL	7.75	8.25	15

1963
FS-25-1963-801

VARIETY: Doubled-Die Reverse
PUP: AMERICA
URS-4 · I-2 · L-2

CONECA: DDR-004

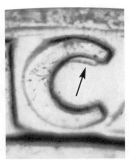

Description: Doubling is evident only left of the left upright on M of AMERICA, inside the upper loop on C of AMERICA, and to the eft of the first T of STATES.

Comments: This is a very unusual variety.

	MS-60	MS-63	MS-65
VARIETY	$75.00	$150.00	$375
NORMAL	7.75	8.25	15

1963, Proof — FS-25-1963-802

VARIETY: Doubled-Die Reverse **CONECA: DDR-006**
PUP: AMERICA
URS-3 · I-2 · L-2

Description: Doubling is evident on all reverse lettering, but strongest on AMERICA and DOLLAR.

Comments: This is one of seven DDR 1963 Proof quarters.

	PF-63	PF-65	PF-66
VARIETY	$55	$75	$125
NORMAL	10	12	20

1963-D — FS-25-1963D-101

VARIETY: Doubled-Die Obverse **CONECA: DDO-004**
PUP: LIBERTY
URS-4 · I-1 · L-3

Description: Doubling is evident on all obverse lettering, strongest on LIBERTY, lesser on IN GOD WE TRUST and the date.

Comments: (Note: Because of its low Interest Factor, this variety will be removed from this chapter in the next edition of this volume, to make room for more popularly collected pieces. The Fivaz-Stanton number will be retained for this variety and it will remain in the cross-references at the back of the book.)

1964 — FS-25-1964-101

VARIETY: Doubled-Die Obverse
PUP: IN GOD WE TRUST
URS-3 · I-1 · L-2

CONECA: UNKNOWN

Description: Doubling is evident on IN GOD WE TRUST, and very slightly on the date and the designer's initials.

Comments: (Note: Because of its low Interest Factor, this variety will be removed from this chapter in the next edition of this volume, to make room for more popularly collected pieces. The Fivaz-Stanton number will be retained for this variety and it will remain in the cross-references at the back of the book.)

1964 — FS-25-1964-801 (024.6)

VARIETY: Doubled-Die Reverse
PUP: QUARTER DOLLAR
URS-4 · I-4 · L-4

CONECA: DDR-001

Description: Doubling is evident on all reverse lettering with a very strong spread, strongest on QUARTER DOLLAR.

Comments: This variety is in extremely high demand by specialists.

	AU-55	MS-60	MS-63	MS-65	MS-66
VARIETY	$40.00	$50.00	$60	$125.00	$250
NORMAL	7.25	7.50	8	8.50	15

211

1964

FS-25-1964-802 (024.5)

VARIETY: Doubled-Die Reverse
PUP: QUARTER DOLLAR
URS-3 · I-3 · L-3

CONECA: DDR-002

Description: Doubling is evident with a nice spread on QUARTER DOLLAR.

Comments: This is one of at least 11 reverse doubled dies for this date.

	AU-55	MS-60	MS-63	MS-65	MS-66
VARIETY	$40.00	$50.00	$60	$110.00	$170
NORMAL	7.25	7.50	8	8.50	15

1964

FS-25-1964-803

VARIETY: Doubled-Die Reverse
PUP: AMERICA
URS-3 · I-3 · L-3

CONECA: DDR-003

Description: Doubling is moderate on UNITED STATES OF AMERICA, being strongest on STATES and AMERICA.

Comments: This variety is very scarce in high grade.

	AU-55	MS-60	MS-63	MS-65	MS-66
VARIETY	$35.00	$50.00	$60	$75.00	$100
NORMAL	7.25	7.50	8	8.50	15

1964

FS-25-1964-804 (024.65)

VARIETY: Doubled-Die Reverse
PUP: QUARTER DOLLAR
URS-3 · I-4 · L-5

CONECA: DDR-004

Description: The doubling is very strong on QUARTER DOLLAR, weaker on UNITED, and very light on STATES.

Comments: This is a rare variety, and always in demand.

	AU-55	MS-60	MS-63	MS-65	MS-66
VARIETY	$100.00	$150.00	$200	$250.00	$350
NORMAL	7.25	7.50	8	8.50	15

1964-D

FS-25-1964D-101 (024.69)

VARIETY: Doubled-Die Obverse
PUP: IN GOD WE TRUST
URS-5 · I-2 · L-2

CONECA: DDO-001

Description: The doubling is most evident on the motto.

Comments: This is very similar to the 1963-(P) FS-101.

	AU-55	MS-60	MS-63	MS-65	MS-66
VARIETY	$25.00	$30.00	$60	$110.00	$150
NORMAL	7.25	7.50	8	8.50	15

1964-D

FS-25-1964D-501

VARIETY: Repunched Mintmark
PUP: Mintmark
URS-3 · I-3· L-3

CONECA: RPM-003

Description: The secondary D mintmark is evident east of the primary D.

Comments: This is one of the nicer RPMs for the date.

	AU-55	MS-60	MS-63	MS-65	MS-66
VARIETY	$10.00	$15.00	$20	$25.00	$35
NORMAL	7.25	7.50	8	8.50	15

1964-D

FS-25-1964D-502

VARIETY: Misplaced Mintmark
PUP: Branch above mintmark
URS-2 · I-4 · L-4

CONECA: N/L

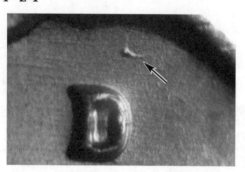

Description: On this very dramatic RPM, a secondary D mintmark is evident protruding from the branch above the mintmark area.

Comments: This is one of the very few totally separated repunched mintmark varieties.

	AU-55	MS-60	MS-63	MS-65	MS-66
VARIETY	$125.00	150.00	$200	300.00	$450
NORMAL	7.25	7.50	8	8.50	15

1964-D

FS-25-1964D-801 (025)

VARIETY: Doubled-Die Reverse
PUP: AMERICA
URS-4 · I-3 · L-4

CONECA: DDR-001

Description: Doubling is very strong on OF AMERICA and DOLLAR, with a medium spread on STATES, QUARTER, and E PLURIBUS UNUM.

Comments: This is a very dramatic doubled-die reverse.

	AU-55	MS-60	MS-63	MS-65	MS-66
VARIETY	$125.00	$150.00	$200	$300.00	$450
NORMAL	7.25	7.50	8	8.50	15

The Cherrypickers' Guide HELPFUL HINTS

Check all the coins in your 1960 and 1968 Proof sets. These are known to have nice doubled dies for each denomination, some on the obverse and some on the reverse. For a complete list of known Mint set and Proof set varieties, refer to appendix D.

1964-D

FS-25-1964D-901

CONECA: RDV-003

VARIETY: Type C Reverse
PUP: Eagle's tail feathers, leaf at arrow tips
URS-4 · I-3 · L-4

Type C

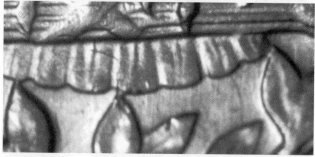

Type C

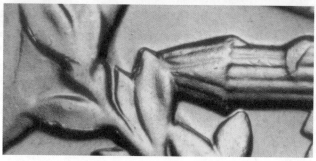

Type B

Description: A very few 1964-D coins are known to have the Type C reverse intended for use starting in 1965. These Type C reverse coins show the leaves above the AR of DOLLAR sharp and almost touching the letters, where the Type A is weak and the Type B is bold, but the one leaf does touch the A of DOLLAR. **The tail feathers on the Type C reverse have a very distinct centerline.** Additionally, the leaves below the tail feathers are sharp and barely touch those tail feathers. The leaf in front of the arrow tips comes to a distinct point in front of the arrow tips. On the Type B reverse, this leaf rises above the top arrow point, and the leaf end tips left. On the Type A it is very weak.

Comments: The Denver Mint coins from 1956 through 1964 are suspected to exist with a Type B reverse. Keep a lookout for these!

	AU-55	MS-60	MS-63	MS-65	MS-66
VARIETY	$125.00	$150.00	$250	$375.00	$500
NORMAL	7.25	7.50	8	8.50	15

1965
FS-25-1965-101 (026)

VARIETY: Doubled-Die Obverse
CONECA: DDO-001
PUP: IN GOD WE TRUST, LIBERTY
URS-3 · I-4 · L-5

Description: The doubling is very strong on all obverse lettering, the eye, and the date.
Comments: This variety is extremely rare, and sells very quickly at auction.

	AU-50	AU-55	MS-60	MS-63	MS-65	MS-66
VARIETY	$475	$575	$650	$850	$1,100	$1,600
NORMAL				1	7	25

1965
FS-25-1965-102

VARIETY: Doubled-Die Obverse
CONECA: DDO-002
PUP: LIBERTY
URS-3 · I-3 · L-3

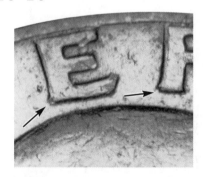
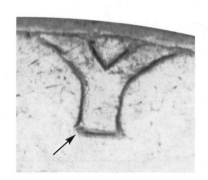

Description: Doubling is very strong on LIBERTY.
Comments: This variety is typical of a Class V doubled die with doubling evident on one area only.

	AU-50	AU-55	MS-60	MS-63	MS-65	MS-66
VARIETY	$50	$60	$80	$140	$250	$350
NORMAL				1	7	25

1965   FS-25-1965-801

VARIETY: Doubled-Die Reverse   **CONECA: DDR-001**
PUP: QUARTER DOLLAR
URS-3 · I-4 · L-3

Description: The doubling is evident on all reverse lettering, some with the Class II spread, and some with the extra thickness normally associated with Class VI.

Comments: This is a relatively new discovery.

	AU-50	AU-55	MS-60	MS-63	MS-65	MS-66
VARIETY	$25	$35	$50	$75	$125	$175
NORMAL				1	7	25

1966   FS-25-1966-801 (026.3)

VARIETY: Doubled-Die Reverse   **CONECA: DDR-001**
PUP: UNITED STATES OF AMERICA, QUARTER DOLLAR
URS-2 · I-5 · L-5

Description: Very strong doubling is evident on all reverse lettering, including E PLURIBUS UNUM.

Comments: Discovered by Roger Gray, this has proven to be a very rare variety. NOTE: This is *not* the Special Mint Set issue!

	AU-55	MS-60	MS-63	MS-65	MS-66
VARIETY	$300	$600	$900	$1,400	$2,250
NORMAL			1	7	25

1967, Special Mint Set — FS-25-1967-101 (026.5)

VARIETY: Doubled-Die Obverse
PUP: IN GOD WE TRUST
URS-5 · I-4 · L-4

CONECA: DDO-002

Description: Strong doubling is evident on the motto and LIBERTY, with moderate doubling evident on the date.

Comments: Most examples of this variety are known with strike doubling. Those specimens without strike doubling will command far more than the values stated.

	MS-60	MS-63	MS-65	MS-66
VARIETY	$100	$150	$225	$350
NORMAL		6	12	22

1967, Special Mint Set — FS-25-1967-801

VARIETY: Doubled-Die Reverse
PUP: QUARTER DOLLAR
URS-3 · I-4 · L-4

CONECA: DDR-002

Description: Moderate doubling is evident on the stems and QUARTER DOLLAR.

Comments: More specimens of this variety are sure to be uncovered.

	MS-60	MS-63	MS-65	MS-66
VARIETY	$50	$75	$100	$150
NORMAL		6	12	22

1968-D

VARIETY: Doubled-Die Reverse
PUP: UNITED STATES OF AMERICA, QUARTER DOLLAR
URS-4 · I-4 · L-4

CONECA: DDR-001

Description: Very strong doubling is evident on all reverse lettering, leaves, branches, and wing tips.
Comments: Keep an eye open for this very strong doubled die.

	AU-55	MS-60	MS-63	MS-65	MS-66
VARIETY	$550	$600	$700	$850	$1,100
NORMAL			1	6	15

1968-S, Proof

VARIETY: Doubled-Die Obverse
PUP: Date, LIBERTY
URS-3 · I-4 · L-4

CONECA: DDO-001

Description: The doubling is evident on the motto, LIBERTY, and the date.
Comments: This is an extremely rare variety!

	PF-63	PF-65	PF-66
VARIETY	$125	$175	$250
NORMAL		3	

1968-S, Proof — FS-25-1968S-501

VARIETY: Repunched Mintmark
PUP: Mintmark
URS-3 · I-3 · L-3

CONECA: RPM-003

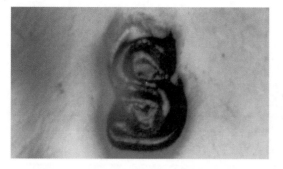

Description: The secondary mintmark is evident north of the primary S.

	PF-63	PF-65	PF-66
VARIETY	$25	$50	$75
NORMAL		3	

1968-S, Proof — FS-25-1968S-801 (027)

VARIETY: Doubled-Die Reverse
PUP: QUARTER DOLLAR
URS-6 · I-3 · L-3

CONECA: DDR-001

Description: The doubling is on all lettering around the rim and the leaf tips.
Comments: Although well known for years, very few examples of this variety have surfaced!

	PF-63	PF-65	PF-66
VARIETY	$125	$165	$190
NORMAL		3	

1969-D

VARIETY: Repunched Mintmark
PUP: Mintmark
URS-5 · I-3 · L-3

CONECA: RPM-001

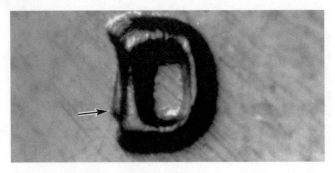

Description: The secondary mintmark is slanted slightly west of the primary D.
Comments: This variety can be found in Mint sets.

	MS-63	MS-65	MS-66
VARIETY	$20.00	$25	$50
NORMAL	2.50	10	25

1969-D

VARIETY: Repunched Mintmark
PUP: Mintmark
URS-4 · I-3 · L-3

CONECA: RPM-003

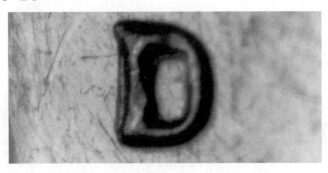

Description: The secondary mintmark is slightly west of the primary D.
Comments: This variety is reported to have been found in Mint sets.

	MS-63	MS-65	MS-66
VARIETY	$20.00	$25	$50
NORMAL	2.50	10	25

1969-S, Proof

FS-25-1969S-101 (027.08)

VARIETY: Doubled-Die Obverse
PUP: Date, LIBERTY
URS-4 · I-5 · L-5

CONECA: DDO-001

Description: The doubling is extremely strong on all obverse lettering and on the date.

Comments: This very rare variety was pictured on the cover of the *Cherrypickers' Guide*, third edition, but omitted from the text of the book. Some eagle-eyed collectors wanted to know more.

	PF-63	PF-65	PF-66
VARIETY	$600	$750	$1,000
NORMAL		3	

1969-S, Proof

FS-25-1969S-501 (27.1)

VARIETY: Repunched Mintmark
PUP: Mintmark
URS-4 · I-3 · L-3

CONECA: RPM-002

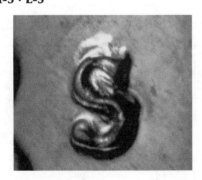

Description: This RPM exhibits an S/S/S, with both secondary punches slightly north of the primary S.

Comments: Very few specimens have been reported.

	PF-63	PF-65	PF-66
VARIETY	$25	$50	$75
NORMAL		3	

223

1970-D

FS-25-1970D-101 (27.3)

Variety: Doubled-Die Obverse
PUP: IN GOD WE TRUST
URS-3 · I-4· L-4

CONECA: DDO-001

Description: A very strong doubled die, with doubling evident on the date, IN GOD WE TRUST, and the ERTY of LIBERTY.

Comments: This variety is considered extremely rare.

	AU-55	MS-60	MS-63	MS-65	MS-66
Variety	$200	$250	$300	$375	$500
Normal			1	5	10

1970-D

FS-25-1970D-102

Variety: Doubled-Die Obverse
PUP: LIBERTY
URS-2 · I-4 · L-4

CONECA: DDO-002

Description: The doubling on this extremely rare variety is evident on the date, the motto, and LIBERTY. Both hubbings were of equal depth, causing the differences in the two to be faint. However, the wide separation, evidenced by the split serifs, is very dramatic.

Comments: This is extremely rare, with only two reported to date.

	AU-55	MS-60	MS-63	MS-65	MS-66
Variety	$125	$150	$250	$375	n/a
Normal			1	5	$10

1970-D FS-25-1970D-801

VARIETY: Doubled-Die Reverse
PUP: QUARTER DOLLAR
URS-6 · I-1 · L-3

CONECA: DDR-001

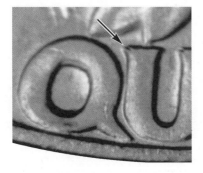

Description: Moderate doubling is evident on the lower letters, branches, and leaves, and slightly on UNITED.

Comments: This variety can be found in Mint sets. (Note: Because of its low Interest Factor, this variety will be removed from this chapter in the next edition of this volume, to make room for more popularly collected pieces. The Fivaz-Stanton number will be retained for this variety and it will remain in the cross-references at the back of the book.)

1970-D FS-25-1970D-802

VARIETY: Doubled-Die Reverse
PUP: AMERICA, DOLLAR
URS-5 · I-1 · L-3

CONECA: DDR-002

Description: Strong doubling is evident around the rim, within the feathers, and on the lower wreath.

Comments: This variety can be found in Mint sets. (Note: Because of its low Interest Factor, this variety will be removed from this chapter in the next edition of this volume, to make room for more popularly collected pieces. The Fivaz-Stanton number will be retained for this variety and it will remain in the cross-references at the back of the book.)

1971-D   FS-25-1971D-801 (027.8)

VARIETY: Doubled-Die Reverse   **CONECA: DDR-001**
PUP: UNITED STATES OF AMERICA
URS-3 · I-4 · L-4

Description: Strong doubling is evident on UNITED STATES OF AMERICA.

Comments: We would love to see a higher-grade specimen!

	AU-55	MS-60	MS-63	MS-65	MS-66
VARIETY	$125	$175	$250	$300	$500
NORMAL			1	4	20

1976-D   FS-25-1976D-101 (028)

VARIETY: Doubled-Die Obverse   **CONECA: DDO-001**
PUP: LIBERTY
URS-6 · I-4 · L-4

Description: Very strong doubling is evident on LIBERTY, and very slight doubling on the motto and date.

Comments: Generally, only early die state specimens will show doubling on the motto.

	AU-55	MS-60	MS-63	MS-65	MS-66
VARIETY	$1,000	$1,250	n/a	n/a	n/a
NORMAL			$1	$5	$15

1976-D   FS-25-1976D-102

VARIETY: Doubled-Die Obverse   **CONECA: DDO-002**
PUP: LIBERTY
URS-4 · I-3 · L-3

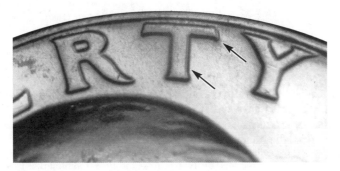

Description: Moderate doubling is evident only on LIBERTY.

Comments: This variety may prove very rare.

	AU-55	MS-60	MS-63	MS-65	MS-66
VARIETY	$25	$50	$75	$100	$150
NORMAL			1	5	15

1979-S, Proof   FS-25-1979S-501

VARIETY: Type II Mintmark   **CONECA: MMS-007**
PUP: Mintmark
URS-10 · I-5 · L-5

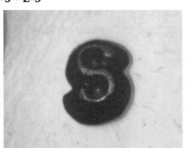

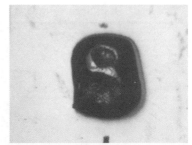

Type I mintmark (common)	Type II mintmark (scarce)

Description: For the 1979-S Proof coins, the mintmark style was changed during the production, creating two distinctly different types. The Type II is the rare variety, and is easily distinguished from the common Type I. The Type I has a very indistinct blob, whereas the Type II shows a well-defined S.

Comments: Complete government-sealed Proof sets in which all six coins are Type II command a substantial premium over the six individual coins. Of the six coins, the quarter dollar is one of the more common pieces.

	PF-63	PF-65	PF-66
VARIETY	$3	$12	$16
NORMAL		3	

1981-S, Proof · FS-25-1981S-501

VARIETY: Type II Mintmark
PUP: Mintmark
URS-10 · I-5 · L-5

CONECA: MMS-008

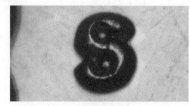

Type I mintmark (common)   Type II mintmark (scarce)

Description: For 1981-S Proofs, the mintmark style was changed during production, creating two distinct types. Type II, the rare variety, is not easily distinguished from the common Type I. For most collectors, the most visible difference is the flatness on the top curve of the Type II S (it is rounded on Type I). Also, the Type II mintmark is frosted, and the openings in the loops slightly larger.

Comments: Complete, *government*-sealed Proof sets with all six coins of Type II command a substantial premium over the six individual coins. (Check the sonically sealed edges for glue or other signs of alteration. Complete 1979-S Type II sets are fairly common and needn't be checked as closely. Of the six coins, the quarter dollar is one of the more common pieces.

	PF-63	PF-65	PF-66
VARIETY	$4	$11	$12
NORMAL		3	

1982-S, Proof · FS-25-1982S-101

VARIETY: Doubled-Die Obverse
PUP: Date
URS-2 · I-3 · L-3

CONECA: MDO-001

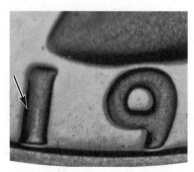

Description: Doubling is visible on the motto, the date, and LIBERTY.

Comments: Because this variety has been classified by CONECA as an example of master-die doubling, it will be removed from the next edition of this volume.

1989-D

FS-25-1989D-501

VARIETY: Repunched Mintmark
PUP: Mintmark
URS-2 · I-3 · L-3

CONECA: RPM-001

Description: The secondary D is evident west of the primary D.
Comments: We'd love to see a higher-grade specimen!

	MS-60	MS-63	MS-65	MS-66
VARIETY	$15	$20.00	$25	$50
NORMAL		0.75	4	20

1990-S, Proof

FS-25-1990S-101

VARIETY: Doubled-Die Obverse
PUP: Date, mintmark
URS-4 · I-4 · L-4

CONECA: DDO-001

Description: Very strong doubling is evident on the date and the mintmark, and slightly on IN GOD WE TRUST.
Comments: Only a few examples have been reported. Check those 1990-S Proof sets!

	PF-63	PF-65	PF-66
VARIETY	$125	$200.00	$300
NORMAL		3.50	

229

1995-S, Proof, Clad — FS-25-1995S-101

VARIETY: Doubled-Die Obverse
PUP: Date, ribbon end
URS-2 · I-3 · L-3

CONECA: DDO-001

Description: Very close doubling is visible on the date, mintmark, ribbon, and hair.

Comments: This may be difficult to pick up, as doubling is often hard to see on coins with heavy frosting.

	PF-63	PF-65	PF-66
VARIETY	$100	$150	$200
NORMAL		10	

1996-P — FS-25-1996P-701

VARIETY: Die Damage

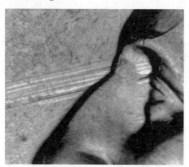

Description: The marks on this coin are due to damage from the feeder-fingers during minting, and not to any die error.

Comments: Because this is not a die variety but a rather common type of damage caused during the minting process, this coin will be removed from the next edition of this volume.

2004-D, Wisconsin   FS-25-2004D-WI-5901

VARIETY: Design Manipulation
PUP: Reverse—corn
URS-12 · I-5 · L-5

Extra Leaf High reverse   Normal reverse

Description: An image was added to the working die, creating an upward line to the left cornhusk.

Comments: It is our belief that the additional lines on this and the next variety of the Wisconsin quarters were deliberately added to the reverse dies. Apparently, a tool with a rounded edge was impressed into the working dies to create images that were not a part of the intended design. Many collectors, dealers, etc., refer to these as an Extra Leaf variety. However, the lines are not the image of a leaf. (Compare with the next variety.)

	AU-55	MS-60	MS-63	MS-65	MS-66
VARIETY	$65	$100	$125	$275	$575
NORMAL				1	10

2004-D, Wisconsin   FS-25-2004D-WI-5902

VARIETY: Design Manipulation
PUP: Reverse—corn
URS-13 · I-5 · L-5

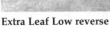

Extra Leaf Low reverse   Normal reverse

Description: Images were added to the working die, creating two downward lines to the left cornhusk.

Comments: See the comments for the previous listing.

	AU-55	MS-60	MS-63	MS-65	MS-66
VARIETY	$45	$80	$125	$250	$400
NORMAL				1	10

2005-P, Minnesota

FS-25-2005P-MN-801

VARIETY: Doubled-Die Reverse
PUP: Portion of "extra tree" right of fourth tree
NEW LISTING

CONECA: DDR-001;
WEXLER: WDDR-001;
PCGS-144227

 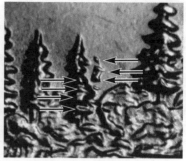

Description: Doubling is seen as a free-floating portion of the fourth evergreen tree east of the state outline.

Comments: This is the one that started the frenzy that led collectors to discover more than 100 other Minnesota doubled-die reverses, most of which are minor to very minor. The arrows at the left side of the second image indicate the point of origin of the doubling, which is indicated by the arrows on the right.

	AU-55	MS-60	MS-63	MS-65	MS-66
VARIETY	n/a	n/a	n/a	n/a	n/a
NORMAL	$0.30		$0.50	$0.75	

THE CHERRYPICKERS' GUIDE HELPFUL HINTS

Study and learn the Pick-Up-Points (PUPs) for each series so that you can focus your initial attention on these areas to find varieties. Don't forget the denticle area and the design above the date (especially on 19th-century coinage such as the Liberty Seated series) for misplaced numbers, etc. They hide, so use a good loupe and good light.

2005-P, Minnesota   FS-25-2005P-MN-802

VARIETY: Doubled-Die Reverse
PUP: Portion of "extra tree" right of fourth tree
NEW LISTING

CONECA: DDR-002;
WEXLER: WDDR-002;
PCGS-144228

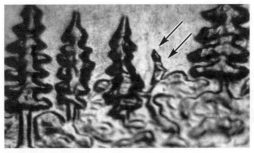

Description: Doubling is seen as a portion of a tree touching the top of the rock at the right of the fourth full evergreen tree east of the state outline.

Comments: On the Minnesota quarters, more than 100 known doubled dies affect the centermost tree (and other centralized areas of the design). They are found on coins from all mints and include the San Francisco Proofs, both clad and in silver. The vast majority are minor but collectible nonetheless. This is one of few Minnesota doubled-die quarters that PCGS designates as an "Extra Tree."

	AU-55	MS-60	MS-63	MS-65	MS-66
VARIETY	n/a	n/a	n/a	n/a	n/a
NORMAL	$0.30		$0.50	$0.75	

2005-P, Minnesota   FS-25-2005P-MN-803

VARIETY: Doubled-Die Reverse
PUP: Portion of "extra tree" right of fourth tree
NEW LISTING

CONECA: DDR-004;
WEXLER: WDDR-004;
PCGS-144419

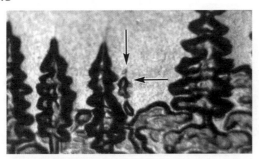

Description: This variety appears almost identical to FS-801, but the doubling is farther to the east and is positioned slightly higher than the "extra tree" found on FS-802.

Comments: This one is found in Mint sets and has a satin finish. On the Minnesota quarters, more than 100 known doubled dies affect the centermost tree (and other centralized areas of the design). They are found on coins from all mints and include the San Francisco Proofs, both clad and in silver. The vast majority are minor but collectible nonetheless. This is one of few Minnesota doubled-die quarters that PCGS designates as an "Extra Tree."

	AU-55	MS-60	MS-63	MS-65	MS-66
VARIETY	n/a	n/a	n/a	n/a	n/a
NORMAL	$0.30		$0.50	$0.75	

2005-P, Minnesota — FS-25-2005P-MN-804

VARIETY: Doubled-Die Reverse
PUP: Portion of "extra tree" left of fourth tree
NEW LISTING

CONECA: DDR-006;
WEXLER: WDDR-006;
PCGS-144232

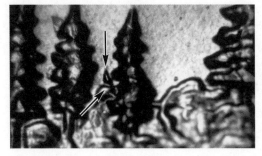

Description: The doubling is shifted predominantly to the *left* of the fourth tree, down to the southwest.

Comments: This one is found in Mint sets and has a satin finish. On the Minnesota quarters, more than 100 known doubled dies affect the centermost tree (and other centralized areas of the design). They are found on coins from all mints and include the San Francisco Proofs, both clad and in silver. The vast majority are minor but collectible nonetheless. This is one of few Minnesota doubled-die quarters that PCGS designates as an "Extra Tree."

	AU-55	MS-60	MS-63	MS-65	MS-66
VARIETY	n/a	n/a	n/a	n/a	n/a
NORMAL	$0.30		$0.50	$0.75	

2005-P, Minnesota — FS-25-2005P-MN-805

VARIETY: Doubled-Die Reverse
PUP: Portion of "extra tree" right of fourth tree
NEW LISTING

CONECA: DDR-007;
WEXLER: WDDR-007;
PCGS-144223

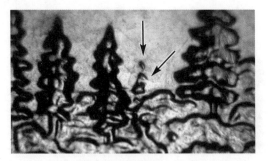

Description: Very similar to FS-801 and FS-802, this one involves a portion of the fourth tree to the right of the state outline with the doubling fully displaced from its point of origin. It appears almost identical to FS-801 but is farther to the east, positioned slightly higher (not touching the rock) than the "extra tree" found on FS-802 (which does touch the rock).

Comments: See the comments under FS-802.

	AU-55	MS-60	MS-63	MS-65	MS-66
VARIETY	n/a	n/a	n/a	n/a	n/a
NORMAL	$0.30		$0.50	$0.75	

2005-P, Minnesota

FS-25-2005P-MN-806

VARIETY: Doubled-Die Reverse
PUP: Portion of "extra tree" right of fourth tree
NEW LISTING

CONECA: DDR-008;
WEXLER: WDDR-008;
PCGS-144234

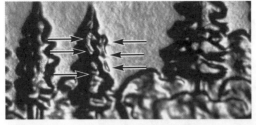

Description: This one involves a portion of the fourth tree east of the state outline; the doubling is fully displaced from its point of origin, but partially tucked in next to the fourth tree.

Comments: On the Minnesota quarters, more than 100 known doubled dies affect the centermost tree (and other centralized areas of the design). They are found on coins from all mints and include the San Francisco Proofs, both clad and in silver. The vast majority are minor but collectible nonetheless. This is one of few Minnesota doubled-die quarters that PCGS designates as an "Extra Tree." The arrows at left indicate the point of origin of the doubling, which is indicated by the arrows at right. See additional comments under FS-802.

	AU-55	MS-60	MS-63	MS-65	MS-66
VARIETY	n/a	n/a	n/a	n/a	n/a
NORMAL	$0.30		$0.50	$0.75	

2005-P, Minnesota

FS-25-2005P-MN-807

VARIETY: Doubled-Die Reverse
PUP: Portion of "extra tree" right of fourth tree
NEW LISTING

CONECA: DDR-012;
WEXLER: WDDR-012;
PCGS-144230

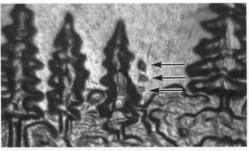

Description: This one involves a portion of the fourth tree east of the state outline with the doubling fully displaced from its point of origin.

Comments: On the Minnesota quarters, more than 100 known doubled dies affect the centermost tree (and other centralized areas of the design). They are found on coins from all mints and include the San Francisco Proofs, both clad and in silver. The vast majority are minor but collectible nonetheless. This is one of few Minnesota doubled-die quarters that PCGS designates as an "Extra Tree."

	AU-55	MS-60	MS-63	MS-65	MS-66
VARIETY	n/a	n/a	n/a	n/a	n/a
NORMAL	$0.30		$0.50	$0.75	

2005-D, Minnesota
FS-25-2005D-MN-801

VARIETY: Doubled-Die Reverse
PUP: Portion of "extra tree" left of fourth tree
NEW LISTING

CONECA: DDR-001;
WEXLER: WDDR-001;
PCGS-144220

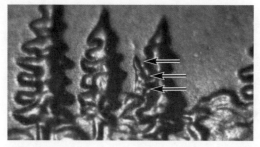

Description: This one involves a portion of a tree to the left of the *fourth* full tree east of the state outline; the doubling is fully displaced from its point of origin, and is tucked in next to the full tree.

Comments: This one is found in Mint sets and has a satin finish. On the Minnesota quarters, more than 100 known doubled dies affect the centermost tree (and other centralized areas of the design). They are found on coins from all mints and include the San Francisco Proofs, both clad and in silver. The vast majority are minor but collectible nonetheless. This is one of few Minnesota doubled-die quarters that PCGS designates as an "Extra Tree."

	AU-55	MS-60	MS-63	MS-65	MS-66
VARIETY	n/a	n/a	n/a	n/a	n/a
NORMAL	$0.30		$0.50	$0.75	

2005-D, Minnesota
FS-25-2005D-MN-802

VARIETY: Doubled-Die Reverse
PUP: Portion of "extra tree" left of fourth tree
NEW LISTING

CONECA: DDR-003;
WEXLER: WDDR-003;
PCGS-144221

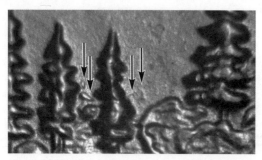

Description: This one involves a portion of a tree placed to the left of the fourth tree east of the state outline; the doubling is fully displaced from its point of origin, and is tucked in next to the full tree. The doubled tree is less complete but farther west than on FS-801. There is also some light doubling of the highest-relief areas of the rock to the right of the primary tree and shifted into the field northwest of the rock (as indicated by the arrows).

Comments: See the comments under FS-803.

	AU-55	MS-60	MS-63	MS-65	MS-66
VARIETY	n/a	n/a	n/a	n/a	n/a
NORMAL	$0.30		$0.50	$0.75	

2005-S, Kansas, Proof, 90% Silver — FS-S25-2005S-KS-901

VARIETY: Large Die Dent Reverse
PUP: Hoof-shaped die dent on bison's hindquarter
NEW LISTING

POTTER: VCR-001

 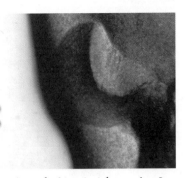

Description: A large, hoof-shaped die dent can be found just above the bison's right rear leg. It appears to be a deliberate addition to the die, but the cause is unknown.

Comments: To date, fewer than two dozen of these have been reported. Surely more exist. The variety is significantly larger in area than the die aberrations found on the two well-known 2004-D "Extra Leaf" Wisconsin quarters, to which this variety is sometimes compared due to the flaw's curved shape.

	PF-63	PF-65	PF-66
VARIETY	n/a	n/a	n/a
NORMAL	$7	$8	$9

2005-P, Oregon — FS-25-2005P-OR-801

VARIETY: Doubled-Die Reverse
PUP: Tallest evergreen tree on right side of coin
NEW LISTING

CONECA: DDR-001;
WEXLER: WDDR-001

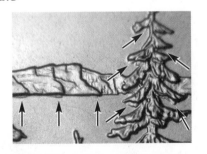 

Normal design for comparison

Description: Very strong doubling appears on many of the branches of the evergreen tree and on the high points of the lower rim of the rocky shoreline (as indicated by the arrows).

Comments: This variety is found in Mint sets.

	AU-55	MS-60	MS-63	MS-65	MS-66
VARIETY	n/a	n/a	n/a	n/a	n/a
NORMAL	$0.30		$0.50	$0.75	

2005-P, Oregon

FS-25-2005P-OR-802

VARIETY: Doubled-Die Reverse
PUP: Two evergreen trees on right side of coin
NEW LISTING

CONECA: DDR-002

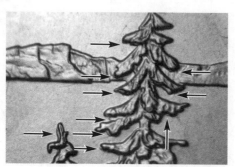

Description: Doubling is present on many of the branches of the evergreen trees. This variety is similar to FS-801, but FS-802 displays its strongest doubling on different leaves. This one also lacks doubling on the rocky rim of the lake; however, it has certain doubling (on the shorter tree and extending into lower areas of the taller tree) that is not present on FS-801. All in all, this variety is equal in desirability.

Comments: This variety is found in Mint sets.

	AU-55	MS-60	MS-63	MS-65	MS-66
VARIETY	n/a	n/a	n/a	n/a	n/a
NORMAL	$0.30		$0.50	$0.75	

2007-P, Wyoming

FS-25-2007P-WY-801

VARIETY: Doubled-Die Reverse
PUP: Saddle horn
NEW LISTING

CONECA: DDR-018;
WEXLER: WDDR-005

 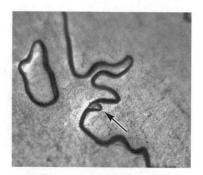

Description: This variety displays very strong doubling of the saddle horn. This one of the strongest of several varieties in which this area of the design is affected.

Comments: Many other doubled dies exist for this date and type, but most of them are less significant.

	AU-55	MS-60	MS-63	MS-65	MS-66
VARIETY	n/a	n/a	n/a	n/a	n/a
NORMAL	$0.30		$0.50	$0.75	

2007-P, Wyoming — FS-25-2007P-WY-802

VARIETY: Doubled-Die Reverse
PUP: Saddle horn
NEW LISTING

WEXLER: WDDR-014

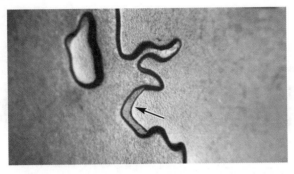

Description: Very strong doubling of the saddle appears just below the saddle horn. This the strongest of several varieties in which this area of the design is affected.

Comments: Many other doubled dies exist for this date and type, but most of them are less significant. These can be found in Mint sets.

	AU-55	MS-60	MS-63	MS-65	MS-66
VARIETY	n/a	n/a	n/a	n/a	n/a
NORMAL	$0.30		$0.50	$0.75	

2007-P, Wyoming — FS-25-2007P-WY-803

VARIETY: Doubled-Die Reverse
PUP: Saddle horn
NEW LISTING

WEXLER: WDDR-002

Description: Very strong doubling of the saddle appears just below the saddle horn. The variety is quite similar to FS-802 but not quite as strong.

Comments: Many other doubled dies exist for this date and type, but most of them are less significant.

	AU-55	MS-60	MS-63	MS-65	MS-66
VARIETY	n/a	n/a	n/a	n/a	n/a
NORMAL	$0.30		$0.50	$0.75	

2009-D, District of Columbia FS-25-2009D-DC-801

VARIETY: Doubled-Die Reverse
PUP: ELL of ELLINGTON
NEW LISTING

CONECA: DDR-001

Description: This variety boasts extremely strong doubling of the ELL of ELLINGTON, as well as some doubling of the two most westerly piano keys, the lower edge of the piano keys, the upper lip of the panel below them, and Duke Ellington's thumb, due to tilt and counterclockwise shift.

Comments: This is the very strongest of the State/Territorial quarter doubled dies and has proven to be very rare. The Mint must have caught this one early. It is also the only doubled-die reverse known from the Denver Mint for this issue.

	AU-55	MS-60	MS-63	MS-65	MS-66
VARIETY	n/a	n/a	n/a	n/a	n/a
NORMAL	$0.40		$0.75	$1	

2009-P, District of Columbia FS-25-2009P-DC-801

VARIETY: Doubled-Die Reverse
PUP: Piano keys
NEW LISTING

CONECA: DDR-012

Description: A strong secondary black key appears centered between the two normal black keys next to Duke Ellington's left arm, in addition to a bit of doubling to the lower left of the E of ELLINGTON.

Comments: This is one of more than a dozen doubled-die reverses known of this date and type for Philadelphia; the others, however, are relatively minor.

	AU-55	MS-60	MS-63	MS-65	MS-66
VARIETY	n/a	n/a	n/a	n/a	n/a
NORMAL	$0.40		$0.75	$1	

2009-P, District of Columbia

FS-25-2009P-DC-802

VARIETY: Doubled-Die Reverse

CONECA: DDR-004

PUP: Piano key below the E of ELLINGTON

NEW LISTING

Description: A strong secondary black key is centered between the two normal black keys next to Ellington's left arm.

Comments: This is one of more than a dozen doubled-die reverses known of this date and type for Philadelphia; the others, however, are relatively minor. This variety is as nice as or nicer than FS-801.

	AU-55	MS-60	MS-63	MS-65	MS-66
VARIETY	n/a	n/a	n/a	n/a	n/a
NORMAL	$0.40		$0.75	$1	

THE CHERRYPICKERS' GUIDE **HELPFUL HINTS**

Don't get discouraged if you haven't found any significant varieties for a while—they're out there, and eventually you'll uncover some. Remember, knowledge is power, but it's only relevant when you use it!

Liberty Seated Half Dollars, 1839–1891

L iberty Seated half dollars contain numerous interesting and valuable die varieties. Significant varieties are known and can be found for virtually every date and mint. From minor repunched mintmarks to major doubled dies, and even major design changes, the varieties are abundant.

Virtually all varieties within the series are in high demand by the large number of Liberty Seated specialists. In general, values for the varieties have been increasing at an even faster rate than for the normal coins. An eagle-eyed cherrypicker can easily earn a significant income by picking the varieties that go unnoticed by most dealers.

The varieties listed in this edition of the *Cherrypickers' Guide* are but a small percentage of those known in the series. More will be included in future editions. Many other varieties are documented in the *Complete Guide to Liberty Seated Half Dollars*, by Randy Wiley and Bill Bugert.

For those seriously interested in the series, we strongly recommend membership in the Liberty Seated Collectors Club (LSCC), which we believe to be one of the very best specialty clubs in numismatics. The club issues its official publication, the *Gobrecht Journal*, three times each year. This fine newsletter is loaded with excellent educational articles. The club has an outstanding web site at www.lsccweb.org. As of this writing, the annual dues are $20—a bargain, considering the amount of information available. If you join the LSCC, you will be connecting with some of the most serious and knowledgeable collectors and dealers in the hobby. For more information, contact

Leonard Augsburger, Secretary-Treasurer
P.O. Box 6114
Vernon Hills, IL 60061
E-mail: leonard_augsburger@hotmail.com

Note: References to Wiley and Bugert (WB) in this volume apply to listings in their *Complete Guide to Liberty Seated Half Dollars*.

1840, Reverse of 1839   FS-50-1840-301

VARIETY: Repunched Date   **WB-102**
PUP: Date
URS-9 · I-3 · L-3

Description: This RPD shows with a secondary 4 and 0 evident south of the primary digits. The 0 is actually slightly southeast.

Comments: This is a reverse of the 1839 variety.

	VG-8	F-12	VF-20	EF-40	AU-50	MS-60
VARIETY	$48	$70	$105	$160	$310	$625
NORMAL	40	60	90	140	275	550

1840, Reverse of 1839   FS-50-1840-302

VARIETY: Repunched Date   **WB-104**
PUP: Date
URS-8 · I-3 · L-3

Description: This RPD shows a secondary 18 slightly west, a secondary 4 slightly north, and a secondary 0 evident north.

Comments: This is a reverse of the 1839 variety.

	VG-8	F-12	VF-20	EF-40	AU-50	MS-60
VARIETY	$48	$70	$105	$160	$300	$625
NORMAL	40	60	90	140	275	550

1840, Reverse of 1839
FS-50-1840-401

VARIETY: Die Crack, Open Claw
PUP: Left claw of eagle
NEW LISTING

Description: A die crack along the northwest edge of the coin touches the fifth through seventh stars. On the reverse, the talons of the claw gripping the branch are open instead of closed.

Comments: This is a major die crack.

	VG-8	F-12	VF-20	EF-40	AU-50	MS-60
VARIETY	n/a	n/a	n/a	n/a	n/a	n/a
NORMAL	$40	$60	$90	$140	$275	$550

1842, Medium Date
FS-50-1842-301

VARIETY: Repunched Date
WB-105
PUP: Date
URS-11 · I-3 · L-3

Description: Another RPD, with secondary digits visible south on the 8, the 4, and the 2.

Comments: There are at least three other RPDs known for the date.

	VG-8	F-12	VF-20	EF-40	AU-50	MS-60
VARIETY	$50	$80	$110	$200	$375	$1,050
NORMAL	40	65	90	150	325	850

1842, Small Date

VARIETY: Doubled-Die Reverse
PUP: UNITED STATES OF AMERICA
URS-7 · I-3 · L-3

WB-103

Description: A very nice doubled die is evident on all reverse lettering, leaves, and arrow tips.

Comments: Very few of this variety have been found.

	VG-8	F-12	VF-20	EF-40	AU-50	MS-60
VARIETY	$90	$125	$175	$275	$475	$1,050
NORMAL	40	65	90	150	325	850

1843-O

VARIETY: Repunched Date
PUP: Date
URS-11 · I-3 · L-3

WB-103

Description: The secondary 1 and 8 are visible south of the primary digits, while the secondary 4 and 3 are visible north of the primary digits.

Comments: This is a reverse of the 1839 variety.

	VG-8	F-12	VF-20	EF-40	AU-50
VARIETY	$48	$58	$75	$140	$260
NORMAL	40	50	65	120	225

1844-O

FS-50-1844o-301 (001)

WB-103

VARIETY: Misplaced Date
PUP: Date
URS-4 · I-4 · L-4

Description: This is one of the more dramatic misplaced dates in this series. All four digits are evident protruding from the rock above the date.

Comments: This variety is considered very rare and highly collectible.

	VG-8	F-12	VF-20	EF-40	AU-50	MS-60
VARIETY	$750	$1,200	$1,600	$2,400	$5,200	$10,500
NORMAL	40	50	60	120	250	750

1845-O

FS-50-1845o-301 (001.5)

WB-104

VARIETY: Repunched Date
PUP: Date
URS-5 · I-4 · L-4

Description: The strong repunched date is evident with a secondary 5 far east of the primary 5. Other secondary numbers are not as visible.

Comments: This variety is sometimes errantly called a tripled date.

	VG-8	F-12	VF-20	EF-40	AU-50	MS-60
VARIETY	$150	$375	$500	$750	n/a	n/a
NORMAL	40	50	70	125	$225	$700

1845-O

FS-50-1845o-302 (002)

VARIETY: Repunched Date
PUP: Date
URS-6 · I-4 · L-4

WB-106

Description: This RPD is clearly tripled on all four digits. Below the primary 8 are three distinct lower loops. Below the primary 4, one can see the bases of two different 4's punched into the die.

Comments: This variety can be detected in low grades.

	VG-8	F-12	VF-20	EF-40	AU-50	MS-60
VARIETY	$75	$125	$225	$450	$750	n/a
NORMAL	40	50	70	125	225	$700

1845-O

FS-50-1845o-303

VARIETY: Repunched Date
PUP: Date
URS-9 · I-3 · L-3

WB-108

Description: Another RPD with all four digits clearly repunched, with the secondary digits west of the primary digits.

Comments: This variety can be detected in low grades.

	VG-8	F-12	VF-20	EF-40	AU-50	MS-60
VARIETY	$50	$75	$175	$300	$750	$1,200
NORMAL	40	50	70	125	225	700

1845-O

FS-50-1845o-501 (002.5)

VARIETY: Repunched Mintmark
PUP: Mintmark
URS-10 · I-3 · L-3

WB-103

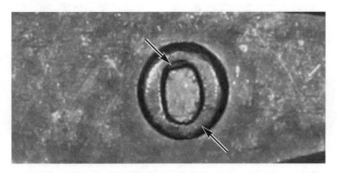

Description: The primary mintmark was punched into the die over a previously punched horizontal mintmark. The underlying horizontal O is evident within the opening at the top.

Comments: This variety can be detected in low grades.

	VG-8	F-12	VF-20	EF-40	AU-50	MS-60
VARIETY	$125	$275	$475	$725	$975	$1,450
NORMAL	40	50	70	125	225	700

1846, 6 Over Horizontal 6

FS-50-1846-301 (003)

VARIETY: Repunched Date
PUP: Date
URS-10 · I-5 · L-5

WB-104

Description: On this RPD, the primary 6 was punched over a 6 previously punched into the die horizontally.

Comments: This variety can be detected in low grades.

	VG-8	F-12	VF-20	EF-40	AU-50	MS-60
VARIETY	$275	$350	$475	$750	$1,750	$3,300
NORMAL	40	55	75	120	250	575

1847   FS-50-1847-101

VARIETY: Doubled-Die Obverse   **WB:** N/L
PUP: Shield, LIBERTY
URS-4 · I-3 · L-3

Description: Doubling is evident on the shield and LIBERTY.
Comments: The next item (1847, 7 Over 6) is listed in WB as a doubled die in early die states. It is unknown at this time whether this listing is a later state (without evidence of the overdate). David Camire is very knowledgeable with varieties and would most likely have noted that when these photos were sent. However, the authors have not seen this coin and can't discount the doubled die being from the overdate die. Liberty Seated coin specialist Larry Briggs stated this is a late die state of the overdate die (FS-50-1847-301), yet still worth a modest premium.

	VG-8	F-12	VF-20	EF-40	AU-50	MS-60
VARIETY	n/a	n/a	n/a	n/a	n/a	n/a
NORMAL	$40	$50	$70	$120	$225	$475

1847, 7 Over 6   FS-50-1847-301 (004)

VARIETY: Overdate   **WB-102**
PUP: Date
URS-3 · I-5 · L-5

Description: Remains of an underlying 6 can be seen below and between the primary 4 and 7.
Comments: The overdate might not be evident on later die states. This is a very popular variety!

	VG-8	F-12	VF-20	EF-40	AU-50	AU-55	MS-60
VARIETY	$3,000	$4,500	$6,000	$9,000	$14,500	$26,500	n/a
NORMAL	40	50	70	120	225	325	$475

1849 FS-50-1849-301 (004.5)

VARIETY: Repunched Date **WB-102**
PUP: Date
URS-6 · I-4 · L-4

Description: The lower portions of all four secondary digits are evident west of the primary digits. Most notable will be the lower 1 and 4 just left of the primary numbers.

Comments: This variety is considered by many to be one of the true rarities of the entire series.

	VG-8	F-12	VF-20	EF-40	AU-50	MS-60
VARIETY	$2,000	$3,000	$4,000	$6,000	$8,500	n/a
NORMAL	40	60	90	175	375	$950

1853, Arrows and Rays FS-50-1853-401

VARIETY: Clashed Obverse Die **WB: N/L**
PUP: Date area
URS-3 · I-3 · L-3

Description: This obverse die was clashed with a reverse die, exhibiting the rays protruding from the rock on the obverse.

Comments: To date we've only heard of a handful of this variety. Remember this is a one-year type coin.

	VG-8	F-12	VF-20	EF-40	AU-50	MS-60
VARIETY	$44	$60	$120	$295	$615	$1,600
NORMAL	40	55	110	275	575	1,500

1853, Arrows and Rays — FS-50-1853-801 (004.7)

VARIETY: Doubled-Die Reverse **WB: N/L**
PUP: UNITED STATES OF AMERICA
URS-4 · I-3 · L-3

Description: The reverse doubling has a clockwise spread on UNITED STATES OF AMERICA, but very little doubling elsewhere.

Comments: To date, only a few specimens have been reported.

	VG-8	F-12	VF-20	EF-40	AU-50	MS-60
VARIETY	$125	$160	$225	$350	$675	$1,650
NORMAL	40	55	110	275	575	1,500

1853, Arrows and Rays — FS-50-1853-802

VARIETY: Doubled-Die Reverse **WB: N/L**
PUP: HALF DOL
URS-3 · I-3 · L-3

Description: The doubling is evident on HALF DOL, AMERICA, and some rays.

Comments: Doubling can also be seen on some of the denticles.

	VG-8	F-12	VF-20	EF-40	AU-50	MS-60
VARIETY	$125	$160	$225	$350	$675	$1,650
NORMAL	40	55	110	275	575	1,500

1853, Arrows and Rays   FS-50-1853-803

VARIETY: Doubled-Die Reverse   **WB:** N/L
PUP: STATES
URS-5 · I-2 · L-3

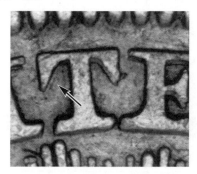 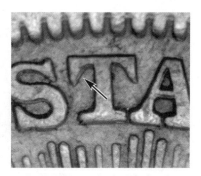

Description: The doubling is evident on UNITED STATES OF AMERICA, with a slight spread toward the center.

Comments: The doubling on this variety is slightly weaker than on FS-802.

	VG-8	F-12	VF-20	EF-40	AU-50	MS-60
VARIETY	$125	$160	$225	$350	$675	$1,650
NORMAL	40	55	110	275	575	1,500

1855, Arrows   FS-50-1855-301 (005)

VARIETY: Overdate   **WB-102**
PUP: Date
URS-7 · I-4 · L-5

Description: The 1855 date was punched over an 854.

Comments: This is one of the top three varieties of the series, and is a Proof die later used for circulation strikes. In February 2011 an MS-64 example sold at auction for $4,888.

	VG-8	F-12	VF-20	EF-40	AU-50	MS-60
VARIETY	$75	$125	$250	$450	$750	$1,650
NORMAL	40	55	80	135	325	750

1855-O

FS-50-1855o-501 (006)

VARIETY: Repunched Mintmark
PUP: Mintmark
URS-6 · I-4 · L-3

WB-102

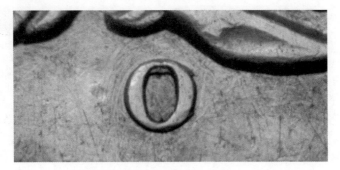

Description: The initial mintmark was punched into the die in a horizontal orientation, visible slightly to the right of the top of the primary O, with a subsequent punch correctly vertical.

Comments: This is listed as CONECA RPM-001.

	VG-8	F-12	VF-20	EF-40	AU-50	MS-60
VARIETY	$125	$200	$300	$450	$750	$1,250
NORMAL	40	55	80	135	325	700

1856-O

FS-50-1856o-301 (006.5)

VARIETY: Repunched Date
PUP: Date
URS-9 · I-3 · L-3

WB-102

Description: The initial date was punched into the die angled slightly upward, with the subsequent punch being more level, creating the repunched date. The secondary 1 is evident south, with a secondary 5 and 6 evident north.

Comments: This variety can be spotted in lower grades! In February 2011 an MS-64 example sold at auction for $2,530. (Note: This variety was incorrectly listed as FS-50-1856o-501 in the fourth edition, volume II.)

	VG-8	F-12	VF-20	EF-40	AU-50	MS-60
VARIETY	$50	$65	$90	$175	$340	$700
NORMAL	40	50	65	100	225	500

1858   FS-50-1858-101

VARIETY: Doubled-Die Obverse   **WB-102**
PUP: Left rock and skirt
URS-6 · I-1 · L-3

Description: Doubling is most evident on the shield, left rock, and skirt; and is also visible on the foot, the hand, and the right side of the rock.

Comments: (Note: Because of its low Interest Factor, this variety will be removed from this chapter in the next edition of this volume, to make room for more popularly collected pieces. The Fivaz-Stanton number will be retained for this variety and it will remain in the cross-references at the back of the book.)

1858   FS-50-1858-301

VARIETY: Repunched Date   **WB-105**
PUP: Date
URS-6 · I-3 · L-3

Description: Evidence of secondary numbers is evident both left and right of the primary 5. Wiley and Bugert indicate the image right of the 5 is an inverted 1, and that may well be accurate.

Comments: This is a very scarce variety.

	VG-8	F-12	VF-20	EF-40	AU-50	MS-60
VARIETY	$50	$75	$150	$250	$450	$675
NORMAL	40	50	65	100	225	450

1858 FS-50-1858-302

VARIETY: Misplaced Date **WB: N/L**
PUP: Date
URS-3 · I-1 · L-3

Description: A portion of an 8 is visible protruding from the skirt above the first 8.

Comments: (Note: Because of its low Interest Factor, this variety will be removed from this chapter in the next edition of this volume, to make room for more popularly collected pieces. The Fivaz-Stanton number will be retained for this variety and it will remain in the cross-references at the back of the book.)

1858-O FS-50-1858o-301

VARIETY: Misplaced Date **WB-108**
PUP: Date
URS-8 · I-3 · L-3

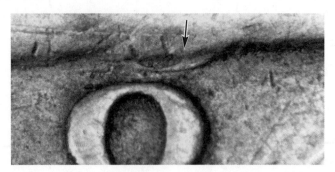

Description: The lower portion of an 8 is evident protruding from the rock above the final primary 8.

Comments: This and other MPDs are abundant in all Liberty Seated coinage series.

	VG-8	F-12	VF-20	EF-40	AU-50	MS-60
VARIETY	$50	$65	$125	$225	$350	$575
NORMAL	40	50	65	100	225	450

1859-O
FS-50-1859o-301

Variety: Repunched Date
PUP: Date
URS-7 · I-1 · L-3

WB-104

Description: A secondary 1 is evident slightly south of the primary, and a secondary 9 is visible very slightly north, showing only as a doubled ball.

Comments: (Note: Because of its low Interest Factor, this variety will be removed from this chapter in the next edition of this volume, to make room for more popularly collected pieces. The Fivaz-Stanton number will be retained for this variety and it will remain in the cross-references at the back of the book.)

1861-O, Die Crack Obverse
FS-50-1861o-401 (007)

Variety: Confederate Obverse
PUP: Die crack in front of head
URS-4 · I-4 · L-4

WB-102

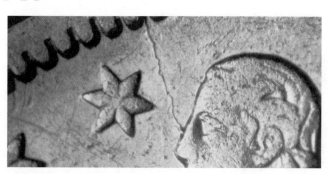

Description: The die crack from the denticles to the right of the seventh star down to Liberty's nose (actually to her shoulder below her jaw) is the diagnostic for this rare variety.

Comments: In 1861, the New Orleans Mint produced a very few half dollars using this obverse die in the striking of Confederate half dollars. This same obverse die, when paired with the normal reverse, is quite desirable, and the higher the grade, the rarer the coin.

	VG-8	F-12	VF-20	EF-40	AU-50	MS-60
Variety	$150	$225	$400	$750	$1,500	$2,500
Normal	40	50	65	115	240	500

1865   FS-50-1865-301

VARIETY: Repunched Date   **WB-102**
PUP: Date
URS-7 · I-3 · L-3

Description: A secondary 1 is evident north of the primary 1, and a secondary 5 is evident south of the primary 5.

Comments: The 8 and 6 are also repunched, although very closely.

	VG-8	F-12	VF-20	EF-40	AU-50	MS-60
VARIETY	$150	$300	$450	$675	$800	$1,050
NORMAL	45	60	80	160	300	800

1866   FS-50-1866-301

VARIETY: Misplaced Date   **WB: N/L**
PUP: Date
URS-3 · I-3 · L-3

Description: The base of three digits (likely an 8 and two 6's) can be seen protruding from the rock. Two images are together above the first 6, and the third is barely visible above the 8.

Comments: This variety is not listed in WB.

	VG-8	F-12	VF-20	EF-40	AU-50	MS-60
VARIETY	$45	$70	$85	$140	$260	$550
NORMAL	40	60	70	120	225	475

1866

FS-50-1866-302

VARIETY: Misplaced Date
PUP: Date
URS-7 · I-3 · L-3

WB-102

Description: The top of a 6 is evident protruding from the denticles below the last 6.

Comments: This variety can be detected in low grades.

	VG-8	F-12	VF-20	EF-40	AU-50	MS-60
VARIETY	$45	$70	$90	$150	$275	$575
NORMAL	40	60	70	120	225	475

1867

FS-50-1867-801

VARIETY: Doubled-Die Reverse
PUP: Eagle's beak
URS-6 · I-4 · L-4

WB-102

Description: The ribbon, IN GOD WE TRUST, and the eagle's beak and eye are all visibly doubled.

Comments: This variety is different from that associated with the 1867-S doubled-die reverse.

	VG-8	F-12	VF-20	EF-40	AU-50	MS-60
VARIETY	$50	$95	$170	$250	$350	$675
NORMAL	40	80	130	200	280	525

1873, Arrows   FS-50-1873-101 (007.1)

VARIETY: Doubled-Die Obverse   **WB-109**
PUP: Shield   *"QUAD STRIPES" VARIETY*
URS-8 · I-4 · L-4

Description: The doubling is evident on Liberty's gown, foot, and shield, the scroll, and the lower stars, but is most notable by the sets of four vertical stripes in the shield.

Comments: This is likely the strongest doubled obverse die in the series.

	VG-8	F-12	VF-20	EF-40	AU-50	MS-60
VARIETY	$75	$125	$250	$425	$585	$1,100
NORMAL	45	60	100	250	400	950

1873, Arrows   FS-50-1873-301 (007.2)

VARIETY: Misplaced Date   **WB: N/L**
PUP: Denticles under right arrow
URS-3 · I-3 · L-3

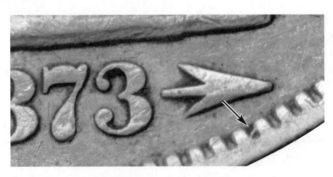

Description: The top of a digit (likely a 3) is evident protruding from the denticles under the tip of the right arrow.

Comments: This variety is not listed in WB.

	VG-8	F-12	VF-20	EF-40	AU-50	MS-60
VARIETY	$75	$125	$250	$425	$585	$1,100
NORMAL	45	60	100	250	400	950

1876   FS-50-1876-301 (007.4)

VARIETY: Large Over Small Date   **WB-106**
PUP: Date
URS-3 · I-4 · L-4

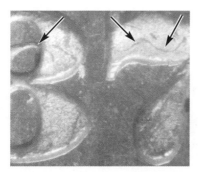 

Description: This repunched date, confirmed by overlays, is a normal (large) date over a smaller date, likely a logo punch intended for a 20-cent or 25-cent denomination. The initial smaller numbers are evident between and on top of the primary numbers.

Comments: This variety is considered very rare.

	VG-8	F-12	VF-20	EF-40	AU-50	MS-60
VARIETY	n/a	n/a	$200	$350	$600	$1,000
NORMAL	$40	$50	65	100	185	500

1876   FS-50-1876-302

VARIETY: Repunched Date   **WB-105**
PUP: Date
URS-4 · I-3 · L-3

Description: The remains of two underlying numbers are evident at the lower left of the 7 and 6 of the primary date.

Comments: This is another very rare variety.

	VG-8	F-12	VF-20	EF-40	AU-50	MS-60
VARIETY	$50	$75	$100	$150	$250	$600
NORMAL	40	50	65	100	185	500

1876 — FS-50-1876-303 (007.3)

VARIETY: Misplaced Date   **WB: N/L**
PUP: Date
URS-5 · I-3 · L-3

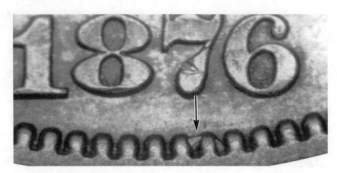

Description: The upper portion of a number (likely a 6) is evident protruding from the denticles below the 7.

Comments: This variety can be detected even in low grades.

	VG-8	F-12	VF-20	EF-40	AU-50	MS-60
VARIETY	$50	$75	$100	$150	$250	$600
NORMAL	40	50	65	100	185	500

1876 — FS-50-1876-304

VARIETY: Misplaced Date   **WB: N/L**
PUP: Date
URS-5 · I-3 · L-3

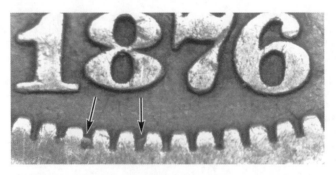

Description: The upper portion of two numbers can be detected protruding from the denticles below the primary 1 and 8.

Comments: This variety can be detected even in low grades.

	VG-8	F-12	VF-20	EF-40	AU-50	MS-60
VARIETY	$50	$75	$100	$150	$250	$600
NORMAL	40	50	65	100	185	500

1876, Proof

FS-50-1876-401

VARIETY: C in Neck
PUP: Neck of Liberty
URS-2 · I-4 · L-4

WB: N/L

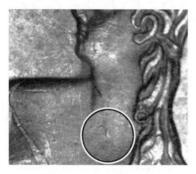
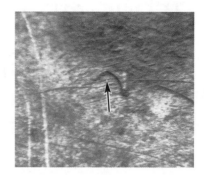

Description: On this Proof die, the remnants of a C are evident in Liberty's neck. The style of the C is identical to that of a CC mintmark.

Comments: Because this variety is a Proof, the chance is very high that several of them will be identified.

	PF-60	PF-63	PF-65
VARIETY	$850	$1,400	n/a
NORMAL	750	1,300	$3,900

1877, 7 Over 6

FS-50-1877-301

VARIETY: Overdate
PUP: Date
URS-4 · I-4 · L-4

WB: N/L

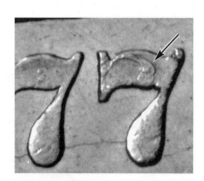

Description: The top portion of a 6 is evident on the upper surface of the last 7.

Comments: This variety is sure to become very popular among Liberty Seated specialists. This type of overdate (surface doubling) is well known in the Morgan dollar series.

	VG-8	F-12	VF-20	EF-40	AU-50	MS-60
VARIETY	$300	$450	$625	$900	$1,350	$2,800
NORMAL	40	50	65	100	185	500

Barber or Liberty Head Half Dollars, 1892–1915

The three series of the Barber design have long been neglected when one considers the typical varieties, such as doubled dies, repunched mintmarks, overdates, and the like. For many collectors, the Barber half dollar series has been somewhat of an afterthought when searching for nice varieties. But all that is changing now that many new varieties are discovered and reported, and some of the known varieties are becoming more popular. We encourage close inspection of all Barber coins.

Only a limited number of varieties in the Barber series were known when the third edition of the *Cherrypickers' Guide* went to press. Furthermore, some varieties were known but were not included in that edition. Since that time a significant number of new varieties have been reported, and there are undoubtedly many varieties yet to be discovered.

To obtain more knowledge of Barber coins in general and Barber varieties in particular, we suggest membership in the Barber Coin Collector's Society. Annual dues are $15. For more information, contact

> BCCS
> Eileen Ribar
> 2053 Edith Place
> Merrick NY 11566
> E-mail: emcrib@optonline.net

The society's quarterly publication, the *Journal*, contains educational information on all denominations of the Barber design. The Web address is www.barbercoins.org. Visitors to the site will find educational articles, membership information, and general information concerning the Barber design, the three Barber series, and Liberty Head nickels.

1892 — FS-50-1892-301 (007.7)

VARIETY: Repunched Date
PUP: Date
URS-3 · I-3 · L-3

LAWRENCE-101

Description: All four digits of the date are dramatically repunched south.

Comments: This impressive RPD has yet to yield many specimens.

	VG-8	F-12	VF-20	EF-40	AU-50	MS-60	MS-63
VARIETY	$75	$100	$200	$300	$425	$650	$1,150
NORMAL	40	70	115	200	350	500	1,000

1892 — FS-50-1892-801 (007.8)

VARIETY: Tripled-Die Reverse
PUP: Reverse lettering
URS-6 · I-3 · L-3

LAWRENCE-102

 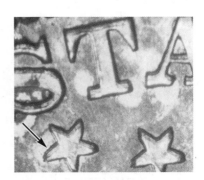

Description: Tripling is evident on all outer lettering, with doubling visible on several stars, the ribbon ends, and the arrows.

Comments: This has become a very popular variety among Barber specialists.

	VG-8	F-12	VF-20	EF-40	AU-50	MS-60	MS-63
VARIETY	$60	$85	$135	$250	$400	$575	$1,100
NORMAL	40	70	115	200	350	500	1,000

1892-O
FS-50-1892o-501 (007.9)

VARIETY: Small O Mintmark
PUP: Mintmark
URS-8 · I-4 · L-3

LAWRENCE-101

Description: Most often referred to as a micro O, this variety was created when an O mintmark punch for quarters was used in place of the regular, larger mintmark intended for use on half dollar dies.

Comments: Many examples show strong strike doubling on reverse.

	F-12	VF-20	EF-40	AU-50	AU-55	MS-60	MS-63
VARIETY	$5,500	$7,500	$12,000	$16,000	$19,000	$23,500	$38,500
NORMAL	500	600	675	750	800	900	1,650

1893
FS-50-1893-801

VARIETY: Tripled-Die Reverse
PUP: Reverse lettering
NEW LISTING

CONECA: DDR-001

Description: Doubling to tripling is evident on all lettering about the rim. The tripling shows best on HALF. Doubling also shows on arrows, stem of olive branch, leaves, wing tips, ribbon, and the stars closest to the rim.

Comments: This is one of the few doubled dies known for the Barber half dollar series.

	VG-8	F-12	VF-20	EF-40	AU-50	MS-60
VARIETY	n/a	n/a	n/a	n/a	n/a	n/a
NORMAL	$30	$80	$160	$200	$325	$550

1909-S

FS-50-1909S-501

VARIETY: Inverted S Mintmark
PUP: Mintmark
URS-5 · I-3 · L-3

LAWRENCE: N/L; CONECA: RPM-001

Description: The S mintmark was punched into the die in an inverted orientation. The base of a correct S is slightly wider than the top.

Comments: Inverted S mintmarks are being discovered more frequently as of late, in many series. This is a very popular variety.

	VG-8	F-12	VF-20	EF-40	AU-50	MS-60	MS-63
VARIETY	$80	$120	$175	$300	$425	$675	$1,550
NORMAL	17	45	95	200	360	600	1,350

1911-S

FS-50-1911S-501

VARIETY: Repunched Mintmark
PUP: Mintmark
URS-7 · I-3 · L-3

LAWRENCE: N/L

Description: The lower serif of the underlying mintmark is evident protruding from the primary serif.

Comments: This is a good example of one of the recently discovered varieties, especially among RPMs.

	VG-8	F-12	VF-20	EF-40	AU-50	MS-60	MS-63
VARIETY	$40	$85	$175	$275	$475	$750	$16,000
NORMAL	20	40	100	210	375	600	1,400

Liberty Walking Half Dollars, 1916–1947

The Liberty Walking half dollars contain many significant and very rare varieties. These include doubled dies, RPMs, and of course missing and hand-carved designer's initials.

Likely the rarest of all the varieties in the series is a very strong obverse doubled die on a 1936-(P) specimen. The specimen we've illustrated in this volume comes to us from Dave Hur. Unknown to us above the grade of Fine, this variety has proven to be very rare and elusive, with fewer than five examples known to exist.

Other significant varieties include visually significant and rare repunched mint-marks, hand-engraved initials on a 1944-D, missing initials on a 1945-(P) and other dates, and an inverted S mintmark on a 1944-S specimen.

As of this publication date there are no clubs devoted strictly to the study of Liberty Walking half dollars. Yet this design is one of the most popular for series collectors, and does hold a number of really nice varieties. For those interested primarily in the varieties within the series, we suggest membership in CONECA, the national error and variety club. Each issue of their bimonthly publication, *ErrorScope*, contains articles on errors and varieties of all types, including those on coins from other countries. For adults, annual dues are $25 (for bulk mailing; contact the Membership Coordinator for current First Class or international rates). For Young Numismatists (under age 18), dues are $7.50 (online membership only, which includes digital access to *ErrorScope*) or $17.50 (online membership plus hard-copy subscription to *ErrorScope*). An application can be obtained online at www.conecaonline.org, or from Rachel Irish at the following address:

CONECA
Rachel Irish
101 W. Prairie #323
Hayden, ID 83835
E-mail: MRirish5@roadrunner.com

1916-D

Variety: Repunched Mintmark
PUP: Mintmark
URS-5 · I-3 · L-3

CONECA: RPM-001; Fox: V-101

Description: The secondary D is evident southwest of the primary D.

Comments: This dramatic RPM has yet to yield many specimens.

	VG-8	F-12	VF-20	EF-40	AU-50	MS-60	MS-63
Variety	$90	$125	$225	$275	$325	$425	$675
Normal	60	85	140	225	250	360	600

1936

Variety: Doubled-Die Obverse
PUP: Date
URS-2 · I-4 · L-4

CONECA: DDO-003; Fox: N/L

Description: Extremely strong doubling is evident on the date. Lesser doubling is evident on IN GOD WE TRUST, the skirt, and some other elements.

Comments: Unknown above Fine, this variety is very elusive.

	VG-8	F-12	VF-20	EF-40	AU-50
Variety	$500	$600.00	n/a	n/a	n/a
Normal	14	14.50	$15	$16	$25

1936   FS-50-1936-102

VARIETY: Doubled-Die Obverse   **CONECA: WHO-001; Fox: V-101**
PUP: Date, IN GOD WE TRUST
URS-11 · I-1 · L-2

Description: Doubling is evident on the date, IN GOD WE TRUST, the lower folds of the skirt, the shoes, and the ground.

Comments: This variety is still easy to locate. Some of the doubled dies of 1936 are from a doubled master die. (Note: Because of its low Interest Factor, this variety will be removed from this chapter in the next edition of this volume, to make room for more popularly collected pieces. The Fivaz-Stanton number will be retained for this variety and it will remain in the cross-references at the back of the book.)

1936-D   FS-50-1936D-101

VARIETY: Doubled-Die Obverse   **CONECA: WHO-001; Fox: V-101**
PUP: Date, IN GOD WE TRUST
URS-11 · I-1 · L-2

Description: Doubling is evident on the date, IN GOD WE TRUST, the lower folds of the skirt, the shoes, and the ground.

Comments: This and the previous variety are from a doubled master die. (Note: Because of its low Interest Factor, this variety will be removed from this chapter in the next edition of this volume, to make room for more popularly collected pieces. The Fivaz-Stanton number will be retained for this variety and it will remain in the cross-references at the back of the book.)

1936-S

FS-50-1936S-101

VARIETY: Doubled-Die Obverse
PUP: Date, IN GOD WE TRUST
URS-11 · I-1 · L-2

CONECA: UNKNOWN; FOX: V-101

Description: Doubling is evident on the date, IN GOD WE TRUST, the lower folds of the skirt, the shoes, and the ground.

Comments: This variety is also from a doubled master die. (Note: Because of its low Interest Factor, this variety will be removed from this chapter in the next edition of this volume, to make room for more popularly collected pieces. The Fivaz-Stanton number will be retained for this variety and it will remain in the cross-references at the back of the book.)

1939-D

FS-50-1939D-101 (008.45)

VARIETY: Doubled-Die Obverse
PUP: Date, IN GOD WE TRUST
URS-11 · I-1 · L-2

CONECA: DDO-001; FOX: V-103

Description: Doubling is evident on the date, IN GOD WE TRUST, the lower folds of the skirt, the shoes, and the ground.

Comments: This variety is extremely similar to the previous three listings. (Note: Because of its low Interest Factor, this variety will be removed from this chapter in the next edition of this volume, to make room for more popularly collected pieces. The Fivaz-Stanton number will be retained for this variety and it will remain in the cross-references at the back of the book.)

1939-D

VARIETY: Repunched Mintmark
PUP: Mintmark
URS-5 · I-3 · L-3

CONECA: RPM-001; Fox: V-101

Description: The secondary mintmark is evident north of the primary mintmark.
Comments: This is a very prominent RPM.

	VG-8	F-12	VF-20	EF-40	AU-50	MS-60	MS-63
VARIETY	$18	$20.00	$25	$30	$35	$55	$95
NORMAL	14	14.50	15	16	25	45	80

1941-D

VARIETY: Repunched Mintmark
PUP: Mintmark
URS-7 · I-3 · L-3

CONECA: RPM-001; Fox: V-101

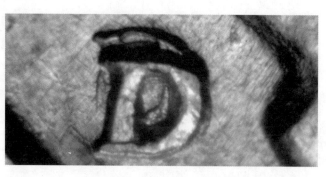

Description: The secondary mintmark is evident northwest of the primary mintmark.
Comments: This is a very prominent repunched mintmark.

	VG-8	F-12	VF-20	EF-40	AU-50	MS-60	MS-63
VARIETY	$19	$25.00	$30	$40	$90	$190	$225
NORMAL	14	14.50	15	16	20	40	60

1941-S

FS-50-1941S-501

VARIETY: Repunched Mintmark
PUP: Mintmark
URS-6 · I-3 · L-3

CONECA: RPM-001; Fox: V-102

Description: The secondary mintmark is evident northwest of the primary mintmark.

Comments: Fox incorrectly lists this variety as an S over horizontal S.

	VG-8	F-12	VF-20	EF-40	AU-50	MS-60	MS-63
VARIETY	$17	$20.00	$23	$25	$40	$85	$130
NORMAL	14	14.50	15	16	20	75	110

1942

FS-50-1942-101 (008.5)

VARIETY: Doubled-Die Obverse
PUP: Liberty's breast
URS-12 · I-2 · L-2

CONECA: DDO-001; Fox: V-103

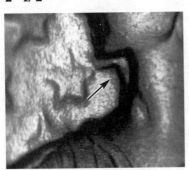 

Description: The doubling is evident on Liberty's breast and neck, and on the bottom of the gown.

Comments: This doubled die is very similar to the San Francisco doubled-die obverse FS-101.

	VG-8	F-12	VF-20	EF-40	AU-50	MS-60	MS-63
VARIETY	$17	$20.00	$23	$25	$30	$80	$120
NORMAL	14	14.50	15	16	20	75	110

1942

VARIETY: Doubled-Die Reverse
PUP: HALF DOLLAR
URS-8 · I-4 · L-4

CONECA: DDR-001; Fox: V-101

Description: Doubling is evident on HALF DOLLAR, UNITED STATES OF AMERICA, the olive branch, and the lower eagle.

Comments: This is one of two very popular DDRs in this series.

	VG-8	F-12	VF-20	EF-40	AU-50	MS-60	MS-63
VARIETY	$20	$25.00	$35	$40	$55	$100	$225
NORMAL	14	14.50	15	16	20	40	50

1942-D

VARIETY: Doubled-Die Obverse
PUP: Liberty's breast

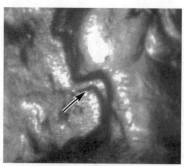 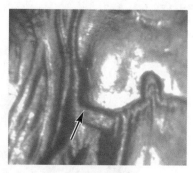

Description: The doubling is evident on Liberty's breast and neck, and on the bottom of the gown.

Comments: Previously listed in error, this variety is now believed to not actually exist. It will be removed from the next edition of this volume.

1942-S
FS-50-1942S-101

VARIETY: Doubled-Die Obverse
PUP: Liberty's breast
URS-4 · I-2 · L-2

CONECA: DDO-001; Fox: V-106

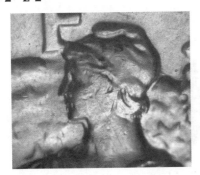

Description: The doubling is evident on Liberty's breast and neck, and on the bottom of the gown.

Comments: This doubling is very similar to the Philadelphia doubled-die obverse FS-101.

	VG-8	F-12	VF-20	EF-40	AU-50	MS-60	MS-63
VARIETY	$18	$20.00	$23	$25	$30	$50	$70
NORMAL	14	14.50	15	16	20	40	60

1943
FS-50-1943-101

VARIETY: Doubled-Die Obverse
PUP: IN GOD WE TRUST, date
URS-20 · I-1 · L-1

Fox: V-101, 102, 103, 106

Description: The doubling is evident on IN GOD WE TRUST and on the date.

Comments: This and many other 1943 doubled dies (from all three mints) are the result of doubled master tooling. Almost all 1943-dated halves exhibit some form of this doubling. On some specimens the last number is clearly doubled. Although some people believe it to be 1943 over 1942, this has not been confirmed. We believe that the upper curve of the underlying digit more closely matches that of a 3.

	VG-8	F-12	VF-20	EF-40	AU-50	MS-60	MS-63
VARIETY	$14	$14.50	$15	$16	$20	$35	$45
NORMAL	14	14.50	15	16	20	35	45

1943-D

FS-50-1943D-101

VARIETY: Doubled-Die Obverse
PUP: IN GOD WE TRUST, date
URS-20 · I-1 · L-1

FOX: V-101, 102, 104, 107

Description: The doubling is evident on IN GOD WE TRUST and on the date.

Comments: This and many other 1943 doubled dies (from all three mints) are the result of working hub doubled dies. Almost all 1943-dated halves exhibit some form of this doubling. (Note: Because of its low Interest Factor, this variety will be removed from this chapter in the next edition of this volume, to make room for more popularly collected pieces. The Fivaz-Stanton number will be retained for this variety and it will remain in the cross-references at the back of the book.)

1943-S

FS-50-1943S-101

VARIETY: Doubled-Die Obverse
PUP: IN GOD WE TRUST, date
URS-20 · I-1 · L-1

FOX: V-101, 102, 103, 105, 107, 108, 115

Description: The doubling is evident on IN GOD WE TRUST and on the date.

Comments: This and many other 1943 doubled dies (from all three mints) are the result of working hub doubled dies. Almost all 1943-dated halves exhibit some form of this doubling. (Note: Because of its low Interest Factor, this variety will be removed from this chapter in the next edition of this volume, to make room for more popularly collected pieces. The Fivaz-Stanton number will be retained for this variety and it will remain in the cross-references at the back of the book.)

1944-D
FS-50-1944D-901

VARIETY: Hand-Engraved Initials
PUP: Designer's initials
URS-4 · I-4 · L-4

CONECA: RED-001; Fox: N/L

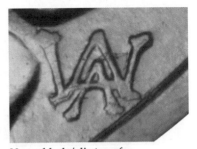

Hand engraved

Normal hub / die transfer

Description: The designer's initials on the reverse were omitted from the original die and were subsequently hand engraved.

Comments: The cause of the missing initials is unclear. The initials are not punched into each die, as many think, but are a part of the master hub and die series, and would normally have been transferred onto the working dies. Other dates and mints within the series are known without the designer's initials, and will be added to our listings as we can examine them.

	VG-8	F-12	VF-20	EF-40	AU-50	MS-60	MS-63
VARIETY	$30	$50.00	$75	$135	$175	$250	$350
NORMAL	14	14.50	15	16	20	40	55

1944-S
FS-50-1944S-501

VARIETY: Repunched Mintmark
PUP: Mintmark
URS-6 · I-3 · L-3

CONECA: RPM-004; Fox: N/L

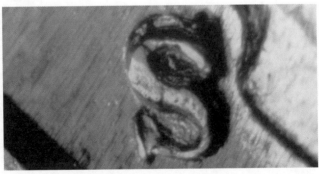

Description: The secondary mintmark is evident north of the primary mintmark.

Comments: This repunched mintmark is very prominent.

	VG-8	F-12	VF-20	EF-40	AU-50	MS-60	MS-63
VARIETY	$18	$20.00	$23	$25	$30	$50	$75
NORMAL	14	14.50	15	16	20	40	65

1944-S
FS-50-1944S-502

VARIETY: Repunched Mintmark
PUP: Mintmark
URS-6 · I-3 · L-3

CONECA: RPM-002; Fox: V-101

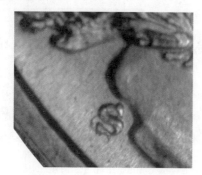 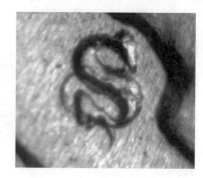

Description: The secondary mintmark is evident southwest, north, and east of the primary mintmark.

Comments: This is a very prominent repunched mintmark.

	VG-8	F-12	VF-20	EF-40	AU-50	MS-60	MS-63
VARIETY	$18	$20.00	$23	$25	$30	$50	$75
NORMAL	14	14.50	15	16	20	40	65

1944-S
FS-50-1944S-511

VARIETY: Possible Inverted Mintmark
PUP: Mintmark
URS-5 · I-3 · L-3

Fox: N/L

 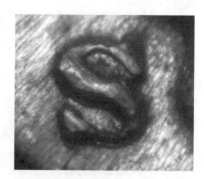

Description: The S mintmark appears to have been punched into the die in an inverted orientation.

Comments: This variety will be removed from this chapter in the next edition of this volume, pending further research into this deceptive variety. Its Fivaz-Stanton number will be retained and it will continue to be listed in the related appendix.

1945
FS-50-1945-901

VARIETY: Missing Designer's Initials
PUP: Designer's initials
URS-5 · I-4 · L-4

Fox: V-102

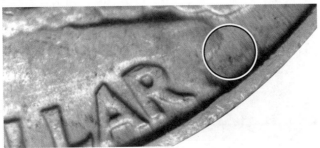

Description: The designer's initials on this die are missing.

Comments: This is a very underrated variety. The MDI error is also found on circulation strikes of 1918-D (Fox-101, Breen-5139), 1929-S (Fox-101, Breen-5154), 1941 (Fox-102), and 1943-S (Fox-106, Breen-5200). It is also found on 1941 Proofs (Fox-P101, Breen-5182) which are actually more common than this Proof date with the initials. The editor has seen two FS-901 coins for the 1943-S in recent years; Breen describes this variety as "presently very rare."

	VG-8	F-12	VF-20	EF-40	AU-50	MS-60	MS-63
VARIETY	$18	$20.00	$35	$65	$100	$150	$250
NORMAL	14	14.50	15	16	20	35	45

1946
FS-50-1946-101

VARIETY: Doubled-Die Obverse
PUP: Fold of flag
URS-3 · I-3 · L-3

CONECA: DDO-001; Fox: N/L

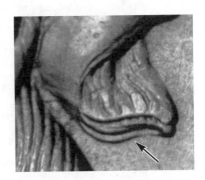

Description: The doubling is evident on Liberty's breast and left arm, and on the fold of the flag.

	VG-8	F-12	VF-20	EF-40	AU-50	MS-60	MS-63
VARIETY	$18	$20.00	$23	$25	$40	$70	$100
NORMAL	14	14.50	15	16	20	40	50

1946

VARIETY: Doubled-Die Reverse
PUP: E PLURIBUS UNUM, feathers
URS-7 · I-4 · L-4

CONECA: DDR-001; Fox: V-101

Description: Very strong doubling is evident on E PLURIBUS UNUM, the eagle's wing feathers, the eagle's left wing, and the branch. The photos above are of a relatively early die state specimen.

Comments: This is the second of the two most popular doubled dies of the series. Early die states command a premium. In July 2011, a PCGS MS-66 sold at public auction for $6,325.

	VG-8	F-12	VF-20	EF-40	AU-50	MS-60	MS-63
VARIETY	$22	$28.00	$40	$65	$125	$275	$550
NORMAL	14	14.50	15	16	20	40	50

Franklin Half Dollars, 1948–1963

Compared with other series, the Franklin half dollars contain few significant varieties, yet one of the rarest Proof doubled reverse dies comes from this series. The 1961 Proof doubled-die reverse (FS-801) is extremely rare and in very high demand, with values continually on the rise. Without a doubt, this is one of the most significant varieties of the last half of the 20th century. It is featured on the cover of this volume.

Other varieties in the series are known, and are highly collectible. However, some of these are on low-mintage dates, such as a quadrupled obverse die on a 1950 Proof. Obviously, being a low-mintage Proof, this variety will likely be found on a relatively large percentage of the population.

Franklin half dollars are perennially popular as a type. We have expanded this volume of the *Cherrypickers' Guide* with extra coverage of the "Bugs Bunny" phenomenon, as well as nearly a dozen new variety listings.

As of this publication date there are no clubs devoted strictly to the study of Franklin half dollars. However, for those interested primarily in the varieties within the series, we suggest membership in CONECA, the national error and variety club. Each issue of their bimonthly publication, *ErrorScope,* contains articles on errors and varieties of all type, and even from other countries. For adults, annual dues are $25 (for bulk mailing; contact the Membership Coordinator for current First Class or international rates). For Young Numismatists (under age 18), dues are $7.50 (online membership only, which includes digital access to *ErrorScope*) or $17.50 (online membership plus hard-copy subscription to *ErrorScope*). An application can be obtained online at www.conecaonline.org, or from Rachel Irish at the following address:

CONECA
Rachel Irish
101 W. Prairie #323
Hayden, ID 83835
E-mail: MRirish5@roadrunner.com

1948–1963

VARIETY: Die-Clash Obverse *"BUGS BUNNY" AND RELATED CLASHES*
PUP: Clash marks in mouth or from nose

Description: Clash marks appear in Franklin's mouth or nose.

Comments: The so-called "Bugs Bunny" die clash on the 1955 Franklin half dollar is perhaps the most well known and most heavily promoted clashed-die variety of all time. The impression of the wing feathers of the small eagle at the right of the Liberty Bell on the reverse was transferred to the obverse during a die clash. The effect made it look like Franklin had buck teeth, and the nickname "Bugs Bunny" caught on. In recent years the collecting of other dates with clashes in the areas of Franklin's mouth and under his nose has caught on, with many dates fetching significant premiums over normal-date half dollars in the same grades.

1948 (nose), FS-401

1950 (mouth), FS-401

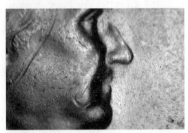

1951 (mouth), FS-401

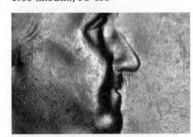

1951 (nose), FS-402

1953-D (nose, Die 1), FS-401

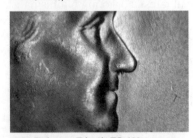

1953-D (nose, Die 2), FS-402

1954 (mouth), FS-401

1954 (nose), FS-402

1948–1963 (continued)   FS-50-[Year]-401/402

VARIETY: Die-Clash Obverse   ***"BUGS BUNNY" AND RELATED CLASHES***
PUP: Clash marks in mouth or from nose

1954-D (mouth), FS-401

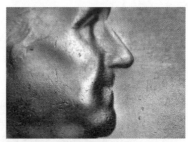

1954-S (mouth), FS-401

1955 (mouth), FS-401

1956 (mouth), FS-401

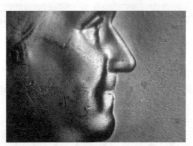

1963 (mouth), FS-401

The following chart lists the known die-clash obverse varieties of this type, their PCGS numbers, and their rarity ratings (including both circulated and Mint State grades).

Date/Mintmark	PCGS No.	Rarity	Date/Mintmark	PCGS No.	Rarity
1948		R-8	1954-D	147872	R-8
1949	408488	R-5	1954-S	507257	R-7
1950		R-8	1955	145357	R-1
1951	147864	R-3	1956	147874	R-3
1952	147866	R-7	1959	501604	R-6
1953	147868	R-7	1960		
1953-D	415695	R-6	1961		R-8
1953-S		R-6	1962		R-8
1954	147870	R-3	1963		R-7

1948   FS-50-1948-801

VARIETY: Doubled-Die Reverse   **CONECA: DDR-001**
PUP: E PLURIBUS UNUM
URS-8 · I-3 · L-3

Description: Doubling is evident on E PLURIBUS UNUM, UNITED, HALF DOLLAR, the dots, and the clapper.

Comments: There are several similar, yet lesser, DDRs for this date.

	EF-40	AU-50	MS-60	MS-63	MS-65	MS-66
VARIETY	$25	$30	$50	$75	$200	$550
NORMAL	16	18	20	25	80	400

1948-D   FS-50-1948D-801

VARIETY: Doubled-Die Reverse   **CONECA: DDR-003**
PUP: E PLURIBUS UNUM
URS-8 · I-3 · L-3

Description: Doubling is evident on E PLURIBUS UNUM, UNITED, HALF DOLLAR, the dots, and the clapper.

Comments: There are several similar, yet lesser, DDRs for this date.

	EF-40	AU-50	MS-60	MS-63	MS-65	MS-66
VARIETY	$25	$30	$35	$50	$175	$1,050
NORMAL	16	18	20	24	125	900

1949-S

FS-50-1949S-501 (011.3)

VARIETY: Repunched Mintmark
PUP: Mintmark
URS-5 · I-3 · L-3

CONECA: RPM-002

 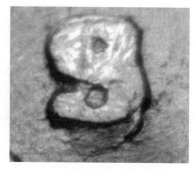

Description: The secondary mintmark is evident south of the primary.

Comments: CONECA has two other RPMs listed for the date.

	EF-40	AU-50	MS-60	MS-63	MS-65	MS-66
VARIETY	$27	$45	$75	$120	$270	$575
NORMAL	20	35	65	105	150	225

1950, Proof

FS-50-1950-101

VARIETY: Quadrupled-Die Obverse
PUP: Date, LIBERTY
URS-4 · I-3 · L-3

CONECA: DDO-001

Description: Quadrupling is evident on the date and LIBERTY.

Comments: Close examination of the R in LIBERTY clearly indicates this is actually a quadrupled obverse die.

	PF-63	PF-65
VARIETY	$375	$550
NORMAL	350	500

1950-D
FS-50-1950D-501

VARIETY: Repunched Mintmark (Possible Over Mintmark)   **CONECA: RPM-001;**
PUP: Mintmark   **WEXLER: WOMM-001;**
NEW LISTING   **POTTER: VCR#1/POMM#1**

Description: What arguably appears to be a light S or D mintmark is evident to the south of the primary D.

Comments: This variety is recognized by many listers as an OMM, but is listed as an RPM in the CONECA Master Listings. The variety needs more study to determine whether it is an OMM or an RPM.

	EF-40	AU-50	MS-60	MS-63	MS-65	MS-66
VARIETY	n/a	n/a	n/a	n/a	n/a	n/a
NORMAL	$15	$20	$25	$35	$250	$900

1951, Proof
FS-50-1951-801

VARIETY: Doubled-Die Reverse   **WEXLER: WDDR-005;**
PUP: PASS AND STOW, disheveled wing feathers on eagle   **CONECA: DDR-010**
NEW LISTING

Description: Class II doubling spread to the center shows on the left side of the bell yoke, on the left side of the upper bell supports, on the upper bell, along the bottom of the bell, on the lettering within the bell, and on the eagle.

Comments: This is a relatively new find. Based on the strength of the doubling on the inscription on the bell, we expect this one to become popular.

	PF-63	PF-65	PF-66
VARIETY	n/a	n/a	n/a
NORMAL	$325	$400	$550

1951-S

FS-50-1951S-501

VARIETY: Repunched Mintmark
PUP: Mintmark
NEW LISTING

CONECA: RPM-001

Description: A very strong secondary S is evident to the south of the primary S.

Comments: This variety was once thought to strengthen in the later die stages, but it has been determined that the earlier die stages are actually stronger. The one shown here is a later die stage.

	EF-40	AU-50	MS-60	MS-63	MS-65	MS-66
VARIETY	n/a	n/a	n/a	n/a	n/a	n/a
NORMAL	$14	$18	$25	$35	$70	$800

1951-S

FS-50-1951S-801

VARIETY: Doubled-Die Reverse
PUP: E PLURIBUS UNUM
URS-6 · I-3 · L-3

CONECA: DDR-002

Description: Doubling is evident on E PLURIBUS UNUM, as well as on the eagle's left wing and tail feathers.

Comments: There is another similar DDR for this date.

	EF-40	AU-50	MS-60	MS-63	MS-65	MS-66
VARIETY	$25	$30	$55	$80	$275	$900
NORMAL	14	18	25	35	70	800

1952   FS-50-1952-402

VARIETY: Die Cracks
PUP: Die crack on face
NEW LISTING

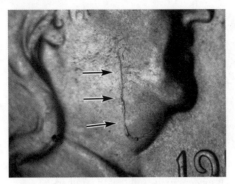

Description: A long die crack is evident on Franklin's face, down into the neck. An additional die crack can be found to a greater or lesser degree on Franklin's lapel.

Comments: Coauthor Bill Fivaz affectionately refers to this variety as "Scarface."

	EF-40	AU-50	MS-60	MS-63	MS-65	MS-66
VARIETY	n/a	n/a	n/a	n/a	n/a	n/a
NORMAL	$14	$15	$16	$20	$70	$250

1952-S   FS-50-1952S-501

VARIETY: Repunched Mintmark   **CONECA: RPM-001**
PUP: Mintmark
NEW LISTING

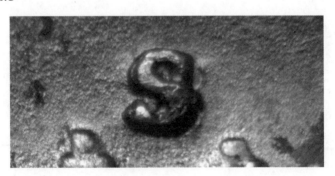

Description: Very strong secondary S's are evident to the east and west of the primary S.

Comments: This is one of the stronger RPMs known in the series. It can still be found with a little searching.

	EF-40	AU-50	MS-60	MS-63	MS-65	MS-66
VARIETY	n/a	n/a	n/a	n/a	n/a	n/a
NORMAL	$16	$24	$50	$70	$100	$300

1953-S
FS-50-1953S-501

VARIETY: Repunched Mintmark
PUP: Mintmark
URS-5 · I-3 · L-3

CONECA: RPM-001

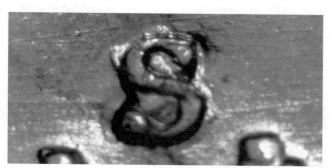

Description: The secondary S is evident northwest of the primary S. Strike doubling can be detected at the top of the primary S on the specimen examined.

Comments: This is an interesting variety that can be found with some hunting.

	EF-40	AU-50	MS-60	MS-63	MS-65	MS-66
VARIETY	$20	$25	$35	$75	$175	$850
NORMAL	14	18	25	35	70	700

1954, Proof
FS-50-1954-101

VARIETY: Doubled-Die Obverse
PUP: UST of TRUST
URS-4 · I-3 · L-3

CONECA: DDO-001

Description: Doubling is evident on the 54 of the date and UST of TRUST.

Comments: This variety is somewhat minor, but rarely found.

	PF-63	PF-65	PF-66
VARIETY	$75	$135	$190
NORMAL	65	90	130

1955 — FS-50-1955-401

VARIETY: Clashed Obverse Die
PUP: Mouth of Franklin
URS-13 · I-3 · L-3

CONECA: N/L
"BUGS BUNNY" VARIETY

Description: This variety is affectionately known as the "Bugs Bunny." There is evidence of clash marks that appear as two buck teeth on Franklin (similar to the buck teeth commonly seen on cartoon characters).

Comments: Although very common, this variety is still in demand! Other "Bugs Bunny" varieties include 1951-P, 1952-P, 1953-P, 1954-P, 1954-D, and 1956. These are discussed in a special section at the beginning of the Franklin half dollar listings.

	AU-50	AU-55	MS-60	MS-63	MS-65	MS-66
VARIETY	$25	$27	$30	$48	$130	$265
NORMAL	22	23	25	40	65	200

1956, Proof — FS-50-1956-101

VARIETY: Doubled-Die Obverse
PUP: Date, TRUST
URS-5 · I-3 · L-3

CONECA: DDO-003

Description: Doubling is evident on the date and WE TRUST, with extra thickness on the letters of IN GOD WE TRUST.

Comments: The Proof varieties in this series have proven to be moderately rare. This is found with the Type II reverse (see FS-50-1956-901).

	PF-65	PF-66
VARIETY	$75	$100
NORMAL	45	60

1956, Proof FS-50-1956-801

VARIETY: Doubled-Die Reverse
PUP: E PLURIBUS UNUM
URS-5 · I-3 · L-3

CONECA: DDR-001

Description: The doubling appears as extreme extra thickness on all perimeter letters, with moderate separation on E PLURIBUS UNUM and the bell clapper.

Comments: The Proof varieties in this series have proven to be moderately rare.

	PF-65	PF-66
VARIETY	$75	$100
NORMAL	45	60

1956, Proof FS-50-1956-802

VARIETY: Doubled-Die Reverse
PUP: Eagle
NEW LISTING

CONECA: DDR-002

Description: Strong doubling to tripling is evident on the eagle's left wing feathers (viewer's right) and the tail feathers. A slight to moderate spread can be seen on HALF DOLLAR and AMERICA, with tripling on the F of HALF and the last A of AMERICA.

Comments: This is a nice one that is barely known to collectors, yet it can still be found with a bit of searching.

	PF-65	PF-66
VARIETY	$75	$100
NORMAL	45	60

1956, Proof
FS-50-1956-901

VARIETY: Type I Reverse
PUP: Eagle
NEW LISTING

CONECA: RDV-001

Type I, low-relief eagle

Type II, normal high-relief eagle;
three feathers left of perch

Description: This variety uses the relief used from 1948 to 1955 for Proof and circulation-strike coinage: a low-relief eagle, four flattened feathers left of the perch, and other minor changes.

Comments: The Type II high-relief eagle was introduced to replace the Type I low-relief eagle on Proof coinage starting in 1956, while the low-relief eagle was maintained for circulation-strike coinage through 1963. Exceptions are circulation strikes dated 1958 and 1959. A significant number of those (20% for 1958 and about 70% for 1959) were struck from retired obverse and reverse Proof dies. This type appears to make up about 5% of the total mintage of 1956 Proof half dollars.

	PF-65	PF-66
VARIETY	n/a	n/a
NORMAL	$45	$60

1957, Proof
FS-50-1957-801

VARIETY: Tripled-Die Reverse
PUP: E PLURIBUS UNUM, HALF DOLLAR
URS-5 · I-3 · L-3

CONECA: DDR-004

Description: A close tripled image can be seen on E PLURIBUS UNUM, on portions of UNITED STATES OF AMERICA, and on HALF DOLLAR.

Comments: This is one of the more collectible reverse varieties of the decade.

	PF-65	PF-66
VARIETY	$90	$150
NORMAL	25	35

1957-D
FS-50-1957D-501

VARIETY: Repunched Mintmark
PUP: Mintmark
URS-6 · I-3 · L-3

CONECA: RPM-001

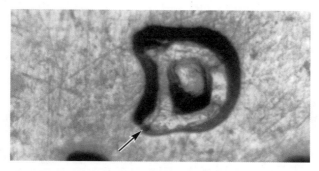

Description: This RPM is rotated slightly, with the secondary D evident at lower left of the primary D.

Comments: As of this writing, this is the only known RPM for the date.

	AU-55	MS-60	MS-63	MS-65	MS-66
VARIETY	$20	$35	$50	$80	$115
NORMAL	15	16	17	60	90

1959
FS-50-1959-402

VARIETY: Die Break
PUP: Die break at throat
NEW LISTING

"GOITER" VARIETY

Description: An interesting die break is found at Franklin's throat.

Comments: This variety is affectionately called the "Goiter" variety by some.

	AU-55	MS-60	MS-63	MS-65	MS-66
VARIETY	n/a	n/a	n/a	n/a	n/a
NORMAL	$15	$16	$18	$70	$1,000

1959

VARIETY: Doubled-Die Reverse
PUP: E PLURIBUS UNUM, eagle, bell hanger, bell striker
URS-5 · I-3 · L-3

CONECA: DDR-001

 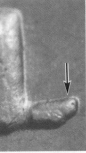 

Description: Doubling shows as disheveled, overlapping feathers on the eagle. Doubling is also apparent on the bell hanger and the striker and in the motto.

Comments: This was one of the earliest doubled dies identified by hobbyists; it was referred to as a "Medium Relief" by Frank Spadone in the early 1960s, before it was known to be a dual hubbing (doubled die). It has become a very popular variety.

	AU-55	MS-60	MS-63	MS-65	MS-66
VARIETY	$25	$50	$85	$120	$1,125
NORMAL	15	16	18	70	1,000

1960, Proof

VARIETY: Doubled-Die Obverse
PUP: Date, TRUST
URS-8 · I-3 · L-3

CONECA: DDO-003

Description: Doubling is evident on LIBERTY, TRUST, and the date.

Comments: This can be found with some searching!

	PF-65	PF-66
VARIETY	$95	$150
NORMAL	20	30

1961, Proof
FS-50-1961-801 (013)

VARIETY: Doubled-Die Reverse
PUP: E PLURIBUS UNUM
URS-7 · I-5 · L-5

CONECA: DDR-003

Description: Very strong doubling is visible on all letters on the left side, especially E PLURIBUS UNUM and UNITED.

Comments: This is by far the strongest doubled die in the series, and is easily sold. This coin—which is also our cover coin—has everything going for it: the doubling is dramatic and naked-eye visible, it's on a large coin, and the issue is a Proof. Very few have been uncovered in the last five or six years, but check those unopened 1961 Proof sets—you may ring the bell if you find one!

	PF-65	PF-66	PF-67
VARIETY	$3,000	$4,000	$7,750
NORMAL	20	35	70

1961, Proof
FS-50-1961-802

VARIETY: Doubled-Die Reverse
PUP: E PLURIBUS UNUM
URS-3 · I-3 · L-3

CONECA: DDR-001

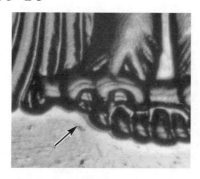

Description: The doubling is evident on all perimeter lettering (with a clockwise spread), and shows very nicely on the eagle's tail and E PLURIBUS UNUM.

Comments: While looking for the previous doubled-die reverse, you may find one of these!

	PF-65	PF-66
VARIETY	$40	$80
NORMAL	20	35

1961, Proof — FS-50-1961-803

VARIETY: Doubled-Die Reverse   **CONECA: DDR-004**
PUP: E PLURIBUS UNUM
URS-6 · I-3 · L-3

Description: Doubling is very evident on E PLURIBUS UNUM, and also visible on the perimeter lettering and the eagle.

Comments: While looking for the biggie (FS-801), you may find one of these!

	PF-65	PF-66
VARIETY	$85	$110
NORMAL	20	35

1962, Proof — FS-50-1962-101

VARIETY: Doubled-Die Obverse   **CONECA: DDO-002**
PUP: Date, TRUST
URS-5 · I-3 · L-3

Description: The doubling is evident on the 62 of the date and on WE TRUST.

Comments: This variety is worthwhile to look for!

	PF-65	PF-66
VARIETY	$30	$60
NORMAL	20	25

1962, Proof

FS-50-1962-901

VARIETY: Possible Misplaced Mintmark
PUP: ST of STOW, Liberty Bell
NEW LISTING

Description: What appears to be a D is punched into the reverse, southeast of STOW.

Comments: This new find could prove to be controversial, but could very well turn out to be an errant D. Even if it is not a Denver mintmark, this could turn out to be as popular as the 1952 so-called "Superbird" Proof quarter due to the character of the flaw, especially if it is rare. We need to see a specimen of this coin for further study.

	PF-65	PF-66
VARIETY	n/a	n/a
NORMAL	$20	$25

1963

FS-50-1963-801

VARIETY: Doubled-Die Reverse
PUP: E PLURIBUS UNUM
NEW LISTING

CONECA: DDR-001

Description: Doubling is evident on E PLURIBUS UNUM; slight doubling shows on UNITED and HALF.

Comments: This variety is found in Mint sets. A diagnostic of this variety in this stage is the presence of numerous horizontal die scratches connecting the tops of the T and E of UNITED; diagnostics for some stages of this variety are the obvious die scratches seen throughout and connecting TED of UNITED.

	AU-55	MS-60	MS-63	MS-65	MS-66
VARIETY	n/a	n/a	n/a	n/a	n/a
NORMAL	$15	$16	$18	$50	$800

Kennedy Half Dollars, 1964 to Date

This series boasts the portrait of one of our most popular presidents. The popularity of the design is likely the result of two important factors—a president assassinated during the lifetime of many budding collectors, and the subsequent removal of silver from most circulating U.S. coinage immediately after the release of the design. Fortunately for collectors, the Kennedy type contains many interesting die varieties.

Coins dated 1964-D display evidence of several different obverse die doublings or triplings; some of these are relatively easy to locate. Proof obverse doubled dies are also dramatic for 1968 and 1969. Certain specimens of a 1968-S Proof half dollar are known with an inverted S mintmark; repunched mintmarks are also known for several dates, most significantly 1964-D.

An excellent reference on these varieties is from James Wiles, who has authored a wonderful, highly detailed book on the entire series, *The Kennedy Half Dollar Book*, which has hundreds of superb photos illustrating almost every known variety within the series. Additionally, a list of the doubled dies and repunched mintmarks can be found on the CONECA Web site (www.conecaonline.org).

As of this publication date there are no clubs devoted strictly to the study of Kennedy half dollars. However, for those interested primarily in the varieties within the series, we suggest membership in CONECA, the national error and variety club. Each issue of their bimonthly publication, the *ErrorScope*, contains articles on errors and varieties of all type, and even from other countries. For adults, annual dues are $25 (for bulk mailing; contact the Membership Coordinator for current First Class or international rates). For Young Numismatists (under age 18), dues are $7.50 (online membership only, which includes digital access to *ErrorScope*) or $17.50 (online membership plus hard-copy subscription to *ErrorScope*). An application can be obtained online at www.conecaonline.org, or from Rachel Irish at the following address:

CONECA
Rachel Irish
101 W. Prairie #323
Hayden, ID 83835
E-mail: MRirish5@roadrunner.com

1964, Proof — FS-50-1964-101 (013.2)

VARIETY: Doubled-Die Obverse
PUP: WE TRUST
URS-7 · I-3 · L-2

CONECA: DDO-002

Description: Doubling is evident on WE TRUST, RTY (of LIBERTY), and the upper hair, with lesser doubling on IN GOD and the date.

Comments: This is a Normal Hair variety. See FS-50-1964-401.

	PF-63	PF-65	PF-66	PF-67
VARIETY	$15	$30	$65	$100
NORMAL	10	15	40	65

1964 — FS-50-1964-102

VARIETY: Doubled-Die Obverse
PUP: WE TRUST
URS-6 · I-3 · L-3

CONECA: DDO-007

Description: Doubling is very strong on WE TRUST, LIBERTY, and the date.

Comments: Extremely high grades (MS-66+) are almost impossible to find.

	MS-63	MS-65	MS-66	MS-67
VARIETY	$35	$65	$250	n/a
NORMAL	13	15	40	$250

1964, Proof
FS-50-1964-103

VARIETY: Doubled-Die Obverse
PUP: IN GOD, LIBERTY
URS-3 · I-3 · L-3

CONECA: DDO-015

Description: Doubling is moderate on IN GOD WE TRUST, LIBERTY, the date, and the upper hair.
Comments: This is an Accented Hair variety. See FS-50-1964-401.

	PF-63	PF-65	PF-66	PF-67
VARIETY	$20	$25	$50	$85
NORMAL	10	15	40	65

1964, Proof, Normal Hair
FS-50-1964-104

VARIETY: Doubled-Die Obverse
PUP: GOD, TRUST
NEW LISTING

CONECA: DDO-021

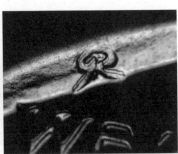

Description: Doubling is evident on IN GOD WE TRUST, the date, the designer's initials, the hair at the back of Kennedy's head, and TY of LIBERTY.
Comments: This is a Normal Hair variety and one of the nicer of the many doubled-die obverses known for the series.

	PF-63	PF-65	PF-66	PF-67
VARIETY	n/a	n/a	n/a	n/a
NORMAL	$10	$15	$40	$65

300

1964, Proof, Normal Hair — FS-50-1964-105

VARIETY: Quadrupled-Die Obverse
PUP: TRUST
NEW LISTING

CONECA: DDO-035

Description: Doubling to quadrupling is evident on WE TRUST, the 4 of the date, RTY of LIBERTY, and the hair on back of the head; very light doubling is visible on the 96 of the date.

Comments: This is the strongest quadrupled die known for the 1964 Proof Kennedy half dollar.

	PF-63	PF-65	PF-66	PF-67
VARIETY	n/a	n/a	n/a	n/a
NORMAL	$10	$15	$40	$65

1964, Proof — FS-50-1964-401

VARIETY: Accented Hair
PUP: Hair, I of LIBERTY
URS-19 · I-5 · L-3

CONECA: ODV-001

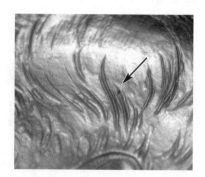

Description: The Accented Hair variety is identifiable by the enhanced hairlines in the central area of the hair, just below the part. However, the easiest way to identify the variety is the weak or broken lower left serif of the I (in LIBERTY).

Comments: Although somewhat common in variety terms, this is a very popular variety.

	PF-65	PF-66	PF-67
VARIETY	$32	$60	$90
NORMAL	15	40	65

1964, Proof, Accented Hair · FS-50-1964-802

VARIETY: Quadrupled-Die Reverse   **CONECA: DDR-003**
PUP: Designer's initials
NEW LISTING

Description: Moderate quadrupling is evident on the stars below UNITED, with a triple spread on almost all lettering and stars around the rim. Very obvious doubling is evident in the designer's initials (FG for Frank Gasparro). Doubling is also evident on the arrows and claws.

Comments: The FG is the most dramatic area of doubling, and the variety may catch on in popularity because of this.

	PF-65	PF-66	PF-67
VARIETY	n/a	n/a	n/a
NORMAL	$15	$40	$65

1964 · FS-50-1964-801

VARIETY: Doubled-Die Reverse   **CONECA: DDR-001**
PUP: UNITED STATES OF AMERICA
URS-4 · I-3 · L-3

Description: Doubling is evident on UNITED STATES OF AMERICA, the rays and stars above E PLURIBUS UNUM, and (slightly) the banner and E PLURIBUS UNUM.

Comments: This is the best of several doubled reverse dies for 1964-(P).

	MS-63	MS-65	MS-66	MS-67
VARIETY	$25	$35	$100	$300
NORMAL	13	15	40	250

1964-D FS-50-1964D-101 (013.4)

VARIETY: Doubled-Die Obverse   **CONECA: DDO-001**
PUP: IN GOD WE TRUST
URS-9 · I-3 · L-3

Description: Doubling is evident on the date, IN GOD WE TRUST, LI and TY (of LIBERTY), and the designer's initials.

Comments: This is a very popular variety. It is extremely rare above MS-65. Note: FS-50-1964D-102 is reserved for future use.

	MS-63	MS-65	MS-66	MS-67
VARIETY	$45	$70	$150	n/a
NORMAL	13	15	40	$400

1964-D FS-50-1964D-103 (013.5)

VARIETY: Tripled-Die Obverse   **CONECA: DDO-003**
PUP: IN GOD WE TRUST
URS-7 · I-4 · L-3

Description: The tripled image is evident on WE TRUST, with strong doubling visible on IN GOD, the L and TY (of LIBERTY), and the date.

Comments: This is well known in grades below MS-65.

	MS-63	MS-65	MS-66	MS-67
VARIETY	$45	$70	$150	n/a
NORMAL	13	15	40	$400

1964-D   FS-50-1964D-104

VARIETY: Doubled-Die Obverse   **CONECA: DDO-004**
PUP: IN GOD
URS-6 · I-2 · L-2

Description: Doubling is evident on IN GOD WE TRUST, but strongest on IN GOD.
Doubling is also evident on letters of LIBERTY and portions of the date.

Comments: All 1964-D halves are very scarce in MS-65 and above.

	MS-63	MS-65	MS-66	MS-67
VARIETY	$30	$55	$100	n/a
NORMAL	13	15	40	$400

1964-D   FS-50-1964D-105 [013.6]

VARIETY: Quadrupled-Die Obverse   **CONECA: DDO-005**
PUP: IN GOD WE TRUST
URS-8 · I-4 · L-3

Description: A quadrupled image is evident on IN GOD WE TRUST, the hair, and
TY (of LIBERTY).

Comments: This is somewhat similar to FS-50-1964D-103. However, the multiple images
on the upper right of U in TRUST are slanted down to the right, whereas
the multiple images on the same area on FS-103 slant straight down.

	MS-63	MS-65	MS-66	MS-67
VARIETY	$35	$70	$150	n/a
NORMAL	13	15	40	$400

1964-D   FS-50-1964D-106

VARIETY: Doubled-Die Obverse   **CONECA: DDO-006**
PUP: WE TRUST
URS-4 · I-2 · L-2

Description: Doubling is evident on WE TRUST and TY (in LIBERTY).

Comments: All 1964-D halves are very scarce in MS-65 and above.
Note: FS-50-1964D-107 is reserved for future use.

	MS-63	MS-65	MS-66	MS-67
VARIETY	$25	$50	$100	n/a
NORMAL	13	15	40	$400

1964-D   FS-50-1964D-108

VARIETY: Doubled-Die Obverse   **CONECA: DDO-008**
PUP: IN GOD WE TRUST
URS-4 · I-2 · L-2

 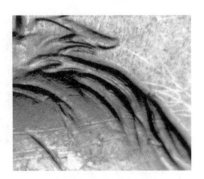

Description: Doubling is evident on IN GOD WE TRUST, the date, and portions of the hair.

Comments: All 1964-D halves are very scarce in MS-65 and above.

	MS-63	MS-65	MS-66	MS-67
VARIETY	$30	$55	$100	n/a
NORMAL	13	15	40	$400

1964-D
FS-50-1964D-501

VARIETY: Repunched Mintmark
PUP: Mintmark
URS-6 · I-4 · L-4

CONECA: RPM-001

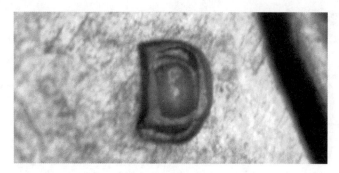

Description: A secondary D mintmark is evident south of the primary D.
Comments: RPMs in the Kennedy series are highly collectible.

	MS-63	MS-65	MS-66	MS-67
VARIETY	$55	$100	$140	n/a
NORMAL	13	15	40	$400

1964-D
FS-50-1964D-502

VARIETY: Repunched Mintmark
PUP: Mintmark
URS-6 · I-4 · L-4

CONECA: RPM-002

Description: A secondary D mintmark is evident north of the primary D.
Comments: This should be slightly more difficult to locate than the preceding.

	MS-63	MS-65	MS-66	MS-67
VARIETY	$45	$65	$125	n/a
NORMAL	13	15	40	$400

1964-D

FS-50-1964D-503

VARIETY: Repunched Mintmark
PUP: Mintmark
URS-7 · I-4 · L-4

CONECA: RPM-003

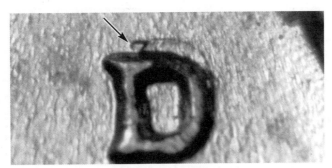

Description: A secondary D mintmark is evident northeast of the primary D.

Comments: This may be the easiest to locate of the three 1964-D RPMs listed.

	MS-63	MS-65	MS-66	MS-67
VARIETY	$45	$65	$125	n/a
NORMAL	13	15	40	$400

1964-D

FS-50-1964D-504

VARIETY: Repunched Mintmark
PUP: Mintmark
NEW LISTING

CONECA: N/L; WEXLER: WRPM-007

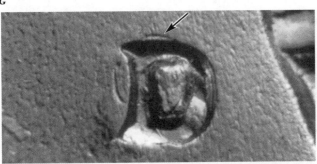

Description: What appears to be a horizontal D can be seen under and to the west of the primary D, along with a D over D north.

Comments: Most specialists consider this a D/Horizontal D West + D/D North; others feel it is a D over diagonal D with the belly of the secondary D showing to the north and west of the primary D. It is a rarity that seldom shows up.

	MS-63	MS-65	MS-66	MS-67
VARIETY	n/a	n/a	n/a	n/a
NORMAL	$13	$15	$40	$400

1965, Special Mint Set FS-50-1965-801

VARIETY: Doubled-Die Reverse
PUP: STATES, DOLLAR
URS-3 · I-3 · L-3

CONECA: DDR-001, DDR-004

Description: Doubling is evident on all outer lettering, all stars, and slightly on E PLURIBUS UNUM.

Comments: This variety is found in the 1965 Special Mint Set.

	SMS-63	SMS-65	SMS-66	SMS-67
VARIETY	n/a	n/a	n/a	n/a
NORMAL	$7	$14	$27	$50

1965 FS-50-1965-802

VARIETY: Doubled-Die Reverse
PUP: Stars
NEW LISTING

CONECA: DDR-004

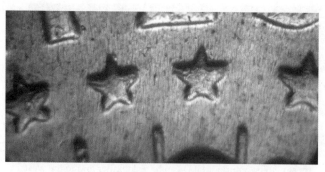

Description: A medium spread exists on the stars in the circle, with the strongest at the top of the coin, the stars above E PLURIBUS UNUM, the stars behind the eagle's head, and the notched lower corners on AMERICA.

Comments: This is one of the strongest doubled-stars varieties.

	MS-63	MS-65	MS-66	MS-67
VARIETY	n/a	n/a	n/a	n/a
NORMAL	$7	$15	$35	$200

1966 — FS-50-1966-101

VARIETY: Doubled-Die Obverse   **CONECA: DDO-005**
PUP: IN GOD WE TRUST
URS-6 · I-4 · L-4

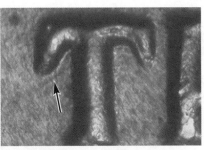

Die marker: scratch from first T of TRUST

Description: Very strong doubling is evident on IN GOD WE TRUST, the date, the designer's initials, and the entire profile. Not all stages of this variety will exhibit the die marker shown.

Comments: This is extremely rare above MS-65.

	MS-63	MS-65	MS-66	MS-67
VARIETY	$25	$35	$45	n/a
NORMAL	7	10	35	$120

1966, Special Mint Set — FS-50-1966-102

VARIETY: Doubled-Die Obverse   **CONECA: DDO-010**
PUP: Profile doubling
URS-4 · I-3 · L-3

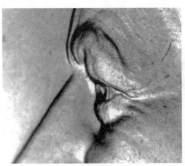

Description: Moderate doubling is evident on IN GOD WE TRUST, the date, the designer's initials, and the eye. Strong doubling shows on the entire profile of Kennedy.

Comments: This variety is extremely rare above MS-65.

	SMS-63	SMS-65	SMS-66	SMS-67
VARIETY	$20	$50	$80	$150
NORMAL	5	8	35	55

1966, Special Mint Set — FS-50-1966-103

VARIETY: Doubled-Die Obverse
PUP: Profile (eye), WE TRUST
URS-8 · I-3 · L-3

CONECA: DDO-013

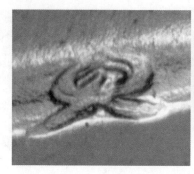

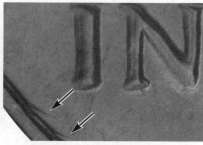

Die marker: gouges next to rim

Description: Strong doubling is evident on the profile, IN GOD WE TRUST, the eye, the hair, and the designer's initials. All stages of this variety exhibit the die marker shown.

Comments: This variety is very similar to the next.

	SMS-63	SMS-65	SMS-66	SMS-67
VARIETY	$35	$85	$125	$200
NORMAL	5	8	35	55

1966, Special Mint Set — FS-50-1966-104

VARIETY: Doubled-Die Obverse
PUP: WE TRUST, date
URS-3 · I-4 · L-4

CONECA: DDO-019

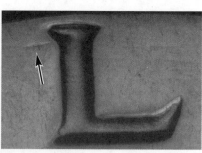

Die marker: gouge near L in LIBERTY

Description: Very strong doubling is evident on IN GOD WE TRUST, the profile, the eye, the hair, and the designer's initials. Additional doubling is evident on the TY of LIBERTY. All stages of this variety exhibit the die marker shown.

Comments: This variety is very similar to the previous.

	SMS-63	SMS-65	SMS-66	SMS-67
VARIETY	$30	$80	$120	$175
NORMAL	5	8	35	55

1966, Special Mint Set
FS-50-1966-105

VARIETY: Doubled-Die Obverse
PUP: Profile, ear
NEW LISTING

CONECA: DDO-007

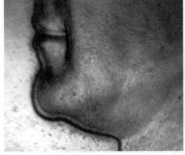
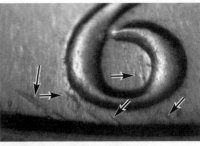

Die marker: gouges at 6

Description: Strong doubling is visible on Kennedy's profile, ear, and eye, the hair above the forehead, and the designer's initials. A light to medium spread is apparent on IN GOD WE TRUST and on portions of LIBERTY and the date. The die marker shown (gouges within and around the first 6 of the date) are visible in the early die states. The reverse is a very minor doubled die not worth listing.

Comments: One of the strongest of the many 1966 doubled dies involving Kennedy's profile.

	SMS-63	SMS-65	SMS-66	SMS-67
VARIETY	n/a	n/a	n/a	n/a
NORMAL	$5	$8	$35	$55

1966, Special Mint Set
FS-50-1966-106

VARIETY: Tripled-Die Obverse
PUP: Profile, ear
NEW LISTING

CONECA: DDO-020

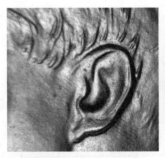

Description: Strong doubling is visible on Kennedy's profile, ear, and eye, and on the designer's initials. Tripling is evident on all of IN GOD WE TRUST. Lesser doubling can be seen on the hair above the forehead and other areas.

Comments: One of the strongest of the many 1966 doubled dies involving Kennedy's profile.

	SMS-63	SMS-65	SMS-66	SMS-67
VARIETY	n/a	n/a	n/a	n/a
NORMAL	$5	$8	$35	$55

1966, Special Mint Set   FS-50-1966-901

VARIETY: Missing Designer's Initials   **CONECA: DDO-002, ADR-001**
PUP: Reverse (between eagle's tail and leg)
URS-7 · I-4 · L-4

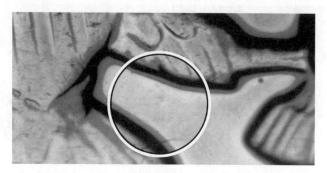

Description: The designer's initials on the reverse are totally missing.

Comments: This variety is very rare and certain to become more popular!

	SMS-63	SMS-65	SMS-66	SMS-67
VARIETY	$45	$125	$400	$500
NORMAL	5	8	35	55

1967, Special Mint Set   FS-50-1967-101

VARIETY: Quintupled-Die Obverse   **CONECA: DDO-006**
PUP: RTY of LIBERTY
URS-5 · I-4 · L-4

Description: A prominent quintupled (at least) spread is evident on RTY of LIBERTY, with strong multiple images on all obverse lettering and portions of the hair.

Comments: This is a very elusive variety!

	SMS-63	SMS-65	SMS-66	SMS-67
VARIETY	$75	$135	$225	n/a
NORMAL	6	9	35	$55

1967
FS-50-1967-102

VARIETY: Doubled-Die Obverse
PUP: WE TRUST
URS-2 · I-3 · L-2

CONECA: DDO-007

Description: Doubling is visible on WE TRUST, on the date, and on portions of the hair under the R of LIBERTY.

Comments: This is a circulation-strike coin.

	MS-63	MS-65	MS-66	MS-67
VARIETY	$15	$25	$75	n/a
NORMAL	7	20	40	$90

1967
FS-50-1967-103

VARIETY: Doubled-Die Obverse
PUP: GOD and LIB of LIBERTY
NEW LISTING

CONECA: DDO-001

Description: Very strong doubling is apparent on IN GOD and LIB of LIBERTY, and on the nostril, forehead, eye, lower lip, and hair. Light doubling is visible on TRUST.

Comments: The doubling on this variety is amazing. It is sure to catch on and be one of the more highly sought-after Kennedy half dollar varieties that are now listed in this guide.

	MS-63	MS-65	MS-66	MS-67
VARIETY	n/a	n/a	n/a	n/a
NORMAL	$7	$20	$40	$90

1967 FS-50-1967-801

VARIETY: Doubled-Die Reverse **CONECA: DDR-001**
PUP: UNITED STATES OF AMERICA, HALF DOLLAR
URS-5 · I-3 · L-2

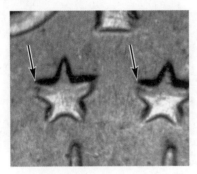 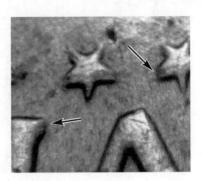

Description: The doubling is evident on all outer reverse lettering, all stars around the rim, and a few rays on the reverse.

Comments: This is one of the stronger DDRs for this date. It is a circulation strike.

	MS-63	MS-65	MS-66	MS-67
VARIETY	$15	$25	$75	n/a
NORMAL	7	20	40	$90

1968-D FS-50-1968D-101

VARIETY: Tripled-Die Obverse **CONECA: DDO-002**
PUP: WE TRUST
URS-3 · I-3 · L-2

Description: A tripled image is visible on IN GOD WE TRUST, the date, and the Y of LIBERTY.

Comments: This is a minor but interesting variety. An early die state will command a premium over values shown. (Note: This variety was incorrectly listed as FS-50-1968D-801 in the fourth edition, volume II.)

	MS-63	MS-65	MS-66	MS-67
VARIETY	$25	$40	$85	n/a
NORMAL	7	20	60	$200

1968-S, Proof · FS-50-1968S-101

VARIETY: Doubled-Die Obverse　　　　　　　　　**CONECA: DDO-002**
PUP: IN GOD WE TRUST
URS-7 · I-4 · L-3

Description: Very strong doubling is evident on all obverse lettering, on the date, and on the designer's initials.

Comments: This is a very popular variety!

	PF-65	PF-66	PF-67
VARIETY	$140	$165	$225
NORMAL	8	10	14

1968-S, Proof · FS-50-1968S-511

VARIETY: Inverted S Mintmark　　　　　　　　　**CONECA: IMM-001**
PUP: Mintmark
URS-6 · I-4 · L-3

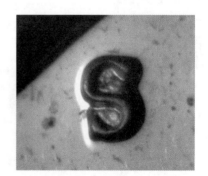

Description: The S mintmark was punched into the die in an inverted orientation.

Comments: This is becoming a highly sought after variety.

	PF-65	PF-66	PF-67
VARIETY	$140	$165	$225
NORMAL	8	10	14

1968-S, Proof
FS-50-1968S-801

VARIETY: Doubled-Die Reverse
PUP: UNITED STATES OF AMERICA
URS-4 · I-3 · L-3

CONECA: DDR-001

Description: Doubling is evident on all lettering around the rim, and some tripled images on OF AMERICA.

Comments: This is a minor but collectible variety.

	PF-65	PF-66	PF-67
VARIETY	$50	$75	$100
NORMAL	8	10	14

1970-S, Proof
FS-50-1970S-101

VARIETY: Doubled-Die Obverse
PUP: WE TRUST
URS-5 · I-3 · L-3

CONECA: DDO-005

Description: Strong doubling is evident on all obverse lettering, especially on WE TRUST.

Comments: Although known for some time, this variety is still very elusive.

	PF-65	PF-66	PF-67
VARIETY	$75	$100	$150
NORMAL	16	23	28

1970-S, Proof
FS-50-1970S-102

VARIETY: Doubled-Die Obverse
PUP: TRUST
NEW LISTING

CONECA: DDO-002

Description: Strong doubling is evident on all obverse lettering and the date; the doubling is strongest on GOD WE TRUST, with tripling on ST of TRUST.

Comments: It's amazing that it took this long for a variety this strong to get discovered and put into the *Cherrypickers' Guide*. Initial reports suggest it is rare.

	PF-65	PF-66	PF-67
VARIETY	n/a	n/a	n/a
NORMAL	$16	$23	$28

1971-D
FS-50-1971D-101

VARIETY: Doubled-Die Obverse
PUP: GOD WE TRUST
URS-6 · I-3 · L-2

CONECA: DDO-004, DDO-002

Description: Very strong doubling is evident on LIBERTY, the 71 of the date, and GOD WE TRUST.

Comments: This variety can be found in Mint sets.

	MS-63	MS-65	MS-66	MS-67
VARIETY	$25.00	$50	n/a	n/a
NORMAL	1.25	10	$18	$50

1971-D

FS-50-1971D-102

VARIETY: Doubled-Die Obverse
PUP: IN GOD WE TRUST
URS-7 · I-3 · L-2

CONECA: DDO-006

Description: Doubling is very evident on IN GOD WE TRUST, the date, and LIBERTY. The lower portions of IN show at least a tripled die.

Comments: As with FS-101 for this date, this can be found in Mint sets.

	MS-63	MS-65	MS-66	MS-67
VARIETY	$25.00	$50	n/a	n/a
NORMAL	1.25	10	$18	$50

1971-S, Proof

FS-50-1971S-101

VARIETY: Doubled-Die Obverse
PUP: TRUST
URS-4 · I-3 · L-2

CONECA: DDO-004

Description: Doubling is most evident on WE TRUST and the last 1 in the date, with lesser doubling on IN GOD and ERTY (of LIBERTY).

Comments: This variety can still be found in Proof sets.

	PF-65	PF-66	PF-67
VARIETY	$35	$50	$90
NORMAL	5	10	15

1971-S, Proof

FS-50-1971S-102

VARIETY: Doubled-Die Obverse
PUP: WE TRUST
URS-6 · I-3 · L-2

CONECA: DDO-006

Description: Doubling is visible on WE TRUST, on the date, and on portions of the hair under the R of LIBERTY.

Comments: This is a strong and very collectible variety.

	PF-65	PF-66	PF-67
VARIETY	$100	$150	$300
NORMAL	5	10	15

1971-S, Proof

FS-50-1971S-103

VARIETY: Doubled-Die Obverse
PUP: TRUST
NEW LISTING

CONECA: DDO-008

Description: Doubling is evident on IN GOD WE TRUST, RTY of LIBERTY, the designer's initials, the hair at back of Kennedy's head, and the date; it is strongest on WE TRUST.

Comments: This is one of several outstanding doubled-die obverses known for this date.

	PF-65	PF-66	PF-67
VARIETY	n/a	n/a	n/a
NORMAL	$5	$10	$15

1971-S, Proof

FS-50-1971S-801

VARIETY: Doubled-Die Reverse
PUP: HALF DOLLAR
URS-4 · I-1 · L-2

CONECA: DDR-001

Description: Doubling is visible on HALF DOLLAR, OF AMERICA, the stars near those letters, the feathers, and the lower arrow shafts.

Comments: (Note: Because of its low Interest Factor, this variety will be removed from this chapter in the next edition of this volume, to make room for more popularly collected pieces. The Fivaz-Stanton number will be retained for this variety and it will remain in the cross-references at the back of the book.)

1972

FS-50-1972-101

VARIETY: Doubled-Die Obverse
PUP: IN GOD WE TRUST
URS-4 · I-3 · L-2

CONECA: DDO-001

Description: The doubling is very evident on IN GOD WE TRUST and the date.

Comments: This variety is very rare above MS-65.

	MS-63	MS-65	MS-66	MS-67
VARIETY	$140	$165	$225	$450
NORMAL	2	15	25	100

1972-D
FS-50-1972D-901

VARIETY: Missing Designer's Initials
PUP: Reverse (between eagle's tail and leg)
URS-2 · I-4 · L-4

CONECA: N/L

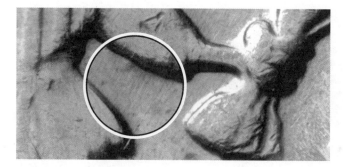

Description: The designer's initials (FG) are totally missing from this stage of the die due to die abrasion.

Comments: This variety is not as well known as others.

	MS-63	MS-65	MS-66	MS-67
VARIETY	$50.00	$75	$150	$250
NORMAL	1.75	8	12	50

1973-D
FS-50-1973D-101 (014.8)

VARIETY: Doubled-Die Obverse
PUP: WE TRUST
URS-6 · I-3 · L-2

CONECA: DDO-001

Description: Doubling is evident on IN GOD WE TRUST, LIBERTY, and the date.

Comments: This is a rare coin, with few found anywhere other than the Kansas City area (where they were released).

	MS-63	MS-65	MS-66	MS-67
VARIETY	$25.00	$50	$75	$150
NORMAL	1.50	10	15	120

1974-D

FS-50-1974D-101 (015)

VARIETY: Doubled-Die Obverse
PUP: WE TRUST
URS-10 · I-3 · L-2

CONECA: DDO-001

Description: Strong doubling is evident on IN GOD WE TRUST, LIBERTY, and the date.

Comments: This variety can still be found in Mint sets. However, most have been searched.

	MS-63	MS-65	MS-66	MS-67
VARIETY	$40.00	$200	$450	n/a
NORMAL	1.50	15	40	$75

1976-S, Unc, 40% Silver

FS-50-1976S-101 (016)

VARIETY: Doubled-Die Obverse
PUP: WE TRUST
URS-4 · I-3 · L-2

CONECA: DDO-001

Description: Doubling is evident on WE TRUST.

Comments: This very rare variety is a 40% silver Uncirculated Mint set coin.

	MS-63	MS-65	MS-66	MS-67
VARIETY	$50	$100	$200	$300
NORMAL	8	10	15	30

1976-S, Clad Proof

FS-50-1976S-801

VARIETY: Doubled-Die Reverse
PUP: Designer's initials
NEW LISTING

CONECA: DDR-001

Description: Strong doubling appears on E PLURIBUS UNUM and the designer's initials; light to moderate doubling appears on INDEPENDENCE and the stars below. Lesser doubling is evident on HALF DOLLAR, AMERICA, and 200 YEARS OF FREEDOM.

Comments: This is an exciting find, as it is the only doubled-die reverse known for the Bicentennial half dollar.

	PF-65	PF-66	PF-67
VARIETY	n/a	n/a	n/a
NORMAL	$5	$10	$13

1977-D

FS-50-1977D-101

VARIETY: Doubled-Die Obverse
PUP: TRUST
NEW LISTING

CONECA: DDO-001

Description: Light to strong doubling is evident on IN GOD WE TRUST, LIBERTY, and the date; it is strongest on TRUST.

Comments: The specimen shown here is in late die state. Earlier die states will show more pronounced doubling.

	MS-63	MS-65	MS-66	MS-67
VARIETY	n/a	n/a	n/a	n/a
NORMAL	$1.50			

1979-S, Proof   FS-50-1979S-501

VARIETY: Type II Mintmark   **CONECA: MMS-003A**
PUP: Mintmark
URS-10 · I-5 · L-5

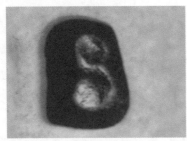

Type I mintmark (common)   Type II mintmark (scarce)

Description: The mintmark style of 1979-S Proof coins was changed during production, creating two different types. Type II (with a well defined S) is rare, and is easily distinguished from the common Type I (with an indistinct blob).

Comments: Complete, *government*-sealed Proof sets with all six coins of Type II command a substantial premium over the six individual coins. (Check the sonically sealed edges for signs of glue or other alterations; this is less commonly seen on 1979-S Type II sets.) Of the six, the half dollar is likely the third most in demand.

	PF-63	PF-65	PF-66	PF-67
VARIETY	$12	$13	$15	$35
NORMAL	11	12	14	30

1981-S, Proof   FS-50-1981S-501

VARIETY: Type II Mintmark   **CONECA: MMS-004**
PUP: Mintmark
URS-10 · I-5 · L-5

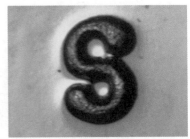

Type I mintmark (common)   Type II mintmark (scarce)

Description: The mintmark style of 1981-S Proof coins was changed during production, creating two different types. Type II is rare, and is not easily distinguished from the common Type I. Type II is flat on the top curve of the S compared to Type I, which has a more rounded top. The surface of the Type II mintmark is frosted, and the openings in the loops are slightly larger.

Comments: Complete government-sealed Proof sets with all six coins of Type II command a substantial premium over the six individual coins.

	PF-63	PF-65	PF-66	PF-67
VARIETY	$13	$18	$20	$30
NORMAL	4	5	10	12

1982 — FS-50-1982-901

Variety: Missing Designer's Initials — **CONECA: ADR-001; Breen-5323**
PUP: Reverse (between eagle's tail and leg)
New Listing

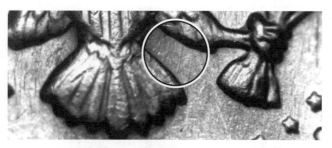

Description: Designer Frank Gasparro's initials, FG, are missing from the reverse due to die
abrasion. The lower serifs of 1 of the date are abraded away on this die. A second
die with missing FG shows some apparent die-clash marks in the area where FG
would normally be, and is listed in CONECA's *The Kennedy Half Dollar Book*, by
James Wiles, as ADR-002. Its date has a normal 1.

Comments: This variety was heavily promoted when it was discovered in the early 1980s.
Another die is known with a missing F of FG. Breen says "at least 50,000 known."

	MS-63	MS-65	MS-66	MS-67
Variety	n/a	n/a	n/a	n/a
Normal	$4.50	$15	$25	$50

1988-S, Proof — FS-50-1988S-101

Variety: Doubled-Die Obverse — **CONECA: DDO-001**
PUP: WE TRUST
URS-3 · I-3 · L-3

Description: Nice doubling is evident on IN GOD WE TRUST, the date, and the
mintmark. Some doubling is also visible on LIBERTY.

Comments: This is one of the most recently discovered doubled dies, with the
mintmark also doubled as a result of the doubled die.

	PF-65	PF-66	PF-67
Variety	n/a	n/a	n/a
Normal	$5	$8	$12

1992-S, Proof, 90% Silver

FS-50-1992S-101

VARIETY: Doubled-Die Obverse
PUP: TRUST
URS-3 · I-3 · L-3

CONECA: DDO-001

Description: Doubling is evident on WE TRUST, RTY of LIBERTY, the 92 of the date, the mintmark, and the designer's initials.

Comments: This variety appears to be rare, with few examples reported since its discovery in the early 1990s.

	PF-65	PF-66	PF-67
VARIETY	n/a	n/a	n/a
NORMAL	$7	$10	$15

THE CHERRYPICKERS' GUIDE HELPFUL HINTS

Check all the coins in your 1960 and 1968 Proof sets. These are known to have nice doubled dies for each denomination, some on the obverse and some on the reverse. For a complete list of known Mint set and Proof set varieties, refer to appendix D.

Liberty Seated Dollars, 1840–1873

Liberty Seated dollars, like all Liberty Seated coinage, are widely collected. Despite the fact that most serious collectors are also astute variety collectors, there is not a definitive reference for varieties within the Liberty Seated dollar series. Nevertheless, longtime members of the Liberty Seated Collectors Club (LSCC) do have access to a tremendous amount of information. LSCC members often publish excellent articles about various Seated dollar varieties in the pages of the club's wonderful newsletter, the *Gobrecht Journal*.

Every few years, the *Gobrecht Journal—Collective Volume* is published by the club and contains all the articles printed in the newsletters since the last compilation. These collective volumes provide excellent reference material on Seated dollars, as well as on the other denominations in the Liberty Seated series. Each new book is offered to members before it is made available to the public. The older volumes are now out of print and are obtainable only through dealers who specialize in used and out-of-print numismatic publications.

We strongly recommend membership in the LSCC, which we believe to be one of the very best specialty clubs in numismatics. As of this writing, the annual dues are $20—a bargain, considering the amount of information available. If you join, you will be connecting with the most serious and knowledgeable collectors and dealers in the hobby. For more information, visit their outstanding web site at www.lsccweb.org, or contact

Leonard Augsburger, Secretary-Treasurer
P.O. Box 6114
Vernon Hills, IL 60061
E-mail: leonard_augsburger@hotmail.com

1865

VARIETY: Doubled-Die Reverse
PUP: U of UNITED
URS-7 · I-3 · L-3

Description: Doubling is evident only on the U of UNITED.

Comments: This is a nice Civil War–era variety.

	F-12	VF-20	EF-40	AU-50
VARIETY	$475	$600	$950	$1,500
NORMAL	375	525	700	1,300

1868

VARIETY: Misplaced Date
PUP: Denticles below date
URS-6 · I-3 · L-3

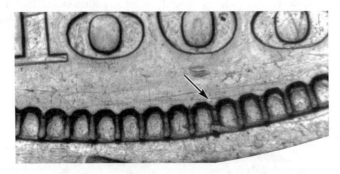

Description: The top portion of an 8 is evident within the denticles below the date.

Comments: This variety can still be located with some searching.

	F-12	VF-20	EF-40	AU-50
VARIETY	$450	$550	$775	$1,250
NORMAL	350	450	650	1,150

1869

VARIETY: Repunched Date
PUP: 1 of date
URS-5 · I-3 · L-3

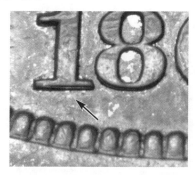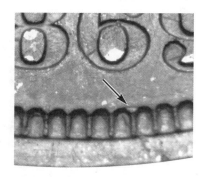

Description: The base of a secondary 1 is visible slightly south of the primary 1. The top of a date digit (likely a 6) is evident protruding from the dentils below the primary 6.

Comments: Other repunched dates for 1869 are also known. In April 2011 a PCGS-graded MS-61 sold at auction for $4,025.

	F-12	VF-20	EF-40	AU-50
VARIETY	$425	$500	$675	$1,100
NORMAL	325	400	500	1,000

1869

VARIETY: Repunched Date
PUP: Between 1 and 8 of date
URS-5 · I-3 · L-3

Description: The top flag of a secondary 1 is evident midway between the primary 1 and the 8.

Comments: Other repunched dates for 1869 are also known.

	F-12	VF-20	EF-40	AU-50
VARIETY	$400	$550	$775	$1,200
NORMAL	325	400	500	1,000

1871

VARIETY: Misplaced Date
PUP: Denticles below 8
URS-5 · I-3 · L-3

Description: The top of a digit (probably an 8) is evident protruding from the denticles below the 8 of the date.

Comments: Other misplaced dates between 1865 and 1873 do exist.

	F-12	VF-20	EF-40	AU-50
VARIETY	$375	$425	$550	$1,100
NORMAL	325	375	500	1,000

THE CHERRYPICKERS' GUIDE **HELPFUL HINTS**

Strike doubling can often be confused with the more valuable die doubling, such as a doubled die or repunched mintmark. To help ensure you know the difference, take time to read, read, and re-read appendix A.

Trade Dollars, 1873–1885

Trade dollars are not widely collected by variety enthusiasts—at least not yet. The coins are relatively expensive for most dates; therefore, few enthusiasts can afford to collect all the varieties. Assembling a complete set can be a daunting task, even with unlimited funds. Nevertheless, significant varieties are known and can be found with some searching. Both minor and major doubled dies, and even over mintmarks, are available. There are also two different design types known for both the obverse and the reverse, as well as various pairings of these two types.

The varieties listed in this edition of the *Cherrypickers' Guide* illustrate most of the known varieties. Breen lists a few varieties, but the best overall reference for the series is *Silver Dollars and Trade Dollars of the United States: A Complete Encyclopedia,* by Q. David Bowers.

Trade dollars are a particular area of study for members of the Liberty Seated Collectors Club (LSCC), which issues its official publication, the *Gobrecht Journal,* three times each year. This newsletter is loaded with excellent educational articles and some of the best photography in the field. We strongly recommend membership in the LSCC, which we believe to be one of the very best specialty clubs in numismatics. As of this writing, the annual dues are $20—a bargain, considering the amount of information available. If you join, you will be connecting with the most serious and knowledgeable collectors and dealers in the hobby. For more information, visit their outstanding web site at www.lsccweb.org, or contact

Leonard Augsburger, Secretary-Treasurer
P.O. Box 6114
Vernon Hills, IL 60061
E-mail: leonard_augsburger@hotmail.com

TWO DIFFERENT DISTINCT OBVERSE AND REVERSE HUBS

There are two different hubs known for both the obverse and reverse of trade dollars. The differences, although somewhat subtle, are relatively easy to distinguish.

Variety	Identifying Characteristics
Type I Obv	LIBERTY ribbon tips point to the left. Hand holding olive branch has three fingers.
Type II Obv	LIBERTY ribbon tips point down. Hand holding olive branch has four fingers.
Type I Rev	Berry visible underneath eagle's sinister claw.
Type II Rev	No berry underneath eagle's sinister claw.

Varying Type I and Type II obverse and reverse marriages are known, with some combinations considerably rarer than others. Type I obverses were used on trade dollars from 1873 to 1876; Type II obverses were used on coins dated 1876 to 1885. Type I reverses were used on coins from 1873 to 1876; Type II reverses were used on coins dated 1875 to 1885. Several assessments of these Type I and Type II combinations have been done and can be found in editions of the *Gobrecht Journal*.

Type I obverse
Hand has three fingers;
scroll points left.

Type II obverse
Hand has four fingers;
scroll points downward.

Type I reverse
Arrowheads end over 0;
berry under eagle's left talon.

Type II reverse
Arrowheads end over 2;
no berry under talon.

1873-CC

FS-T1-1873CC-301

VARIETY: Misplaced Date
PUP: Denticles below date
URS-6 · I-3 · L-3

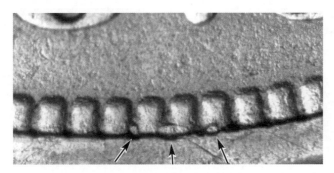

Description: The top portion of a 7 is evident protruding from the denticles below the date, centered between the 8 and 7.

Comments: This variety is very prominent.

	F-12	VF-20	EF-40	AU-50	MS-60
VARIETY	$350	$425	$650	$1,500	$10,000
NORMAL	350	425	650	1,500	10,000

1875-S, S Over CC

FS-T1-1875S-501 (012.5)

CONECA: OMM-001

VARIETY: Over Mintmark
PUP: Mintmark
URS-8 · I-3 · L-3

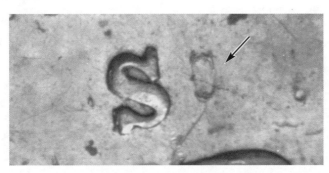

Description: The S mintmark is evident over a previously punched CC mintmark. The weak C from the underlying mintmark is evident right of the S.

Comments: This is one of the more popular varieties in the series.

	F-12	VF-20	EF-40	AU-50	MS-60
VARIETY	$425	$650	$850	$1,200	$1,800
NORMAL	150	175	225	300	1,050

1875-S, S Over CC　　　　　　　　　　FS-T1-1875S-502

VARIETY: Over Mintmark
PUP: Mintmark
URS-5 · I-5 · L-4

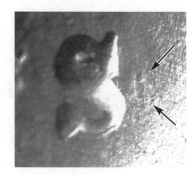

Description: The S mintmark is evident over a previously punched CC mintmark. The C is very weak, but visible, right of the S.

Comments: This variety is slight, but significantly different from the previous listing.

	F-12	VF-20	EF-40	AU-50	MS-60
VARIETY	$425	$675	$950	$1,800	$4,675
NORMAL	150	175	225	300	1,050

1876-CC　　　　　　　　　　FS-T1-1876CC-801 (014)

VARIETY: Doubled-Die Reverse
PUP: Right branch, E PLURIBUS UNUM
URS-7 · I-4 · L-4

Description: Doubling is evident on the branches on the right, the eagle's talons, the right wing tip, and the eagle's beak, and is very strong on E PLURIBUS UNUM. Weaker doubling can be detected on UNITED STATES OF AMERICA.

Comments: Considered by most to be the strongest reverse doubled die in the series, this variety is one of the highlights of the trade dollar varieties and is thought to be extremely rare in grades above AU. Counterfeits are common; beware.

	F-12	VF-20	EF-40	AU-50	MS-60
VARIETY	$350	$475	$850	$1,750	$7,750
NORMAL	275	400	600	1,200	$7,500

1876-S   FS-T1-1876S-101 (013)

VARIETY: Doubled-Die Obverse
PUP: Liberty's hand and foot
URS-4 · I-4 · L-4

 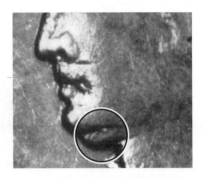

Description: Doubling is evident on Liberty's hand, chin, and left foot, and on the olive branch.

Comments: This DDO is easily the rarest doubled die in the series, and is considered extremely rare in grades above AU. Most known examples are cleaned. The variety is known as the king of the trade dollar varieties. Fewer than a dozen are known.

	F-12	VF-20	EF-40	AU-50	MS-60
VARIETY	$650	$850	$1,400	$1,750	$2,200
NORMAL	150	170	200	300	1,075

1876-S   FS-T1-1876S-301

VARIETY: Repunched Date
PUP: 6 of date
URS-7 · I-2 · L-3

Description: The lower loop of a secondary 6 is evident within the loop of the primary 6.

Comments: Surface doubling is also evident on the lower left of the 8 and the top of the 7.

	F-12	VF-20	EF-40	AU-50	MS-60
VARIETY	$175	$200	$250	$350	$1,150
NORMAL	150	170	200	300	1,075

1877
FS-T1-1877-101

VARIETY: Doubled-Die Obverse
PUP: LIBERTY, wheat stalks
URS-5 · I-3 · L-3

Description: The doubling is visible on the wheat stalks, LIBERTY, IN GOD WE TRUST, and stars 11, 12, and 13.

Comments: This is still considered a rare variety.

	F-12	VF-20	EF-40	AU-50	MS-60
VARIETY	$185	$225	$300	$400	$1,250
NORMAL	150	170	190	300	1,100

1877-S
FS-T1-1877S-301

VARIETY: Repunched Date
PUP: 7 of date
URS-6 · I-3 · L-3

Description: A secondary 7 is evident protruding south from the last 7.

Comments: This variety is probably the most prominent RPD in the series.

	F-12	VF-20	EF-40	AU-50	MS-60
VARIETY	$180	$200	$240	$365	$1,275
NORMAL	150	170	190	300	1,075

1877-S
FS-T1-1877S-801 (014.5)

Variety: Doubled-Die Reverse
PUP: E PLURIBUS UNUM, UNITED STATES OF AMERICA
URS-5 · I-4 · L-4

Description: Doubling is evident on E PLURIBUS UNUM, on UNITED STATES OF AMERICA, and on the ribbon.

Comments: Considered a highlight of the trade dollar varieties, this is another very rare variety.

	F-12	VF-20	EF-40	AU-50	MS-60
Variety	$225	$325	$500	$700	$1,600
Normal	150	170	190	300	1,075

1877-S
FS-T1-1877S-802

Variety: Doubled-Die Reverse
PUP: 420, TRADE
URS-8 · I-3 · L-3

Description: Minor doubling is evident on virtually all reverse lettering, especially on 420 GRAINS.

Comments: This is one of the more common trade dollar varieties.

	F-12	VF-20	EF-40	AU-50	MS-60
Variety	$180	$225	$275	$375	$1,200
Normal	150	170	190	300	1,075

1878-S   FS-T1-1878S-801 (015)

VARIETY: Doubled-Die Reverse
PUP: Arrows, 420
URS-7 · I-4 · L-3

Description: Strong doubling is evident on the entire lower left side, on the arrow points and shafts, on 420 GRAINS, and slightly on the motto.

Comments: This variety is very difficult to find in AU and above.

	F-12	VF-20	EF-40	AU-50	MS-60
VARIETY	$180	$210	$230	$360	$1,300
NORMAL	150	170	190	300	1,100

1878-S   FS-T1-1878S-802

VARIETY: Doubled-Die Reverse
PUP: UNITED, E PLURIBUS UNUM
URS-4 · I-3 · L-2

Description: Doubling with a close spread is evident on UNITED STATES, on E PLURIBUS UNUM, and on the ribbon.

Comments: The doubling is somewhat minor, but very interesting.

	F-12	VF-20	EF-40	AU-50	MS-60
VARIETY	$180	$210	$230	$360	$1,300
NORMAL	150	170	190	300	1,100

Morgan Dollars, 1878–1921

In the world of variety collecting, no other series will touch the popularity of Morgan silver dollars. Both the Morgan and Peace dollar varieties are known as VAMs, an acronym derived from the first letters of the last names of Leroy Van Allen and George Mallis, the two gentlemen who popularized collecting silver dollar die varieties.

VAMs are collected by thousands of enthusiasts. Often, a silver dollar valued at less than $40 could in fact be worth several thousand dollars because of some relatively minor, yet very rare, abnormality. A variation might be a die chip, an image from one side lightly visible on the other, a doubled or tripled die, a repunched mintmark or date, or even a slight die gouge. There are even some dramatic overdates. In recent editions we have expanded this section of the *Cherrypickers' Guide* to give collectors more information about this specialized category of variety collecting.

In addition, in the Morgan dollar and Peace dollar sections we have included the most recent condition census (as of this writing) for each listing. These notations give the known grades of the top examples of the variety and help to emphasize its rarity. Having this information helps the collector find those examples that are true rarities.

For those interested in learning more about the varieties of Morgan dollars, we highly recommend membership in the Society of Silver Dollar Collectors (SSDC). At the time of publication, membership was $21.95 per year. The club has a web site at www.vamlink.com, or you may write to

SSDC
c/o Mike Andrew
680 Grackle Drive
Casselberry, FL 32707

1878, 8 Tail Feathers — FS-S1-1878-005

VARIETY: Doubled-Die Obverse   **VAM-5**
PUP: RIB of PLURIBUS
URS-5 · I-4 · L-4

Description: Doubling is visible on much of the obverse lettering, but is most evident on E PLURIBUS UNUM.

Comments: The reverse, which is designated an "A^1c", is shared with eight other 8TF varieties. All but two are quite rare.

Census: 65, 64, 64, 64, 64, 64, 64, 64

	VF-20	EF-40	AU-50	MS-60	MS-63	MS-65
VARIETY	$65	$100	$150	$385	$775	$7,500
NORMAL	40	45	75	150	190	1,450

1878, 8 Tail Feathers — FS-S1-1878-009

VARIETY: First Die Pair   **VAM-9**
PUP: Engraved left wing feather
URS-5 · I-4 · L-4

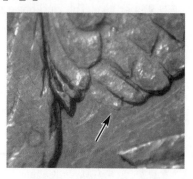 

Description: An additional feather in the shape of a kidney bean is evident under the eagle's left wing (viewer's right).

Comments: The obverse and reverse dies of this variety are known to be the first pair of dies used to strike Morgan dollars on March 11, 1878. This is an important 8TF rarity!

Census: 64PL, 64, 64, 63, 63, 63, 62, 62

	VF-20	EF-40	AU-50	MS-60	MS-63	MS-65
VARIETY	$300	$475	$925	$3,250	$8,500	n/a
NORMAL	40	45	75	150	190	$1,450

1878, 8 Tail Feathers · FS-S1-1878-014.11

VARIETY: Obverse Die Gouge
PUP: Liberty's eye
URS-7 · I-5 · L-5

VAM-14.11
"DOUBLED EYELID" VARIETY

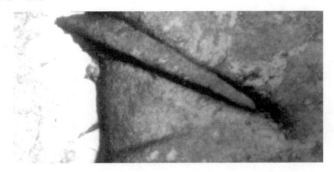

Description: Two spikes are visible protruding from the front of Liberty's eye.

Comments: Like VAM-5, this major rarity (sometimes called the "Wild Eye" variety) has the "A^1c" reverse. Fifteen to 20 specimens are known of this Top 100 variety and any sale is a landmark event.

Census: 67, 65, 65, 64, 63, 63, 63, 63

	VF-20	EF-40	AU-50	MS-60	MS-63	MS-65
VARIETY	$3,250	$4,750	$8,000	$13,000	$24,000	n/a
NORMAL	40	45	75	150	190	$1,450

1878, 8 Tail Feathers · FS-S1-1878-015

VARIETY: Doubled-Die Obverse, Doubled-Die Reverse
PUP: LIBERTY, eye, date
URS-6 · I-5 · L-4

VAM-15

Description: Strong doubling is evident on LIBERTY. A spike is visible in front of the eye and there is metal die fill in the loops of the first 8.

Comments: There are other doubled LIBERTY 8TF varieties, but only this one has this particular configuration of engraved feathers on the reverse under the eagle's wings. Refer to the VAM book for additional diagnostics.

Census: 65DM, 65DM, 64DM, 64DM, 64DM, 64PL, 64PL, 64PL

	VF-20	EF-40	AU-50	MS-60	MS-63	MS-65
VARIETY	$150	$260	$375	$775	$1,300	n/a
NORMAL	40	45	75	150	190	$1,450

1878, 7 Over 8 Tail Feathers — FS-S1-1878-032

VARIETY: 7 Over 3 Tail Feathers **VAM-32**
PUP: Tail feathers
URS-8 · I-5 · L-4

Description: Three extra tail feather tips protrude from under the seven tail feathers of the primary design. There is also a small die scratch in the field to the right of the cotton bolls and leaf on the obverse.

Comments: This is the second rarest of the 7 Over 8TF varieties and commands a significant premium.

Census: 64DM, 64DM, 64DM, 64DM, 64DM, 64DM, 64DM, 64DM

	VF-20	EF-40	AU-50	MS-60	MS-63	MS-65
VARIETY	$115	$275	$500	$850	n/a	n/a
NORMAL	33	45	80	150	$290	$2,200

1878, 7 Over 8 Tail Feathers — FS-S1-1878-044 (001)

VARIETY: Tripled-Die Obverse, Doubled-Die Reverse **VAM-44**
PUP: Tripled leaves, LIBERTY, cotton bolls, tail feathers *"KING OF VAMs" VARIETY*
URS-7 · I-5 · L-5

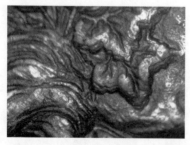
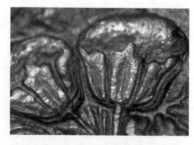

Description: This variety shows three to five weak tail feathers under the seven primary tail feathers. The obverse exhibits a tripled image on the cotton bolls and the leaves, and doubling on LIBERTY.

Comments: Known as the King of VAMs, this variety is considered the top VAM and carries a premium commensurate with the title. There are fewer than a dozen Mint State specimens known. The same reverse die was used on VAM-33, which is the most common of the 7 Over 8TF varieties.

Census: 63PL, 63, 62PL, 62PL, 62, 62, 62, 61PL

	VF-20	EF-40	AU-50	MS-60	MS-63	MS-65
VARIETY	$2,250	$3,850	$5,900	$12,000	$23,000	n/a
NORMAL	33	45	80	150	290	$2,200

1878, 7 Tail Feathers

VARIETY: Tripled-Die Obverse, Doubled-Die Reverse   **VAM-115**
PUP: Cotton bolls
URS-7 · I-4 · L-4

Description: Tripling is evident on the right edges of the cotton bolls in Liberty's bonnet.

Comments: Note that there are two different reverses with this obverse: VAM-115 and VAM-198. Both are equally rare and valuable. VAM-115 shows design detail where the eagle's right wing (viewer's left) joins the body, whereas the VAM-198 does not. VAM-115 and VAM-198 are both ultra-rare in all Mint State grades.

Census: 64, 64, 63, 62, 62, 62, 62, 62

	VF-20	EF-40	AU-50	MS-60	MS-63	MS-65
VARIETY	$75	$125	$215	$575	n/a	n/a
NORMAL	32	38	55	80	$125	$1,200

1878, 7 Tail Feathers

VARIETY: Broken Letters Obverse   **VAM-145**
PUP: UNUM, TRUST
URS-8 · I-4 · L-4

Description: The lower right serifs of the N (not shown) and the lower right serifs of the M of UNUM are broken.

Comments: This is actually a doubled-die obverse. The U and R of PLURIBUS and stars 3 and 5 are hub doubled; the 1 and 7 of the date are repunched right. On the reverse, the upper O of GOD is broken. The R of TRUST is *not* broken on VAM-145, but is on VAM-166 (also included in this guide). VAM-145 and VAM-166 are very scarce in Mint State.

Census: 65, 64, 64, 64, 64, 63, 63, 63

	VF-20	EF-40	AU-50	MS-60	MS-63	MS-65
VARIETY	$38	$45	$65	$100	$190	n/a
NORMAL	32	38	55	80	125	$1,200

1878, 7 Tail Feathers   FS-S1-1878-162

VARIETY: Broken Letters   **VAM-162**
PUP: M of UNUM
URS-7 · I-4 · L-4

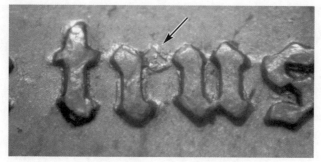

Description: The bottom serifs of the N and M in UNUM are broken off.

Comments: This and the preceding listing have the same obverse, but a different reverse. Here the arm of the R in TRUST on the reverse motto is broken, whereas this is not the case with VAM-145. VAM-162 is very scarce in Mint State.

Census: 63, 62, 62, 62, 62, 62, 62, 62

	VF-20	EF-40	AU-50	MS-60	MS-63	MS-65
VARIETY	$40	$50	$90	$165	$365	n/a
NORMAL	32	38	55	80	125	$1,200

1878, 7 Tail Feathers   FS-S1-1878-166

VARIETY: Tripled Eye   **VAM-166**
PUP: Liberty's eye   *"SPIKES" VARIETY*
URS-5 · I-4 · L-4

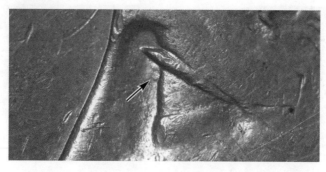

Description: The front of Liberty's eye shows two tiny spikes under the eyelid.

Comments: This VAM is one of the sleepers of the 1878 7TF set, and is missing from the collections of most VAM specialists. It is included here, not for its dramatic features, but for its rarity. This one is worth finding!

Census: 64, 63, 61, 50, 45, 45, 45, 45

	VF-20	EF-40	AU-50	MS-60	MS-63	MS-65
VARIETY	$650	$1,250	n/a	n/a	n/a	n/a
NORMAL	32	38	$55	$80	$125	$1,200

1878, 7 Tail Feathers — FS-S1-1878-168

VARIETY: Doubled-Die Obverse, Doubled-Die Reverse **VAM-168**
PUP: Liberty's eye
URS-4 · I-4 · L-3

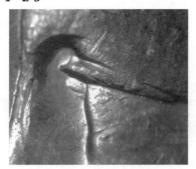 

Description: A doubled spike is evident in front of Liberty's eye, just below the eyelid. The P in PLURIBUS is doubled above the serifs on its base and at the top.

Comments: No Mint State specimens have been confirmed to date. This VAM is a desirable variety sought by many collectors. The finest known, an AU-58, sold on January 7, 2011, for $1,153.

Census: 58, 58, 58, 55, 55, 53, 53, 53

	VF-20	EF-40	AU-50	MS-60	MS-63	MS-65
VARIETY	$70	$125	$300	n/a	n/a	n/a
NORMAL	32	38	55	$80	$125	$1,200

1878, 7 Tail Feathers — FS-S1-1878-188

VARIETY: Weak L in LIBERTY **VAM-188**
PUP: L in LIBERTY
URS-4 · I-4 · L-4

Description: The L in LIBERTY is over-polished. The front leaf atop Liberty's headband is shortened. On the reverse, the arm of the R in TRUST is broken.

Comments: The rarity of this VAM is under-appreciated. Now is the time to acquire one grading EF or above!

Census: 63, 62, 62, 58, 58, 58, 55, 55

	VF-20	EF-40	AU-50	MS-60	MS-63	MS-65
VARIETY	$150	$325	$650	n/a	n/a	n/a
NORMAL	32	38	55	$80	$125	$1,200

1878-CC
FS-S1-1878CC-006

VARIETY: Doubled-Die Obverse, Wide CC
PUP: Obverse leaves, widely spaced CC
URS-6 · I-4 · L-4

VAM-6

Description: Very strong doubling is evident on the leaves in Liberty's headdress and strong doubling on Liberty's ear. The date shows dramatic doubling to the right. The CC mintmark is level and widely spaced.

Comments: The VAM-6 mintmark is important, because the right C of the CC is widely spaced and actually touches the bottom of the wreath. There are only two such cases in the entire Morgan dollar series. Both are very scarce and desirable.

Census: 64, 64, 64, 64, 64, 64, 64, 64

	VF-20	EF-40	AU-50	MS-60	MS-63	MS-65
VARIETY	$115	$165	$185	$300	$675	n/a
NORMAL	95	140	155	225	325	$1,650

1878-CC
FS-S1-1878CC-018

VARIETY: Doubled-Die Obverse, Narrow CC
PUP: Obverse leaves, closely spaced CC
URS-7 · I-4 · L-5

VAM-18

 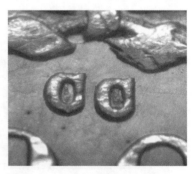

Description: Strong doubling is evident on the leaves, on Liberty's ear, and on the date. The reverse shows an uneven and closely spaced CC.

Comments: This variety has the same obverse as VAM-6, but the reverse is different. Although both are highly prized, VAM-18 is even rarer than VAM-6. VAM-18 specimens often resemble Proofs.

Census: 64PL, 62PL, 63PL, 63PL, 63PL, 62PL, 62, 61PL

	VF-20	EF-40	AU-50	MS-60	MS-63	MS-65
VARIETY	$175	$375	$700	$1,500	$2,500	n/a
NORMAL	95	140	155	225	325	$1,650

1878-S

FS-S1-1878S-050

VARIETY: Tripled-Die Obverse
PUP: Liberty's eye, junction of wing and body
URS-7 · I-3 · L-3

VAM-50
"TRIPLED EYELID" VARIETY

Description: Two spikes are evident in front of Liberty's eye, below the eyelid. The junction of the eagle's right wing (viewer's left) and the eagle's body shows areas suggesting that molten metal had been poured onto the struck coin.

Comments: This VAM is extremely interesting, but is not listed in either the Top 100 or Hot 50 books. Also interesting is that there was a second reverse die used with this same obverse.

Census: 64, 63, 63, 63, 63, 63, 63, 62

	VF-20	EF-40	AU-50	MS-60	MS-63	MS-65
VARIETY	$90	$185	$250	$475	$1,450	n/a
NORMAL	33	38	50	60	70	$250

1879-O

FS-S1-1879o-004

VARIETY: Repunched Mintmark
PUP: Mintmark, date
URS-7 · I-4 · L-3

VAM-4

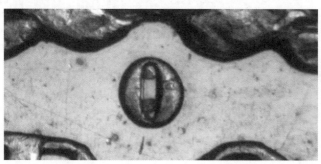

Description: An O is evident far north, and another far south, of the primary O.

Comments: Long considered an O Over Horizontal O, we feel this VAM is actually an O/O/O. Two different obverses are known paired with this reverse. Both are desirable Top 100 varieties. (See the VAM-28 listing for differences.)

Census: 63, 63, 63, 63, 63, 63, 63, 63

	VF-20	EF-40	AU-50	MS-60	MS-63	MS-65
VARIETY	$60	$80	$130	$335	$750	n/a
NORMAL	33	38	42	90	190	$3,000

1879-O FS-S1-1879o-028

VARIETY: Repunched Mintmark **VAM-28**
PUP: Mintmark
URS-7 · I-5 · L-4

Description: Doubling is visible on the 9 in the date.

Comments: VAM-28 has the same reverse as the previously listed VAM-4 (O/O/O), but is paired with a different obverse die. On VAM-4, the left side of the 9 is not doubled and there is no doubling on the 7. On VAM-28, however, the right side of the 7 is doubled and there is doubling on the upper left loop of the 9. Unlike VAM-4, only a few Mint State VAM-28 specimens have been reported. These specimens are in great demand.

Census: 64, 63, 62, 62, 58, 58, 58, 58

	VF-20	EF-40	AU-50	MS-60	MS-63	MS-65
VARIETY	$625	$1,175	$1,750	n/a	n/a	n/a
NORMAL	33	38	42	$90	$190	$3,000

THE CHERRYPICKERS' GUIDE **HELPFUL HINTS**

Keep in mind that as the numismatic value of a coin increases, the premiums attached to its varieties tend to decrease. A doubled die on a 1901-S Barber quarter would add no significant value to the coin because of the already high numismatic value, and very few dies were used to produce that date. Another so-called white elephant would be an RPM on a Mint State 1936-D Washington quarter.

1879-S, Second Reverse

FS-S1-1879S-901

VARIETY: B Reverse (Type of 1878)
PUP: Top arrow feather, eagle's breast
URS-10 · I-4 · L-4

VAM: SEVERAL

B reverse: flat breast, parallel feather

C reverse: rounded breast, slanted feather

Description: The Type B reverse shows the top arrow feather parallel to the arrow shaft, and the eagle's breast flat or concave. The C reverse exhibits slanted arrow feathers, and a more convex breast on the eagle.

Comments: This variety is highly collectible, even by non-variety specialists. At present there are 17 different die pairs that together represent the 1879-S Flat Breast (B-reverse) varieties.

Census: 66PL, 66, 66, 66, 66, 66, 66, 66

	VF-20	EF-40	AU-50	MS-60	MS-63	MS-65
VARIETY	$40	$50	$65	$130	$475	$5,500
NORMAL	32	35	38	50	65	175

349

1880   FS-S1-1880-006 (003)

VARIETY: Overdate   **VAM-6**
PUP: Second 8 of the date   *"SPIKES" VARIETY*
URS-7 · I-4 · L-3

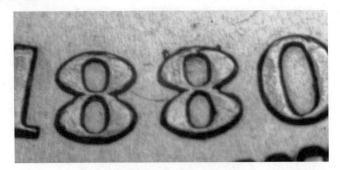

Description: Spikes can be seen above the second 8 in the date. The incomplete crossbar inside the 8 denotes the remains of the 7 in the underlying date.

Comments: VAM-6 is one of the easiest 1880 overdates to detect. It is available in circulated grades, but is sometimes difficult to find in Mint State condition.

Census: 64, 64, 64, 63, 62, 62, 62, 62

	VF-20	EF-40	AU-50	MS-60	MS-63	MS-65
VARIETY	$75	$145	$300	$750	n/a	n/a
NORMAL	32	35	38	50	$65	$750

1880   FS-S1-1880-007 (004)

VARIETY: Overdate   **VAM-7**
PUP: Second 8 of date   *"CROSSBAR" VARIETY*
URS-6 · I-5 · L-4

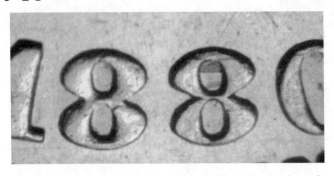

Description: The clear remains of an underlying 7 are visible as a recessed crossbar inside the second 8 at the top.

Comments: This VAM is very rare in AU and unknown in any Uncirculated grade. A PCGS AU-58 sold on January 7, 2011, for $2,760.

Census: 63, 58, 58, 58, 58, 58, 58, 58

	VF-20	EF-40	AU-50	MS-60	MS-63	MS-65
VARIETY	$175	$300	$1,050	n/a	n/a	n/a
NORMAL	32	35	38	$50	$65	$750

1880

VARIETY: Overdate
PUP: Second 8 of date
URS-6 · I-5 · L-4

VAM-8
"EARS" VARIETY

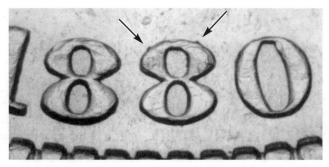

Description: The remains of an underlying date are visible as small bumps on the top right side of the second 8.

Comments: In general, VAM-8 may be going unnoticed because of its less-than-dramatic variety feature. As a key part of the 1880-(P) overdate set, however, this variety is in tremendous demand.

Census: 62, 58, 58, 58, 58, 58, 58, 58

	VF-20	EF-40	AU-50	MS-60	MS-63	MS-65
VARIETY	$750	$1,500	$3,000	n/a	n/a	n/a
NORMAL	32	35	38	$50	$65	$750

1880, 80 Over 79

VARIETY: Overdate
PUP: Last 8 and 0 of the date
URS-7 · I-4 · L-4

VAM-23

Description: An underlying 79 is visible on the *surface* of the last 8 and 0. The 8 has a small ear of metal at the top left surface, and the 0 has metal remnants on the surface at 8 o'clock and 9 o'clock.

Comments: In the previous edition, only one Mint State specimen had been reported to date, making high-grade AU examples highly desirable. Since that time, numerous Mint State examples have come to light.

Census: 62, 62, 62, 61, 61, 61, 61, 60

	VF-20	EF-40	AU-50	MS-60	MS-63	MS-65
VARIETY	$200	$500	$850	n/a	n/a	n/a
NORMAL	32	35	38	$50	$65	$750

1880-CC, 80 Over 79, Second Reverse · FS-S1-1880CC-004

VARIETY: Overdate · **VAM-4**
PUP: 80 of the date, Flat Breast reverse
URS-7 · I-5 · L-5

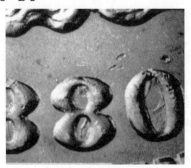

Description: The top crossbar and diagonal stem of an underlying 79 are clearly visible within the 8. Extensive polishing marks are evident within the 0.

Comments: To add further excitement, the reverse is a B-reverse, Flat Breast leftover from 1878! VAM-4 can be obtained in grades up through MS-66; nevertheless, it enjoys tremendous popularity at a time when all CC dollars remain the darlings of numismatics.

Census: 66, 66, 66, 66, 66, 66, 66, 65DM

	VF-20	EF-40	AU-50	MS-60	MS-63	MS-65
VARIETY	$250	$290	$335	$550	$625	$2,150
NORMAL	210	250	300	460	515	1,100

1880-CC, 8 Over High 7, Third Reverse · FS-S1-1880CC-005 (005.2)

VARIETY: Overdate · **VAM-5**
PUP: Last 8 of the date
URS-7 · I-5 · L-5

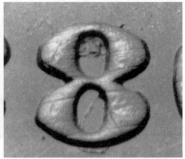

Description: An almost complete 7 can be seen inside the last 8 of the date. The top edge of the 7 touches the top inside of the 8.

Comments: The clear overdate markings are icing on the cake in the current runaway bull market for Carson City dollars!

Census: 67, 67, 66DM, 66, 66, 66, 66, 66

	VF-20	EF-40	AU-50	MS-60	MS-63	MS-65
VARIETY	$235	$300	$350	$525	$600	$1,250
NORMAL	210	250	300	460	515	1,100

1880-CC, 8 Over Low 7, Third Reverse   FS-S1-1880CC-006

VARIETY: Overdate   **VAM-6**
PUP: Last 8 of the date
URS-7 · I-5 · L-5

Description: A complete 7 is evident inside the last 8 of the date. The crossbar of
the underlying 7 is visible in the top loop and the diagonal of the 7
is visible in the lower loop.

Comments: The remnants of the underlying 7 on VAM-5 are set higher than on
VAM-6. There is little or no controversy regarding claims that VAM-6
is an overdate. If you are seeking a clear Morgan dollar overdate, this
may be the one for you!

Census: 66, 66, 66, 66, 66, 65PL, 65PL, 65

	VF-20	EF-40	AU-50	MS-60	MS-63	MS-65
VARIETY	$240	$325	$375	$575	$640	$1,275
NORMAL	210	250	300	460	515	1,100

1880-CC, 8 Over 7, Second Reverse   FS-S1-1880CC-007

VARIETY: Overdate   **VAM-7**
PUP: Dash under last 8, Flat Breast reverse
URS-7 · I-4 · L-5

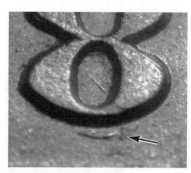

Description: This 1880-CC specimen has a Flat Breast reverse, no overdate markings, and a dash
under the last 8.

Comments: VAM-7 is one of only two 1880-CC varieties that have a Flat Breast (B) reverse. All the
known 1880 dies used at the Carson City branch mint were overdates. Hence VAM-7,
which shows no decisive markings within the last 8, is still considered an overdate.

Census: 66, 65, 65, 65, 65, 65, 65, 65

	VF-20	EF-40	AU-50	MS-60	MS-63	MS-65
VARIETY	$250	$335	$400	$650	$850	$2,075
NORMAL	210	250	300	460	515	1,100

1880-O FS-S1-1880o-004

VARIETY: Overdate **VAM-4**
PUP: Ears above 8, metal within upper loop of second 8
URS-8 · I-4 · L-4

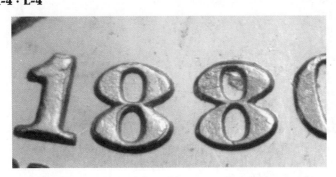

Description: Excess metal representing the crossbar of an underlying 7 is evident within the upper loop. The 1 and the first 8 are slightly doubled to the right.

Comments: The variety also has a micro-O mintmark, which has no effect on its value.

Census: 64DM, 64DM, 64DM, 64DM, 64DM, 64DM, 64DM, 64DM

	VF-20	EF-40	AU-50	MS-60	MS-63	MS-65
VARIETY	$40	$48	$60	$150	$625	n/a
NORMAL	32	35	40	75	365	$22,500

1880-O FS-S1-1880o-005

VARIETY: Overdate **VAM-5**
PUP: Ear above 8, metal within upper loop of second 8
URS-8 · I-4 · L-4

 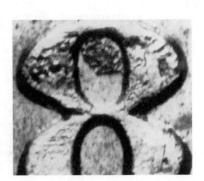

Description: There is excess metal inside the upper loop, similar to VAM-4.

Comments: This VAM is different from the previous one in that it has an O over O mintmark.

Census: 64PL, 64PL, 64PL, 64PL, 64, 64, 63DM, 63PL

	VF-20	EF-40	AU-50	MS-60	MS-63	MS-65
VARIETY	$43	$50	$80	$200	$600	n/a
NORMAL	32	35	40	75	365	$22,500

1880-O

VARIETY: Repunched Date
PUP: Eagle's right tail feather
URS-7 · I-4 · L-3

VAM-49
"HANGNAIL" VARIETY

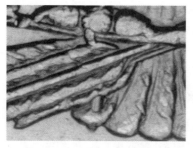 

Description: On the reverse, a die gouge runs from the bottom of the arrow feather, across the feathers, and out the eagle's rightmost tail feather. On the obverse the top left of the second 8 has a spike. (Another variety, VAM-48, does *not* have a spiked 8; that variety is worth less.)

Comments: Formerly listed as VAM-6B. All specimens with this reverse should be carefully checked.

Census: 63, 63, 63, 62, 62, 60, 60, 58

	VF-20	EF-40	AU-50	MS-60	MS-63	MS-65
VARIETY	$225	$450	$800	n/a	n/a	n/a
NORMAL	32	35	40	$75	$365	$22,500

1881-O

VARIETY: Repunched Mintmark
PUP: Mintmark
URS-6 · I-3 · L-3

VAM-5

Description: A diagonal image, the remains of one or two additional O mintmark punches, is evident within the primary O.

Comments: Amazingly similar to the OMMs of the popular 1882-O Over S varieties, VAM-5 is gaining in popularity with variety specialists.

Census: 65, 65, 65, 64DM, 64PL, 64, 64, 64

	VF-20	EF-40	AU-50	MS-60	MS-63	MS-65
VARIETY	$40	$60	$100	$150	$250	n/a
NORMAL	32	35	40	50	65	$1,250

1881-O
FS-S1-1881o-027

VARIETY: Doubled-Die Obverse
PUP: Ear
URS-7 · I-5 · L-4

VAM-27

Description: Clear doubling is visible on the back outside of Liberty's ear.

Comments: This Hot 50 variety is similar to the popular 1891-(P) VAM-2 and is at least as scarce. It can be very difficult to locate.

Census: 64, 63, 62, 62, 62, 62, 61, 61

	VF-20	EF-40	AU-50	MS-60	MS-63	MS-65
VARIETY	$40	$75	$200	$450	n/a	n/a
NORMAL	32	35	40	50	$65	$1,250

1882-O
FS-S1-1882o-003 (005.25)

VARIETY: Over Mintmark
PUP: Mintmark
URS-8 · I-5 · L-5

VAM-3
"O OVER S FLUSH" VARIETY

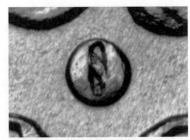

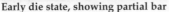

Early die state, showing partial bar   Later die state, showing full bar

Description: The top surface of what is considered an S is level with the top surface of the O.

Comments: This RPM is quite evident and has been nicknamed the O Over S Flush. Further study may determine this to be an O Over O, much like FS-S1-1880o-005.

Census EDS: 63, 63, 63, 62, 62, 62, 62, 61
Census LDS: 64, 64, 63, 63, 63, 63, 63, 63

	VF-20	EF-40	AU-50	MS-60	MS-63	MS-65
VARIETY EDS	n/a	$135	$200	$375	$1,950	n/a
VARIETY LDS	$55	83	100	225	600	n/a
NORMAL	32	35	40	50	65	$1,000

1882-O
FS-S1-1882o-004

VARIETY: Over Mintmark
PUP: Mintmark
URS-8 · I-5 · L-5

VAM-4
"O OVER S RECESSED" VARIETY

Description: The top surface of what is probably an S is lower than the O.

Comments: This RPM is known as the O Over S Recessed. While it is the most common of the 1882-O Over S varieties overall, this VAM is the rarest of them all in an early-die-state (EDS) example.

Census EDS: 63, 62, 58, 55, 55, 45
Census LDS: 64, 64, 64, 64, 64, 64, 64, 64

	VF-20	EF-40	AU-50	MS-60	MS-63	MS-65
VARIETY EDS	n/a	$4,000	$6,000	n/a	n/a	n/a
VARIETY LDS	$50	75	95	$225	$650	n/a
NORMAL	32	35	40	50	65	$1,000

1882-O, O Over S
FS-S1-1882o-005

VARIETY: Over Mintmark
PUP: Mintmark
URS-8 · I-5 · L-5

VAM-5
"BROKEN S" VARIETY

Description: The top right portion on an underlying S mintmark is evident within the opening of the primary O mintmark.

Comments: This OMM had been nicknamed the Broken S. This is more common than the two previous listings. The three OMMs for 1882-O are all nice finds.

Census EDS: 63, 62DM, 62, 62, 62, 62, 61DM, 60DM
Census LDS: 65, 65, 65, 64, 64, 64, 64, 64

	VF-20	EF-40	AU-50	MS-60	MS-63	MS-65
VARIETY EDS	n/a	$135	$225	$385	n/a	n/a
VARIETY LDS	$55	80	225	225	$675	n/a
NORMAL	32	35	40	50	65	$1,000

1884
FS-S1-1884-003

VARIETY: Large Dot
VAM-3
PUP: Designer's initial
URS-9 · I-5 · L-5

Description: A dot is visible after the designer's initial.

Comments: These dots varieties are thought to have been used as some type of identifier. This VAM is called the Large Dot variety, with the next listing, VAM-4, known as the Small Dot variety.

Census: 66, 66, 65, 65, 65, 64, 64, 64

	VF-20	EF-40	AU-50	MS-60	MS-63	MS-65
VARIETY	$38	$43	$58	$90	$250	n/a
NORMAL	32	35	39	50	65	$275

1884
FS-S1-1884-004

VARIETY: Small Dot
VAM-4
PUP: Designer's initial
URS-7 · I-5 · L-5

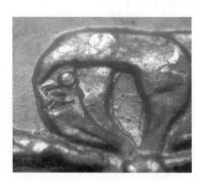

Description: A raised dot is evident after the designer's initial.

Comments: This VAM is considered the Small Dot variety, while the previous listing, VAM-3, is known as the Large Dot variety. The dots are reported to have been used as some type of identifier.

Census: 66, 65, 65, 65, 65, 65, 65, 65

	VF-20	EF-40	AU-50	MS-60	MS-63	MS-65
VARIETY	$40	$55	$65	$95	$350	n/a
NORMAL	32	35	39	50	65	$275

1885   FS-S1-1885-022

Variety: Die Chip   **VAM-22**
PUP: Date
URS-8 · I-5 · L-5

Description: There is a large, raised die chip below the second 8. The area above the "dash" below the second 8 has broken away on the die to create this character effect. All specimens found so far have a doubled arrowshaft on the reverse which indicates VAM-22.

Comments: This is the most desirable of the several P-Mint dash varieties.

Census: 64, 63, 62, 62, 62, 61, 50

	VF-20	EF-40	AU-50	MS-60	MS-63	MS-65
Variety	$50	$60	$70	$100	$550	n/a
Normal	32	35	39	50	65	$175

1885-CC   FS-S1-1885CC-004

Variety: Die Chip   **VAM-4**
PUP: Date
URS-8 · I-5 · L-5

Description: There is a large, raised die chip below the second 8, as on the 1885-(P) VAM-22.

Comments: The space above the dash has broken away on the die.

Census: 67, 67, 66, 66, 66, 66, 66, 66

	VF-20	EF-40	AU-50	MS-60	MS-63	MS-65
Variety	$600	$650	$675	$725	$800	$1,250
Normal	475	510	540	575	635	1,000

1886

FS-S1-1886-001c

VARIETY: Clashed Die
PUP: Reverse, right field
URS-9 · I-5 · L-5

VAM-1C

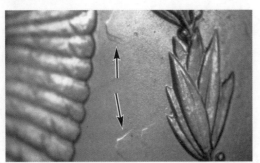

Description: Five heavy clash marks from the obverse die show on the right side of the reverse.

Comments: This variety is available for modest premiums.

Census: 67, 67, 67, 67, 67, 67, 66, 66

	VF-20	EF-40	AU-50	MS-60	MS-63	MS-65
VARIETY	$40	$45	$50	$60	$80	$275
NORMAL	32	35	39	50	65	175

1886

FS-S1-1886-020

VARIETY: Repunched Date
PUP: Date
URS-3 · I-5 · L-5

VAM-20

Description: The repunched date is evident in the loop of the lower 6. The other digits are also repunched, especially the lower base of the 1.

Comments: This is a recently reported and very rare variety!

Census: 64, 64, 63, 63, 63, 63, 63, 63

	VF-20	EF-40	AU-50	MS-60	MS-63	MS-65
VARIETY	n/a	$1,250	$2,250	$3,500	$5,750	n/a
NORMAL	$32	35	39	50	65	$175

1886-O

FS-S1-1886o-001a (005.27)

VARIETY: Clashed Die E Reverse
PUP: Reverse below eagle's tail feathers
URS-9 · I-5 · L-5

VAM-1A

Description: A clashed die is evident from the E of LIBERTY on the obverse, between the eagle's tail feathers and the bow on the wreath.

Comments: This popular VAM variety is always in demand.

Census: 63, 63, 62, 62, 62, 62, 62, 62

	VF-20	EF-40	AU-50	MS-60	MS-63	MS-65
VARIETY	$50	$175	$300	$1,000	$5,750	n/a
NORMAL	34	43	100	725	3,250	$165,000

1887

FS-S1-1887-001b

VARIETY: Clashed Die E Reverse
PUP: Reverse below eagle's tail feathers
URS-4 · I-5 · L-5

VAM-1B

 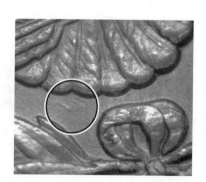

Description: The clashed die is evident from the E of LIBERTY. It is partially evident between the eagle's tail feathers and the bow.

Comments: This is a variety very much in demand. Fewer than 10 are known at this time.

Census: 64, 58, 55, 55, 55, 55, 50, 50

	VF-20	EF-40	AU-50	MS-60	MS-63	MS-65
VARIETY	$1,250	$2,500	$4,500	n/a	n/a	n/a
NORMAL	32	35	39	$50	$65	$175

1887, 7 Over 6

FS-S1-1887-002 (005.3)

VARIETY: Overdate
PUP: Date
URS-7 · I-5 · L-5

VAM-2

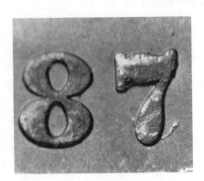

Description: The 7 of the date is punched over a 6. The lower loop of the 6 is clearly evident near the bottom of the 7.

Comments: This is one of the most sought after varieties in the series, but it can still be cherrypicked!

Census: 66PL, 66, 66, 66, 66, 66, 66, 66

	VF-20	EF-40	AU-50	MS-60	MS-63	MS-65
VARIETY	$45	$60	$145	$325	$475	$2,000
NORMAL	32	35	39	50	65	175

1887

FS-S1-1887-012

VARIETY: Doubled-Die Obverse
PUP: Eye
NEW LISTING

VAM-12, VAM-12A
"ALLIGATOR EYE" VARIETY

Doubling on leaf tip of leaf pointing to I in LIBERTY

Description: Doubling is visible on the eye, portions of LIBERTY, and other areas. VAM-12A is a later die state than VAM-12 and exhibits extensive die clashing on the obverse and reverse.

Comments: Known by collectors as the Alligator Eye, this variety is relatively minor but very popular due to its nickname. It can be found with a bit of searching.

Census: 67, 67, 67, 67, 67, 67, 67, 67

	VF-20	EF-40	AU-50	MS-60	MS-63	MS-65
VARIETY	n/a	n/a	n/a	n/a	n/a	n/a
NORMAL	$29	$32	$36	$50	$65	$175

1887-O
FS-S1-1887o-002 (005.7)

VARIETY: Repunched Date
PUP: Date
URS-8 · I-5 · L-4

VAM-2

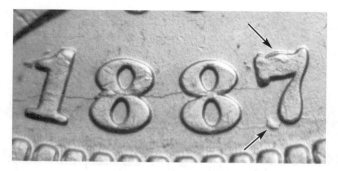

Description: The top flag of the secondary 1 is evident left of the primary 1. The lower foot of the secondary 7 is visible left of the primary 7. Tripling is evident on the top of the 7.

Comments: This variety is in the Top 100 VAM listings!

Census: 64, 64, 64, 64, 64, 64, 64, 64

	VF-20	EF-40	AU-50	MS-60	MS-63	MS-65
VARIETY	$60	$78	$95	$115	$250	n/a
NORMAL	34	39	50	68	105	$2,150

1887-O, 7 Over 6
FS-S1-1887o-003 (005.5)

VARIETY: Overdate
PUP: Date
URS-7 · I-5 · L-5

VAM-3

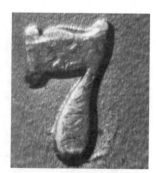

Description: The 7 of the date is punched over a 6. The lower loop of the 6 is clearly evident near the bottom of the 7.

Comments: This variety is very similar to the P-Mint variety. It is another of the more popular VAM varieties and is always in demand. An MS-64 example sold at auction in January 2011 for $3,910.

Census: 65, 64, 64, 64, 64, 64, 64, 64

	VF-20	EF-40	AU-50	MS-60	MS-63	MS-65
VARIETY	$45	$75	$175	$385	$2,000	n/a
NORMAL	34	39	50	68	105	$2,150

1887-O

FS-S1-1887o-030

VARIETY: Clashed Die

VAM-30

PUP: Entire reverse

URS-4 · I-5 · L-5

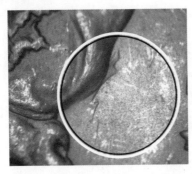
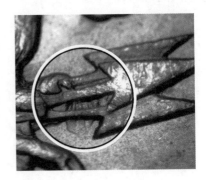

Description: Clashed details are clearly visible on the obverse and the reverse.

Comments: A relatively new, yet highly sought after variety, this is a superb clashed die.

Census: 63, 63, 63, 63, 63, 63, 63, 63

	VF-20	EF-40	AU-50	MS-60	MS-63	MS-65
VARIETY	$50	$75	$150	$290	$550	n/a
NORMAL	34	39	50	68	105	$2,150

1888-O

FS-S1-1888o-001a

VARIETY: Clashed Die E Reverse

VAM-1A

PUP: Reverse below eagle's tail feathers

URS-6 · I-5 · L-5

Description: On the reverse, the E of LIBERTY is faintly visible below the left side of the eagle's tail feathers. On the late die state, a strong die crack is evident on the obverse, from the rim through the R of PLURIBUS and down to the lower left of the L in LIBERTY.

Comments: This variety commands strong premiums over the normal coin.

Census: 65, 65, 64, 64, 64, 64, 64, 64

	VF-20	EF-40	AU-50	MS-60	MS-63	MS-65
VARIETY	n/a	n/a	$90	$125	$315	n/a
NORMAL	$32	$35	39	50	60	$500

1888-O
FS-S1-1888o-001b

VARIETY: Die Crack
PUP: Cheek
URS-5 · I-5 · L-5

VAM-1B
"SCARFACE" VARIETY

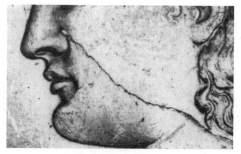

Description: There is a major die crack on the obverse, running from the rim between the E and P, through the field, and all the way across Liberty's face and neck.

Comments: This is the largest die crack reported in the Morgan dollar series, and is very rare in all grades. The "Scarface" was the cover coin of the fourth edition.

Census: 64, 64, 63, 63, 63, 63, 63, 63

	VF-20	EF-40	AU-50	MS-60	MS-63	MS-65
VARIETY	n/a	n/a	$2,250	$3,750	$8,650	n/a
NORMAL	$32	$35	39	50	60	$500

1888-O
FS-S1-1888o-004 (006)

VARIETY: Doubled-Die Obverse
PUP: Lips
URS-8 · I-5 · L-5

VAM-4
"HOT LIPS" VARIETY

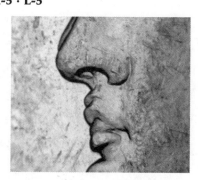

Description: Doubling is evident on the lips, nose, eye, chin, entire profile, and part of the hair.

Comments: Only a few of this very dramatic doubled die known in Mint State. Find an MS-65 and name your price! This variety is affectionately known as "Hot Lips." (Note: This variety was incorrectly listed as FS-S1-1888o-002 in the fourth edition.)

Census: 62, 62, 62, 61, 61, 61, 60DM, 60

	VF-20	EF-40	AU-50	MS-60	MS-63	MS-65
VARIETY	$145	$290	$900	$20,000	n/a	n/a
NORMAL	32	35	39	50	$60	$500

1888-O

VARIETY: Oval O Mintmark
PUP: Mintmark
URS-9 · I-5 · L-5

VAM: VARIOUS

Oval O

Normal O

Description: Oval O mintmark.

Comments: The following VAMs are included with this listing: 2, 5, 6, 17, 18, 21, and 24. All are very scarce in circulated grades, and extremely rare in Mint State.

Census: 63, 63, 63, 63, 63, 63, 63, 63

	VF-20	EF-40	AU-50	MS-60	MS-63	MS-65
VARIETY	$50	$85	$150	$450	$750	n/a
NORMAL	32	35	39	50	60	$500

1889

VARIETY: Die Break
PUP: Top of eagle's right wing (viewer's left)
URS-9 · I-5 · L-5

VAM-19A
"BAR WING" VARIETY

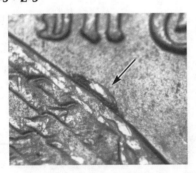

Description: VAM-19A has the same reverse die as VAM-22, yet paired with a different obverse die. VAM-19A has an obverse with a normal date, and VAM-22 has an obverse with the date set to the right of normal.

Comments: The nicknames for many VAMs, a practice begun many years ago, are still used today. This die break variety is nicknamed the Bar Wing.

Census: 65, 65, 65, 65, 65, 65, 65, 65

	VF-20	EF-40	AU-50	MS-60	MS-63	MS-65
VARIETY	$40	$60	$90	$165	$285	n/a
NORMAL	32	35	39	50	60	$275

1889 FS-S1-1889-022

VARIETY: Die Break
PUP: Top of eagle's right wing (viewer's left)
URS-9 · I-5 · L-5

VAM-22
"BAR WING" VARIETY

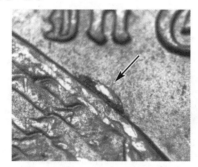 

Description: This VAM has this same reverse die as VAM-19A, yet paired with different obverse dies. VAM-22 has an obverse with a far date, and VAM-19A has an obverse with a normal date.

Comments: Many of the older popular VAMs have become known by their nicknames. This die break variety is nicknamed the Bar Wing.

Census: 65, 65, 65, 65, 64, 64, 64, 64

	VF-20	EF-40	AU-50	MS-60	MS-63	MS-65
VARIETY	$40	$60	$80	$135	$200	n/a
NORMAL	32	35	39	50	60	$275

1889 FS-S1-1889-023a

VARIETY: Obverse Clashed Die
PUP: Field under jaw by neck
URS-3 · I-5 · L-5

VAM-23A

Description: The IN of IN GOD WE TRUST shows clear evidence of a clashed die just beneath Liberty's jaw at her neck.

Comments: The coin shown here is one of fewer than a dozen known examples of the full IN variety. Find an MS-65 and you can name your price!

Census: 58, 58, 58, 58, 58, 58, 45

	VF-20	EF-40	AU-50	MS-60	MS-63	MS-65
VARIETY	n/a	n/a	n/a	n/a	n/a	n/a
NORMAL	$32	$35	$39	$50	$60	$275

1889-O
FS-S1-1889o-001a (006.5)

VARIETY: Clashed Die E Reverse
PUP: Reverse in field under tail feathers
URS-4 · I-5 · L-5

VAM-1A

Description: The E of LIBERTY is evident in the field below the eagle's tail feathers and slightly left of the bow.

Comments: Another of the famous and popular reverse clashed dies, this variety is extremely rare in Mint State, and unknown above MS-61.

Census: 61, 61, 61, 60, 58, 55, 55, 55

	VF-20	EF-40	AU-50	MS-60	MS-63	MS-65
VARIETY	$275	$375	$975	$2,000	n/a	n/a
NORMAL	32	35	50	160	$375	$6,000

1890-CC
FS-S1-1890CC-004 (007)

VARIETY: Die Gouge
PUP: Field between arrow feathers and wreath
URS-7 · I-5 · L-5

VAM-4
"TAILBAR" VARIETY

Description: A heavy die gouge extends from between the eagle's first tail feather and the lowest arrow feather to the leaves in the wreath below.

Comments: This is an extremely popular and highly marketable variety, especially in Mint State.

Census: 65, 65, 65, 64DM, 64DM, 64DM, 64DM, 64DM

	VF-20	EF-40	AU-50	MS-60	MS-63	MS-65
VARIETY	$225	$375	$650	$1,150	$2,950	n/a
NORMAL	125	175	200	400	725	$4,750

1890-O

VARIETY: Die Gouges
PUP: Area to the right of date
URS-9 · I-5 · L-5

VAM-10
"COMET" VARIETY

VAM-10

VAM-10a, weaker die state

Description: Die gouges are evident to the right of the date.

Comments: This so-called Comet Variety is an old variety that has been popular for 25 years. The weaker die state (VAM-10a) does not command as much of a premium as VAM-10.

Census: 65, 65, 65, 65, 65, 65, 64, 64

	VF-20	EF-40	AU-50	MS-60	MS-63	MS-65
VARIETY	$43	$55	$65	$90	$260	$1,650
NORMAL	32	35	44	68	115	1,550

1891-CC

VARIETY: Die Gouge
PUP: Gouge in front of eagle's beak
NEW LISTING

VAM-3
"SPITTING EAGLE" VARIETY

Description: A die gouge is evident below the eagle's beak.

Comments: Very common but popular, this variety is affectionately referred to as the Spitting Eagle by VAM collectors.

Census: 66+, 66, 65, 65, 65, 65, 65, 65

	VF-20	EF-40	AU-50	MS-60	MS-63	MS-65
VARIETY	n/a	n/a	n/a	n/a	n/a	n/a
NORMAL	$125	$180	$250	$350	$800	$4,750

1891-O

VARIETY: Clashed Die E Reverse **VAM-1A**
PUP: Reverse in field under tail feathers
URS-5 · I-5 · L-5

Description: The evidence of a clashed die is seen below the eagle's tail feathers and slightly left of the bow, where the E in LIBERTY has been clashed from the obverse die.

Comments: The most evident and popular of the E Reverse clashed dies, only two are known in MS-63 and none are known higher.

Census: 63, 63, 62, 62, 62, 62, 62, 61

	VF-20	EF-40	AU-50	MS-60	MS-63	MS-65
VARIETY	$60	$150	$215	$370	$1,500	n/a
NORMAL	35	38	50	140	300	$7,250

1891-O

VARIETY: Pitted Reverse Die **VAM-1B**
PUP: Bottom of reverse
URS-4 · I-5 · L-5

Description: The pitting on the reverse is visible around the ONE and on the bottom of the wreath above and between ONE and DOLLAR.

Comments: Discovered in 1997, this variety is rare in circulated grades, and unknown above AU.

Census: 58, 58, 58, 55, 55, 55, 55, 55

	VF-20	EF-40	AU-50	MS-60	MS-63	MS-65
VARIETY	$110	$190	$370	n/a	n/a	n/a
NORMAL	35	38	50	$140	$300	$7,250

1895-S

VARIETY: Repunched Mintmark　　　　　　　　　　**VAM-3**
PUP: Mintmark
URS-5 · I-5 · L-5

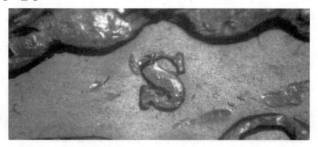

Description: A dramatic repunched mintmark is evident, with the secondary S northwest of the primary S. This secondary S only shows in the southwest quadrant of the upper loop outside of the primary S, with some elements of the secondary letter within the loops of the primary.

Comments: This is a very dramatic RPM for this series. The variety is very expensive because of the rare date. The date also accounts for a relatively large percentage of the surviving coins likely being this RPM.

Census: 64, 63, 63, 63, 63, 63, 62PL, 62

	VF-20	EF-40	AU-50	MS-60	MS-63	MS-65
VARIETY	$875	$1,400	$1,950	$3,900	n/a	n/a
NORMAL	750	1,200	1,800	3,600	$5,750	$25,000

1896

VARIETY: Repunched Date　　　　　　　　　　　**VAM-20**
PUP: 6 of the date
URS-8 · I-5 · L-5

Description: The strong repunched date is evident only on the secondary 6. The left lower loop of the secondary 6 is evident within the lower loop of the primary 6.

Comments: This variety is one of the widest RPDs in the series.

Census: 67, 65, 65, 65, 65, 65, 65, 65

	VF-20	EF-40	AU-50	MS-60	MS-63	MS-65
VARIETY	$43	$48	$55	$70	$115	$450
NORMAL	32	35	39	50	65	175

1896-O FS-S1-1896o-004 (008)

VARIETY: Micro O Mintmark   **VAM-4**
PUP: Mintmark
URS-8 · I-5 · L-5

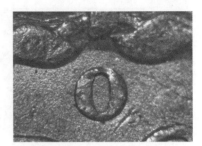

Micro O   Normal O, for comparison

Description: The O mintmark is smaller than the mintmark normally seen.

Comments: This variety has been found to be made from counterfeit dies. Although it is very popular and collectible among VAM enthusiasts, it will be deleted from this chapter in the next edition to make room for genuine varieties. Its Fivaz-Stanton number will be retained, and it will continue to be listed in the cross-reference appendix.

Census: 58, 55, 50, 45, 15 (none reported by PCGS or NGC)

	VF-20	EF-40	AU-50	MS-60	MS-63	MS-65
VARIETY	n/a	n/a	n/a	n/a	n/a	n/a
NORMAL	35	$43	$145	$1,300	$7,000	$175,000

1896-O FS-S1-1896o-019

VARIETY: Repunched Date   **VAM-19**
PUP: Date
URS-7 · I-5 · L-5

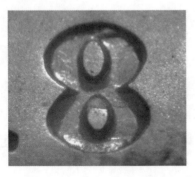

Description: A strong repunched date is evident with the secondary image north and east of the primary image. The secondary images are evident within the lower loops of the 8, the 9, and the 6.

Comments: This variety was previously listed as VAM-1A. It is very rare in any grade.

Census: 62, 62, 62, 61, 61, 58, 58, 55

	VF-20	EF-40	AU-50	MS-60	MS-63	MS-65
VARIETY	n/a	$225	$450	n/a	n/a	n/a
NORMAL	$35	43	145	$1,300	$7,000	$175,000

1898-O

Variety: Repunched Date
PUP: Date
URS-1 · I-5 · L-5

VAM-20

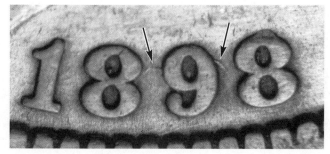

Description: A secondary 8 is evident between the primary first 8 and the 9, and a secondary 9 evident between the primary 9 and the last 8.

Comments: Discovered in 1995 by Jerry Sajbel, this is one of the strongest repunched dates of this series. To our knowledge, only two specimens are known. There is only one sales report to date. This variety was listed as FS-301 in the previous edition.

Census: 45, 35

	VF-20	EF-40	AU-50	MS-60	MS-63	MS-65
VARIETY	$400	n/a	n/a	n/a	n/a	n/a
NORMAL	32	$35	$39	$50	$65	$175

1899-O

Variety: Micro O Mintmark
PUP: Mintmark
URS-8 · I-5 · L-5

VAM-4, 5, 6, 31, AND 32

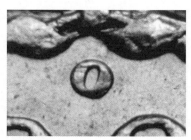 

Micro O   Normal O, for comparison

Description: The O mintmark is smaller than the mintmark normally seen.

Comments: The O mintmark used for this 1899-O die was probably from a punch intended for a Barber half dollar. There are five different dies known, including VAM-5, but all are very scarce—and very desirable. This and the 1880-O Micro O are the only two Micro O varieties considered genuine.

Census: 66, 65, 65, 65, 65, 64, 64, 64

	VF-20	EF-40	AU-50	MS-60	MS-63	MS-65
VARIETY	$45	$70	$140	$375	$1,000	n/a
NORMAL	32	35	39	50	65	$175

1900 — FS-S1-1900-016

VARIETY: Doubled-Die Reverse (C4 Over C3 Reverse)   **VAM-16**
PUP: Left olive on branch
URS-10 · I-4 · L-4

Description: Doubling is most evident as an extra olive to the right of the olive connected to the branch (illustrated). Doubling is also evident on the upper feathers of the eagle's left wing and on the inside of the OF in UNITED STATES OF AMERICA.

Comments: Two different hubs were used when producing the die. The first hub was the C3 reverse, and the second, and final, hub was the C4 reverse. VAM-18 is very similar. We suggest using the VAM book or www.VAMworld.com to determine the difference.

Census: 66, 66, 65, 65, 65, 65, 65, 65

	VF-20	EF-40	AU-50	MS-60	MS-63	MS-65
VARIETY	$43	$48	$55	$68	$75	$250
NORMAL	32	35	39	50	65	185

1900-O — FS-S1-1900o-005 (009)

VARIETY: Micro O Mintmark   **VAM-5**
PUP: Mintmark
URS-6 · I-5 · L-5

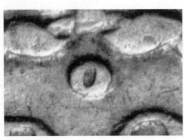 

Micro O   Normal O, for comparison

Description: The O mintmark is smaller than the mintmark normally seen.

Comments: This variety has been found to be made from counterfeit dies. Although it is very popular and collectible among VAM enthusiasts, it will be deleted from this chapter in the next edition to make room for genuine varieties. Its Fivaz-Stanton number will be retained, and it will continue to be listed in the cross-reference appendix.

Census: 58, 50, 50, 50, 45, 45, 45, 45 (none reported by PCGS or NGC)

	VF-20	EF-40	AU-50	MS-60	MS-63	MS-65
VARIETY	n/a	n/a	n/a	n/a	n/a	n/a
NORMAL	$32	$35	$39	$50	$65	$200

1900-O

VARIETY: Obverse Die Crack **VAM-29A**
PUP: Date area
URS-6 · I-5 · L-5

Description: A die crack is visible from the rim through the date to just below the lower point of the bust.

Comments: This variety is often confused with VAM-35. Look for any VAM-29a above VF-20.

Census: 63, 62, 62, 62, 61, 61, 58, 58

	VF-20	EF-40	AU-50	MS-60	MS-63	MS-65
VARIETY	$150	$275	$700	n/a	n/a	n/a
NORMAL	32	35	39	$50	$65	$200

1900-O

VARIETY: Over Mintmark **VAM: VARIOUS**
PUP: Mintmark
URS-9 · I-5 · L-5

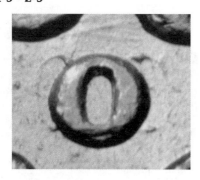 

Description: An O mintmark has been punched into the die over a previously punched CC mintmark.

Comments: There are at least seven different dies, and therefore different VAMs, included in this listing. VAM-9, shown on the right, is extremely rare.

Census: 67, 67, 67, 66, 66, 66, 66, 66

	VF-20	EF-40	AU-50	MS-60	MS-63	MS-65
VARIETY	$73	$100	$190	$325	$675	$1,775
NORMAL	32	35	39	50	65	200

1901   FS-S1-1901-003 (010)

VARIETY: Doubled-Die Reverse   **VAM-3**
PUP: Tail feathers   *"SHIFTED EAGLE" VARIETY*
URS-6 · I-5 · L-5

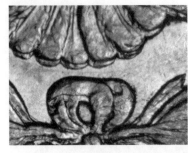 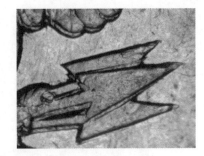

Description: Doubling is evident on IN GOD WE TRUST, as well as on the arrows, wreath, and bow, but it is the doubling on the eagle's tailfeathers that gives this variety the "Shifted Eagle" nickname.

Comments: Historically one of the more popular and important Morgan dollar varieties, the few Mint State coins that are known are in low grades.

Census: 62, 62, 61, 61, 61, 60, 58, 58

	VF-20	EF-40	AU-50	MS-60	MS-63	MS-65
VARIETY	$550	$1,250	$2,500	n/a	n/a	n/a
NORMAL	50	125	325	$2,300	$15,000	$325,000

1902-O   FS-S1-1902o-003

VARIETY: Micro O Mintmark   **VAM-3**
PUP: Mintmark
URS-5 · I-5 · L-5

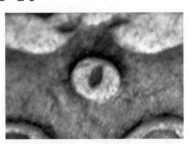 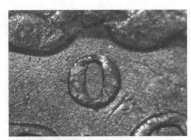

Micro O   Normal O, for comparison

Description: The O mintmark is smaller than the mintmark normally seen.

Comments: This variety has been found to be made from counterfeit dies. Although it is very popular and collectible among VAM enthusiasts, it will be deleted from this chapter in the next edition to make room for genuine varieties. Its Fivaz-Stanton number will be retained, and it will continue to be listed in the cross-reference appendix.

Census: 53, 50, 45, 45, 45, 45, 45, 45 (none reported by PCGS or NGC)

	VF-20	EF-40	AU-50	MS-60	MS-63	MS-65
VARIETY	n/a	n/a	n/a	n/a	n/a	n/a
NORMAL	$32	$35	$39	$50	$65	$200

1903-S

FS-S1-1903S-002 (011.5)

VARIETY: Small S Mintmark
PUP: Mintmark
URS-8 · I-5 · L-5

VAM-2

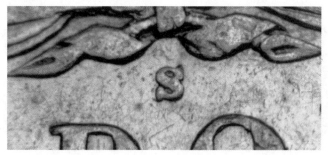

Description: The S mintmark is smaller than usual.

Comments: The S mintmark punched into this die may have been intended for the Barber half dollar series, but it is certainly not the normal mintmark for a Morgan dollar. This is the only known Morgan die with this small mintmark. Only one is known in Mint State. Find another and you can pay for a year of college!

Census: 62, 58, 58, 58, 58, 58, 58, 58

	VF-20	EF-40	AU-50	MS-60	MS-63	MS-65
VARIETY	$675	$2,000	$6,400	n/a	n/a	n/a
NORMAL	200	375	1,600	$4,000	$6,300	$10,500

1921-D

FS-S1-1921D-001x

VARIETY: Large Cud
PUP: Obverse at 10 o'clock
URS-1 · I-5 · L-5

VAM-1x

Description: A double major die break is evident above the E and P on E PLURIBUS UNUM. The breaks have progressed to the point where they have joined. In addition to the double major die break, there is a pre-cud die crack extending from the rim at 7 o'clock, through two stars, then back to the rim at 6 o'clock.

Comments: A major die break of this magnitude, commonly referred to as a *cud*, is extremely rare on a Morgan dollar. To have a Morgan dollar with two die breaks is exponentially rarer. Only one specimen is known to date. The die crack may have progressed to a cud, with the die being removed from service afterward. No sales records exist for this coin.

Census: 40

	VF-20	EF-40	AU-50	MS-60	MS-63	MS-65
VARIETY	n/a	n/a	n/a	n/a	n/a	n/a
NORMAL	$32	$33	$34	$45	$65	$350

1921-S   FS-S1-1921S-001b7

VARIETY: Die Gouges
PUP: Y of LIBERTY
NEW LISTING

VAM-1B7
"THORNHEAD" VARIETY

Gouge through the Y, diagnostic of VAM-1B7

Gouge through cap, seen on all stages

Gouge ("thorn") from cap, visible only on VAM-1B1

Abraded wheat leaf, visible on VAM-1B3A and later stages

Description: Several die gouges are present on this coin, with the one that runs through the Y of LIBERTY diagnostic to this stage.

Comments: One of ten stages of VAM-1B, this is the most desirable. It is known by VAM collectors as the Thornhead due to a "spike" that can be seen emanating from Liberty's Phrygian cap on the first stage (VAM-1B1). In addition to the discovery coin, shown in the census below, two other circulated specimens of VAM-1B7 have been reported by a reputable Internet seller. Check www.VAMWorld.com or other, more detailed, references for more information on the other stages.

Census: 50

	VF-20	EF-40	AU-50	MS-60	MS-63	MS-65
VARIETY	n/a	n/a	n/a	n/a	n/a	n/a
NORMAL	$28	$30	$31	$45	$65	$1,300

Peace Dollars, 1921–1935

The Peace dollar series has been greatly overlooked until somewhat recently; however, there are many very interesting die varieties in this short and relatively inexpensive series. Both the Peace and Morgan dollar varieties are classified as VAMs, an acronym derived from the first letters of the last names of Leroy Van Allen and George Mallis, the two gentlemen who first popularized the varieties of the series.

VAMs are collected by thousands of enthusiasts. Often, a silver dollar valued at less than $40 could in fact be worth several thousand dollars because of some minor, yet very rare, abnormality. A variation might be a die chip, an image from one side lightly visible on the other, a doubled or tripled die, a repunched mintmark or date, or even a slight die gouge. There are even some dramatic overdates.

In the *Cherrypickers' Guide,* third edition, there was only one listing for Peace dollars. In the fourth edition we expanded the listings to 20 varieties, all of which are very popular.

In addition, in the Morgan dollar and Peace dollar sections we have included a condition census, current as of this writing, for each listing. These notations give the known grades of the top examples of the variety and help to emphasize its rarity. Having this information helps the collector find those examples that are true rarities.

For those interested in learning more about the varieties of Peace dollars, we highly recommend membership in the Society of Silver Dollar Collectors (SSDC). Dues are $22 per year. The club has a web site at www.vamlink.com, or you may write to

SSDC
c/o Mike Andrew
680 Grackle Drive
Casselberry, FL 32707
E-mail: ssdc@vamlink.com

1921 — FS-S1-1921-003

VARIETY: Line Through L **VAM-3**
PUP: Ray through DOLLAR
URS-7 · I-5 · L-5

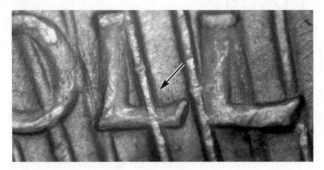

Description: The ray that runs across the first L in DOLLAR cuts through the L, rather than appearing behind it.

Comments: Because of the unusual nature of the design change, this relatively new discovery often attracts a lot of attention.

Census: 65, 65, 65, 65, 65, 65, 65

	EF-40	AU-50	MS-60	MS-63	MS-65
VARIETY	$175	$225	$325	$500	$3,000
NORMAL	140	180	285	450	1,850

1922 — FS-S1-1922-001f

VARIETY: Die Break in Field **VAM-1F**
PUP: Field above DOLLAR
URS-5 · I-4 · L-4

Description: A die break is evident in the field above DOLLAR.

Comments: This variety has turned out to be much rarer than previously thought, and is very scarce in grades above EF. Therefore, as soon as the occasional specimen enters the market, collectors rush to buy it. Prices have risen to reflect its popularity.

Census: 64, 63, 63, 63, 63, 62, 62

	EF-40	AU-50	MS-60	MS-63	MS-65
VARIETY	$200	$400	$800	$2,500	n/a
NORMAL	32	33	35	42	$180

1922

FS-S1-1922-002a

VARIETY: Die Break
PUP: Area at ear
URS-8 · I-5 · L-5

VAM-2A
"EARRING" VARIETY

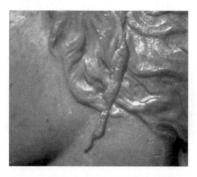 

Description: A major die break is located near Liberty's ear, dangling down to the neck.

Comments: The whimsically named variety is listed in the *Official Guide to the Top 50 Peace Dollar Varieties*. It is one of the largest Peace dollar die breaks known and is highly sought after.

Census: 65, 64, 64, 64, 63, 63, 63

	EF-40	AU-50	MS-60	MS-63	MS-65
VARIETY	$160	$300	$650	$2,300	n/a
NORMAL	32	33	35	42	$180

1922

FS-S1-1922-002c

VARIETY: Die Break
PUP: Die break at lower hair
URS-8 · I-5 · L-5

VAM-2C
"EXTRA HAIR" VARIETY

Description: An irregular line of raised metal runs along the back of Liberty's hair.

Comments: As is true for other die breaks, several different die states are known and all are desirable. This VAM is also listed in the *Official Guide to the Top 50 Peace Dollar Varieties*.

Census: 65, 65, 64, 64, 64, 64, 64

	EF-40	AU-50	MS-60	MS-63	MS-65
VARIETY	$65	$110	$200	$400	n/a
NORMAL	32	33	35	42	$180

1922 — FS-S1-1922-005a

VARIETY: Die Break
PUP: Die break at cheek, level with mouth
URS-7 · I-5 · L-5

VAM-5A
"Scar Cheek" Variety

Description: Liberty's cheek shows a raised, almost triangular, chunk of metal along a vertical break in the die. The reverse is lightly tripled.

Comments: Originally listed as VAM-2G, this so-called Scar Cheek variety is popular and very scarce in Uncirculated grades.

Census: 64, 64, 64, 64, 63, 63, 63

	EF-40	AU-50	MS-60	MS-63	MS-65
VARIETY	$80	$190	$400	n/a	n/a
NORMAL	32	33	35	$42	$180

1922 — FS-S1-1922-012a

VARIETY: Die Break
PUP: Cheek
URS-8 · I-5 · L-5

VAM-12A
"Moustache" Variety

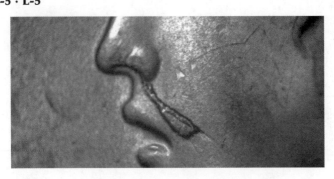

Description: A die break is evident on the cheek, level with the mouth.

Comments: Originally listed as VAM-2B, this popular item is among the top five Peace dollar varieties and is listed in the *Official Guide to the Top 50 Peace Dollar Varieties*.

Census: 65, 64, 64, 64, 64, 64, 64

	EF-40	AU-50	MS-60	MS-63	MS-65
VARIETY	$70	$90	$200	$500	n/a
NORMAL	32	33	35	42	$180

1922

FS-S1-1922-401

VARIETY: High Relief – Design of 1921   **VAM: N/A**
PUP: Date
URS-1 · I-5 · L-5+

Description: The high relief on the date shows a 9 more closed than that of the regular 1922 specimens; the 2s of the date have curled bases. On the reverse, there is a distinct additional ray above the N in ONE.

Comments: The existence of a 1922 Peace dollar with high relief design has long been the subject of journal articles and conversations among specialists. This is likely one of the rarer U.S. coins known to date.

Census: Unique: NGC Photoproof AU-55, ID-1625701-001

	EF-40	AU-50	MS-60	MS-63	MS-65
VARIETY	n/a	n/a	n/a	n/a	n/a
NORMAL	$32	$33	$35	$42	$180

1923

FS-S1-1923-001a

VARIETY: Die Break   **VAM-1A**
PUP: Cheek and jaw   *"WHISKER JAW" VARIETY*
URS-9 · I-5 · L-5

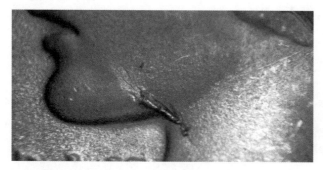

Description: A die break is evident bridging Liberty's cheek and jaw.

Comments: This is one of the more popular Peace dollar varieties, and is available in Mint State with little searching.

Census: 66, 66, 65, 65, 65, 65, 65

	EF-40	AU-50	MS-60	MS-63	MS-65
VARIETY	$50	$80	$125	$240	$500
NORMAL	32	33	35	42	180

1923 FS-S1-1923-001b

VARIETY: Die Break
PUP: Hair near nape of neck
URS-8 · I-5 · L-5

VAM-1B
"EXTRA HAIR" VARIETY

Description: A significant die break is visible in Liberty's hair running diagonally across the strands of hair. Die breaks may also be evident toward the back of Liberty's hair.

Comments: This VAM is listed in the *Official Guide to the Top 50 Peace Dollar Varieties*.

Census: 65, 65, 65, 65, 64, 64, 64

	EF-40	AU-50	MS-60	MS-63	MS-65
VARIETY	$75	$125	$225	$450	n/a
NORMAL	32	33	35	42	$180

1923 FS-S1-1923-001c

VARIETY: Die Break (Tail on O of DOLLAR)
PUP: O of DOLLAR
URS-6 · I-5 · L-5

VAM-1C

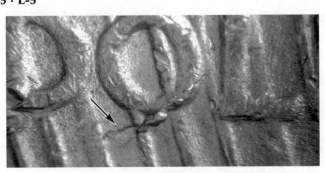

Description: A die break is evident trailing from the O of DOLLAR.

Comments: This variety is exceedingly rare in any grade!

Census: 64, 64, 64, 64, 63, 63, 63

	EF-40	AU-50	MS-60	MS-63	MS-65
VARIETY	$165	$235	$600	$1,700	n/a
NORMAL	32	33	35	42	$180

1923

FS-S1-1923-001d

Variety: Die Break
PUP: Cheek by nose and mouth
URS-8 · I-5 · L-5

VAM-1D
"Whisker Cheek" Variety

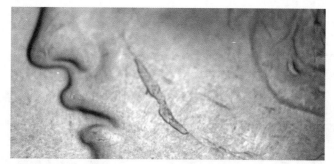

Description: The die break runs down Liberty's cheek toward the junction of the chin and neck.

Comments: Bill Fivaz discovered this variety three decades ago. It is a favorite with specialists, and is listed in the *Official Guide to the Top 50 Peace Dollar Varieties*.

Census: 65, 64, 64, 64, 64, 64, 64

	EF-40	AU-50	MS-60	MS-63	MS-65
Variety	$80	$150	$230	$475	n/a
Normal	32	33	35	42	$180

1923

FS-S1-1923-002

Variety: Doubled-Die Obverse
PUP: Rays of tiara
URS-8 · I-5 · L-5

VAM-2
"Double Tiara" Variety

Description: The DDO is most evident in the wide spread on the rays of Liberty's tiara, especially those under the BER of LIBERTY.

Comments: This VAM is listed in the *Official Guide to the Top 50 Peace Dollar Varieties*.

Census: 66, 66, 66, 65, 65, 65, 64

	EF-40	AU-50	MS-60	MS-63	MS-65
Variety	$45	$58	$75	$125	n/a
Normal	32	33	35	42	$180

1923-S

VARIETY: Pitted Reverse

PUP: Right of mintmark to N of ONE

URS-7 · I-5 · L-5

VAM-1C

Description: Pitting runs from the eagle's back tail-feathers, just to the right of the mintmark, upward to the N in ONE.

Comments: This is the most important Pitted Reverse variety in the Peace dollar series and is listed in the *Official Guide to the Top 50 Peace Dollar Varieties*.

Census: 64, 64, 64, 63, 63, 63, 63

	EF-40	AU-50	MS-60	MS-63	MS-65
VARIETY	$65	$125	$250	n/a	n/a
NORMAL	32	33	35	$90	$5,500

1924

VARIETY: Die Break

PUP: Eagle's wing

URS-9 · I-5 · L-5

VAM-5A

"BROKEN WING" VARIETY

Description: The die break runs down and across the entire width of the eagle's back.

Comments: This die break is incredible to behold. Most would consider it one of the premier Peace dollar varieties. It is listed in the *Official Guide to the Top 50 Peace Dollar Varieties*.

Census: 65, 65, 64, 64, 64, 64, 64

	EF-40	AU-50	MS-60	MS-63	MS-65
VARIETY	$80	$130	$200	$550	n/a
NORMAL	32	33	35	42	$180

1925

VARIETY: Missing Ray
VAM-5
PUP: Field between eagle's wing and talon
URS-8 · I-5 · L-4

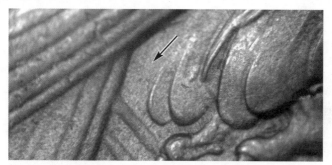

Description: The partially effaced remains of bold clash marks are showing, but the topmost internal ray is missing.

Comments: This over-polished reverse is a unique variety type among Peace dollars. It fascinates collectors and is listed in the *Official Guide to the Top 50 Peace Dollar Varieties*.

Census: 65, 65, 65, 65, 65, 65, 65

	EF-40	AU-50	MS-60	MS-63	MS-65
VARIETY	$45	$58	$80	$135	$350
NORMAL	32	33	35	42	180

1926-S

VARIETY: Dot
VAM-4
PUP: Field below olive leaves
*"**EXTRA BERRY**" VARIETY*
URS-8 · I-5 · L-5

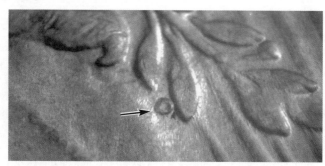

Description: A raised circular dot of metal appears just to the left of the bottom olive leaf.

Comments: Listed in the *Official Guide to the Top 50 Peace Dollar Varieties*, this VAM is also known as the Extra Berry variety. There is nothing else like it in the series!

Census: 66, 65, 65, 65, 64, 64, 64

	EF-40	AU-50	MS-60	MS-63	MS-65
VARIETY	$43	$50	$85	$200	n/a
NORMAL	33	35	52	115	$900

1927-S

VARIETY: Repunched Mintmark
PUP: Mintmark
URS-3 · I-5 · L-5

VAM-4; CONECA: RPM-001

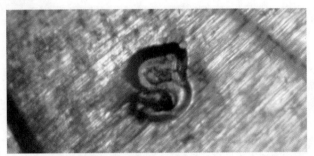

Description: The secondary S is slightly skewed counter-clockwise and overlaps the primary S. Doubling is most evident in the upper serif of the S.

Comments: Until this S Over S mintmark was reported to us in December of 1997, we were unaware of the variety. The specimen examined was Mint State, but others have since been reported.

Census: 65, 65, 64, 64, 64, 64, 64

	EF-40	AU-50	MS-60	MS-63	MS-65
VARIETY	$50	$90	$215	$525	n/a
NORMAL	39	80	160	375	$9,000

1928-S

VARIETY: Doubled-Die Obverse
PUP: WE TRUST
URS-8 · I-5 · L-5

VAM-3

Description: Strong doubling is evident on the OD of GOD, on WE, and on the TR of TRUST. Doubling is also evident on the right-most rays of the tiara, the designer's initials (AF), and some of the hair toward the right side of the coin.

Comments: Although not rare, its "wow factor" makes this a popular variety. VAM-3 should not be confused with the very similar VAM-4, on which the mintmark is higher than normal. VAM-3 is listed in the *Official Guide to the Top 50 Peace Dollar Varieties*.

Census: 64, 64, 64, 64, 64, 64, 64

	EF-40	AU-50	MS-60	MS-63	MS-65
VARIETY	$55	$95	$220	$485	n/a
NORMAL	45	70	190	425	$21,000

1934-D

VARIETY: Doubled-Die Obverse, Medium D
PUP: WE TRUST, profile, mintmark
URS-11 · I-5 · L-5

VAM-3

Filled, Medium D mintmark

Description: Doubling is evident on most letters of IN GOD WE TRUST, on Liberty's profile, and on some of the rays on the right side of the coin. The reverse exhibits a filled medium D mintmark.

Comments: VAM-3 is somewhat common, but the wonderful doubled die adds some value. The same doubled die is paired with a small D mintmark in the next listing, which is considerably rarer.

Census: 66, 66, 65, 65, 65, 65, 65

	EF-40	AU-50	MS-60	MS-63	MS-65
VARIETY	$50	$105	$200	$575	n/a
NORMAL	38	55	130	350	$1,400

1934-D

VARIETY: Doubled-Die Obverse, Small D
PUP: WE TRUST, mintmark
URS-7 · I-5 · L-5

VAM-4

Clear, Small D mintmark

Description: The obverse is the same as on VAM-3. The mintmark on the reverse die is a small D, shaped much like that of the 1920s-era D punches.

Comments: This VAM is quite rare and in very high demand by specialists.

Census: 64, 64, 64, 64, 64, 63, 63

	EF-40	AU-50	MS-60	MS-63	MS-65
VARIETY	$185	$375	$675	$1,650	n/a
NORMAL	38	55	130	350	$1,400

Modern Dollars
Eisenhower Dollars, 1971–1978
Susan B. Anthony Dollars, 1979–1981 and 1999
Sacagawea and Presidential Dollars, 2000 to Date

Because of modern changes in the die-making process in the United States Mint, very few significant varieties are known in these series, which began with the Eisenhower dollar in 1971. However, those that are known are generally in very high demand, especially those with a visually attractive difference. The edge lettering of the recent golden dollars is the focal point of several modern varieties.

Eisenhower dollars are known with somewhat strong obverse and reverse doubled dies, and a couple repunched mintmarks. The Anthony series contains a slight change in the obverse design (in 1979), changes in the mintmarks (in 1979 and 1981), and a possible repunched mintmark for the 1980-S Proof. Another variety for the Sacagawea dollar is known; it appears on the reverse, with lines of an unknown origin appearing to breach the breast of the eagle. To date, only the Eisenhower dollar has been the topic of reference books, but more information on all can be found in the Red Book.

As of this publication date, there are no clubs devoted strictly to the study of Susan B. Anthony and golden dollars, yet these series hold a number of nice varieties and are popular among collectors. For those interested in modern dollar varieties, we suggest membership in CONECA, the national error and variety club.
For adults, annual dues are $25 (for bulk mailing; contact the Membership Coordinator for current First Class or international rates). For Young Numismatists (under age 18), dues are $7.50 (online membership only, which includes digital access to *ErrorScope*) or $17.50 (online membership plus hard-copy subscription to *ErrorScope*). An application can be obtained online at www.conecaonline.org, or from Rachel Irish at the following address:

> CONECA
> Rachel Irish
> 101 W. Prairie #323
> Hayden, ID 83835
> E-mail: MRirish5@roadrunner.com

Those interested primarily in Eisenhower varieties can also contact Rob Ezerman of The Ike Group, 542 Hemlock Road, St. George, VT 05495.

1971-D
FS-C1-1971D-901

VARIETY: Low-Relief Reverse
PUP: Area above eagle's eye
NEW LISTING

CONECA: RDV-006
"FRIENDLY EAGLE" VARIETY

Description: This variety lacks the furrowed brow line over the eagle's eye. Earth is fully round, and the Gulf is rounded; the islands form a string; and the design details around the crater above LLA of DOLLAR are very distinct.

Comments: This variety is affectionately referred to as the Friendly Eagle by the Ike Group. The details are naked-eye visible, with six features that are different than on the common 1971-D reverse with the furrowed brow line. According to the Ike Group, the mintage is around 250,000. The Friendly Eagle can be found clustered in original rolls.

	MS-65	MS-66	MS-67
VARIETY	n/a	n/a	n/a
NORMAL	$50	$150	

1971-S, Proof
FS-S1-1971S-103 (015.8)

VARIETY: Doubled-Die Obverse
PUP: IN GOD WE TRUST
URS-4 · I-4 · L-3

CONECA: DDO-003

Description: Strong doubling is evident on IN GOD WE TRUST, the date, and LIBER of LIBERTY.

Comments: This obverse is also paired with a minor doubled-die reverse.

	PF-63	PF-65	PF-66	PF-67
VARIETY	$75	$90	$100	$115
NORMAL	9	12	13	15

1971-S, Proof
FS-S1-1971S-106

VARIETY: Doubled-Die Obverse
PUP: IN GOD WE TRUST
URS-4 · I-4 · L-3

CONECA: DDO-006

Description: *Very* strong doubling is evident on IN GOD WE TRUST, the date, and LIBERTY.

Comments: This listing is every bit as nice as the previous.

	PF-63	PF-65	PF-66	PF-67
VARIETY	$75	$90	$100	$115
NORMAL	9	12	13	15

1971-S, Proof, 40% Silver
FS-S1-1971S-801

VARIETY: Doubled-Die Reverse
PUP: UNITED STATES OF AMERICA,
E PLURIBUS UNUM, ONE DOLLAR
NEW LISTING

WEXLER: WDDR-010;
CONECA: DDR-005

Description: An extremely strong counterclockwise spread from a pivot at 7 o'clock shows on UNITED STATES OF AMERICA, E PLURIBUS UNUM, ONE DOLLAR, the stars, the designer's initials, Earth, the eagle's left wing feathers, the tail feathers, the olive branch and leaves, and the craters, with the strongest spread on the right side of the reverse.

Comments: This is a relatively new discovery that should make every owner of a 1971-S Proof Ike dollar take a second look.

	PF-63	PF-65	PF-66	PF-67
VARIETY	n/a	n/a	n/a	n/a
NORMAL	$9	$12	$13	$15

1971-S, Mint State, 40% Silver — FS-S1-1971S-401

VARIETY: Polished Die
PUP: R of LIBERTY
URS-6 · I-4 · L-4

CONECA: ODV-002, DDO-009
"PEGLEG R" VARIETY

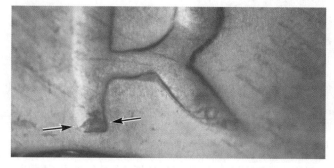

Description: The left leg on the R of LIBERTY has been over polished.
Comments: Affectionately referred to as the "Pegleg R."

	MS-65	MS-66	MS-67
VARIETY	$150	$250	$450
NORMAL	20	40	300

1971-S, Mint State, 40% Silver — FS-S1-1971S-501

VARIETY: Repunched Mintmark
PUP: Mintmark
URS-6 · I-4 · L-4

CONECA: RPM-001

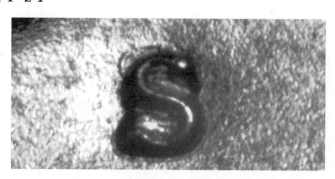

Description: A secondary S is evident protruding northwest of the primary S.
Comments: This is one of fewer than a half dozen RPMs known for the entire Eisenhower series. (Note: This variety was incorrectly listed as FS-S1-1971S-40 in the fourth edition, volume II.)

	MS-65	MS-66	MS-67
VARIETY	$225	$350	$475
NORMAL	20	40	300

1972, Variety II   FS-C1-1972-901

VARIETY: B Reverse
PUP: Earth northwest of eagle's head
NEW LISTING

CONECA: RDV-002; BREEN-5749
"KING OF IKES" VARIETY

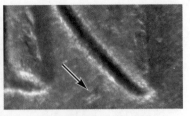

Shiny die gouge under N of IN on March 1972 releases

Description: Earth is rounded and the Caribbean Islands are blended into a single area that is difficult to detect among the general markings along the eastern United States. On all other reverse varieties the Caribbean Islands are raised and distinctive.

Comments: This variety is referred to as the King of Ikes by the Ike Group. Called the B Reverse when it was first discovered, it was later called the Type-I Reverse by Breen, RDV-002 by CONECA, and Type-2 by the Ike Group. Specimens released in March 1972 have a shiny die gouge under the N of IN; specimens released in August 1972 have die cracks through the upper ATE of STATES.

	MS-65	MS-66	MS-67
VARIETY	n/a	n/a	n/a
NORMAL	$5		

1972-S, Proof   FS-S1-1972S-101

VARIETY: Doubled-Die Obverse
PUP: IN GOD WE TRUST
URS-5 · I-1 · L-3

CONECA: UNKNOWN

Description: A medium spread can be detected on IN GOD WE TRUST, LIBERTY, and slightly on the date.

Comments: (Note: Because of its low Interest Factor, this variety will be removed from this chapter in the next edition of this volume, to make room for more popularly collected pieces. The Fivaz-Stanton number will be retained for this variety and it will remain in the cross-references at the back of the book.)

1973-S, Proof, 40% Silver — FS-S1-1973S-101

VARIETY: Doubled-Die Obverse
PUP: IN GOD WE TRUST
URS-5 · I-1 · L-3

CONECA: UNKNOWN

Description: A medium spread can be detected on IN GOD WE TRUST, LIBERTY, and slightly on the date.

Comments: (Note: Because of its low Interest Factor, this variety will be removed from this chapter in the next edition of this volume, to make room for more popularly collected pieces. The Fivaz-Stanton number will be retained for this variety and it will remain in the cross-references at the back of the book.)

1979-P — FS-C1-1979P-301 (016)

VARIETY: Wide Rim
PUP: Date
URS-11 · I-4 · L-3

CONECA: ODV-002
"NEAR DATE" VARIETY

Wide Rim (Near Date)   **Narrow Rim (Far Date)**

Description: The rim on some later 1979-P SBA dollars is wider than on earlier issues, making the date appear to be closer to the rim.

Comments: This variety, created in 1979 by a slight design alteration, carries the nickname "Near Date."

	MS-65	MS-66	MS-67
VARIETY	$55	$135	n/a
NORMAL	10	20	

1979-S, Proof, Clear S
FS-C1-1979S-501

VARIETY: Type II Mintmark
PUP: Mintmark
URS-9 · I-5 · L-5

CONECA: MMS-002

Common "Type I" mintmark   **Rare "Type II" mintmark**

Description: The S-mintmark punch was changed in 1979 to create a clearer S.

Comments: The Type II mintmark is far rarer than the Type I. Any 1979-S Proof set in which all six coins bear the Type II mintmark is extremely rare and will command a higher value than six individual coins.

	PF-65	PF-66	PF-67	PF-68
VARIETY	$58	$60	$63	$68
NORMAL	8			

1980-S, Proof
FS-C1-1980S-501

VARIETY: Repunched Mintmark
PUP: Mintmark
URS-3 · I-4 · L-4

CONECA: N/L

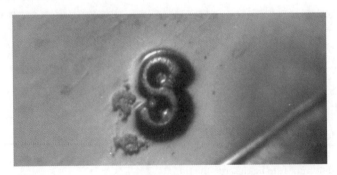

Description: The possible remnants of a previously punched S appear left of the primary S.

Comments: Although this has been listed as an S/S, there is speculation in the collecting community that it's actually a damaged or rusted die. Very few specimens of this variety have surfaced to date.

	PF-65	PF-66	PF-67	PF-68
VARIETY	n/a	n/a	n/a	n/a
NORMAL	$8			

1981-S, Proof, Clear S
FS-C1-1981S-501

VARIETY: Type II Mintmark
PUP: Mintmark
URS-8 · I-5 · L-5

CONECA: MMS-003

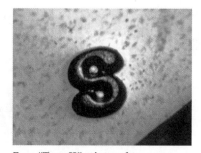

Common "Type I" mintmark

Rare "Type II" mintmark

Description: The S-mintmark punch was changed in 1981 to create a clearer S. The Type II mintmark for 1981 has a flat, frosty surface, while the mintmark on the Type I is rounded.

Comments: As with the 1979 Proof set, any 1981-S set with all six coins bearing the Type II mintmark is very rare and will command a higher value than six individual coins.

	PF-65	PF-66	PF-67	PF-68
VARIETY	$100	$110	$130	$140
NORMAL	8			

2000-P
FS-C1-2000P-901

VARIETY: Reverse Die Aberrations
PUP: Eagle's breast
URS-6 · I-4 · L-4

CONECA: N/L
"SPEARED EAGLE" VARIETY

Description: There are two spikes appearing through the breast of the eagle on the reverse.

Comments: Some collectors have nicknamed this variety the "Speared Eagle."

	MS-65	MS-66	MS-67	MS-68
VARIETY	$775	$1,500	$2,500	n/a
NORMAL	3	12		

2000-P, Boldy Detailed Tail Feathers · FS-C1-2000P-902

VARIETY: Enhanced Reverse Die
PUP: Tail Feathers
URS-14 · I-5 · L-5

CONECA: N/L
"CHEERIOS" VARIETY

Enhanced feathers   Normal feathers

Description: The feathers of the eagle are greatly enhanced, as evidenced in the photos.

Comments: This variety is affectionately known as the "Cheerios" variety, as it was included as a promotion in boxes of Cheerios cereal. (Note: This variety was incorrectly listed as FS-S1-2000P-901 in the fourth edition.) An MS-68 example was auctioned in August 2000 for $5,750.

	MS-65	MS-66	MS-67	MS-68
VARIETY	$2,500	$3,000	$3,750	$6,000
NORMAL	3	12		

(2007), Washington · FS-C1-(2007)-GW-701

VARIETY: Missing Edge Inscription
PUP: Edge of coin
NEW LISTING

"PLAIN EDGE" VARIETY

Description: The date, mintmark, E PLURIBUS UNUM, IN GOD WE TRUST, and delimiter dots are missing from the edge, due to the coin's not being run through an edge-lettering machine.

Comments: Thousands of these escaped the Mint, with some estimates being higher than 100,000. (Adams and Jefferson dollars were also released in significant, but smaller, quantities.) Most were found in Florida, with smaller numbers scattered throughout several other states. Plain Edge dollars with other presidents are also known in very small to moderate numbers; some are found among Mint sets. Issues that approach or exceed 1,000 released are the (2008) Harrison, (2009) Tyler, and (2009) Polk.

	MS-65	MS-67
VARIETY	n/a	n/a
NORMAL	$3	

(2007), Adams

FS-C1-(2007)-JA-701

VARIETY: Missing Edge Inscription
PUP: Edge of coin
NEW LISTING

"PLAIN EDGE" VARIETY

Description: The date, mintmark, E PLURIBUS UNUM, IN GOD WE TRUST, and delimiter dots are missing from the edge, due to the coin's not being run through an edge-lettering machine.

Comments: Thousands (by some estimates, 10,000 or more) of these escaped the Mint, more than 99% of them in Philadelphia rolls. Most were found in southeastern Michigan, but a small number were found in Florida. Plain Edge Washington and Jefferson dollars were also released in significant quantities, with the Washington being the more common; the variety is known in very small to moderate numbers with other Presidential obverses (some found in Mint sets). Issues that may be close to or exceed 1,000 released are the (2008) Harrison, (2009) Tyler, and (2009) Polk. Many thousands of John Adams dollars with doubled edge lettering were also released—in even larger quantities than the Plain Edge variety; many were found in the same rolls as the plain-edgers.

	MS-65	MS-67
VARIETY	n/a	n/a
NORMAL	$3	

(2007), Jefferson

FS-C1-(2007)-TJ-701

VARIETY: Missing Edge Inscription
PUP: Edge of coin
NEW LISTING

"PLAIN EDGE" VARIETY

Description: The date, mintmark, E PLURIBUS UNUM, IN GOD WE TRUST, and delimiter dots are missing from the edge, due to the coin's not being run through an edge-lettering machine.

Comments: More than 1,000 of these escaped the Mint. Plain Edge Washington and Adams dollars were also released in significant quantities, with the Washington being the more common; the variety is known in very small to moderate numbers with other Presidential obverses (some found in Mint sets). Issues that may be close to or exceed 1,000 released are the (2008) Harrison, (2009) Tyler, and (2009) Polk. The coin shown here is the discovery coin.

	MS-65	MS-67
VARIETY	n/a	n/a
NORMAL	$3	

2007-S, Jefferson, Proof — FS-C1-2007S-TJ-701

VARIETY: Out-of-Sequence Edge Inscription
PUP: Edge of coin
NEW LISTING

Description: The edge inscription reads, 2007 S - IN GOD WE TRUST - E PLURIBUS UNUM instead of the proper 2007 S - E PLURIBUS UNUM - IN GOD WE TRUST.

Comments: Five of these coins were found within a group of two hundred 2007 four-coin Presidential dollar Proof sets early in the ordering period. One was sent to and authenticated by *Coin World*. Mint spokesman Michael White, in a March 20, 2008, statement, said: "It was a simple mistake in the hand placement of the segments for the mottos to appear out-of-order." A week later the Mint said: "100,000 of the errors may have been produced early in the production run before measures were taken to prevent the error from occurring." To date, only those first five specimens are known. Surely more exist. The image here is a mock-up depicting how the inscription is sequenced on the actual variety.

	PF-65	PF-67
VARIETY	n/a	n/a
NORMAL	$10	

(2010), Native American, Satin Finish — FS-C1-(2010)-NA-701

VARIETY: Missing Edge Inscription
PUP: Edge of coin
NEW LISTING

"PLAIN EDGE" VARIETY

Description: The date, mintmark, E PLURIBUS UNUM, and stars are missing due to the coin's not being run through an edge-lettering machine.

Comments: This one is found in Mint sets and appears to be very scarce to rare.

	MS-65	MS-67
VARIETY	n/a	n/a
NORMAL	$2.80	

Gold Coin Varieties

When considering gold varieties of any denomination, keep in mind one of our Helpful Hints: **"A good point to remember and consider is that, generally speaking, as the numismatic or bullion value of a coin increases, the premium one might expect to be associated with that variety will go down."**

If you will, compare these two coins: an 1888 Liberty Head $20 gold piece featuring a doubled reverse die, and a 1943-S Washington quarter exhibiting a doubled obverse die. Both show dramatic doubling of the images. Yet the 1888 $20 DDR will command little if any premium for a knowledgeable enthusiast, while the 1943-S quarter with the DDO will command a hefty premium.

The 1888 Liberty Head $20 coin is listed with a value of $1,700 in AU-50, a common grade for the coin. The listed price for the doubled reverse die is $1,800, virtually the same as the normal coin. The 1943-S Washington quarter is listed at $50 in MS-65. The same coin with a doubled obverse die is listed at $2,250 in MS-65. That represents a premium of $2,200, or a 4,500% premium for the doubled die.

The 1888 $20 piece has a total mintage of 226,161. Based upon average die-life estimates, there would have been about six to 10 reverse dies used for the entire mintage. Using those estimates, the 1888 Liberty Head $20 coin with the doubled reverse die would make up at least 10% of the total mintage.

The 1943-S Washington quarter has a total mintage of 21,700,000. Based upon average die-life estimates, there would have been about 434 obverse dies used for the entire mintage. Using those estimates, the 1943-S quarter with the doubled obverse die would make up less than 4% of the total mintage.

There is also another consideration when comparing mintage estimates. During the time of gold-coin production, the dies were not inspected very closely for abnormalities. Therefore, a doubled die in 1943 was more likely to be pulled from service than in 1888.

The important factor to consider is the percent of the total population having the die abnormality. The higher that percentage, the lower any premium percentage one might expect. This same analogy will hold true for commemorative coins, and any other coinage with a low regular-issue mintage.

One last comment: many of the gold varieties will bring a small premium in lower grades. However, as the value of the normal coin reaches higher, any premium will soon evaporate.

With a very few exceptions, a doubled die, repunched mintmark, or overdate on a gold coin is less likely to command any premium over the value of the normal coin.

Note: The "Normal" values listed in this chapter were figured with gold's bullion value at $1,600 per ounce.

1854, Type 2 — FS-G1-1854-101

VARIETY: Doubled-Die Obverse
PUP: UNITED STATES OF AMERICA
URS-9 · I-3 · L-2

CONECA: N/L

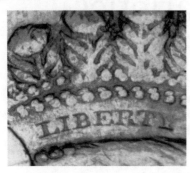 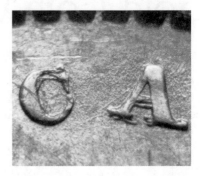

Description: Very strong doubling is evident on UNITED STATES OF AMERICA, the beads in the headdress, the feathers, and portions of LIBERTY. Strong clash marks on the reverse are evident on the specimens we've seen.

Comments: A slight premium can be expected for the lower grades.

	VF-20	EF-40	AU-50	MS-60	MS-63
VARIETY	$375	$525	$660	$2,050	$10,000
NORMAL	350	500	625	1,850	9,500

1854, Type 2 — FS-G1-1854-301

VARIETY: Repunched Date
PUP: Date
URS-7 · I-3 · L-2

CONECA: N/L

Description: Secondary date digits are evident, with the secondary 1 slightly north of the primary, and the secondary 8, 5, and 4 slightly right of the primary.

Comments: The doubling visible on the word DOLLAR is the typical doubling known for James B. Longacre's designs, such as Indian Head cents, Shield nickels, and others. This is not the result of a doubled die.

	VF-20	EF-40	AU-50	MS-60	MS-63
VARIETY	$350	$500	$625	$1,850	$9,500
NORMAL	350	500	625	1,850	9,500

1856-S, Type 2 — FS-G1-1856S-501

VARIETY: Repunched Mintmark   **CONECA: RPM-001**
PUP: Mintmark
URS-10 · I-2 · L-2

Description: This bold repunched mintmark exhibits the secondary S wide to the northeast of the primary S.

Comments: Due to this being a better date and a more expensive coin, little to no premium might be expected for this variety. Additionally, a larger percentage of the surviving coins of this date and mint would likely be this RPM.

	VF-20	EF-40	AU-50	MS-60	MS-63
VARIETY	$950	$1,450	$2,350	$8,000	$30,000
NORMAL	950	1,450	2,350	8,000	30,000

1862, Type 3 — FS-G1-1862-101 (G-001)

VARIETY: Doubled-Die Obverse   **CONECA: DDO-001**
PUP: UNITED STATES OF AMERICA
URS-7 · I-3 · L-2

Description: Doubling is evident on the entire obverse, including UNITED STATES OF AMERICA and the entire profile of Lady Liberty, most evident of which are the tops of the hair curls and the feathers.

Comments: This is a visually appealing DDO.

	VF-20	EF-40	AU-50	MS-60	MS-63
VARIETY	$275	$300	$350	$600	$1,350
NORMAL	225	245	265	400	1,100

1851 FS-G2.5-1851-301

VARIETY: Repunched Date
CONECA: N/L
PUP: Date
URS-6 · I-3 · L-2

Description: A secondary 1 is visible west of the primary first 1, and at the base slightly north on the second 1.

Comments: Being one of the more common dates, this variety may bring little to no premium, especially in the better "collector" grades below MS-63.

	VF-20	EF-40	AU-50	MS-60	MS-63
VARIETY	$350	$375	$385	$450	$1,450
NORMAL	350	375	385	450	1,450

1853 FS-G2.5-1853-301

VARIETY: Repunched Date
CONECA: N/L
PUP: Date
URS-7 · I-3 · L-2

Description: A secondary 1 is evident slightly north on the primary 1, and the upper loop of a secondary 8 is barely visible within the upper loop of the primary 8.

Comments: Repunched dates are known throughout all gold coins of the 19th century.

	VF-20	EF-40	AU-50	MS-60	MS-63
VARIETY	$350	$375	$385	$450	$1,450
NORMAL	350	375	385	450	1,450

1854-O
FS-G2.5-1854o-301 (G-002)

Variety: Misplaced Date   **CONECA: N/L**
PUP: Date
URS-7 · I-3 · L-2

Description: The 4 is repunched, with just an upright of a secondary 4 evident right of the primary 4. Additionally, the tip of the crosslet of a 4 is evident protruding from the bust, just below the lower hair curl.

Comments: In a better market, the values for this overdate would represent an exception to the rule that gold varieties don't command much premium. As of press time, however, the variety follows the pattern typical of other gold coins.

	VF-20	EF-40	AU-50	MS-60	MS-63
Variety	$385	$400	$575	$1,550	$8,250
Normal	385	400	575	1,550	8,250

1862, 2 Over 1
FS-G2.5-1862-301 (G-002)

Variety: Overdate   **CONECA: N/L**
PUP: Date
URS-5 · I-3 · L-2

Description: This overdate exhibits a 2 over a 1. The 1 is evident between the ball of the 2 and the lower left leg.

Comments: The values for this overdate represent an exception to the rule that gold varieties don't command much premium.

	VF-20	EF-40	AU-50	MS-60	MS-63
Variety	$950	$1,950	$3,100	$7,000	n/a
Normal	400	600	900	2,000	$7,000

1891 FS-G2.5-1891-801

VARIETY: Doubled-Die Reverse   **CONECA: DDR-001**
PUP: AMERICA
URS-6 · I-3 · L-2

Description: Doubling is evident on most reverse elements, especially on the lower right side. The doubling is especially strong on AMERICA, the arrow tips, the eagle's claw, and the feathers.

Comments: This is a really dramatic doubled die! Possibly, most if not all of the 1891 quarter eagles exhibit this doubled die.

	VF-20	EF-40	AU-50	MS-60	MS-63
VARIETY	$385	$420	$445	$545	$1,250
NORMAL	365	400	425	520	1,150

1882 FS-G3-1882-301

VARIETY: Repunched Date   **CONECA: N/L**
PUP: Date
URS-7 · I-3 · L-2

Description: A secondary 2 is evident north of the primary 2. This secondary 2 has obviously been polished, with only the right portion of the upper loop and the base visible.

Comments: Although this is a very appealing $3 gold variety, little to no premium should be expected due to the high value of the "normal" coin.

	VF-20	EF-40	AU-50	MS-60	MS-63
VARIETY	$1,250	$1,500	$2,350	$4,250	$10,500
NORMAL	1,250	1,500	2,350	4,250	10,500

1802, 2 Over 1   FS-G5-1802-301

VARIETY: Overdate   **CONECA: N/L**
PUP: Date
URS-10 · I-4 · L-4

Description: The 2 is clearly punched over a 1.

Comments: There were no 1801-dated $5 gold pieces, and all known 1802-dated pieces are the overdate, 2 Over 1.

	VF-20	EF-40	AU-50	MS-60	MS-63
VARIETY	$5,000	$7,000	$10,000	$14,500	$31,500
NORMAL	5,000	7,000	10,000	14,500	31,500

1819, 5D Over "50"   FS-G5-1819-901

VARIETY: Repunched Letters   **CONECA: N/L**
PUP: 5D on reverse
URS-6 · I-3 · L-3

Description: The 5D (for "Five Dollars") on the reverse is listed in most references as 5D/50. The authors believe this is actually a 5D with the D over an inverted D.

Comments: This reverse variety is actually more common than the 1819 without the repunching of the letter. "Normal" values shown are for the 1819 coin without the repunching.

	VF-20	EF-40	AU-50	MS-60	MS-63
VARIETY	n/a	$50,000	$65,000	$105,000	$150,000
NORMAL	n/a	50,000	65,000	105,000	150,000

1847, Top of Extra 7 Very Low at Border   FS-G5-1847-301 (G-003)

VARIETY: Misplaced Date   **CONECA: N/L**
PUP: Denticles below date
URS-5 · I-3 · L-2

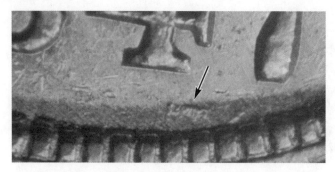

Description: The top of a 7 is clearly evident protruding from the denticles below the 4.

Comments: Remember, the premium will reduce as the normal coin's value increases.

	VF-20	EF-40	AU-50	MS-60	MS-63
VARIETY	$575	$585	$600	$2,000	$7,500
NORMAL	475	485	500	1,650	6,000

1847   FS-G5-1847-302 (G-004)

VARIETY: Misplaced Date   **CONECA: N/L**
PUP: Front of neck
URS-4 · I-3 · L-2

Description: A misplaced 1 is evident protruding from the front of the neck.

Comments: Remember, the premium will reduce as the normal coin's value increases.

	VF-20	EF-40	AU-50	MS-60	MS-63
VARIETY	$575	$585	$600	$2,000	$7,500
NORMAL	475	485	500	1,650	6,000

1847 — FS-G5-1847-303

VARIETY: Repunched Date
PUP: Date
URS-5 · I-3 · L-2

CONECA: N/L

Description: The date is clearly repunched, with a secondary 1 south of the primary 1; the secondary 8 slightly south of the primary 8; and remnants of a secondary 7 far right of the primary 7.

Comments: Further study may prove this to be a triple-punched date.

	VF-20	EF-40	AU-50	MS-60	MS-63
VARIETY	$475	$485	$500	$1,650	$6,000
NORMAL	475	485	500	1,650	6,000

1847 — FS-G5-1847-304

VARIETY: Misplaced Date
PUP: Base of bust above 1
URS-4 · I-3 · L-2

CONECA: N/L

Description: The base of an errantly placed 1 is evident protruding from the very low, front portion of the bust, immediately above the primary 1.

Comments: This is a relatively recent discovery.

	VF-20	EF-40	AU-50	MS-60	MS-63
VARIETY	$475	$485	$500	$1,650	$6,000
NORMAL	475	485	500	1,650	6,000

1848-D FS-G5-1848D-501

VARIETY: Repunched Mintmark
PUP: Mintmark
NEW LISTING

BREEN: N/A; CONECA: RPM-001

Description: A strong secondary D is evident to the south of the primary D.

Comments: This is one of the strongest RPMs known on a gold coin variety.

	VF-20	EF-40	AU-50	MS-60	MS-63
VARIETY	n/a	n/a	n/a	n/a	n/a
NORMAL	$475	$485	$500	$1,650	$6,000

1854 FS-G5-1854-101 (004.5)

VARIETY: Doubled-Die Obverse
PUP: Ear
URS-5 · I-3 · L-2

CONECA: DDO-001
"EARRING" VARIETY

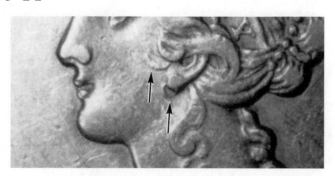

Description: This is a fairly strong doubled die, with the doubling evident on the front hair curl above the ear, and the earlobe.

Comments: This is known as the "Earring" variety.

	VF-20	EF-40	AU-50	MS-60	MS-63
VARIETY	$500	$525	$600	$2,250	n/a
NORMAL	475	485	550	2,000	$6,500

1881   FS-G5-1881-301 (005)

VARIETY: Overdate   **CONECA: N/L**
PUP: Date
URS-6 · I-3 · L-2

Description: The 1881 date is clearly punched over an 1880 date. From the appearance of the repunching, each date was part of a four-digit logo punch.

Comments: This is a fairly well-known variety.

	VF-20	EF-40	AU-50	MS-60	MS-63
VARIETY	$450	$460	$475	$525	$1,025
NORMAL	450	460	475	525	1,025

1881   FS-G5-1881-302

VARIETY: Repunched Date   **CONECA: N/L**
PUP: Date
URS-7 · I-3 · L-2

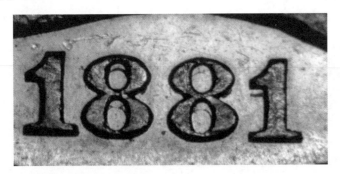

Description: Secondary digits are evident south on both 8's and the final 1.

Comments: This RPD is very easy to spot.

	VF-20	EF-40	AU-50	MS-60	MS-63
VARIETY	$450	$460	$475	$525	$1,025
NORMAL	450	460	475	525	1,025

1881
FS-G5-1881-303

VARIETY: Repunched Date
CONECA: N/L
PUP: Date
URS-6 · I-3 · L-2

Description: All four secondary digits are evident north of the primary date.

Comments: This is a very eye-appealing variety.

	VF-20	EF-40	AU-50	MS-60	MS-63
VARIETY	$450	$460	$475	$525	$1,025
NORMAL	450	460	475	525	1,025

1881
FS-G5-1881-304

VARIETY: Repunched Date
CONECA: N/L
PUP: Date
URS-7 · I-3 · L-2

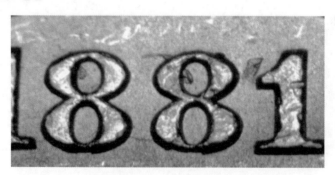

Description: The secondary digits are evident far left of the primary digits.

Comments: This is another very attractive repunched date.

	VF-20	EF-40	AU-50	MS-60	MS-63
VARIETY	$485	$500	$525	$575	$1,100
NORMAL	450	460	475	525	1,025

1881   FS-G5-1881-305

VARIETY: Repunched Date   **CONECA: N/L**
PUP: Date
URS-7 · I-3 · L-2

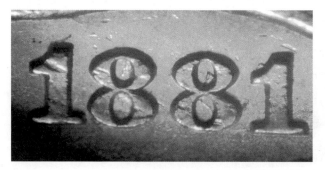

Description: The secondary digits are evident slightly left of the primary digits.
Comments: The weaker second 8 appears slanted slightly downward.

	VF-20	EF-40	AU-50	MS-60	MS-63
VARIETY	$450	$460	$475	$525	$1,025
NORMAL	450	460	475	525	1,025

1899   FS-G5-1899-301

VARIETY: Repunched Date   **CONECA: N/L**
PUP: Date
URS-7 · I-3 · L-2

Description: The secondary digits are evident slightly northwest of the primary digits.
Comments: This is another very attractive repunched date.

	VF-20	EF-40	AU-50	MS-60	MS-63
VARIETY	$450	$460	$475	$525	$1,025
NORMAL	450	460	475	525	1,025

1901-S, Final 1 Over 0　　　　FS-G5-1901S-301

VARIETY: Overdate　　　　　　　　　　　　**CONECA: N/L**
PUP: Date
URS-7 · I-3 · L-2

Description: A secondary 0 is evident at the upper right outside of the last 1 of the date.

Comments: This is a very eye-appealing overdate and a well-known variety.

	VF-20	EF-40	AU-50	MS-60	MS-63
VARIETY	$475	$500	$525	$575	$1,200
NORMAL	450	460	475	525	1,025

1901-S　　　　　　　　　　　　　　　FS-G5-1901S-501

VARIETY: Repunched Mintmark　　　　　　**CONECA: RPM-002**
PUP: Mintmark
URS-7 · I-3 · L-2

Description: The primary S mintmark is clearly punched over a smaller S.

Comments: This is a very interesting variety, and not well known.

	VF-20	EF-40	AU-50	MS-60	MS-63
VARIETY	$450	$460	$475	$525	$1,025
NORMAL	450	460	475	525	1,025

1905-S

VARIETY: Misplaced Mintmark **CONECA: RPM-001**
PUP: Mintmark
URS-4 · I-3 · L-3

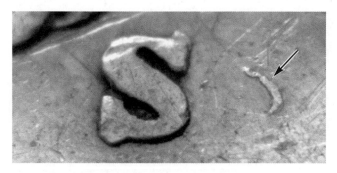

Description: A secondary S mintmark is evident right of the primary S.
Comments: This is a very, very interesting variety.

	VF-20	EF-40	AU-50	MS-60	MS-63
VARIETY	$450	$460	$475	$575	$1,750
NORMAL	450	460	475	575	1,750

1906

VARIETY: Repunched Date **CONECA: N/L**
PUP: Date
URS-7 · I-3 · L-2

 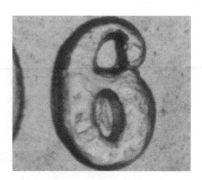

Description: A secondary 6 is evident within the lower loop of the primary 6.
Comments: This is an interesting variety but does not command a premium.

	VF-20	EF-40	AU-50	MS-60	MS-63
VARIETY	$450	$460	$475	$525	$1,025
NORMAL	450	460	475	525	1,025

1911-S

VARIETY: Repunched Mintmark
PUP: Mintmark
URS-7 · I-3 · L-2

CONECA: RPM-001

Description: A secondary S is evident south of the primary S.

Comments: This is an interesting and readily available variety.

	VF-20	EF-40	AU-50	MS-60	MS-63
VARIETY	$460	$475	$485	$850	$5,750
NORMAL	460	475	485	850	5,750

1911-S

VARIETY: Repunched Mintmark
PUP: Mintmark
NEW LISTING

VP-001

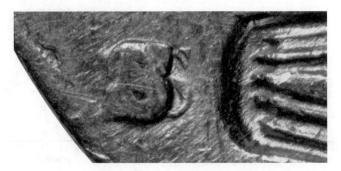

Description: A secondary S is evident to the east of the primary S.

Comments: This new variety was reported by a grading service just months before press time.

	VF-20	EF-40	AU-50	MS-60	MS-63
VARIETY	n/a	n/a	n/a	n/a	n/a
NORMAL	$460	$475	$485	$850	$5,750

1846-O
FS-G10-1846o-301

VARIETY: Repunched Date, Repunched Mintmark
PUP: Date, mintmark
URS-5 · I-3 · L-2

CONECA: N/L

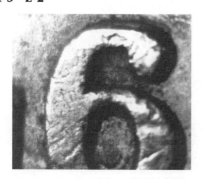 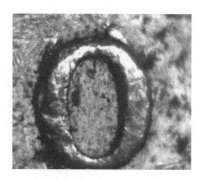

Description: The 6 is slightly repunched, with the secondary 6 visible slightly north of the primary 6. The mintmark is also slightly repunched, with the secondary O evident protruding from the top of the primary O.

Comments: This variety is not very dramatic, but interesting.

	VF-20	EF-40	AU-50	MS-60
VARIETY	$900	$1,200	$4,200	$13,500
NORMAL	900	1,200	4,200	13,500

1854-S
FS-G10-1854S-301

VARIETY: Misplaced Date
PUP: Area below date
URS-5 · I-3 · L-2

CONECA: N/L

Description: The base of a 1 is evident below the 1 and the 8.

Comments: This MPD is very dramatic!

	VF-20	EF-40	AU-50	MS-60
VARIETY	$900	$950	$1,300	$9,500
NORMAL	900	950	1,300	9,500

1883-S

VARIETY: Misplaced Date
PUP: Denticles below date
URS-7 · I-6 · L-2

CONECA: N/L

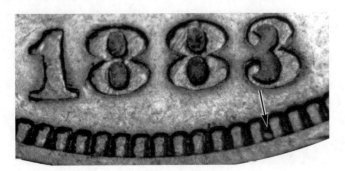

Description: A 3 is visible in the denticles below the date.

Comments: This is not a very dramatic MPD.

	VF-20	EF-40	AU-50	MS-60	MS-63
VARIETY	$800	$825	$835	$1,150	$9,000
NORMAL	800	825	835	1,150	9,000

1889-S

VARIETY: Repunched Mintmark, Doubled-Die Reverse
PUP: Mintmark, OF AMERICA
URS-6 · I-3 · L-2

**CONECA: DDR-001,
RPM-001**

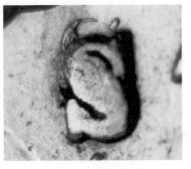 

Description: Doubling on the reverse is most evident on STATES OF AMERICA, WE TRUST, and portions of the ribbon. But the S/S north is the more dramatic of the two diagnostics, with the secondary S strong above the primary S.

Comments: The mintmark is the really interesting portion of this variety.

	VF-20	EF-40	AU-50	MS-60	MS-63
VARIETY	$800	$825	$835	$900	$1,500
NORMAL	800	825	835	900	1,500

1891-CC
FS-G10-1891CC-501

Variety: Repunched Mintmark
PUP: Mintmark
URS-6 · I-3 · L-2

CONECA: RPM-001

Description: A secondary C is evident protruding from the right side of the second C of the primary CC mintmark.

Comments: Any CC mintmark variety is interesting.

	VF-20	EF-40	AU-50	MS-60	MS-63
VARIETY	$950	$1,050	$1,150	$1,750	$5,750
NORMAL	950	1,050	1,150	1,750	5,750

1892-CC
FS-G10-1892CC-501

Variety: Tripled-Die Reverse
PUP: IN GOD WE TRUST
New Listing

VP-001

Description: Tripling is evident within IN GOD WE TRUST, and in other lettering about the rim.

Comments: This was first reported by a grading service several months before press time; it is surprising it was not reported sooner, considering that the 1892-CC is a low-mintage coin.

	VF-20	EF-40	AU-50	MS-60	MS-63
VARIETY	n/a	n/a	n/a	n/a	n/a
NORMAL	$950	$1,050	$1,150	$3,750	$10,000

1852   FS-G20-1852-301

VARIETY: Repunched Date   **CONECA: N/L**
PUP: Date
URS-7 · I-3 · L-2

Description: The weaker digits of the first date punch are all evident north of the primary digits.

Comments: This is a very evident repunched date.

	VF-20	EF-40	AU-50	MS-60	MS-63
VARIETY	$1,850	$1,900	$2,050	$4,750	n/a
NORMAL	1,700	1,750	1,900	4,250	$16,500

1853, 3 Over 2   FS-G20-1853-301 (G-008)

VARIETY: Overdate   **CONECA: N/L**
PUP: Date
URS-7 · I-4 · L-4

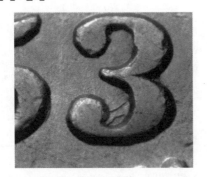 

Description: The 3 of the primary date is punched over a clearly visible 2. There is a rust spot under the R of LIBERTY.

Comments: This is a well-known variety.

	VF-20	EF-40	AU-50	MS-60	MS-63
VARIETY	$2,000	$2,600	$4,350	$30,000	n/a
NORMAL	1,700	1,750	1,900	5,000	$25,000

1857

FS-G20-1857-301

VARIETY: Misplaced Date

CONECA: N/I.

PUP: Date

URS-6 · I-3 · L-2

Description: What appears to be a 1 is evident protruding from the left side of the 5.

Comments: This is a very interesting variety, with a 1 so far misplaced.

	VF-20	EF-40	AU-50	MS-60	MS-63
VARIETY	$1,700	$1,800	$1,900	$4,500	$27,500
NORMAL	1,700	1,800	1,900	4,500	27,500

1859-S

FS-G20-1859S-101 (G-011)

VARIETY: Doubled-Die Obverse

CONECA: DDO-001

PUP: LIBERTY, profile

URS-5 · I-3 · L-3

Description: Doubling is evident on LIBERTY, the eye, the hair curls, and the profile.

Comments: This variety commands the modest premium typical of gold-coin varieties.

	VF-20	EF-40	AU-50	MS-60
VARIETY	$1,900	$2,000	$2,250	$8,600
NORMAL	1,750	1,850	2,100	8,000

1866 FS-G20-1866-801

Variety: Doubled-Die Reverse
PUP: IN GOD WE TRUST
URS-7 · I-3 · L-2

CONECA: N/L

Description: This reverse die was created with a small-letter hub over a large-letter hub. The N of the IN on the motto is clearly doubled.

Comments: This variety is fairly well known among specialists.

	VF-20	EF-40	AU-50	MS-60	MS-63
Variety	$2,000	$2,150	$2,400	n/a	n/a
Normal	1,700	1,750	1,900	$9,000	$30,000

1866-S, With Motto FS-G20-1866S-301

Variety: Misplaced Date
PUP: Denticles just left of date
URS-5 · I-3 · L-2

CONECA: N/L

Description: The top of an 8 is evident protruding from the denticles left of the 1.

Comments: This is a very evident variety.

	VF-20	EF-40	AU-50	MS-60
Variety	$1,700	$1,750	$2,100	$18,500
Normal	1,700	1,750	2,100	18,500

1871-S   FS-G20-1871S-301

VARIETY: Misplaced Date   **CONECA: N/L**
PUP: Denticles below date
URS-6 · I-3 · L-2

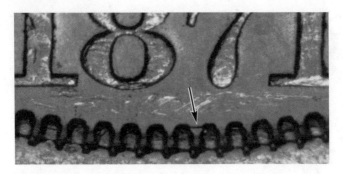

Description: The top of a digit, likely an 8, is evident protruding from the denticles below and between the 8 and 7.

Comments: This is another magical misplaced date.

	VF-20	EF-40	AU-50	MS-60	MS-63
VARIETY	$1,700	$1,750	$1,800	$5,000	$23,500
NORMAL	1,700	1,750	1,800	5,000	23,500

1873   FS-G20-1873-101

VARIETY: Doubled-Die Obverse   **CONECA: DDO-001**
PUP: LIBERTY
URS-6 · I-3 · L-2

Description: Doubling is evident on LIBERTY, the beads around the headband, and portions of the hair.

Comments: This is another very attractive doubled die.

	VF-20	EF-40	AU-50	MS-60	MS-63
VARIETY	$1,700	$1,750	$1,775	$2,000	$11,500
NORMAL	1,700	1,750	1,775	2,000	11,500

1879
FS-G20-1879-801

VARIETY: Doubled-Die Reverse
PUP: LIBERTY
URS-6 · I-3 · L-2

CONECA: DDR-001

Description: Strong doubling is evident on all reverse lettering, including E PLURIBUS UNUM, and the banner.

Comments: This is an extremely strong doubled-die reverse.

	VF-20	EF-40	AU-50	MS-60	MS-63
VARIETY	$1,650	$1,675	$1,700	$1,850	$15,000
NORMAL	1,650	1,675	1,700	1,850	15,000

1883-S
FS-G20-1883S-501

VARIETY: Misplaced Date
PUP: Denticles below date
URS-7 · I-3 · L-2

CONECA: N/L

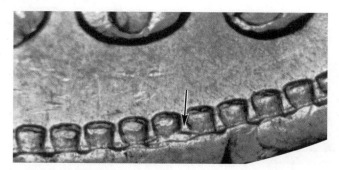

Description: The top of an 8 is evident protruding from the denticles below the second 8.

Comments: Remember to look in the denticles for other misplaced dates.

	VF-20	EF-40	AU-50	MS-60	MS-63
VARIETY	$1,650	$1,675	$1,700	$1,850	$7,500
NORMAL	1,650	1,675	1,700	1,850	7,500

1888
FS-G20-1888-801

VARIETY: Doubled-Die Reverse
PUP: TWENTY DOLLARS
URS-6 · I-3 · L-2

CONECA: DDR-001

Description: Doubling is evident on most reverse lettering, but strongest on TWENTY DOLLARS, and the lower ribbon.

Comments: This is another very strong doubled die.

	VF-20	EF-40	AU-50	MS-60	MS-63
VARIETY	$1,750	$1,775	$1,800	$1,950	n/a
NORMAL	1,650	1,675	1,700	1,850	$9,500

1896
FS-G20-1896-301

VARIETY: Repunched Date
PUP: Date
URS-7 · I-3 · L-2

CONECA: N/L

Description: Doubling is evident with all four digits, evident north of the primary date.

Comments: This is a very strong repunched date.

	VF-20	EF-40	AU-50	MS-60	MS-63
VARIETY	$1,650	$1,675	$1,700	$1,850	$2,750
NORMAL	1,650	1,675	1,700	1,850	2,750

1909, 9 Over 8 — FS-G20-1909-301

VARIETY: Overdate
PUP: 9 of date
URS-8 · I-3 · L-2

CONECA: N/L

Description: The 9 in the date is punched over an 8.

Comments: This is a very well-known overdate, and relatively scarce.

	VF-20	EF-40	AU-50	MS-60	MS-63
VARIETY	$1,800	$1,825	$1,850	$1,950	$3,900
NORMAL	1,650	1,675	1,700	1,750	3,500

1909-S — FS-G20-1909S-501

VARIETY: Repunched Mintmark
PUP: Mintmark
URS-6 · I-3 · L-2

CONECA: RPM-001

Description: The underlying S mintmark is evident below the primary S. There is a slight rotation to the underlying S compared with the primary S.

Comments: This is a very interesting RPM.

	VF-20	EF-40	AU-50	MS-60	MS-63
VARIETY	$1,650	$1,675	$1,700	$1,750	$1,850
NORMAL	1,650	1,675	1,700	1,750	1,850

1911-D

VARIETY: Repunched Mintmark

CONECA: RPM-001

PUP: Mintmark

URS-6 · I-3 · L-2

Description: A secondary D mintmark is evident east of the primary D.

Comments: Although interesting, this RPM will not command a premium.

	VF-20	EF-40	AU-50	MS-60	MS-63
VARIETY	$1,650	$1,675	$1,700	$1,750	$1,850
NORMAL	1,650	1,675	1,700	1,750	1,850

1922

VARIETY: Doubled-Die Reverse

CONECA: DDR-001

PUP: IN GOD WE TRUST

URS-6 · I-3 · L-2

Description: Doubling is evident on most reverse elements, but most visible on IN GOD WE TRUST, the rays, the eagle's talon, and DOLLARS.

Comments: This is a really super DDR! But as with most numismatically high-priced varieties, it is worth little or no premium.

	VF-20	EF-40	AU-50	MS-60	MS-63
VARIETY	$1,650	$1,675	$1,700	$1,750	$1,850
NORMAL	1,650	1,675	1,700	1,750	1,850

1925 FS-G20-1925-801

VARIETY: Doubled-Die Reverse
CONECA: N/L
PUP: Feathers, rays
URS-6 · I-3 · L-2

Description: Doubling is evident on the eagle's feathers, the rays, and IN GOD WE TRUST.

Comments: These doubled dies are generally well known. (See comments for FS-G20-1922-801.)

	VF-20	EF-40	AU-50	MS-60	MS-63
VARIETY	$1,650	$1,675	$1,700	$1,750	$1,850
NORMAL	1,650	1,675	1,700	1,750	1,850

1926 FS-G20-1926-101

VARIETY: Tripled-Die Obverse
CONECA: DDO-001
PUP: Rays, designer's initials
URS-7 · I-3 · L-2

Description: Tripling is evident on the date, rays, and designer's initials.

Comments: This is a well-known and common variety. (See comments for FS-G20-1922-801.)

	VF-20	EF-40	AU-50	MS-60	MS-63
VARIETY	$1,650	$1,675	$1,700	$1,750	$1,850
NORMAL	1,650	1,675	1,700	1,750	1,850

Classic Commemoratives, 1892–1954

M*uch like the gold coin varieties, commemoratives will hold very little, if any, premium for die varieties.* Generally, fewer dies were used on the commemoratives than with gold coinage. If one die is doubled, you can expect a large percentage of the available coins to show that doubling. A very good example is the Stone Mountain Memorial half dollar with the doubled obverse die. Almost 1 in 10 specimens show evidence of the doubled die. Therefore, you can expect no premium associated with these.

Although the varieties may be common, they are interesting, nonetheless. If you are able to locate a very early-die-state specimen in very high grade, you might get a very small premium over the value of the regular coin. But, you might have to wait to find that one person who is willing to pay just a little more.

1892, World's Columbian Exposition   FS-C50-1892-301

VARIETY: Repunched Date   **CONECA: N/L**
PUP: Date
URS-7 · I-3 · L-2

 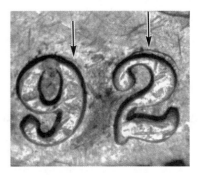

Description: This RPD shows secondary images evident protruding to the northeast from the 9 and 2. The secondary 2 is more evident than the 9.

Comments: Compare this variety with the next.

	AU-50	MS-60	MS-63	MS-65
VARIETY	$19	$32	$85	$475
NORMAL	19	32	85	475

1892, World's Columbian Exposition   FS-C50-1892-302

VARIETY: Repunched Date   **CONECA: N/L**
PUP: Date
URS-7 · I-3 · L-2

Description: This RPD shows secondary images evident protruding to the northeast from the 9 and 2, but slightly more eastward than the previous listing.

Comments: Compare this with the previous listing. They are slightly different.

	AU-50	MS-60	MS-63	MS-65
VARIETY	$19	$32	$85	$475
NORMAL	19	32	85	475

1892, World's Columbian Exposition   FS-C50-1892-303

VARIETY: Repunched Date   **CONECA: N/L**
PUP: Date
URS-7 · I-3 · L-2

Description: Unlike the previous two listings, this RPD is evident only on the 9, with the secondary image protruding to the east of the primary 9.

Comments: There seems to be no distinct difference in the rarity of the three 1892 listings.

	AU-50	MS-60	MS-63	MS-65
VARIETY	$19	$32	$85	$475
NORMAL	19	32	85	475

1893, World's Columbian Exposition   FS-C50-1893-301

VARIETY: Repunched Date   **CONECA: N/L**
PUP: Date
URS-7 · I-3 · L-2

Description: With this RPD, there are secondary images evident north on the 9 and 3.

Comments: The 3, especially, on this RPD is fairly significant.

	AU-50	MS-60	MS-63	MS-65
VARIETY	$25	$38	$85	$500
NORMAL	25	38	85	500

1915-S, Panama-Pacific Exposition   FS-C50-1915S-501

VARIETY: Repunched Mintmark   **CONECA: RPM-002**
PUP: Mintmark
URS-16 · I-3 · L-3

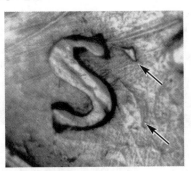 

Description: There is a secondary S protruding to the right of the primary S.

Comments: There is no premium to be expected from this variety. Another RPM, an S/S north, also exists.

	AU-50	MS-60	MS-63	MS-65
VARIETY	$475	$515	$725	$2,400
NORMAL	475	515	725	2,400

1915-S, Panama-Pacific Exposition   FS-C50-1915S-502

VARIETY: Repunched Mintmark   **CONECA: RPM-001**
PUP: Mintmark
NEW LISTING

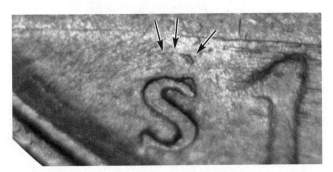

Description: A secondary S can be seen to the north of the primary S.

Comments: This is the second nice variety for the date and type.

	AU-50	MS-60	MS-63	MS-65
VARIETY	n/a	n/a	n/a	n/a
NORMAL	$475	$515	$725	$2,400

1920, Pilgrim Tercentenary — FS-1920-C50-1920-901

VARIETY: Die Crack/Break
PUP: Reverse
NEW LISTING

Early die state (FS-901a)

Middle die state (FS-901b)

Late die state (FS-901c)

Description: A long die crack or break runs vertically between the ship's two forward masts.

Comments: The images show how the crack/break progresses in size through the stages. (A die *crack* is a fracture in the surface of the die with no loss of metal; once the crack widens enough that a piece of metal falls out of the die, it becomes a die *break*.) Other cracks can be found on this coin in all stages.

	AU-50	MS-60	MS-63	MS-65
VARIETY	n/a	n/a	n/a	n/a
NORMAL	$85	$110	$125	$360

1925, Stone Mountain Memorial · FS-C50-1925-101

VARIETY: Doubled-Die Obverse · **CONECA:** DDO-002
PUP: Date
URS-9 · I-3 · L-2

Description: Doubling is strongly visible on STONE MOUNTAIN and 1925.

Comments: A significant percentage of all Stone Mountain Memorial half dollars have this doubled obverse die. There is also a doubled reverse die known, and it is also common.

	AU-50	MS-60	MS-63	MS-65
VARIETY	$60	$70	$85	$275
NORMAL	60	70	85	275

1925, Fort Vancouver Centennial · FS-C50-1925-102

VARIETY: Doubled-Die Obverse · **CONECA:** N/L
PUP: Date, WE TRUST
URS-8 · I-3 · L-2

Description: The doubling is evident on the date and WE TRUST.

Comments: This is another commemorative variety that is very common and well-known.

	AU-50	MS-60	MS-63	MS-65
VARIETY	$340	$400	$450	$1,200
NORMAL	340	400	450	1,200

1933-D, Oregon Trail Memorial   FS-C50-1933D-801

VARIETY: Tripled-Die Obverse   **CONECA: DDO-001**
PUP: HALF DOLLAR, UNITED STATES OF AMERICA
URS-9 · I-3 · L-2

Description: A tripled image is evident on HALF DOLLAR, UNITED STATES OF AMERICA, and the lower portions of the map.

Comments: This is a very attractive, yet common, variety. 1934-D Oregon halves also exhibit this characteristic. Formerly listed as FS-C50-1933D-101.

	AU-50	MS-60	MS-63	MS-65
VARIETY	$360	$380	$400	$500
NORMAL	360	380	400	500

1935, Daniel Boone Bicentennial   FS-C50-1935-101

VARIETY: Doubled-Die Obverse   **CONECA: DDO-001**
PUP: UNITED STATES OF AMERICA, HALF DOLLAR
URS-10 · I-3 · L-2

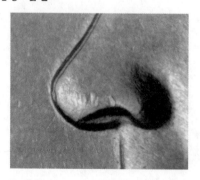 

Description: Doubling is evident on UNITED STATES OF AMERICA, HALF DOLLAR, and the profile.

Comments: This exact same doubled die is also known on the 1937-D Boone half dollar. Most likely, this is a master-die doubled die, and will be found on other Boone issues.

	AU-50	MS-60	MS-63	MS-65
VARIETY	$125	$135	$150	$275
NORMAL	125	135	150	275

1936-D, California Pacific Expo   FS-C50-1936D-101

VARIETY: Quadrupled-Die Obverse, Repunched Mintmark
PUP: LIBERTY, mintmark
NEW LISTING

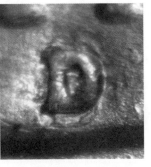

Description: Quadrupling is evident on LIBERTY, and lesser doubling can be seen on HALF DOLLAR and OF AMERICA.

Comments: The RPM is also known paired with a normal obverse die without hub doubling, listed as FS-501.

	AU-50	MS-60	MS-63	MS-65
VARIETY	n/a	n/a	n/a	n/a
NORMAL	$100	$130	$140	$175

1936-D, California Pacific Expo   FS-C50-1936D-501

VARIETY: Repunched Mintmark   **CONECA: RPM-001**
PUP: Mintmark
URS-9 · I-3 · L-2

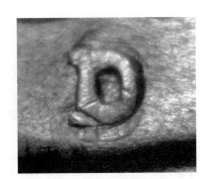

Description: A secondary D is evident south of the primary D.

Comments: This dramatic yet somewhat common repunched mintmark is sometimes seen on the California Pacific International Exposition (often called the San Diego) half dollar.

	AU-50	MS-60	MS-63	MS-65
VARIETY	$100	$130	$140	$175
NORMAL	100	130	140	175

1951, Carver/Washington

FS-C50-1951-801

VARIETY: Doubled-Die Reverse
PUP: AMERICANISM
URS-9 · I-3 · L-2

CONECA: N/L

 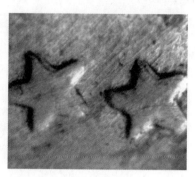

Description: The doubling is evident on all outer reverse lettering.

Comments: This is another doubled die that is likely a master-die doubled die.

	AU-50	MS-60	MS-63	MS-65
VARIETY	$15	$21	$24	$75
NORMAL	15	21	24	75

1953-S, Carver/Washington

FS-C50-1953S-801

VARIETY: Doubled-Die Reverse
PUP: AMERICANISM
URS-9 · I-3 · L-2

CONECA: DDR-001

Description: As with the previous listing, the doubling is evident on all outer reverse lettering.

Comments: This is another doubled die that is likely a master-die doubled die. No doubt this doubling is on other Carver/Washington issues.

	AU-50	MS-60	MS-63	MS-65
VARIETY	$15	$21	$24	$75
NORMAL	15	21	24	75

Bullion Coinage, 1986 to Date

The United States' bullion-coinage program was launched in 1986. Since then, American silver, gold, and platinum coins have become among the most popular precious-metal investment vehicles in the world.

To date, two known mistakes in regular Uncirculated gold bullion coinage have occurred at the Philadelphia Mint. In 1999, two obverse dies with the W mintmark intended for Proof production were processed as Uncirculated (matte-finish) dies, resulting in tenth-ounce and quarter-ounce gold Philadelphia-minted coins with West Point mintmarks.

Platinum Proofs of 2007 were designed so that the word FREEDOM appeared incuse on a ribbon draped across the shield. Because the word had the same, frosted finish as the ribbon on the prototypes, it was difficult to see, so the letters on the dies were polished to a mirror-like finish to achieve greater contrast—but not before a handful of quarter-ounce, half-ounce, and one-ounce platinum Proofs with the original frosted letters were struck and released to the public in error.

Beginning in 2006, the West Point Mint produced Uncirculated "Burnished" coins, so-called because their distinctive finish—richer than on a regular Uncirculated coin, but not quite frosted, as on a Proof—resulted from the burnishing of the coin blanks. After 2007 the Mint changed some of the design details on the reverse, but in 2008 numerous Burnished $1 Silver Eagles were struck and released with a reverse style distinctive to the 2007 issues before anyone realized the error.

Bullion coins have an intrinsic value based on their weight in precious metal; unlike for circulating coins, however, there is scant *numismatic* value for bullion coins (except for some special collector versions and regular versions in exceptional grades, like PF-70DC). Thus, the market for the coins in this section will grow in a sort of "numismatic vacuum" that is unique in the world of die varieties. It will be interesting to see how the premiums develop.

2008-W, Silver Eagle, Burnished — FS-SE1-2008W-901

VARIETY: Reverse of 2007
PUP: U of UNITED
NEW LISTING

2008 reverse, with spur on U, blunt terminus at bottom right of N, wider spacing between N and I

Description: The U of UNITED on the 2007 reverse lacks the stem or spur at the bottom right of the U, while the new reverse introduced in 2008 bears a very prominent spur. Other variations are many, and involve differences in the style of characters, the size and spacing of the stars above the eagle, the distance of characters from the rim and from each other, and the style of the tilde that separates the word SILVER from the word ONE.

Comments: This variety was first reported in 2008. Mint spokesman Michael White suggested that 47,000 such pieces were minted, this number representing about three shifts of production at the West Point facility.

	Unc.
VARIETY	n/a
NORMAL	$45

1999-W, Tenth-Ounce, Uncirculated — FS-G5-1999W-401

VARIETY: Proof W-Mintmark Obverse
PUP: Mintmark and obverse finish
NEW LISTING

Description: Struck as a bullion piece at the Philadelphia Mint, this coin used a West Point–mintmarked obverse die that had been processed as an Uncirculated (matte-finish) die in error.

Comments: This is a Red Book variety of very high interest. PCGS, NGC, and ANACS have certified more than 3,300 of these in various grades.

	Unc.
VARIETY	n/a
NORMAL	$200

1999-W, Quarter-Ounce, Uncirculated — FS-G10-1999W-401

VARIETY: Proof W-Mintmark Obverse
PUP: Mintmark and obverse finish
NEW LISTING

Description: A bullion piece from the Philadelphia Mint, this variety was struck with a West Point–mintmarked obverse die that had been processed as an Uncirculated (matte-finish) die in error.

Comments: This is a Red Book variety of very high interest. PCGS, NGC, and ANACS have certified more than 2,500 of these. (Note: This is the same image as that used for the $5).

	Unc.
VARIETY	n/a
NORMAL	$500

2007-W, Quarter-Ounce, Proof — FS-P25-2007W-901

VARIETY: FREEDOM on Shield Frosted
PUP: FREEDOM on shield
NEW LISTING

Variety, with frosted FREEDOM	Normal coin, with mirrored FREEDOM

Description: This is one of 21 specimens that the Mint produced with a frosted finish on the word FREEDOM; on later issues, the word was polished to a mirror finish to create better contrast. The 21 original specimens were released with the normal run in error.

Comments: This is a recent discovery that many will consider a type of pattern coin—but the fact that examples were released to collectors makes them fair game for cherrypickers.

	PF
VARIETY	n/a
NORMAL	$500

2007-W, Half-Ounce, Proof   FS-P50-2007W-901

VARIETY: FREEDOM on Shield Frosted
PUP: FREEDOM on shield
NEW LISTING

The normal style, with mirrored FREEDOM (here, on the quarter-ounce Proof)

Description: This is one of 21 specimens that the Mint produced with a frosted finish on the word FREEDOM; on later issues, the word was polished to a mirror finish to create better contrast. The 21 original specimens were released with the normal run in error.

Comments: This is a recent discovery that many will consider a type of pattern coin—but the fact that examples were released to collectors makes them fair game for cherrypickers.

	PF
VARIETY	n/a
NORMAL	$1,000

2007-W, One Ounce, Proof   FS-P100-2007W-901

VARIETY: FREEDOM on Shield Frosted
PUP: FREEDOM on shield
NEW LISTING

The normal style, with mirrored FREEDOM (here, on the quarter-ounce Proof)

Description: According to the Treasury, this is one of 12 specimens that the Mint produced with a frosted finish on the word FREEDOM; on later issues, the word was polished to a mirror finish to create better contrast. The 12 original specimens were then released with the normal run in error.

Comments: This is a recent discovery that many will consider a type of pattern coin—but the fact that examples were released to collectors makes them fair game for cherrypickers.

	PF
VARIETY	n/a
NORMAL	$2,100

Appendix A
Doubled Dies vs. Other Forms of Doubling

The difference between die doubling (doubled dies, repunched dates, and repunched mintmarks, among others) and the more confusing forms of doubling can be very challenging to explain, and even more difficult for a novice to comprehend. Additionally, there are times when determining the difference can be frustrating even for a very experienced collector. This section will help you learn the differences. But reading alone will not do it all; you must examine numerous coins before you can expect to have a solid grasp of the differences between die doubling and other forms of doubling.

DIE DOUBLING: THOSE ABNORMALITIES WE LOVE TO COLLECT!

Die doubling is the type of doubling that exhibits a doubled image on the die itself, even before the coin is struck. Die doubling includes doubled dies, repunched dates, repunched mintmarks, overdates, over mintmarks, and repunched letters. It almost always exhibits splits in the serifs of the letters and/or numerals, with rounded, secondary images.

On this Jefferson nickel, the distinctive splits in the serifs are evident, and the secondary images are "rounded" and can easily be detected.

The photograph shown here of a true 1969-S doubled-die Lincoln cent exhibits the typical rounded secondary images. Notice also the "crease" between the images.

Many 19th-century coins have letters and numerals that are flat on their top surfaces as compared to the rounded appearance of most 20th-century letters and numerals. Therefore, the key to identifying true die doubling on 19th-century coins is the distinctive splits in the serifs.

There is one class of doubled die that would not exhibit the normal characteristics mentioned for die doubling. Known as Class VI doubled dies, these exhibit extra thickness

The splits in the serifs on this 1887 Indian Head cent doubled-die obverse are typical of what one would expect for most 19th-century coins with true die doubling.

on some letters and numbers. Most widely known on Lincoln cents, the doubling sometimes exhibits letters that are slightly misshapen, such as the lower bar of an E being curved. This curved shape often is convex. Although some specialists may disagree, Class VI doubled dies *generally* command very small premiums—except in rare cases.

Notice the extra thickness of the letters in LIBERTY. This is typical of a Class VI doubled die, shown here on a Lincoln cent.

STRIKE DOUBLING

Strike doubling is the type of doubling most often confused with, and very often misidentified as, a doubled die or repunched mintmark. Not only do novices confuse this type of doubling with doubled dies, but specialists disagree as to what the correct terminology should be.

Strike doubling (the term we prefer) is generally accepted to be caused by die bounce due to looseness in the tooling-to-die

This LIBERTY on a Lincoln cent exhibits typical strike doubling. Notice the flat, shelf-like appearance of the secondary image.

assembly, the die holder, or the die(s) within that holder. This causes excessive vibration during press operation, much as excessive vibration may set up in a running automobile with a broken motor mount. In effect, the vibration causes a coin to bounce or slide against the die within the split second after it is struck, just before or during ejection. In its most common form, strike doubling is characterized by a flat, shelf-like area of doubling bordering a design; this represents metal from the original raised image that has been smashed by the die down into the field of the coin. According to Mint technicians, strike doubling is usually eliminated when loose bolts, etc., are tightened.

Some might argue that the striking of the coin ends when the hammer die reaches the very end of its stroke. By this argument, this should not be called *strike doubling,* but rather *mechanical* or *machine doubling.* In our opinion, this is like trying to split a hair. Additionally, we feel that *machine* or *mechanical* doubling can be even more confusing, as neither term indicates in which part of the minting process this happens. Either of those terms could refer to the coin counters at the end of the process! We feel *strike doubling* is best suited to indicate the point of the minting process in which this doubling occurs.

Furthermore, numismatists agree there are three basic areas of the minting process: planchet, die, and striking. This doubling occurs during the striking process, and not in the die-making or planchet-making process. (We don't refer to incomplete planchets as a machine problem, although a machine causes them.)

Whether you refer to this as *strike doubling, machine doubling, mechanical doubling,* or *ejection doubling,* your primary focus should be to understand the differences and educate others.

Typically, strike doubling exhibits a flat, shelf-like secondary image, not like the rounded secondary images of true die doubling. Usually this secondary image is low to the field. There are no splits in the serifs. On most Uncirculated and Proof coins, strike doubling gives the appearance that the metal has been "moved," much like that on hobo nickels or love tokens, and has a very shiny appearance. (Other less common forms of strike doubling exist that are not covered here.)

On this 1937 Buffalo nickel, the secondary images exhibit the flat, shelf-like doubling typical of strike doubling. The secondary image is low, close to the field.

Strike doubling can affect all lettering on one or both sides, or could be detected on only one letter or a small portion of a device. Proof coins often exhibit strike doubling due to the excessive force employed in their manufacture. Strike doubling can also be evident on a coin with a true doubled die or true repunched mintmark.

There are several dates (and runs of dates) in several series that are well known for strike doubling. Examples include Mercury dimes from 1936 through 1942 and Lincoln cents from 1968 through 1972.

Compare this 1969-S Lincoln cent doubled die with the strike-doubling specimen to the right.

In this 1969-S cent, strike doubling is evident on the date and mintmark. Whenever the date and mintmark both are doubled, odds are that the doubling is strike doubling.

Although it can be difficult for a novice to understand, strike doubling might affect only the mintmark on a coin, creating what some may interpret as a repunched mintmark. In fact, this is fairly common, especially on Franklin halves and Washington quarters. This is often because strike doubling first affects the deepest part of the die (the highest part of the coin), which in many cases is the deeply punched mintmark.

This is a genuine repunched mintmark on a Kennedy half dollar. Compare the doubling here with the next, which was caused by strike doubling.

This mintmark on a Franklin half dollar is the result of strike doubling. Notice the flat, shelf-like doubling, which is the primary characteristic of strike doubling.

OTHER FORMS OF DOUBLING

In addition to strike doubling, there are other forms of doubling that are often mistaken for die doubling. Among these are doubling caused by die deterioration, and doubling that is typical on coins designed by James B. Longacre, possibly intentionally.

Die Deterioration

Die deterioration doubling is very often confused with doubled dies, repunched mint-marks, and other collectible forms of die doubling. In general, as a die deteriorates, its letters and numerals (among other design elements) will develop doubling, twisting, mushrooming, and similar effects. The exact result often depends on the type of die steel used, composition of planchets struck, geometry of die design, and length of time the die(s) remain in service. These effects normally begin on elements closest to the rim and move inward to a point of leaving random die-deterioration patches that may appear to be misplaced mintmarks in strange places (e.g., on Roosevelt's cheek). This is due to stress in the metal of the die. This doubling will often, but not always, occur in combination with an "orange-peel" effect on the fields of the coin, created by the stress in the metal on the dies.

Die deterioration is very evident and extreme in this Jefferson nickel. Notice the secondary images on both sides of the letters, and the "orange-peel" effect on the field.

Here is another example of die deterioration. Notice the edges of the I and T appearing to merge into the field. Also, the letters have less definition than one would expect.

Die deterioration is very common on Washington quarters from the 1980s and 1990s, Jefferson nickels from 1955 to date, and Roosevelt dimes from 1965 to date. Die deterioration is a prime example of what can happen when the Mint tries to get maximum production out of every single die.

Die deterioration doubling is found on many Lincoln cents, in particular those of the 1950s and earlier. One such deteriorated 1955 cent was often promoted by dealers as "the poor man's doubled die."

"Longacre" Doubling

This term was coined by J.T. Stanton as an easy way to describe the doubling that is typical on many coins designed by James Barton Longacre. These include Indian Head cents, nickel three-cent pieces, Shield nickels, and many gold issues. We're certain many readers have seen this doubling before; almost all of the letters are doubled,

In this Indian Head cent, the doubling that is typical on many of Longacre's designs is evident. Notice that the secondary image is visible on both sides of the letters.

with the secondary image appearing on both sides of the letters. Some specialists believe this is from the shoulder of the punch penetrating the die, causing the secondary step. Others feel it was an intentional design on Longacre's part, to help the metal flow into the tight crevices of the die. Although this doubling is evident on many of the coins that Longacre designed, it is not seen on all of his coins. This would likely remove the theory that the secondary or "stepped" image was planned to help with metal flow.

Longacre doubling does not add premium to a coin's value.

SUMMARY

We hope this long, but educational, article will help our readers learn the difference between die doubling and other forms of doubling. However, the best learning tool is experience. In that light, we suggest that you look—and look carefully—at as many coins as possible, especially in the date ranges mentioned. Look especially carefully at Proof quarters from 1968 and 1969 for strike doubling, Indian Head cents from the 1860s, 1870s, and 1880s for "Longacre" doubling, nickels from the 1980s for die deterioration, and Franklin half dollars for strike doubling on the mintmark. Don't pass up the opportunity to buy a good example of one of these for your reference, if it's not too expensive.

DIE-DOUBLING I.Q. TEST

The 10 photographs here exhibit some examples of die doubling, strike doubling, and even some other forms of doubling. Take a few minutes to see for yourself whether you can accurately identify the various forms of doubling.

Note: Most variety collectors feel coins exhibiting other forms of doubling should not command a premium. However, some collectors believe they are collectable and actively seek them. We feel there is absolutely nothing wrong with this and encourage those who decide to take this course. The question is and should be, "Are you having *fun* in your collecting pursuits?"

Test photo 1

Test photo 2

Test photo 3

Test photo 4

Test photo 5

Test photo 6

Test photo 7

Test photo 8

Test photo 9

Test photo 10

Answers to the test photographs:
1. strike doubling; 2. strike doubling; 3. doubled die; 4. strike doubling; 5. doubled die; 6. die deterioration; 7. strike doubling; 8. repunched mintmark; 9. doubled die; 10. strike doubling.

In test photo 10, notice that the date and the mintmark both exhibit similar doubling. This should be a red flag. There are very few examples on which a doubled die and a repunched mintmark both are evident on the same side of the same coin. Keep in mind that until very recently, the mintmark was punched into the die after the die was made. Therefore, if the die is doubled, the mintmark is not necessarily doubled.

Appendix B
The Minting Process

WHY STUDY THE MINTING PROCESS?

In the study of Mint errors and varieties—and the study of the "regular" segment of numismatics, as well—a basic knowledge of the minting process is vital. If you do not understand how an error or variety occurred, you will not be able to determine whether it is genuine. The description that follows is an abbreviated one, but the basics remain the same.

There are four basic processes that take place at the U.S. Mint, and it is during the second through fourth processes that all errors and varieties occur. First is the design process, in which the coin is designed and a model is engraved. Next is the die-making process, whereby the design is transferred to a "die steel" to strike the coin. The third process is the making of planchets—coin blanks that are created and specially prepared for striking. The last process is the striking of these planchets to make them into coins. The last three processes—die making, planchet production, and striking—are where errors occur. Some have described this trio of areas as "P-D-S" (planchets, dies, and striking); the resemblance of these initials to the P, D, and S mintmarks of the three primary minting facilities (Philadelphia, Denver, and San Francisco) makes it easy to remember these areas of production.

Error vs. Variety

Occasionally there is disagreement as to whether a certain aberrant coin is an error or a variety. Generally speaking, most specialists consider an error a one-time occurrence that is not repeated in exactly the same way, and a variety an occurrence that *is* repeated in exactly the same way. An off-center strike, therefore, would be considered an error. True, some off-center strikes look quite similar, but generally speaking, each one will be different. However, a doubled die will repeat exactly with each strike, and is thus considered a variety.

THE DESIGN PROCESS

Sculptors and engravers are employed by the Mint to design coins and medals and to sculpt and engrave other designs into workable subjects for coining. These highly trained specialists take a design from a drawing, painting, or other two-dimensional object and transform it onto a plaster model, approximately 15 inches in diameter, that will ultimately be transferred to a coin or medal. The design on the model is always raised above the surrounding area (i.e., it is "positive" or "in relief"), just as it will appear on the finished coin. This plaster sculpture, after slight changes and improvements, is coated with epoxy resins that act as a preservative and a hardener. The epoxy-coated plaster sculpture is called a *galvano* and is forwarded to the die-making area of the Mint.

The Die-Making Process

Since the galvano is usually many times larger than the intended coin, its design must be reduced. To accomplish this, the galvano is placed onto a Janvier transfer-reducing machine. This machine traces the design on the galvano and, using the principle of the fulcrum, transfers the design onto the end of a piece of steel bar the actual size of the coin to be produced. This is called the *reducing* stage of die production, and this finished piece of steel is called the *master hub.* When the master hub has been produced, it is heated to extreme temperature, then quenched (cooled) quickly in a vat of oil. This heating-and-cooling process, called *tempering,* hardens the steel even further.

The master hub has the design in the same relief design as on the galvano and as it will appear on the finished coin. It is

The large galvano is reduced on a Janvier transfer-reducing machine to create a master hub (a "positive") that is the actual size of the coin.

placed into a hydraulic hubbing press, opposite a piece of die steel that is about four inches long. When each is seated into the press, hydraulic force brings the two together, transferring the image from the master hub onto the end of the die steel. When complete, this is called the *master die,* with the design pressed (incused) into its surface.

This operation, known as *hubbing,* used to take several impressions to bring the design to the depth specifications. After each hubbing, the die would be annealed to make the steel even more hardened. If the die were to receive the image deep enough in the first hubbing, stress on the die steel would result and very likely create cracks, or at least would weaken the die. Strength and durability are stringent requirements. This process is now done by the "single-squeeze method," using one high-pressure compression.

After the master die is produced, it is placed into the hubbing press to create the working hub in the same manner. Several working hubs are produced. These working hubs then produce working dies in the manner described before. The working dies are then placed into the coining presses to strike coins and medals.

Traditionally, all dies were made in the Philadelphia Mint. Until 1987 the dies were produced without mintmarks, which were added by hand with punches before the dies were shipped to the branch-mint facilities for completion. However, beginning in 1987 the mintmark was added to the master die, and in 1990 it was added to the original plaster sculpture. Subsequently, the mintmark is transferred to the master hub and on down the die-production chain. Beginning in 1996, the Denver Mint started producing dies for its own use and for the San Francisco Mint's production facilities.

Remember that the plaster sculpture, the galvano, the master hub, and the working hub all have the image of the coin in relief, or positive, just as the finished coin will appear. Master dies and working dies have the image coin incuse, or negative—a mirror image of the finished coin.

Planchet Making

Cent and nickel planchets are primarily made outside the Mint, as is the sheet metal for the other denominations. However, the process is much the same as when the Mint produced its own planchets and metal. Raw metal, after being melted, is rolled into long sheets until it is the proper thickness for the intended coin. These long sheets are then coiled for storage, shipping, and eventual use. The sheets are uncoiled and fed into a blanking press—which is nothing more than a series of punches that cut blanks out of the metal coils—either at the outside facility or at the Mint. Notice the word "blank" instead of "planchet": Technically speaking, a *blank* is a disc of metal that has not yet been prepared for striking, whereas a *planchet* is a blank that has been further prepared for striking, as described below.

Once the blanks are produced, they pass through what is known as a *riddler*, which passes the blanks over a three-tiered, vibrating screen, with holes in the first tier slightly larger than the intended blanks. The blanks that are of proper diameter drop through, and blanks that are too large are retained on the upper tier and carried to a scrap bin. The second-tier screen has holes slightly smaller than a proper-sized blank. Blanks that are too small pass through these holes to the third tier, from which they are carried away to the scrap bin. The blanks that remain on the second tier are presumed to be of accurate size, and are forwarded to the next process.

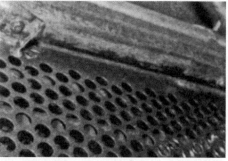

Once the blanks are produced, they pass through what is known as a riddler, which removes imperfectly-sized blanks.

At this point, the blanks must be annealed and cleaned. The annealing process softens the blanks to improve striking and reduce wear on the dies. After annealing, they are passed through a wash for cleaning, then through a dryer to remove any soap or water (which might cause spots).

The blanks are then ready for the *upset mill.* This is a machine with two primary components: (1) a stationary die with V-shaped grooves, and (2) a rotating die in the center, also with V-shaped grooves. Blanks are fed into one end of the upset mill, fitting into the grooves. As the center die rotates, the blanks pass between the outer, stationary die and the inner, rotating die. As the blanks go through the mill, the spacing between the two dies is gradually reduced, forcing the metal on the edge of the blank to be raised above the flat surfaces. When the disc of metal exits the upset mill, generally with raised metal all around the edge, it is considered a planchet.

The reason for putting raised edges on planchets before striking is that it greatly helps in coin production: it helps force the metal, during striking, toward the center of the coin and then into the crevices of the die; it also helps the coins stack neatly as they are struck.

A blank remains a blank until it has been through the upsetting mill and received a raised edge, at which time it becomes a planchet. Blanks are frequently (and erroneously) referred to as "Type 1 planchets," but because they do not have raised edges, they should not be called planchets of any kind. There are no Type 1 or Type 2 planchets; the disc of metal is either a blank or a planchet, period.

The planchets are then fed into a furnace. This furnace is much like a long dryer with the planchets being fed in one end and tumbled as they travel through the furnace. Planchets are heated in the furnace to make them softer, which helps with striking. When the planchets exit the furnace, they are washed in a chemical bath and slowly tumbled dry. By the end of this process, most planchets made of nickel will have a yellowish tint.

STRIKING

The striking process begins with the planchets' being brought to the coining presses via overhead conveyors with small bins. These conveyors deposit the planchets into a hopper above the coining presses. From that point the planchets are fed by gravity through feeder tubes and down into the *coining chamber* (the area of the coining press where striking takes place).

The planchets drop from the feeder tubes into *feeder fingers,* each of which has a slot in the end to push out the struck coin and a hole a couple of inches back that holds the next planchet to be deposited into the chamber. These fingers slide back and forth over a smooth steel surface.

The coining chamber consists primarily of the anvil (lower) die, hammer (upper) die, collar, and feeder fingers. The *anvil die,* which usually strikes the reverse of the coin, moves only when coins are being ejected and planchets received. The *hammer die,* which usually strikes the obverse, comes down and strikes the planchet. The *collar* is a metal ring that retains the planchet during the strike, preventing the metal from expanding outside the desired diameter. The collar also serves as a third die, creating the reeding or lettering on coins intended to have reeded or lettered edges.

When the planchet is deposited on the anvil die and within the collar by the feeder finger, the finger retracts and the hammer die comes down and strikes the planchet. As the hammer die retracts, the anvil die (riding on a cam) rises; the feeder finger pushes the struck coin out of the chamber, continues forward, and deposits another planchet onto the anvil die. The feeder finger retracts and the striking process begins again. The finished coins pass through an additional riddler to catch errors; this has greatly reduced the number of error coins escaping the Mint.

COUNTING AND BAGGING

Once the coins are ejected from the coining press, they fall down a chute and are carried to the counting room on conveyors. In the counting room, the coins are counted, packaged, and weighed. Some coins are bagged in the well-known Mint-sewn bags, while others (usually cents) are placed in large totes containing 1,500 pounds of coins within a heavy plastic liner. The bagged coins are then shipped to the various Federal Reserve banks.

Appendix C
What Are the Best Magnifiers?

"What level of magnification should I use when searching for varieties?" "Which magnifier is the best to use?" "Do I need a microscope?" These are three of the more common questions ever broached concerning this subject. All too often a collector will believe *more* magnification is better—when in fact less is usually best. With coin collecting in general and variety collecting in particular, the strength of the magnification is not as important as the *quality.*

Virtually every variety of any significance can be detected with a 7x glass, if it's of good quality. (A good 7x magnifier is also the recommended loupe for the most accurate coin grading.) A lesser-quality magnifier will only distort the image, making proper identification even more difficult. On the other hand, a good-quality glass with too much magnification is almost always overkill, as it can cause you to overlook key identification points.

An H.E. Harris magnifier (or *loupe,* pronounced "loop") is a common sight at coin shows. You will see dealers and collectors slip them out of their pocket to examine interesting coins. (Some wear them on a chain or string around their neck, for constant easy access.) These magnifiers fold into their chrome cases to protect the lens, which is usually 4x to 8x or greater strength.

Most serious collectors and almost all dealers use a Hastings triplet magnifier; usually a 7x or 10x power is preferred. "Hastings" is not a brand but a method of manufacture. The Hastings triplet has a three-glass (or plastic) optic, which ensures clarity throughout the entire lens and produces virtually no distortion.

Some manufacturers use 10x or 17x designations. However, without good-quality optics, the 10x or 17x means nothing. We've seen some magnifiers marked as 17x, compared to which a 10x Hastings triplet provides more detail, better clarity, and a wider field of view. And remember, if you can't see a variety with a 7x glass, it's likely not worth searching for.

A good 7x Bausch & Lomb Hastings triplet will normally run about $45. However, with some searching on the Internet, you can find a good 7x Hastings triplet for less than $25.

Stereoscopes (microscopes) are handy, fun, and very educational, but these are not absolutely necessary for the study of varieties. Should you have the desire to add one to your array of collecting tools, a good stereoscope can be obtained for as little as $250 (though most will run around $500 or more). Be sure to get a stereoscope—one that has two eyepieces. This will allow the very best in clarity and use. A stereoscope is great for taking photographs, and for studying the minute differences evident on every coin.

Check with your local supplier or favorite online dealers. See what they recommend. We strongly advise spending a little more for a good-quality product. You'll reap the rewards soon afterward.

Appendix D

Popular Varieties From Proof and Mint Sets

This list, of Proof sets and Mint sets that contain significant varieties, should be useful for all collectors. Beginning with those modern Mint sets from 1947, and Proof sets from 1950, there are many years of one or the other that are absent of a significant variety. Not all of the known varieties are significant. Should you encounter a significant variety that is not listed, please contact the publisher so the list can be updated.

Again, this list is just to be used as a guide. Those Proof listings in **bold type** are considered the most desirable.

Mint Sets

Year	Denom	Variety
1949	5¢	D/S–over mintmark (although known, most have already been removed)
1954, Small Date	25¢	doubled-die reverse
1960, Small Date	5¢	(P)–doubled-die obverse (found in sets labeled as Small Date)
1960, Small Date	10¢	(P)–doubled-die obverse (found in sets labeled as Small Date)
1960, Small Date	25¢	(P)–doubled-die obverse (found in sets labeled as Small Date)
1961	50¢	D/D–repunched mintmark
1963	10¢	(P)–doubled-die obverse
1963	25¢	(P)–doubled-die obverse (P)–doubled-die reverse
1963	50¢	(P)–doubled-die obverse (P)–doubled-die reverse
1968	10¢	(P)–doubled-die obverse
1968	25¢	D–doubled-die reverse
1969	5¢	D/D–repunched mintmark
1969	10¢	D/D–repunched mintmark
1969	25¢	D/D–repunched mintmark
1969	50¢	D–doubled-die reverse
1970	1¢	D/D–repunched mintmark D–doubled-die obverse
1970	10¢	D–doubled-die reverse
1970	25¢	D–doubled-die reverse
1970, Small Date	50¢	D–doubled-die reverse
1971	5¢	D/D–repunched mintmark
1971	10¢	D/D–repunched mintmark D–doubled-die reverse
1971	50¢	D–doubled-die obverse D–doubled-die reverse
1972	1¢	(P)–doubled-die obverse
1972	5¢	D–doubled-die reverse
1972	50¢	D–doubled-die reverse
1973	50¢	(P)–doubled-die obverse D–doubled-die obverse
1974	50¢	D–doubled-die obverse
		D–doubled-die reverse
1981	5¢	D–doubled-die reverse
1984	50¢	D/D–repunched mintmark
1987	5¢	D/D–repunched mintmark
1987	10¢	D/D–repunched mintmark
1989	5¢	D–doubled-die reverse
1989	10¢	P–doubled-die reverse
1989	50¢	D/D–repunched mintmark
1991	5¢	D–doubled-die obverse

Proof Sets

1950	10¢	doubled-die reverse
1950	50¢	doubled-die obverse
1951	1¢	doubled-die obverse
1951	**5¢**	**doubled-die obverse**
1952	**25¢**	**"Superbird"**
1953	1¢	doubled-die obverse
1953	**5¢**	**doubled-die obverse**
1953	25¢	doubled-die obverse recut tail feathers
1954	1¢	doubled-die obverse
1954	10¢	doubled-die obverse
1954	50¢	doubled-die obverse
1955	1¢	doubled-die obverse doubled-die reverse
1955	**5¢**	**tripled-die reverse**
1956	1¢	doubled-die reverse
1956	10¢	doubled-die obverse
1956	50¢	doubled-die obverse doubled-die reverse
1957	**5¢**	**quadrupled-die obverse**
1957	50¢	doubled-die reverse
1959	25¢	doubled-die obverse
1960, Small Date	**1¢**	**doubled-die obverse** (Large/Small) **doubled-die obverse** (Small/Large)
1960	5¢	doubled-die reverse
1960	10¢	doubled-die obverse
1960	**10¢**	**doubled-die reverse**
1960	**25¢**	**doubled-die reverse**
1960	50¢	doubled-die obverse
1961	5¢	doubled-die reverse
1961	25¢	doubled-die obverse
1961	**50¢**	**doubled-die reverse**
1962	25¢	doubled-die obverse
1962	50¢	doubled-die obverse
1963	**10¢**	**doubled-die reverse**
1963	25¢	doubled-die reverse
1964	10¢	doubled-die obverse
1964	50¢	doubled-die obverse
1968-S	1¢	doubled-die obverse
1968-S	5¢	repunched mintmark
1968-S	10¢	doubled-die obverse
1968-S	**10¢**	**doubled-die reverse doubled-die obverse**
1968-S	**10¢**	**No S**
1968-S	25¢	repunched mintmark
1968-S	**25¢**	**doubled-die reverse**
1968-S	**50¢**	**doubled-die obverse**
1969-S	25¢	doubled-die obverse
1969-S	**25¢**	**repunched mintmark**
1970-S	**10¢**	**No S**
1970-S	50¢	doubled-die obverse
1971-S	1¢	doubled-die obverse
1971-S	**5¢**	**No S**
1971-S	50¢	doubled-die obverse
1975-S	10¢	doubled-die reverse
1975-S	**10¢**	**No S**
1979-S	1¢	Type II mintmark
1979-S	5¢	Type II mintmark
1979-S	10¢	Type II mintmark
1979-S	25¢	Type II mintmark
1979-S	50¢	Type II mintmark
1979-S	$1	Type II mintmark
1981-S	1¢	Type II mintmark
1981-S	5¢	Type II mintmark
1981-S	10¢	Type II mintmark
1981-S	25¢	Type II mintmark
1981-S	50¢	Type II mintmark
1981-S	$1	Type II mintmark
1982-S	25¢	doubled-die obverse
1983-S	**10¢**	**No S**
1990-S	**1¢**	**No S**
1990-S	25¢	doubled-die obverse
1995-S	25¢	doubled-die obverse

Appendix E

When Cherrypickin', Use Courtesy and Respect!

Many years ago, a dealer friend of ours indicated he would never let anyone, other than a few people, cherrypick his stock (fortunately, we were among that select group). He had legitimate complaints regarding most of those who try to cherrypick varieties. His experiences are not unlike those of many dealers. Too often, collectors who are most interested in cherrypickin' varieties disregard the dealer's other (and potentially more profitable) customers. Many cherrypickers will take up space and time, and then walk away without a single purchase. Is that right? Is that fair to the dealer?

Before we get directly into the *courtesy* aspect of this article, we would like to remind you that there is nothing wrong with cherrypickin'. We use our knowledge just as another dealer or collector would use their knowledge to buy the best deal. A dealer trying to buy an 1892-S Barber quarter in Fine condition for a client will usually cherrypick to get the best possible value. Dealers with excellent grading skills can cherrypick undergraded coins, making a nice profit in a later sale. That has been occurring for decades in our hobby.

When the term *cherrypick* is used today, most hobbyists automatically think of those who search for varieties among a stock of normal coins. Those of us involved with varieties have studied long and hard for our knowledge. However, to make the most of this knowledge, we must use some common sense, and we must *always* respect a dealer's main objective—to earn a living. Dealers are at shows and in the coin business to make money to support their families. This is their livelihood, and we must always respect their time and space. If you don't feel you can afford them this courtesy, don't consider cherrypickin' for varieties. Those of us who do respect a dealer's time and space do not want a few inconsiderate people to ruin the pickings for the rest of us.

There are a few "courtesy" pointers that we'd like you to keep in mind. Remember that you are very likely a small customer for the typical dealer. They can almost certainly make more money from another customer in a tenth of the time they might spend with you. Remember that *you need the dealers* for cherrypickin'—they could make their living without cherrypickers!

If you're at a show and you've spotted a dealer whose stock you would like to search, and that dealer is busy, simply go to another dealer for a while. If you are seated at a dealer's table looking over their stock, and they start to get busy, let them know in a respectful way that you realize you're taking up their space and time, and that you will come back when they aren't as busy. We promise the dealer will remember your courtesy and respect, and you're more likely to be welcomed back when time permits.

We've often had dealers ask what we're looking for. We generally tell them that we're looking for various varieties, and that will usually suffice. Don't lie. Never lie!

But you don't have to tell everything. If the dealer persists, you might tell them about a few of the more scarce varieties, and explain that there is a market for those varieties. Remember most dealers couldn't care less about the popular varieties that aren't listed in the Red Book. They will usually say "fine," and you can continue looking.

However, the best-case scenario is that you can teach this dealer something about varieties. As you become better acquainted, the dealer might start to look for some of the varieties, and save them for you. Sure, you'll likely pay a little more for them than the price of the normal coin, but far less than the actual value of the variety. In short, you'll have added a pair of eyes to *your* cherrypickin'. You'll get a new supply for varieties and at prices that will enable you to realize a very nice profit. We've even had dealers tell us to name the price, and we've had dealers ask for only the value of the normal coin.

Here's a tip that we think is extremely important. If you're at a dealer's table, and if for some reason you need to reach into your pocket or lap, plainly open your hands above the table, turn them over and rub them together, then do what you need to do. You don't need to say anything, and don't make a big deal of it, but make sure it's obvious. Why? The dealer will know for sure that you are not "palming" a coin. Do this with dealers you know well, and with dealers you don't know. Make it a habit. The main point here is to *never* give any dealer any opportunity to even think you are doing something wrong. We've seen people who hold a want list or magnifier in their lap, then take the coin below the table's surface, out of view of the dealer. That is very wrong, whether cherrypickin' or not, and will often discourage a dealer from welcoming you back. Always think of how you would want a customer to act if you were the dealer, and *always be respectful*—even if the dealer may seem rude.

Here are some other important points: Never let a dealer feel cheated when you buy a coin, or you'll never be welcomed back. Never brag about what you've purchased from a dealer if there is any way possible it could get back to the dealer. Always be polite and courteous—and being friendly doesn't hurt, either. Try to put yourself in their shoes once in a while. Usually, a dealer's main objective is to sell for a profit coins they have and know best. Many dealers specialize in certain areas, and leave other coins to others. We cherrypickers are the ones who know varieties best, and so they will usually leave this area for us.

One last tip: Suppose you find a super variety for the price of a regular coin, and for some reason you don't want the dealer to key in on that one coin. You might buy a few other coins at the same time to draw less attention to the coin you really want. Who cares about the added expense? You'll make a bundle on that nice cherry! And if the extra coins are ones with firm markets, such as an MS-63 Morgan dollar or a Proof set, you'll be able to turn around and sell them quickly.

Above all, *always use courtesy and respect* in all your dealings, be honest, and always act in a professional manner. You'll make some friends along the way, and we guarantee you'll come out ahead in the long run!

Appendix F
1979-S and 1981-S Proof-Mintmark Varieties

The Type I and Type II mintmark varieties for the 1979-S and 1981-S Proof sets are very well known, yet many people become confused when trying to differentiate them. This appendix illustrates the four mintmark styles for each denomination.

Compare these descriptions to the photos, and you'll be able to identify the correct types:

- The *1979-S Type I* mintmark has a squared, filled S, very indistinct.
- The *1979-S Type II* mintmark is clear and well formed.
- The *1981-S Type I* is a worn version of the 1979-S Type II.
- The *1981-S Type II*, although somewhat similar to the Type I, is distinguishable by the flattened top surface of the S. Some specialists argue that the S must be clear in both loops. Most agree that the S can show some slight filling, but the mintmark punch must show that flattened top surface. This is usually the most difficult type to comprehend. But the key is really very simple—that flatness on the top surface.

Cents

| 1979-S Type I | 1979-S Type II | 1981-S Type I | 1981-S Type II |

Nickels

| 1979-S Type I | 1979-S Type II | 1981-S Type I | 1981-S Type II |

Dimes

  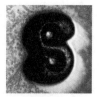

1979-S Type I   1979-S Type II   1981-S Type I   1981-S Type II

Quarter Dollars

1979-S Type I   1979-S Type II   1981-S Type I   1981-S Type II

Half Dollars

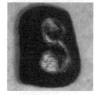   

1979-S Type I   1979-S Type II   1981-S Type I   1981-S Type II

Dollars

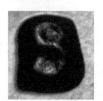   

1979-S Type I   1979-S Type II   1981-S Type I   1981-S Type II

Appendix G
Recommended Reading

The axiom "Buy the book before the coin" applies even more strongly to the error/variety collector than to the regular segment of the hobby. The following is a list of recommended readings. It can by no means stay complete—new books become available regularly—but it gives you an excellent foundation for building your knowledge. Most of these books are available online, or through any coin dealer. The abbreviation OOP indicates the book is out of print.

GENERAL

The following books cover not only errors and varieties, but regular coins as well. These books should be included in any numismatist's library:

A Guide Book of United States Coins, by R.S. Yeoman, edited by Kenneth Bressett. Popularly known as the "Red Book," this is the book with which any numismatic library should begin.

Walter Breen's Complete Encyclopedia of U.S. and Colonial Coins. This is undoubtedly the best book anyone interested in die varieties can add to their library. It's not cheap, but much of the information it contains cannot be found anywhere else.

Walter Breen's Encyclopedia of Early United States Cents, 1793–1814.

Walter Breen's Encyclopedia of United States Half Cents, 1793–1857.

SERIES TOPICS

The following books highlight a specific series or subject. Each is a tremendous asset for anyone seriously interested in its topic.

The Flying Eagle and Indian Cent Attribution Guide, second ed., vols. 1–4, by Richard E. Snow.

Flying Eagle and Indian Cent Die Varieties, by Larry R. Steve and Kevin Flynn. (OOP)

Flying Eagle, Indian Cent, Two-Cent, and Three-Cent Doubled Dies, by Kevin Flynn. (OOP)

A Guide Book of Flying Eagle and Indian Head Cents, by Richard Snow.

Treasure Hunting in the Flying Eagle and Indian Head Cents, by Kevin Flynn. (OOP)

The Authoritative Reference on Lincoln Cents, by John Wexler and Kevin Flynn. (OOP)

The Complete Guide to Lincoln Cents, by David Lange.

The Complete Price Guide and Cross Reference to Lincoln Cent Mint Mark Varieties, by Brian Allen and John A. Wexler. (OOP)

The Comprehensive Guide to Lincoln Memorial Cent Repunched Mintmark Varieties: 1959, by John A. Wexler and John W. Bordner.

The Comprehensive Guide to Lincoln Repunched Mintmark Varieties: Wheat Cents, 1909–1939, by John A. Wexler, Brian Allen, and John W. Bordner.

A Detailed Analysis of Lincoln Cents, vol. 1, by Billy Crawford. 2003. (OOP)

A Guide Book of Lincoln Cents, by Q. David Bowers.

The Lincoln Cent Doubled Die, by John Wexler. (OOP)

The Lincoln Cent RPM Book, third ed., vol. 1, by James Wiles. (e-Book)

The Lincoln Cent RPM Book Update, 1997–2002, by James Wiles. (OOP)

Lincoln Cent Varieties, 1909–2009, by Billy G. Crawford. (e-Book)

Looking Through Lincoln Cents, by Charles Daughtrey.

A Quick Reference to the Top Lincoln Cent Varieties, by Gary Waggnon, Karen Peterson, and Kevin Flynn.

The RPM Book: Lincoln Cents, second ed., by James Wiles.

The Top 100 Lincoln Cent RPMs and OMMs, by James Wiles. (e-Book)

The Wexler Doubled Die Files: Lincoln Cents, vols. 1–3, by John A. Wexler.

The Authoritative Reference on Two-Cent Coins, by Kevin Flynn.

Getting Your Two Cents Worth, by Kevin Flynn.

Longacre's Two-Cent Piece, 1864: Attribution Guide, by Frank Leone.

The Authoritative Reference on Three Cent Nickels, by Kevin Flynn and Edward Fletcher.

The Authoritative Reference on Three-Cent Silver Coins, by Kevin Flynn and Winston Zack.

The Complete Guide to Shield and Liberty Nickels, by Gloria Peters and Cynthia Mohon. (OOP)

A Guide Book of Shield and Liberty Head Nickels, by Q. David Bowers.

The Shield Five Cent Series, by Ed Fletcher. (OOP)

Treasure Hunting Liberty Head Nickels, by Kevin Flynn and Bill Van Note. (OOP)

Buffalo Nickels: The Abraded Die Varieties, by Ron Pope.

The Complete Guide to Buffalo Nickels, second ed., by David W. Lange.

A Guide Book of Buffalo and Jefferson Nickels, by Q. David Bowers.

Treasure Hunting Buffalo Nickels, by John Wexler, Ron Pope, and Kevin Flynn. (OOP)

The Best of the Jefferson Nickel Doubled Dies, by John Wexler and Brian Ribar.

The Jefferson Nickel Analyst, second ed., by Bernard A. Nagengast.

The Jefferson Nickel RPM Book and *The Jefferson Nickel RPM Book Update: 2001–2002,* by James Wiles.

The Complete Guide to Liberty Seated Half Dimes, by Al Blythe. (OOP)

The Complete Guide to Liberty Seated Dimes, by Brian Greer. (OOP)

The Authoritative Reference on Barber Dimes, by Kevin Flynn.

The Complete Guide to Barber Dimes, by David Lawrence. (OOP)

The Complete Guide to Mercury Dimes, second ed., by David W. Lange.

Treasure Hunting Mercury Dimes, by Kevin Flynn. (OOP)

The Authoritative Reference on Roosevelt Dimes, by John Wexler and Kevin Flynn.

Richard's Roosevelt Dime Review: The Silver Years, 1946–1965, by Richard Bateson.

The Early Quarter Dollars of the United States, 1796–1838, by A.W. Browning.

The Comprehensive Encyclopedia of United States Liberty Seated Quarters, by Larry Briggs. (OOP)

Standing Liberty Quarters, third ed., by J. H. Cline.

Standing Liberty Quarters: Varieties and Errors, by Robert H. Knauss.

The Authoritative Reference on Barber Quarters, by Kevin Flynn.

The Complete Guide to Barber Quarters, by David Lawrence. (OOP)

The Best of the Washington Quarter Doubled Dies, by John Wexler and Kevin Flynn. (OOP)

A Guide Book of Washington and State Quarters, by Q. David Bowers.

The Washington Quarter Dollar Book, vols. 1–3, by James Wiles.

Early Half Dollar Varieties, by Al C. Overton (now credited to Don L. Parsley as author).

Bust Half Fever, 1807–1836, by by Edgar E. Sounders.

The Top 100 R4 and R5 Capped Bust Half Dollar Varieties and Sub-Varieties, by Edgar E. Sounders.

The Ultimate Guide to Attributing Bust Half Dollars, by Glenn R. Peterson.

The Complete Guide to Liberty Seated Half Dollars, by Randy Wiley and Bill Bugert. (OOP)

The Complete Guide to Barber Halves, by David Lawrence. (OOP)

The Complete Guide to Walking Liberty Half Dollars, by Bruce Fox. (OOP)

Treasure Hunting Walking Liberty Half Dollars, by Kevin Flynn and Brian Raines.

A Guide Book of Franklin and Kennedy Half Dollars, by Rick Tomaska.

Treasure Hunting Franklin and Kennedy Half Dollar Doubled Dies, by Kevin Flynn and John Wexler.

The Kennedy Half Dollar, by James Wiles.

Comprehensive Catalog and Encyclopedia of Morgan and Peace Dollars, fourth ed., by Leroy C. Van Allen and George Mallis.

A Guide Book of Morgan Silver Dollars, by Q. David Bowers.

Top 100 Morgan Dollar Die Varieties: The VAM Keys, by Michael Fey and Jeff Oxman.

A Guide Book of Peace Dollars, by Roger W. Burdette.

The Authoritative Reference on Eisenhower Dollars, by John Wexler, Bill Crawford, and Kevin Flynn.

Collectable Ike Varieties: Facts—Photos—Theories, by the Ike Group

Little Book of Collectible Eisenhower Dollars, by the Ike Group, edited by Bill Sanders.

A Guide Book of Gold Dollars, by Q. David Bowers.

The United States $3 Gold Pieces, 1854–1889, by Douglas Winter and Q. David Bowers.

An Insider's Guide to Collecting Type One Double Eagles, by Douglas Winter and Adam Crum.

Type Three Double Eagles, 1877–1907: A Numismatic History and Analysis, by Mike Fuljenz.

Gold Coins of the Carson City Mint: 1870–1893, by Douglas Winter.

Gold Coins of the Charlotte Mint: 1838–1861, third ed., by Douglas Winter.

Gold Coins of the Dahlonega Mint: 1838–1861, second ed., by Douglas Winter.

Gold Coins of the New Orleans Mint: 1839–1909, second ed., by Douglas Winter.

The Authoritative Reference on Commemorative Coins, 1892–1954, by Kevin Flynn.

Commemorative Coins of the United States—A Complete Encyclopedia, by Q. David Bowers. (OOP)

A Guide Book of United States Commemorative Coins, by Q. David Bowers.

100 Greatest U.S. Error Coins, by Nicholas P. Brown, David J. Camire, and Fred Weinberg.

Error Coins From A to Z, by Arnold Margolis.

The Error Coin Encyclopedia, by Arnold Margolis.

Error-Variety News Classics, books I and II, by John A. Wexler and Robert Wilharm.

Official Price Guide to Mint Errors, seventh ed., by Alan Herbert.

World's Greatest Mint Errors, by Mike Byers.

The Cud Book, by Sam Thurman and Arnold Margolis.

The Encyclopedia of Doubled Dies, vols. 1 and 2, by John Wexler.

Over Mintmarks and Hot Repunched Mintmarks, by Kevin Flynn and John Wexler.

A Quick Reference to the Top Misplaced Dates, by Kevin Flynn

The RPM Book, by John Wexler and Tom Miller. (OOP)

Strike It Rich With Pocket Change: Error Coins Bring Big Money, third ed., by Ken Potter and Brian Allen.

Two Dates Are Better Than One: A Collector's Guide to Misplaced Dates, by Kevin Flynn.

What Are Die Varieties? by James Wiles. (e-book)

Periodicals

These magazines regularly feature varieties and errors.

ERRORSCOPE. The bi-monthly magazine of CONECA (Combined Organizations of Numismatic Error Collectors of America), the national error/variety club. Membership information is available online at www.conecaonline.org

Error Trends Coin Magazine. This highly educational monthly magazine is devoted to the error/variety hobby, weighted toward errors. Subscription information is available from Arnold Margolis, P.O. Box 158, Oceanside, New York, 11572-0158.

The Hub. This is the bi-monthly magazine of the National Collectors Association of Die Doubling. Membership information is at http://www.ncadd98.org.

Appendix H
Coin Clubs

Joining a coin club is an important part of your hobby fulfillment. Membership brings many advantages, most important of which are camaraderie and the accumulation of knowledge. We all need both.

Even if you can't travel to meeting locations and shows, most clubs produce newsletters that are highly educational and encourage members to contribute articles. This is one of the best ways to learn about a specific numismatic subject. With every article you write, you'll travel new avenues of research and add to your numismatic knowledge. It never fails.

Many specialized coin clubs have been born in the virtual environment of the Internet. These clubs often are interactive, offering all members a great opportunity to ask questions of specialists, share knowledge, and meet others with similar interests.

This appendix lists numismatic organizations dedicated to subjects that should interest most of our readers. The information noted, including membership fees and addresses, is as accurate as possible at the time of publication. A visit to a group's Web site can provide the latest information.

NATIONWIDE CLUBS AND GROUPS

The American Numismatic Association. This is the largest coin-collecting group in the world. The monthly magazine, *The Numismatist*, contains articles submitted by members on a wide array of topics. Additionally, the ANA's library is second to none and is available to all members. Other great benefits are also included as a part of your membership.

American Numismatic
   Association
818 N. Cascade Ave.
Colorado Springs, CO 80903-3279
Phone: 719-632-2646
Fax: 719-634-4085
E-mail: ana@money.org
Web site: www.money.org

CONECA (Combined Organizations of Numismatic Error Collectors of America). CONECA is a worldwide organization that specializes in the study of errors and varieties. Its bimonthly newsletter, *ErrorScope,* is filled with educational topics. Additionally, CONECA's Web site has a huge listing with descriptions of several thousand repunched mintmarks and doubled dies. And access to that is free to all!

CONECA
c/o Rachel Irish
101 W. Prairie #323
Hayden, ID 83835
Web site: www.conecaonline.org

NCADD (National Collectors Association of Die Doubling). NCADD is a group devoted to collecting coins with die doubling, repunched mintmarks, over mintmarks, doubled dies, overdates, etc. *The Hub,* NCADD's bi-monthly newsletter, is loaded with features and general educational articles.

NCADD
c/o John Bordner
P.O. Box 15
Lykens, PA 17048-0015
Web site: http://ncadd98.org

ONLINE CLUBS AND GROUPS

Variety Coins. This is a great online group with a very active discussion board. Most variety specialists belong and are active on the boards. Ask a question, get several answers, each of which will prove useful. Membership is free.

> Web site: groups.msn.com/
> VarietyCoins /

Coin Varieties. Much like the above, this is a discussion group for those with an interest in coin varieties. Many variety specialists and enthusiasts hold membership (free) and are active in the discussions.

> Web site: http://groups.yahoo.com/
> group/coinvarieties

Shield Nickels. Another excellent online group for enthusiasts of Shield nickels. Like many of the others, the discussion groups are filled with excellent information. There is no better discussion group available for the variety enthusiast. And best of all, you can join free!

> Web site: groups.yahoo.com/
> group/Shield_Nickels

SPECIALIZED CLUBS AND GROUPS

John Reich Collectors Society. "The purpose of the John Reich Collectors Society is to encourage the study of numismatics, particularly United States gold and silver coins minted before the introduction of the Liberty Seated design, and to provide technical and educational information concerning such coins." JRCS has a great newsletter and conducts meetings at various times throughout the year.

> John Reich Collectors Society
> Attn: Stephen A. Crain
> P.O. Box 1680
> Windham, ME 04062
> Web site: http://logan.com/jrcs

Liberty Seated Collectors Club. LSCC is one of the strongest groups dedicated to any coin design or series. LSCC members receive the quarterly *Gobrecht Journal*, which is filled with some of the most educational numismatic articles available anywhere.

> LSCC
> Leonard Augsburger, Secretary-
>   Treasurer
> P.O. Box 6114
> Vernon Hills, IL 60061
> E-mail: leonard_augsburger
>   @hotmail.com
> Web site: www.lsccweb.org

Appendix I
Fivaz-Stanton Numbers Cross-Reference Chart

The Fivaz-Stanton numbering system changed in the fourth edition of the *Cherry-pickers' Guide*. The earlier numbering system was very confined, limiting the number of new listings that could be added. The newer system is rational and infinite. For details, consult the "How to Use This Book" section.

This chart cross-references the current FS numbers assigned to all previous listings. The first column indicates the *new* FS number, with other columns showing the old FS number (if there was a listing), the date and mint of the coin, and a brief description. (Abbreviations listed in the date/mint column include L for Longacre's initial; LL for Large Letters; br for bronze; and NC for No Cents.) Due to space limitations, the description is very short and should not be used in an attempt to identify a variety.

These numbers can easily be used in an abbreviated format, by using only the final three or four digits in the full number. A variety is always described with the denomination and date, so duplicating that number in a description is not really necessary. The final digits will describe the variety's FS number when the denomination and date are identified.

FS#	Old FS#	Date/Mint	Brief Description
HALF CENTS			
HC-1804-301	001	1804	Cohen 2
HC-1804-302	002	1804	Cohen 4
HC-1805-301	003	1805	Cohen 2
HC-1806-301	004	1806	Cohen 3
HC-1808-301	005	1808	Cohen 1
HC-1809-301	006	1809 L	Cohen 1
LARGE CENTS			
LC-1843-301	001	1843	Newcomb 17
LC-1846-301	002	1846	Newcomb 23
LC-1846-302	002.5	1846	Newcomb 25
LC-1847-301	003	1847	Newcomb 36
LC-1847-302	004	1847	Newcomb 43
LC-1849-301	005	1849	Newcomb 25
LC-1850-301	005.5	1850	Newcomb 24
LC-1851-301	006	1851	Newcomb 42
LC-1851-302	006.5	1851	Newcomb 44
LC-1856-301	007	1856	Newcomb 22
FLYING EAGLE CENTS			
01-1857-101	002	1857	DDO 2-0-I; UNITED STATES OF AMERICA, beak, eye, tail
01-1857-102	002.3	1857	DDO 3-0-I; UNITED STATES OF AMERICA, beak, eye, tail; not as strong as 101

FS#	Old FS#	Date/Mint	Brief Description
01-1857-103	002.7	1857	DDO 6-0-I and RPD; doubling on UNITED STATES OF AMER-ICA, beak, and eye
01-1857-104	002.8	1857	DDO 5-0-II; doubling evident on UNITED STATES OF AMERICA, beak, and wing
01-1857-105	002	1857	DDO; doubling evident on UNITED STATES OF AMERICA, beak, eye, and tail
01-1857-301	001.5	1857	RPD very strong south on all four digits
01-1857-401	001	1857	Obv of '56; rectangular opening of O, long center serifs of F
01-1857-402	003	1857	Ohverse clashed with Liberty Seated half dollar obverse
01-1857-403	004	1857	Obverse clashed with Liberty Head $20 gold obverse
01-1857-901	005	1857	Reverse clashed with Liberty Seated quarter reverse
01-1858-101	005.5	1858LL	Snow 2, DDO
01-1858-301	006	1858LL	Snow 1, Overdate 8/7 Die 1
01-1858-302	006.1	1858LL	Snow 7, Overdate 8/7 Die 2
INDIAN HEAD CENTS			
01-1859-301	006.3	1859	Snow 1, RPD
01-1859-302	006.2	1859	Snow 2, RPD
01-1859-303	006.35	1859	Snow 3, RPD

FS#	Old FS#	Date/Mint	Brief Description
01-1860-401	006.4	1860	Transitional design; Pointed Bust of 1860
01-1861-301	006.45	1861	Snow 1, RPD
01-1862-301		1862	Snow 2, MPD
01-1862-801		1862	Snow 5, DDR
01-1863-301		1863	Snow 2, RPD
01-1863-302		1863	MPD
01-1863-801	006.46	1863	Snow 10, DDR
01-1864-401		1864	Snow 5, Polished Die
01-1864-1101	006.47	1864 br	Snow 4, DDO, RPD
01-1864-1301	006.48	1864 br	Snow 2, RPD
01-1864-2301	006.7	1864 L	Snow 1, RPD
01-1864-2302	006.71	1864 L	Snow 3, RPD
01-1864-2303	006.72	1864 L	Snow 4, RPD
01-1864-2304	006.5, 006.55	1864 L	Snow 5, RPD
01-1864-2305		1864 L	Snow 2, RPD
01-1864-2306	006.73	1864 L	Snow 10, RPD
01-1865-301	007.4	1865	Snow 1, Plain 5–RPD
01-1865-302	007.45	1865	Plain 5–RPD
01-1865-303	007.5	1865	Snow 3, Plain 5–RPD
01-1865-304	007.56	1865	Snow 2, Plain 5–MPD
01-1865-1301	007.3	1865	Snow 1, Fancy 5–RPD
01-1865-1302	007.55	1865	Snow 4, Fancy 5–RPD
01-1865-1401	007.2	1865	Snow 14, Fancy 5–Obverse Die Gouge
01-1865-1801	007	1865	Snow 2, Fancy 5–DDR
01-1866-101	007.6	1866	Snow 1, DDO, Multiple MPD
01-1866-301	007.7	1866	Snow 2, RPD
01-1866-302	007.9	1866	Snow 3, RPD
01-1866-303	007.8	1866	Snow 9, RPD
01-1867-301	008	1867	Snow 1, RPD
01-1867-302	008.1	1867	Snow 4, RPD
01-1868-101	008.2	1868	Snow 1, DDO
01-1868-102	008.26	1868	Snow 4, DDO, RPD
01-1868-103	008.25	1868	Snow 5, DDO. RPD, MPD
01-1868-301	008.23	1868	Snow 8, MPD
01-1869-301	008.3	1869	Snow 3, RPD (formerly believed to be 1869/8)
01-1869-302	008.5	1869	Snow 1, RPD
01-1870-101	008.6	1870	Snow 1, 2, 13, 22, 28, DDO
01-1870-102	008.82	1870	Snow 5, DDO, RPD, MPD
01-1870-301	008.81	1870	Snow 4, RPD
01-1870-302	008.8	1870	Snow 8, MPD, DDR
01-1870-801	008.7	1870	Snow 2, 3, 14, DDR
01-1870-901		1870	Shallow N reverse
01-1871-901		1871	Shallow N reverse
01-1872-301	008.9	1872	Snow 1, RPD
01-1872-901		1872	Shallow N reverse
01-1873-101	009	1873	Snow 1, Close 3 DDO
01-1873-102	009.1	1873	Snow 2, Close 3 DDO
01-1873-1301	009.3	1873	Snow 1, Open 3 RPD
01-1874-101	009.33	1874	Snow 1, DDO
01-1875-301		1875	Snow 1, RPD
01-1875-302		1875	Snow 2, RPD
01-1875 303		1875	Snow 3, RPD
01-1875-801		1875	Snow 16, Die Alteration
01-1878-301	009.4	1878	Snow 2, MPD
01-1880-101	009.41	1880	Snow 1, DDO, MAD Reverse
01-1882-401	009.43	1882	Snow 6, MPD
01-1883-401	009.45	1883	Snow 8, MPD
01-1883-402		1883	Snow 7, MPD
01-1883-403		1883	Snow 1, MPD
01-1883-801	009.46	1883	Snow 6, DDR
01-1884-401	009.48	1884	Snow 1, MPD
01-1887-101	009.5	1887	Snow 1, DDO
01-1888-301	010	1888/7	Snow 1, Overdate
	010.5	1888	No variety–delisted
01-1888-302	010.7	1888/7	Snow 2, RPD
01-1888-303	010.73	1888	MPD; base of 1 in ribbon
01-1888-304	010.74	1888	MPD; 8 in hair curl
01-1888-305	010.75	1888	MPD; two 8's in hair curl
01-1889-301	010.8	1889	Snow 3, RPD
01-1889-801	010.81	1889	Snow 1, DDR
01-1889-802		1889	Snow 11, DDR
01-1890-101	010.85	1890	Snow 1, TDO
01-1890-401	010.82	1890	Snow 3, MPD
01-1890-402	010.84	1890	Snow 6, MPD
01-1891-101	010.88	1891	Snow 1, DDO
01-1891-301	010.87	1891	Snow 3, RPD
01-1892-301	010.89	1892	Snow 8, RPD
01-1892-302	010.9	1892	Snow 1, RPD, DDR
01-1892-401	010.91	1892	Heavy die scratches
01-1893-301	010.95	1893	Snow 2, RPD
01-1894-301	011	1894	Snow 1, RPD
01-1894-402	011.2	1894	Snow 2, MPD
01-1895-301	011.3	1895	Snow 1, RPD
01-1895-302	011.31	1895	Snow 9, RPD
01-1896-301	011.4	1896	Snow 1, RPD
01-1897-401	011.5	1897	Snow 1, MPD
01-1897-402	011.6	1897	Snow 8, RPD
01-1898-401	011.65	1898	MPD; 8 in denticles
01-1898-402	011.66	1898	Snow 5, MPD
01-1899-301	011.7	1899	Snow 1, RPD
01-1899-302	011.75	1899	Snow 13, RPD
01-1899-303		1899	Snow 9, RPD
01-1900-301	011.751	1900	Snow 1, RPD
01-1900-302		1900	Snow 3, RPD
01-1901-301		1901	Snow 19, RPD
01-1902-401		1902	Snow 4, Die gouge
01-1903-301	011.76	1903	Snow 10, MPD
01-1903-302	011.765	1903	Snow 6, MPD
01-1903-303		1903	Snow 7, RPD
01-1903-304		1903	Snow 3, RPD
01-1904-301		1904	Snow 10, RPD
01-1905-301		1905	Snow 1, RPD
01-1906-301		1906	Snow 7, RPD
01-1906-302		1906	Snow 14, MPD, RPD
01-1906-303		1906	Snow 20, RPD

FS#	Old FS#	Date/Mint	Brief Description
01-1907-301		1907	Snow 1, RPD
01-1907-302		1907	Snow 2, RPD
01-1907-303		1907	Snow 27, RPD
01-1908-201		1908	Snow 1, RPM
01-1908-301	011.77	1908	Snow 4, MPD
01-1908-302	011.79	1908	Snow 9, MPD
01-1909-101	011.9	1909	Snow 1, Doubled L

LINCOLN CENTS

FS#	Old FS#	Date/Mint	Brief Description
01-1909-1101	012	1909 V.D.B.	DDO, 1-0-IV
01-1909-1102	012.1	1909 V.D.B.	DDO, 2-0-VI
01-1909S-1501	012.2	1909-S	S/S RPM
01-1909S-1502	012.3	1909-S	S/S, Horizontal S, RPM
01-1910S-501		1910-S	RPM
01-1910S-502	012.7	1910-S	S/S, RPM
01-1911D-501	012.8	1911-D	D/D, RPM
01-1911D-502	012.81	1911-D	D/D, RPM
01-1911D-503	012.82	1911-D	D/D, RPM
01-1911D-504	012.83	1911-D	D/D, RPM
01-1911S-501	012.85	1911-S	S/S, RPM
01-1917-101	013	1917	DDO, 1-0-V
01-1922-401	013.2	1922	"No D" Variety; Die Pair #2 only
01-1925S-101	013.3	1925-S	DDO, 1-0-VI
01-1925S-501	013.31	1925-S	S/S RPM
01-1927-101	013.5	1927	DDO, 1-0-I
01-1927D-501	013.51	1927-D	D/D, RPM
01-1928S-501	013.6	1928-S	Large S mintmark variety
01-1929S-501	013.65	1929-S	S/S, RPM
01-1930D-501		1930-D	RPM
01-1930D-502	013.7	1930-D	D/D, RPM
01-1930S-501	013.73	1930-S	S/S, RPM
01-1934-101	013.79	1934	DDO
01-1934D-503	013.81	1934-D	D/D/D/D, RPM
01-1934D-504	013.8	1934-D	D/D, RPM
01-1935-101	013.9	1935	DDO, 1-0-V
01-1936-101	014	1936	DDO, 1-0-IV
01-1936-102	015	1936	DDO, 2-0-V
01-1936-103	016	1936	DDO, 3-0-V
01-1938D-501	016.4	1938-D	D/D, RPM
01-1938S-501	016.51	1938-S	S/S, RPM
01-1938S-502	016.5	1938-S	S/S/S, RPM
01-1939-101	017	1939	DDO, 1-0-I
01-1941-101	018	1941	DDO, 1-0-I
01-1941-102	018.1	1941	DDO, 2-0-I
01-1941-103	018.3	1941	DDO, 5-0-IV
01-1942-102	018.7	1942	DDO, 4-0-V
01-1942-103	018.9	1942	DDO, 6-0-IV
01-1942D-502	018.91	1942-D	D/D, RPM
01-1942D-504	018.92	1942-D	D/D, RPM
01-1942S-101	018.94	1942-S	DDO, 1-0-IV and S/S RPM
01-1942S-512	018.93	1942-S	S/S/S, RPM; very strong north and west
01-1943-101	018.97	1943	DDO, 1-0-VI; very strong class VI

FS#	Old FS#	Date/Mint	Brief Description
01-1943D-501	019	1943-D	D/D, RPM; very strong D/D southwest
01-1943D-513	019.1	1943-D	D/D, RPM
01-1943S-101	019.5	1943-S	DDO, 1-0-IV
01-1944D-502	021.1	1944-D	D/D, RPM
01-1944D-507	021.11	1944-D	D/D, RPM
01-1944D-511	020	1944-D	D/S, OMM; very wide north
01-1944D-512	021	1944-D	D/S, OMM; centered under D
01-1946S-511	021.2	1944-S	S/D, OMM; D well centered under S
01-1947-101	021.3	1947	DDO, 1-0-I
01-1947S-504	021.31	1947-S	S/S, RPM
01-1949D-501	021.33	1949-D	D/D/D, RPM
01-1950S-504	021.34	1950-S	S/S, RPM
01-1951-101	021.35	1951 PF	DDO, 1-0-II
01-1951D-101	021.4	1951-D	DDO, 1-0-V
01-1951D-511	021.5	1951-D	D/S, OMM; S well centered under D
01-1951D-512	021.52	1951-D	D/S, OMM; S slightly south of being centered under D
01-1951D-521	021.51	1951-D	Misplaced D mintmark in date
01-1952D-511	021.6	1952-D	D/S, OMM; very likely over S mintmark
01-1953-101	021.7	1953 PF	DDO, 1-0-II
01-1953D-501	021.73	1953-D	D/D, RPM
01-1954D-501	021.76	1954-D	D/D/D, RPM; very strong north and south of primary D
01-1955-101	021.8	1955	DDO, 1-0-I
01-1955-102	021.9	1955	2-0-II+V
01-1955D-101	021.93	1955-D	DDO, 1-0-IV+VII
01-1955D-503	021.94	1955-D	D/D/D, RPM; secondary D centered and wide east
01-1955D-504	021.95	1955-D	D/Horizontal D (presently unique)
01-1955S-501	021.97	1955-S	S/S/S, RPM; both secondary stepped northwest
01-1956D-501	022.1	1956-D	D/D, RPM
01-1956D-508	022	1956-D	D/D, RPM; separated south
01-1958-101	022.15	1958	DDO, 1-0-I
01-1959-101	022.2	1959	DDO, 1-0-II
01-1959-104	022.3	1959	DDO, 4-0-II
01-1959D-501	022.5	1959-D	D/D/D, RPM
01-1960-101	025	1960 PF	DDO, Large/Small Date 1-0-III
01-1960-102	024	1960 PF	DDO, Small/Large Date 2-0-III
01-1960-103	023	1960 PF	TDO, Large/Small Date 3-0-III
01-1960D-101	025.5	1960-D	DDO, Small/Large Date, RPM
01-1961D-501		1961-D	RPM, D/Horizontal D
01-1963D-101	025.8	1963-D	DDO
01-1964-801	026	1964	DDR, 1-R-I
01-1964-802	027	1964	DDR, 58-R-II
01-1964-803		1964	DDR
01-1966-101		1966	DDO
01-1968D-501	027.3	1968-D	RPM
01-1968D-801	027.4	1968-D	DDR, 1-R-V
01-1968S-101	027.5	1968-S PF	DDO
01-1969D-901		1969-D	Missing Designer's Initials

FS#	Old FS#	Date/Mint	Brief Description
01-1969S-101	028	1969-S	DDO, 1-0-I
01-1970S-101	029	1970-S	DDO, 1-0-I
01-1970S-102	030	1970-S PF	DDO, 3-0-III, Large/Small Date
01-1970S-103	030.1	1970-S	DDO, 5-0-VII
01-1970S-107	030.4	1970-S PF	DDO, 7-0-I
01-1970S-113	030.6	1970-S PF	DDO, 13-0-I
01-1970S-1401		1970-S	Small Date; circulation strike
01-1970S-1402	030.2	1970-S PF	Small Date; Proof
01-1971-101	031	1971	DDO, 1-0-II
01-1971-102	030.7	1971	DDO
01-1971S-101	032	1971-S PF	DDO, 1-0-II
01-1971S-102	033	1971-S PF	DDO, 2-0-II+V
01-1971S-103	033.1	1971-S PF	DDO, 4-0-V
01-1972-101	033.3	1972	DDO, 1-0-I
01-1972-102	033.52	1972	DDO, 2-0-I
01-1972-103	033.53	1972	DDO, 3-0-I
01-1972-104	033.54	1972	DDO, 4-0-I
01-1972-105	033.55	1972	DDO, 5-0-I
01-1972-106	033.56	1972	DDO, 6-0-I
01-1972-107	033.57	1972	DDO, 7-0-I
01-1972-108	033.58	1972	DDO, 8-0-I
01-1972-109	033.59	1972	DDO, 9-0-VII
01-1972S-101	033.7	1972-S PF	DDO, 1-0-I 3
	034.1	1980-D	removed listing
01-1980-101	034	1980	DDO, 1-0-V
01-1982-101	034.5	1982	CLD, DDO, 2-0-V
01-1982-1801		1982	ZSD, DDR
01-1983-101	035	1983	DDO, 1-0-V
01-1983-102	035.1	1983	DDO, 2-0-V
01-1983-103	035.2	1983	DDO, 3-0-V
01-1983-401	035.3	1983	Obverse die clash
01-1983-801	036	1983	DDR, 1-R-IV
01-1984-101	037	1984	DDO, 1-0-IV
01-1984-102	038	1984	DDO, 2-0-II
01-1984D-101	039	1984-D	DDO, 1-0-II+VI
01-1990-101		1990-(S) PF	No mintmark
01-1992D-901		1992-D PF	Type 1 reverse; touching AM of AMERICA
01-1994-801	039.9	1994	DDR, 1-R-IV
01-1995-101	040	1995	DDO, 1-0-V
01-1995D-103	041	1995-D	DDO, 3-0-V
01-1997-101	043	1997	DDO (?); Doubled Ear
01-1998-901		1998	Type 2 reverse; wide AM of AMERICA
01-1999-901		1999	Type 2 reverse; wide AM of AMERICA
01-1999S-901		1999-S PF	Type 1 reverse; close AM of AMERICA
01-2000-901		2000	Type 2 reverse; wide AM of AMERICA
01-2000S-901		2000-S PF	Type 1 reverse; close AM of AMERICA

TWO-CENT PIECES

FS#	Old FS#	Date/Mint	Brief Description
02-1864-401	000.5	1864	Small Motto

FS#	Old FS#	Date/Mint	Brief Description
02-1864-1101	001	1864	DDO, 1-0-II (Leone-64Lg-06G)
02-1864-1301	001.5	1864	RPD (Leone 64Lg-100E)
02-1864-1302	001.7	1864	RPD (Leone 64-Lg-24H)
02-1864-1901	001.8	1864	Reverse die clashed with obverse of Indian Head cent
02-1865-101	002	1865	Plain 5; DDO 2-0-III (Leone 65P-1o1r)
02-1865-301	002.3	1865	Plain 5; RPD (Leone 65P-5o1r)
02-1865-1301	002.5	1865	Fancy 5; RPD (Leone 65F-1o1r)
02-1865-1302	002.7	1865	Fancy 5; RPD (Leone 65F-2o1r)
02-1865-1303	002.8	1865	Fancy 5; RPD
02-1865-1304	002.9	1865	Fancy 5; MPD (6 or 8 in digits below primary 8)
02-1867-101	003	1867	DDO, 1-0-V
02-1868-301	003.5	1868	MPD (6 in digits below primary 6)
02-1868-302		1868	Possible overdate
02-1869-101	004.2	1869	DDO
02-1869-301	003.9	1869	RPD and MPD (6 in digits below primary 6)
02-1869-302	004	1869	RPD
02-1870-101	004.3	1870	DDO
02-1871-101	005	1871	DDO; circulation strike
02-1871-102		1871 PF	DDO; common
02-1872-101	006	1872	DDO

THREE-CENT SILVER PIECES

FS#	Old FS#	Date/Mint	Brief Description
3S-1851-301	001	1851	RPD
3S-1851-302	001.5	1851	RPD
3S-1852-301	002	1852	1852/inverted date
3S-1852-302	002.3	1852	RPD
3S-1852-801	002.5	1852	Doubled-Die Reverse
3S-1853-301	003	1853	RPD
3S-1854-301	004	1854	RPD–wide west
3S-1862-301	007	1862	2/1 overdate

NICKEL THREE-CENT PIECES

FS#	Old FS#	Date/Mint	Brief Description
3N-1865-101	003.5	1865	DDO
3N-1865-102		1865	DDO
3N-1865-301	001	1865	MPD; flag of 5 in denticles
3N-1865-302	001.5	1865	RPD; wide west
3N-1865-303	002	1865	MPD; flag of 5 deep in denticles
3N-1865-304	002.5, 003	1865	RPD; strong south (blunt tip 5)
3N-1865-305		1865	RPD
3N-1866-101	004	1866	DDO
3N-1866-301		1866	RPD
3N-1869-301	004.3	1869	RPD
3N-1869-302	004.5	1869	RPD
3N-1869-801	004.7	1869	DDR
3N-1870-101	005	1870	DDO, RPD
3N-1870-301	005.5	1870	MPD
3N-1870-302	005.6	1870	MPD, DDR
3N-1871-101	006	1871	TDO, 1-0-I

FS#	Old FS#	Date/Mint	Brief Description
3N-1871-301		1871	RPD
3N-1875-301	006.5	1875	MPD; 1 in neck; very common (~1 in 3)
3N-1881-301	006.8	1881	RPD
3N-1887-301	007	1887	Overdate 7/6; circulation-strike version only
3N-1887-302	007	1887 PF	Overdate 7/6; Proof version
3N-1888-301		1888	MPD

SHIELD NICKELS

FS#	Old FS#	Date/Mint	Brief Description
05-1866-101	001.7	1866	DDO, F-22
05-1866-102	001.5	1866	DDO, F-21
05-1866-301	001	1866	RPD, F-08
05-1866-302	001.1	1866	RPD, F-10
05-1866-303	001.2	1866	RPD, F-20
05-1866-304	001.3	1866	RPD, F-16
05-1866-305	001.4	1866	RPD, F-13
05-1866-901		1866	Clashed reverse, RPD, F-09a
05-1867-301	002.1	1867	With Rays; RPD, F-8; likely a small/large date
05-1867-302	002.4	1867	With Rays; RPD, F-9
05-1867-303	002.7	1867	With Rays; RPD, F-2
05-1867-304	002.6	1867	With Rays; MPD, F-01
05-1867-305	002.75	1867	With Rays; 1 punched in shield
05-1867-901		1867	With Rays; rev die clashed with obv; date showing very strong; super!
05-1867-1101	001.8	1867	No Rays; DDO, 3-0-III F-59
05-1867-1102	002	1867	NR; DDO, 1-0-IV and RPD
05-1867-1301	001.9	1867	No Rays; RPD, F-23
05-1867-1302	002.15	1867	No Rays; RPD, F-25
05-1867-1303	002.2	1867	No Rays; RPD, F-21
05-1867-1304	002.25	1867	No Rays; RPD, F-20
05-1867-1305	002.3	1867	No Rays; RPD, F-22
05-1867-1306	002.35	1867	No Rays; RPD, DDO, F-08.01
05-1867-1307	002.5	1867	No Rays; RPD, F-38
05-1867-1308	002.9	1867	No Rays; RPD, F-46
05-1867-1309	002.45	1867	No Rays; MPD, F-01.01
05-1867-1401		1867	Obverse die clash, F-69
05-1868-101	003	1868	DDO, 1-0-IV
05-1868-102	003.65	1868	TDO, 10-0-III+IV; Reverse of '68
05-1868-103	003.8	1868	DDO, 6-0-III
05-1868-104	003.9	1868	DDO, 9-0-IV
05-1868-105	003.95	1868	DDO, DDR
05-1868-106	003.96	1868	DDO, 3-0-IV; Reverse of '68
05-1868-107	003.97	1868	DDO, 11-0-IV and RPD
05-1868-109		1868	DDO, RPD
05-1868-110		1868	DDO
05-1868-301	003.2	1868	RPD, F-19
05-1868-302	003.3	1868	RPD; Reverse of '68
05-1868-303	003.35	1868	RPD, south, F-28.05
05-1868-304	003.4	1868	RPD, east, F-25
05-1868-305	003.45	1868	RPD, multiple
05-1868-306	003.5	1868	RPD, date touching ball, F-24

FS#	Old FS#	Date/Mint	Brief Description
05-1868-307	003.7	1868	RPD
	003.75	1868	duplicate, removed listing
05-1868-309	003.85	1868	RPD
05-1868-310	003.98	1868	RPD, F-20
05-1868-311	003.985	1868	RPD and missing leaf
05-1868-312	003.1	1868	MPD; 1 in ball of shield; Reverse of '68
	003.55	1868	removed listing; photo was an Indian Head cent
05-1868-313	003.6	1868	MPD; 6 or 8 in denticles; F-2
05-1868-401	003.99	1868	Missing leaf and circular scribe mark
05-1868-901	002.94	1868	Variety 1 has a fully broken C of CENTS
05-1868-902	002.95	1868	Variety 2 has a broken C and S of CENTS
05-1868-903	002.96	1868	Variety 3 has a broken C and S of CENTS, plus the S of STATES
05-1868-904	002.97	1868	Variety 4 is same as #903 plus a broken D of UNITED
05-1868-905	002.98	1868	Variety 5 has no broken letters; earliest die state
05-1868-906	002.99	1868	Variety 5.5 has a partially broken C of CENTS
05-1869-301	005	1869	Narrow Date
05-1869-1101	004	1869	Wide Date, DDO 1-0-III
05-1869-1102	004.5	1869	Wide Date, DDO 2-0-V and RPD (tripled)
05-1869-1103	005.67	1869	Wide Date, DDO 3-0-IV+V and RPD
05-1869-1104		1869	Wide Date, DDO and RPD
05-1869-1301		1869	Normal or "wide" date as opposed to the narrow date FS-301
05-1869-1302	005.3	1869	Wide Date, RPD, F-104
05-1869-1303	005.4	1869	Wide Date, RPD, F-202
05-1869-1304	005.5	1869	Wide Date, RPD, F-408
05-1869-1305	005.6	1869	Wide Date, RPD, F-408
05-1869-1306	005.68	1869	Wide Date, RPD, F-105
05-1869-1307	005.2	1869	Wide Date, MPD; 1 in ball above date
05-1870-101	005.7	1870	DDO, 1-0-III and RPD, F-03
05-1870-102	005.74	1870	DDO, F-12
05-1870-103	005.75	1870	DDO and RPD, very wide east
05-1870-301	005.77	1870	RPD, wide southwest, and die clash
05-1870-302	005.76	1870	MPD with 0 in denticles southwest of primary 0
05-1870-801	005.9	1870	DDR 2-R-III rev of '70 over rev of '67
05-1871-101	006	1871	DDO
05-1871-301	006.5	1871	RPD, F-02
05-1872-101	007	1872	DDO, F-121
05-1872-102	007.1	1872	DDO, F-123
05-1872-103	007.2	1872	DDO, 1-0-III, F-124
05-1872-104	007.3	1872	DDO, 4-0-III, F-109
05-1872-105	007.4	1872	TDO, F-05

FS#	Old FS#	Date/Mint	Brief Description
05-1872-106	007.5	1872	DDO, F-116
05-1872-301	007.6	1872	RPD, F-104; moderate north
05-1872-302	007.65	1872	RPD; very strong with 7 south 3x
05-1872-303	007.7	1872	RPD, F-103
05-1872-304	007.76	1872	RPD, 72 repunched north
05-1872-305	007.77	1872	RPD, MPD
05-1872-306	007.9	1872	RPD, F-02
05-1872-307	007.75	1872	MPD; 2 north right of ball
05-1872-308	007.8	1872	Small over large date
05-1873-101	008, 008.85	1873	Close 3; DDO, 2-0-IV, F-04
05-1873-102	008.7	1873	Close 3; DDO, 3-0-IV, F-05
05-1873-103	008.8	1873	Close 3; DDO, F-06
05-1873-1101	008.3	1873	Open 3; DDO, F-113
05-1873-1102	008.5	1873	Open 3; DDO, MPD, F-102
05-1873-1301	009	1873	Open 3; RPD, Large Date over Small Date
05-1873-1302	009.3	1873	Open 3; RPD, F-103
05-1873-1303	009.5	1873	Ooen 3; RPD, F-110
05-1873-1304	009.7	1873	Open 3; RPD
05-1874-101	010	1874	DDO, F-05
05-1874-102	010.4	1874	DDO, F-12; very strong on shield and motto
05-1874-103	010.5	1874	DDO, 4-0-V, F-08
05-1874-104	010.6	1874	DDO; very strong south; full annulet separation
05-1874-301	010.7	1874	RPD, F-02
05-1874-302	010.8	1874	RPD, F-01
05-1875-101	011	1875	DDO, 1-0-III, F-04
05-1875-102	011.3	1875	DDO, 2-0-V, F-05
05-1875-103	011.5	1875	DDO, RPD, F-03
05-1876-101	012	1876	TDO, 1-0-II+III, F-04
05-1876-102	012.1	1876	DDO, 2-0-III
05-1876-103		1876	DDO, RPD, F-08
05-1882-101		1882	DDO, F-19
05-1882-301	012.5	1882	RPD
05-1882-302		1882	RPD, F-02
05-1882-999		1882	Die chip
05-1883-301	013	1883	Overdate Die #1, F-08
05-1883-302	013.1	1883	Overdate Die #2, F-09
05-1883-303	013.2	1883	Overdate Die #3, F-10
05-1883-304	013.3	1883	Overdate Die #4, F-08.01
05-1883-305		1883	Overdate Die #5, F-07
05-1883-311	012.8	1883	RPD, F-04
05-1883-312	012.9	1883	RPD, F-02

LIBERTY HEAD NICKELS

FS#	Old FS#	Date/Mint	Brief Description
05-1883-1301	013.7	1883	No cents; RPD; base of 1 low and left from first 8
05-1883-1302		1883	No cents; RPD; base of 1 low and left from first 8
05-1884-301	013.8	1884	RPD
05-1886-301	013.9	1886	RPD
05-1887-801	014	1887	DDR, 1-R-III
05-1888-101		1888	DDO; most evident on Liberty's ear

FS#	Old FS#	Date/Mint	Brief Description
05-1889-301		1889	RPD
05-1890-301	014.3	1890	RPD
05-1897-301	014.48	1897	RPD
05-1898-301	014.49	1898	RPD
05-1898-302	014.495	1898	RPD; very strong east of primary date
05-1899-301	014.5	1899	RPD; some believe to be a 9/8
05-1900-801	014.7	1900	DDR; moderate on all reverse elements

BUFFALO NICKELS

FS#	Old FS#	Date/Mint	Brief Description
05-1913-901	014.85	1913	Type 1; 3-1/2 leg reverse
05-1913-1101	014.8	1913	Type II; DDO, 1-0-VI (listed in CPG 4-1 as Type I)
05-1913-1801	014.86	1913	Type II; DDR, 1-R-II+VI
05-1913D-401	014.861	1913-D	Two Feather Variety
05-1914-101	014.87	1914	DDO; Overdate 4/3
05-1914S-101	014.89	1914-S	DDO; Overdate 4/3
05-1915-101	014.9	1915	DDO, 1-0-IV
05-1915-401	014.91	1915	Two Feather Variety
05-1915D-501	015	1915-D	RPM, D/D north
05-1915S-501	015.5	1915-S	RPM
05-1915S-502	015.6	1915-S	RPM
05-1916-101	016	1916	DDO, 1916/1916
05-1916-401	016.3	1916	No F; missing designer's initial
05-1917-401	016.411	1917	Two Feather Variety
05-1917-801	016.4	1917	DDR, 1-R-III
05-1917-802	016.41	1917	DDR, 2-R-IV
05-1917D-401	016.43	1917-D	Two Feather Variety
05-1917D-901	016.42	1917-D	3-1/2 leg reverse
05-1917S-401	016.44	1917-S	Two Feather Variety
05-1918-401	016.46	1918	Two Feather Variety
05-1918-801	016.45	1918	DDR, 1-R-II
05-1918D-101	016.5	1918-D	Overdate
05-1918S-401	016.6	1918-S	Two Feather Variety
05-1919-401	016.61	1919	Two Feather Variety, Missing initial
05-1920D-501	016.63	1920-D	RPM
05-1920S-401	016.631	1920-S	Two Feather Variety
05-1921-401	016.633	1921	Two Feather Variety
05-1921S-401	016.635	1921-S	Two Feather Variety
05-1925D-401	016.638	1925-D	Two Feather Variety
05-1925S-401	016.641	1925-S	Two Feather Variety
05-1925S-501	016.64	1925-S	RPM
05-1927D-501	016.7	1927-D	RPM
05-1927D-901	016.65	1927-D	3-1/2 leg reverse
05-1927S-101	016.75	1927-D	DDO
05-1929-101	016.8	1929	DDO
05-1930-101	017	1930	DDO, 1-0-IV
05-1930-801	017.5	1930	DDR, 1-R-IV
05-1930-802	017.3	1930	DDR, 2-R-IV
05-1930-803	017.4	1930	DDR, 3-R-IV
05-1930S-401	017.711	1930-S	Two Feather Variety
05-1930S-501	017.71	1930-S	S/S, RPM

FS#	Old FS#	Date/Mint	Brief Description
05-1935-801	018	1935	DDR, 1-R-V
05-1935-803	018.1	1935	DDR, 3-R-V
05-1935D-502	018.5	1935-D	D/D/D/D, RPM
05-1935S-801	018.6	1935-S	DDR, 1-R-IV
05-1936-101	018.7	1936	DDO, 1-0-VI
05-1936-801	018.8	1936	DDR, 1-R-II+VI (4)
05-1936D-502	019.5	1936-D	D/D/D, RPM
05-1936D-511	019.8	1936-D	D/D/S, OMM; actually D/D/D/S
05-1936D-901	019	1936-D	3-1/2 leg reverse
05-1936S-501	020	1936-S	S/S south; RPM
05-1937D-901	020.2	1937-D	3-legged variety
05-1938D-511	020.5	1938-D/S	D/D/D/S, OMM

JEFFERSON NICKELS

FS#	Old FS#	Date/Mint	Brief Description
05-1938-1101	021	1938	DDO, 1-0-III
05-1938-1105	021.5	1938	DDO, 5-0-II-(4)
05-1939-801	022	1939	DDR, 1-R-IV
05-1939-802	022.5	1939	DDR, 2-R-II+VI
05-1939-901	023	1939 PF	Reverse of 1940; Type II Steps
05-1940-901	024	1940 PF	Reverse of 1938; Type I Steps
05-1941D-501	024.3	1941-D	RPM; D/D southeast
05-1941S-501	024.5	1941-S	Large S mintmark
05-1941S-502		1941-S	Large S; RPM, S/S overlapping
05-1941S-503	024.6	1941-S	Inverted mintmark
05-1942-101	025	1942	DDO, 2-0-IV
05-1942-102	026	1942	DDO, 3-0-IV
05-1942D-501	027	1942-D	RPM, D/Horizontal D
05-1943P-101	028	1943-P	DDO, 1943/2-P
05-1943P-106	029	1943-P	DDO, 6-0-I; Doubled Eye variety
05-1945P-801	030	1945-P	DDR, 1-R-III
05-1945P-803	030.3	1945-P	DDR, 3-R-II+VI
05-1945P-804	030.5	1945-P	DDR, 4-R-II-(6), RPM
05-1946D-501	031	1946-D	D/Inverted D, RPM
05-1946S-101	031.5	1946-S	DDO, 1-0-V
05-1949D-501	032	1949-D	D/S, OMM
05-1951-101	032.5	1951 PF	DDO, 1-0-V
05-1953-101	032.7	1953 PF	DDO, 1-0-I
05-1954D-501	032.9	1954-D	RPM; some believe this to be an OMM, D/S
05-1954S-501	033	1954-S	OMM, D/S
05-1954S-502	033.1	1954-S	S/S, RPM
05-1955D-501		1955-D	OMM
05-1955-801	035	1955 PF	DDR, 1-R-II-(3)
05-1956-102	035.4	1956 PF	DDO
05-1956-801	035.2	1956	QDR, 18-R-II-(4)
05-1956-802	035.6	1956	TDR
05-1957-101	035.8	1957 PF	QDO
05-1960-801	036	1960 PF	DDR, 1-R-II
05-1961-801	037	1961 PF	DDR, 13-R-II
05-1963-801	037.3	1963	TDR
05-1964D-501	037.5	1964-D	RPM
05-1968S-501	038	1968-S PF	S/S east; RPM

BUST HALF DIMES

FS#	Old FS#	Date/Mint	Brief Description
H10-1829-301	000.1	1829	1829/8; 8 on top surface of 9
H10-1834-301	000.3	1834	3 Over Inverted 3 in date
H10-1836-301		1836	RPD; Breen 3003

LIBERTY SEATED HALF DIMES

FS#	Old FS#	Date/Mint	Brief Description
H10-1838-901		1838	Rusted die reverse; rusting evident at about K-3 and K-4
H10-1839o-501		1839-O	Rev. of '38 (large O mintmark); "Blundered Date" variety; Breen 3414
H10-1840o-901	000.5	1840-O	Transitional reverse; Large Letter reverse with open buds
H10-1842o-301		1842-O	Repunched Date; evident on 8 and 2
H10-1843-301	000.6	1843	RPD; 1 and 8 evident south of primary, 4 visible light south
H10-1844-301	000.63	1844	RPD; 1, 8, and 4 south of primary, also 1 north of primary
H10-1845-301	000.65	1845	RPD; 84 protruding south from base of rock
H10-1845-302	000.66	1845	RPD; all 4 digits doubled WNW of the primary date
H10-1848-301	001	1848	Large Date
H10-1848-302	001.3	1848	Overdate; 1848/7/6
H10-1849-301	001.5	1849	Overdate; 1849/8
	001.55	1849	Overdate; 1849/6 (?)
H10-1853-301	001.8	1853	MPD; date protruding from rock; Blythe says 1853/2
H10-1853-401		1853	Arrows; Dot Below 5 of Date
H10-1855-101		1855	DDO (lower edge of skirt), die clash
H10-1856-301	001.9	1856	MPD; 8 in rock above primary 8
H10-1858-301	002	1858	RPD; Breen 3090
H10-1858-302	003	1858	RPD; date over inverted date
H10-1861-301	003.6	1861	1861/0 overdate
H10-1865-301	003.8	1865	RPD; circulation strike of V-1
H10-1871-301	003.9	1871	MPD; portion of a digit in rock
H10-1872-101	004	1872	DDO
H10-1872S-301	005	1872-S	MPD; 1 in skirt right of ribbon end
H10-1872S-302		1872-S	Mmk Below Bow; MPD (left of and below pendant)

BUST DIMES

FS#	Old FS#	Date/Mint	Brief Description
10-1824-901		1824	Broken wing reverse; relatively common
10-1829-301	001	1829	Curl Base 2
10-1829-901	002	1829	Small/Large 10c
10-1830-301	003	1830	Overdate 30/29

LIBERTY SEATED DIMES—NO STARS (1838 ONLY)

FS#	Old FS#	Date/Mint	Brief Description
10-1838o-501		1838-O	Normal mintmark
10-1838o-502		1838-O	RPM south

FS#	Old FS#	Date/Mint	Brief Description
LIBERTY SEATED DIMES–SMALL STARS OBVERSE, NO DRAPERY, CLOSED BUD REVERSE–1838–1840			
10-1838-801	003.27	1838	DDR; all of this type are the DDR
LIBERTY SEATED DIMES–LARGE STARS OBVERSE, NO DRAPERY, CLOSED BUD REVERSE–1838–1840			
10-1838-401		1838	Cracked obverse die #1
10-1838-402		1838	Cracked obverse die #2
10-1838-403		1838	Cracked obverse die #3
10-1838-802	003.27	1838	Doubled-Die Reverse; same reverse die as 1838-801
10-1838-901		1838	Die flaw rev; large chip between N and M of ONE DIME
10-1840-401		1838	Whiskers at chin; "Whiskers" variety
LIBERTY SEATED DIMES–LARGE STARS OBVERSE, PARTIAL DRAPERY, CLOSED BUD REVERSE–1838–1839			
10-1839o-501	003.28	1839-O	RPM; O/O southeast
10-1839o-502		1839-O	Huge O mintmark
LIBERTY SEATED DIMES–LARGE STARS OBVERSE, WITH DRAPERY, OPEN BUD REVERSE–1840–1853, 1856–1860-S			
10-1841-301		1841	Repunched Date; repunched 184
10-1841-302		1841	Repunched Date; repunched 841
10-1841o-301		1841-O	Small O mintmark
10-1841o-302		1841-O	Large O mintmark
10-1841o-901	003.3	1841-O	Transitional reverse; closed bud; Small O mintmark
10-1841o-902		1841-O	Transitional reverse; closed bud; Large O mintmark
10-1843-301		1843	Repunched Date
LIBERTY SEATED DIMES–ARROWS ADDED			
10-1853-1301		1853	Repunched Date
10-1854o-501		1854-O	Incomplete mintmark punch, "U" shaped; Breen 3286
10-1856-1101		1856 SD	Small date; Doubled-Die Obverse
10-1856-301		1856	Repunched Date
10-1856o-2301		1856-O	Large O; Repunched Date
10-1872-301	003.45	1872	Repunched Date
10-1872-302		1872	MPD (outer curve of 2)
10-1872-801		1872	New DDR; entire reverse rotated about 175 degrees
LIBERTY SEATED DIMES–NO ARROWS, CLOSE 3			
10-1873-301		1873	Repunched Date; secondary images west of primary images
LIBERTY SEATED DIMES–WITH ARROWS			
10-1873-2101	003.5	1873	Doubled-Die Obverse
10-1875-301		1875	MPD; strong 1 in denticles
10-1876CC-101	004	1876-CC	Doubled-Die Obverse; level CC mintmark
10-1876CC-102	004	1876-CC	Doubled-Die Obverse; right C high

FS#	Old FS#	Date/Mint	Brief Description
10-1876CC-103	004	1876-CC	Doubled-Die Obverse; right C low
10-1876CC-301	003.7	1876-CC	MPD; digits in skirt by shield (#301 listed in *CPG* #3 as P-Mint coin, actually CC-Mint coin)
10-1876CC-901	005	1876-CC	Type II Reverse
10-1876S-301		1876-S	RPD (18 of date)
10-1877CC-301		1877-CC	Overdate
10-1887S-501		1887-S	Repunched mintmark; S/S slightly north
10-1888S-501		1888-S	Repunched mintmark; S/S Greer 101
10-1889-801	005.3	1889	DDR, RPD
10-1890-301	005.5	1890	MPD
10-1890-302	005.6	1890	MPD; multiple digits in drapery
10-1890S-501		1890-S	Repunched mintmark; Greer 105
10-1890S-502		1890-S	Repunched mintmark; wrong photo in *CPG* #3
10-1891-301		1891	MPD; multiple digits in denticles
10-18910-501	008	1891-O	Repunched mintmark; O/Horizontal O
10-1891S-501	007	1891-S	Repunched mintmark; Greer 101
BARBER DIMES			
10-1892-301	008.3	1892	RPD
10-1892-302	008.4	1892	RPD
10-18920-301	008.5	1892-O	RPD
10-1893S-501	009	1893-S	RPM
10-1895S-301	009.2	1895-S	RPD; secondary image north of primary on 9 and 5
10-1896-301	009.3	1896	RPD; secondary image south on 8, 9, and 6
10-1897-301		1897	RPD
10-1897-302		1897	RPD
10-1897-303		1897	RPD
10-18990-501		1899-O	RPM
10-19000-501		1900-O	RPM
10-19010-501	010	1901-O	RPM
10-1903-301		1903	RPD
10-19030-301		1903-O	RPD; some think 3/2– we doubt it
10-1904S-501		1904-S	Slanted S mintmark
10-1906-301		1906	RPD
10-1906D-301		1906-D	RPD, RPM
10-1906D-302		1906-D	RPD, RPM; different from above
10-1906D-303		1906-D	RPD, MPD
10-19060-301		1906-O	RPD, MPD
10-1906S-301		1906-S	RPD, RPM; Breen 3552
10-1907-301		1907	RPD
10-1907D-301		1907-D	RPD
10-19070-501		1907-O	RPM
10-1908-301		1908	RPD
10-1908-302		1908	Possible overdate 08/07 low
10-1908-303		1908	RPD; multiple punches

FS#	Old FS#	Date/Mint	Brief Description
10-1908D-301	010.220	1908-D	RPD; possible overdate
10 1908D-302	010.210	1908-D	RPD
10-1908D-303	010.200	1908-D	Overdate
10-1908D-304	010.225	1908-D	RPD
10-1908D-305	010.230	1908-D	RPD
10-1908D-306	010.235	1908-D	RPD
10-1908D-307	010.240	1908-D	RPD
10-19080-301	010.250	1908-O	RPD; wide right
10-19080-302	010.260	1908-O	RPD
10-1912S-101		1912-S	DDO; obverse letters, date, and ribbon ends

MERCURY DIMES

FS#	Old FS#	Date/Mint	Brief Description
10-1928S-501		1928-S	Large S mintmark
10-1929S-101	010.3	1929-S	Doubled-Die Obverse
10-1931D-101		1931-D	DDO/DDR
10-1931S-101		1931-S	Doubled-Die Obverse
10-1934D-501		1934-D	RPM; CONECA RPM-001
10-1935S-501		1935-S	RPM south (strike doubling on N side of mintmark)
10-1936-101	010.5	1936	Doubled-Die Obverse
10-1936S-110		1936-S	Very likely 1936/192
10-1937-101		1937	Doubled-Die Obverse
10-1937S-101		1937-S	Doubled-Die Obverse
10-1939-101		1939	Doubled-Die Obverse
10-1939D-501		1939-D	D/D south
10-1940S-501		1940-S	RPM west and serifs–S/S/S/S
10-1940S-901		1940-S	DDO, DDR; CONECA DDO-002, DDR-001
10-1941-101		1941	Doubled-Die Obverse
10-1941D-101	010.58	1941-D	DDO/DDR, 1-O-V+1-R-II
10-1941S-501	010.6	1941-S	RPM
10-1941S-502		1941-S	Unknown RPM; CPN #13
10-1941S-511	010.65	1941-S	Large S mintmark
10-1941S-801		1941-S	Doubled-Die Reverse; minor
10-1942-101	010.7	1942/1	1942/1 Doubled-Die Obverse
10-1942D-101	010.8	1942/1-D	1942/1-D Doubled-Die Obverse, RPM 4
10-1942D-501		1942-D	1942-D/D RPM 5
10-1942S-501		1942-S	Inverted Mintmark
10-1943S-501		1943-S	S/S RPM
10-1943S-511		1943-S	Large S, Trumpet Tail S
10-1944D-501		1944-D	RPM
10-1945-901		1945	DDO (date); CONECA DDO-002
10-1945D-501		1945-D	RPM, D/D northeast
10-1945D-506	010.95	1945-D	D/Horizontal D
10-1945S-503	011	1945-S	S/Horizontal S
10-1945S-511		1945-S	Possible S/D
10-1945S-512		1945-S	Micro S variety

ROOSEVELT DIMES

FS#	Old FS#	Date/Mint	Brief Description
10-1946-101	011.4	1946	Doubled-Die Obverse and Doubled-Die Reverse (4-O-V + 3-R-II)
10-1946-102		1946	Doubled-Die Obverse; same obverse die as above, but no DDR
10-1946-103	011.5	1946	Doubled-Die Obverse
10-1946-104		1946	Doubled-Die Obverse
10-1946-801		1946	Doubled-Die Reverse
10-1946-802		1946	DDR; very unusual, strong at only a couple of positions
10-1946D-501		1946-D	D/D south; unlisted
10-1946D-502		1946-D	D/D south
10-1946D-503		1946-D	D/D south
10-1946S-501	011.7	1946-S	RPM and DDR 1-R-II+V; illustrated in CPN 11
10-1946S-502	011.6	1946-S	RPM and DDR 2-R-IV
10-1946S-503		1946-S	Possibly CONECA RPM 13; actually tripled, S/S/S
10-1946S-504		1946-S	Sans serif S; very rare
10-1947-101	011.9	1947	Doubled-Die Obverse; illustrated in CPN 13
10-1947D-101		1947-D	DDO; CONECA DDO-003
10-1947D-102		1947-D	DDO (on LIBERTY, IGWT); CONECA DDO-001
10-1947S-501	013	1947-S	S mintmark over D mintmark
10-1947S-502	012	1947-S	S mintmark over D mintmark
10-1947S-503		1947-S	Repunched mintmark; S over S north
10-1947S-504		1947-S	Repunched mintmark; S over S rotated clockwise
10-1947S-801	013.5	1947-S	Doubled-Die Reverse
10-1948-801		1948	Doubled-Die Reverse
10-1948S-501		1948-S	RPM; CONECA RPM-001
10-1950-801		1950 PF	Proof; Doubled-Die Reverse
10-1950D-501		1950-D	New D/S OMM
10-1950D-801	014	1950-D	Doubled-Die Reverse; very strong
10-1950S-501	014.5	1950-S	S over inverted S
10-1951D-501		1951-D	RPM; CONECA RPM-001
10-1952S-501		1952-S	RPM; CONECA RPM-001
10-1953D-501		1953-D	D/Horizontal D MM RPM
10-1953S-501		1953-S	RPM; CONECA RPM-002
10-1954-101		1954 PF	Doubled-Die Obverse
10-1954-801		1954	Unusual Doubled-Die reverse; base of torch and oak stem
10-1954S-501		1954-S	Repunched mintmark
10-1954S-901		1954-S	Missing Designer's Initials; Breen 3736
10-1956-101		1956 PF	Doubled-Die Obverse
10-1959D-501	014.8	1959-D	D/Inverted D mintmark
10-1959D-502		1959-D	Repunched mintmark; D/D west
10-1959D-503		1959-D	Repunched mintmark; D/D northwest
10-1959D-504		1959-D	RPM; CONECA RPM-001
10-1960-101		1960 PF	Doubled-Die Obverse
10-1960-102A	015	1960 PF	Doubled-Die Obverse; early die state
10-1960-102B	015	1960 PF	Doubled-Die Obverse; late die state
10-1960-103		1960 PF	DDO (designer's initials, TRUST); CONECA DDO-004

FS#	Old FS#	Date/Mint	Brief Description
10-1960-104		1960 PF	DDO (like FS-101 but stronger on N); CONECA DDO-007
10-1960-105		1960 PF	DDO (TRUST); CONECA DDO-008
10-1960-801	015.5	1960 PF	Doubled-Die Reverse
10-1960D-501		1960-D	Repunched mintmark; D/D/D east
10-1961D-801	015.8	1961-D	Doubled-Die Reverse
10-1962D-505		1962-D	D/Horizontal D
10-1963-101	016	1963	Doubled-Die Obverse
10-1963-801	017	1963 PF	Doubled-Die Reverse (listed incorrectly in CPG #3 as 5-R-II+V)
10-1963-802	017.5	1963 PF	Doubled-Die Reverse
10-1963-803	018	1963 PF	Doubled-Die Reverse
10-1963-804		1963 PF	Doubled-Die Reverse
10-1963-805		1963	Doubled-Die Reverse
10-1963D-801	018.2	1963-D	Doubled-Die Reverse
10-1964-101	018.4	1964 PF	Doubled-Die Obverse
10-1964-801		1964	Doubled-Die Reverse
10-1964-802	018.3	1964	Doubled-Die Reverse
10-1964D-101	018.45	1964-D	Doubled-Die Obverse
10-1964D-501		1964-D	Repunched mintmark; D/D northeast
10-1964D-502	018.7	1964-D	Misplaced mintmark; D protruding from torch
10-1964D-503		1964-D	Repunched mintmark; D/D south
10-1964D-504		1964-D	Repunched mintmark; D/D south
10-1964D-505		1964-D	Repunched mintmark; D/D south
10-1964D-506		1964-D	Repunched mintmark; D/D south
10-1964D-801	018.5	1964-D	DDR
10-1964D-802		1964-D	DDR
10-1964D-803		1964-D	DDR
10-1967-101	019	1967	DDO
10-1968-101	019.5	1968	DDO
10-1968S-101	020	1968-S PF	DDO
10-1968S-102	020.2	1968-S PF	DDO
10-1968S-501		1968-S PF	No S mintmark
10-1968S-502		1968-S PF	Repunched Mintmark; also a very minor Doubled-Die obverse
10-1968S-801	020.3	1968-S PF	DDR
10-1968S-802		1968-S PF	DDR
10-1969-901		1969	Rev. of '68 (deeper lines in flame); CONECA RDV-002
10-1969D-501	020.4	1969-D	Repunched mintmark; D/D wide northeast
10-1970-801	020.6	1970	DDR
10-1970-901		1970	Rev. of '68 (deeper lines in flame); CONECA RDV-002
10-1970D-801		1970-D	DDR
10-1970D-802		1970-D	DDR
10-1970D-901		1970-D	Rev. of '68 (deeper lines in flame); CONECA RDV-002

FS#	Old FS#	Date/Mint	Brief Description
10-1975S-501		1975-S PF	Repunched mintmark; S/S north
10-1982-501	021	1982	No "P" mintmark; circulation strike; strong obverse
10-1982-501		1982	No "P" mintmark; circulation strike; weak obverse
10-1983D-501		1983-D	Repunched mintmark; D/D north
10-1985P-501		1985-P	Ghost in neck; similar to a P
10-1986P-501		1986-P	Ghost in field; similar to a P
10-1987P-501		1987-P	Ghost in field; similar to a P
10-2004D-101		2004-D	DDO; doubled ear, rotated

TWENTY-CENT PIECES

FS#	Old FS#	Date/Mint	Brief Description
20-1875S-301		1875-S	MPD, 8 in denticles; RPM
20-1875S-302		1875-S	Possible MPD in denticles below 7; RPM

BUST QUARTERS

FS#	Old FS#	Date/Mint	Brief Description
25-1831-301		1831	RPD; 1 and 8 south
25-1833-801		1833	DDR
25-1834-901		1834	Recut "OF A" in UNITED STATES OF AMERICA

LIBERTY SEATED QUARTERS

FS#	Old FS#	Date/Mint	Brief Description
25-18400-501		1840-O	WD; Large O mintmark
25-18410-101	001	1841-O	Doubled-Die Obverse, CONECA 1-O-III
25-18430-301		1843-O	Repunched Date; 1 and 8 north
25-18430-501	001.5	1843-O	Large O mintmark
25-1845-301		1845	Repunched Date; Large 5/Small 5
25-1847-301	002.3	1847	MPD; 8 protruding from base of rock
25-1847-801	002	1847	RPD, Doubled-Die Reverse, 1-R-II
25-1850-301		1850	RPD; 1 in denticles
25-1853-301		1853	RPD; 5 and 3 evident slightly below the primary digits, slanted

LIBERTY SEATED QUARTERS–ARROWS AND RAYS

FS#	Old FS#	Date/Mint	Brief Description
25-1853-1301	003	1853	1853/4 Overdate
25-18530-501		1853-O	O Over Horizontal O
25-18540-501	004	1854-O	Huge O mintmark
25-1856-301		1856	MPD; 1 and 6 punched in gown
25-1856S-501	005	1856-S	Large S / Small S mintmark
25-1857-401		1857	Die Gouge on Liberty's fingers resembles a cigar
25-1857-901	006	1857	Reverse clashed die; clashed with reverse of Flying Eagle cent
25-18570-301	006.2	1857-O	MPD; 1 and 8 in denticles
25-1872-301		1872	RPD; 1 and 8 repunched south of the primary digits
25-1875-301	006.75	1875	MPD; 1 and 7 in denticles
25-1876-301		1876	MPD; top of a 6 in denticles below 6

FS#	Old FS#	Date/Mint	Brief Description
25-1876-302	006.8	1876	MPD; 1 evident south and west of primary 1 and S and W of primary 8

LIBERTY SEATED QUARTERS

FS#	Old FS#	Date/Mint	Brief Description
25-1876-303	06.85	1876	MPD; 6 in rock
25-1876-304		1876	RPD; triple 6
25-1876-305		1876	MPD; top of 1 and 8 in denticles
25-1876CC-301		1876-CC	RPD; 1, 8, and 7 close south
25-1876S-301	006.88	1876-S	MPD; 7 and 6 in denticles
25-1876S-302		1876-S	MPD; digit in denticles under 8
25-1877CC-301		1877-CC	RPD; 1, 8, and 7 close south
25-1877S-501	007	1877-S	RPM, S/Horizontal S
25-1891-301	007.5	1891	MPD

BARBER QUARTERS

FS#	Old FS#	Date/Mint	Brief Description
25-1892-101	007.7	1892	Doubled-Die Obverse; IN GOD WE TRUST
25-1892-301		1892	Tripled-Die Obverse, RPD; very minor TDO, very nice RPD
25-1892-801		1892	Tripled-Die Reverse
25-1892O-101	007.8	1892-O	Doubled-Die Obverse; IN GOD WE TRUST
25-1892O-301	007.9	1892-O	RPD; very strong south
25-1892o-901		1892-O, Covered E Reverse	Clashed Dies, visible in Liberty's profile
25-1899-901		1899	DDR, visible on DOLLAR, arrows, claws
25-1892S-501		1892-S	RPM; S/S northwest
25-1902O-301		1902-O	MPD; digit evident in denticles below O of date
25-1907D-301		1907-D	Doubled-Die Obverse, RPD
25-1907S-501		1907-S	RPM; S/S southeast
25-1908D-301		1908-D	MPD; 8 in denticles between 0 and 8 (likely an O)
25-1914D-101	007.99	1914-D	Doubled-Die Obverse
25-1916D-501	008	1916-D	D/D, RPM

STANDING LIBERTY QUARTERS

FS#	Old FS#	Date/Mint	Brief Description
25-1917D-801		1917-D, Type 1	DDR (motto); CONECA DDR-001;
25-1918S-101	008.5	1918-S	Overdate Doubled-Die obverse; 1918/7-S
25-1920-401		1920	Double Clashed Obv. Die; inverted doubled E visible in drapery
25-1920S-401		1920-S	Clashed Obv. Die; inverted doubled E visible in drapery
25-1928S-501		1928-S	Inverted S mintmark
25-1928S-502		1928-S	Repunched mintmark
25-1929S-401		1929-S	Very interesting and bold die clash
25-1930S-501		1930-S	Interesting mintmark; likely a small S over large S

WASHINGTON QUARTERS

FS#	Old FS#	Date/Mint	Brief Description
25-1932-101		1932	DDO; doubled earlobe
25-1934-101	009	1934	DDO, 1-O-I
25-1934-401		1934	Light Motto

FS#	Old FS#	Date/Mint	Brief Description
25-1934-402		1934	Medium Motto (common)
25-1934-403		1934	Large Motto (common)
25-1934D-501	009.5	1934-D	Small D; D of 1932
25-1935-101	010	1935	DDO, 1-O-II+V
25-1936-101	011	1936	DDO, 1-O-I
25-1937-101	012	1937	DDO, 1-O-IV
25-1939D-501	012.3	1939-D	D/S (D over S mintmark)
25-1939S-101		1939-S	DDO
25-1940D-101	012.5	1940-D	DDO, 1-O-III
25-1940D-501	012.4	1940-D	RPM; D wide left of primary D
25-1941-101	012.7	1941	Doubled-Die Obverse
25-1941-102	012.9	1941	Doubled-Die Obverse
25-1941-103		1941	DDO, on date and IGWT; CONECA DDO-004
25-1941-801	013	1941	TDR, 4-R-III+V
25-1941D-101		1941-D	DDO, on date and IGWT; Breen 4309; CONECA DDO-001
25-1941D-801		1941-D	1-R-V; strong on OF AMERICA, weak QUARTER DOLLAR
25-1941S-501		1941-S	Large mintmark; Trumpet Tail style
25-1941S-502		1941-S	S/S, far north; small style mintmark
25-1942-101		1942	Doubled-Die Obverse
25-1942-801	014	1942	Doubled-Die Reverse
25-1942-802	014.3	1942	Doubled-Die Reverse
25-1942-803		1942	Doubled-Die Reverse
25-1942D-101	015	1942-D	Doubled-Die Obverse
25-1942D-801	016	1942-D	Doubled-Die Reverse
25-1943-101	016.5	1943	DDO; strong on motto, weaker on LIB and date
25-1943-102		1943	DDO; strong on LIBERTY, weaker on motto and date
25-1943-103	016.7	1943	DDO; strong on motto, weaker on LIB and date
25-1943D-101		1943-D	DDO; eye, hair curls, initials, lip, chin
25-1943S-101	017	1943-S	Doubled-Die Obverse
25-1943S-401		1943-S	Die Deformation at Washington's throat; "Goiter" variety
25-1943S-501	017.3	1943-S	Trumpet Tail S
25-1943S-502		1943-S	Slightly smaller and slightly different S (Large S is common)
25-1943S-503		1943-S	South, with filled upper loop of primary mintmark
25-1943S-504		1943-S	Knob evident south of primary mintmark
25-1944-101		1944	DDO; light spread on IGWT and minor on date and LIB
25-1944D-101		1944-D	Doubled-Die Obverse– most evident on LIBERTY
25-1944S-101	017.5	1944-S	Doubled-Die Obverse
25-1945-101	018	1945	Doubled-Die Obverse
25-1945S-101		1945-S	Doubled-Die Obverse; IGWT, date, and TY of LIBERTY
25-1945S-102		1945-S	Doubled-Die Obverse; thick on IGWT, Liberty

FS#	Old FS#	Date/Mint	Brief Description
25-1946-101		1946	Doubled-Die Obverse; IGWT, date, and slightly on LIBERTY
25-1946-801		1946	DDR and DDO; UNITED STATES OF AMERICA, EPU, slightly on QD
25-1946D-501		1946-D	Secondary mintmark weak but evident north of the primary
25-1946S-501		1946-S	S/S north, RPM
25-1947-101		1947	Doubled-Die Obverse; LIBERTY only
25-1947S-501		1947-S	S/S west, RPM
25-1947S-502		1947-S	S/S south
25-1948S-501	018.4	1948-S	S/S/S/S, N and N and very wide northeast
25-1949D-501		1949-D	D/D/D–One D north, another horizontal west
25-1949D-601		1949-D	Possible D/S; several dies reported; only this appears to be D/S
25-1950-801	019	1950	Doubled-Die Reverse; eagle's beak, wings, etc.
25-1950D-801	020	1950-D	Doubled-Die Reverse; talons, feathers, and arrow tips
25-1950D-802		1950-D	DDR; extra thickness on all lettering, especially QUARTER DOLLAR
25-1950D-502		1950-D	D/D, RPM
25-1950D-601	021	1950-D	D/S, OMM
25-1950S-501		1950-S	S/S, north, RPM
25-1950S-601	022	1950-S	S/D, OMM
25-1950S-801		1950-S	Joe Miller
25-1951D-101		1951-D	DDO; nice on LIBERTY, okay on IGWT, weak on date
25-1951D-501		1951-D	RPM; CONECA RPM-004
25-1952-901		1952 PF	"Superbird"; unusual S evident on breast of eagle
25-1952-902		1952 PF	"Superbird," plus recut tail feathers and DDO
25-1952D-101		1952-D	DDO, Class I; nice on all obverse lettering
25-1952D-501		1952-D	Huge D mintmark
25-1952S-501		1952-S	S/S/S, serifs and far north
25-1952S-502		1952-S	S/S, north
25-1953-101		1953 PF	All obverse lettering and date
25-1953-901		1953 PF	Recut tail feathers
25-1953D-801	022.2	1953-D	All reverse lettering, strongest USA and E PLURIBUS UNUM
25-1953D-501		1953-D	Inverted D over D
25-1953D-601		1953-D	OMM, D/S (actually D/D/D/S/S)
25-1956-701		1956 PF	Unusual reverse die gouges
25-1956-701		1956	Reverse die gouge
25-1956-901		1956	Type B reverse on circ strike; intended for Proofs; rare
25-1956D-501		1956-D	D over inverted D mintmark
25-1957-901		1957	Type B reverse on circ strike; intended for Proofs; rare

FS#	Old FS#	Date/Mint	Brief Description
25-1957D-501		1957-D	RPM (Master Die); separate D above olive branch
25-1957D-901		1957-D	Recut tail feathers
25-1958-901		1958	Type B reverse on circ strike; intended for Proofs; rare
25-1959-101	022.45	1959 PF	DDO Strong on IGWT, weaker on other elements
25-1959-901		1959	Type B reverse on circ strike; intended for Proofs; rare
25-1959D-501		1959-D	D/D mintmark, interesting as secondary mintmark tilted slightly
25-1960-801	022.5	1960 PF	DDR all reverse elements; small/large design
25-1960-901		1960	Type B reverse on circ strike; intended for Proofs; rare
25-1961-101		1961 PF	IGWT, LIBERTY, date, queue; PUP is IGWT
25-1961-901		1961	Type B reverse on circ strike; intended for Proofs; rare
25-1961D-501		1961-D	RPM, D/D northeast; secondary is wide northeast
25-1961D-502		1961-D	D/D north
25-1962-101		1962 PF	Strong on all obverse lettering, similar to class VI
25-1962-901		1962	Type B reverse on circ strike; intended for Proofs; rare
25-1962D-501		1962-D	Unl RPM D/D strong north, 1/2 letter height
25-1963-101	023	1963	Date, motto, and LIBERTY
25-1963-102		1963	Obverse like 101; reverse on all rim lettering
25-1963-103		1963	Only on 63 of date; strongest on 6
25-1963-801		1963	Doubling evident on C and M of AMERICA, first T of STATES
25-1963-802		1963 PF	Doubling on all reverse lettering, strong spread on AMERICA
25-1963-901		1963	Type B reverse on circ strike; intended for Proofs; rare
25-1963D-101		1963-D	DDO 4-O-II+V; all lettering and date, weakest on IGWT
25-1964-101		1964	DDO evident on IN GOD WE TRUST; similar to 63 die 1
25-1964-801		1964	DDR all reverse lettering
25-1964-802	024.5	1964	Evident on QUARTER DOLLAR
25-1964-803		1964	Doubling strongest on STATES OF AMERICA
25-1964-804		1964	DDR evident on UNITED with light doubling
25-1964-901		1964	Type B reverse on circ strike; intended for Proofs; rare
25-1964-902		1964	Type C reverse
25-1964D-101		1964-D	Doubling most evident on IN GOD WE TRUST
25-1964D-501		1964-D	D/D east; 1/2 letter width
25-1964D-502		1964-D	D and second D far north protruding from branch

FS#	Old FS#	Date/Mint	Brief Description
25-1964D-801	025	1964-D	Evident on STATES OF AMERICA, QUARTER DOLLAR
25-1964D-901		1964-D	Type B reverse on circ strike; intended for Proofs; *rare*
25-1964D-902		1964-D	Type C reverse; intended for production beginning in 1965
25-1965-101	026	1965	DDO, very strong, evident on all obverse lettering
25-1965-102		1965	Doubled-Die Obverse; very strong on LIBERTY
25-1965-801		1965	Doubled-Die Reverse; primarily on QUARTER DOLLAR
25-1966-801	026.3	1966	DDR; very rare and very strong on all lettering
25-1967-101	026.5	1967 SMS	Doubled-Die Obverse; evident on all obverse lettering
25-1967-801		1967 SMS	DDR; light on lower branches, leaves, QUARTER DOLLAR
25-1968D-801		1968-D	Doubled-Die Reverse; very strong on all reverse lettering
25-1968S-101		1968-S PF	DDO; evident on all lettering, 1/2 letter width
25-1968S-501		1968-S PF	S/S, north
25-1968S-801	027	1968-S PF	Doubled-Die Reverse; very strong on all lettering
25-1969D-501	027.06	1969-D	D/D slanted west; found in Mint Sets
25-1969D-502		1969-D	D/D slightly west
25-1969S-101	027.08	1969-S PF	Doubled-Die Obverse; very strong on all lettering and date
25-1969S-501	027.1	1969-S PF	Repunched mintmark; S/S/S north and south
25-1970D-101	027.3	1970-D	DDO; evident on all lettering, weaker on LIBERTY
25-1970D-102		1970-D	DDO; evident most on LIBERTY, slightly on date and IGWT
25-1970D-801		1970-D	DDR; evident on all reverse lettering; *strong*
25-1970D-802		1970-D	Doubled-Die Reverse; evident on all reverse lettering
25-1971-801	027.7	1971	Doubled-Die Reverse; very strong on all reverse lettering
25-1971D-801	027.8	1971-D	DDR; very strong on UNITED STATES OF AMERICA
25-1976D-101	028	1976-D	DDO; most on LIBERTY, and in EDS on motto and date
25-1976D-102		1976-D	DDO, 2-0-V CCW; evident on LIBERTY only
25-1979S-501		1979-S PF	Type II mintmark
25-1981S-501		1981-S PF	Type II mintmark
25-1982S-101		1982-S PF	DDO; IGWT, date, and slightly on LIBERTY
25-1989D-501		1989-D	D/D, west
25-1990S-101		1990-S PF	Slight doubling on date and mintmark
25-1995S-101		1995-S PF	DDO on date, mintmark, ribbon, hair, west on LIBERTY and IGWT

FS#	Old FS#	Date/Mint	Brief Description
25-1996P-701		1996-P	Strange; die abraded through bust (must see photos)
25-2004D-5901		2004-D WI	Wisconsin quarter, Extra Leaf High (lines pointing up)
25-2004D-5902		2004-D WI	Wisconsin quarter, Extra Leaf Low (lines pointing down)
25-2005P-MN-801		2005-P, CONECA MN	DDR (right of 4th tree); DDR-001; PCGS-144227
25-2005P-MN-802		2005-P, CONECA MN	DDR (right of 4th tree); DDR-002; PCGS-144228
25-2005P-MN-803		2005-P, CONECA MN	DDR (right of 4th tree); DDR-004; PCGS-144419
25-2005P-MN-804		2005-P, MN	DDR (left of 4th tree); CONECA DDR-006; PCGS-144232
25-2005P-MN-805		2005-P, CONECA MN	DDR (right of 4th tree); DDR-007; PCGS-144223
25-2005P-MN-806		2005-P, CONECA MN	DDR (right of 4th tree); DDR-008; PCGS-144234
25-2005P-MN-807		2005-P, CONECA MN	DDR (right of 4th tree); DDR-012; PCGS-144230
25-2005D-MN-801		2005-D, MN	DDR (left of 4th tree); CONECA DDR-001; PCGS-144220
25-2005D-MN-802		2005-D, MN	DDR (left of 4th tree); CONECA DDR-003; PCGS-144221
S25-2005S-KS-901		2005-S, KS, PF, 90% Silver	Large Die Dent Reverse (on bison's hindquarter)
25-2005P-OR-801		2005-P, OR	DDR (tallest tree, right side of coin); CONECA DDR-001
25-2005P-OR-802		2005-P, OR	DDR (two trees on right side of coin); CONECA DDR-002
25-2007P-WY-801		2007-P, WY	DDR (saddle horn); CONECA DDR-018
25-2007P-WY-802		2007-P, WY	DDR (saddle horn)
25-2007P-WY-803		2007-P, WY	DDR (saddle horn)
25-2009D-DC-801		2009-D, DC	DDR (ELL of ELLINGTON); CONECA DDR-001
25-2009P-DC-801		2009-P, DC	DDR (piano keys); CONECA DDR-012
25-2009P-DC-802		2009-P, DC	DDR (piano key below ELL); CONECA DDR-004

BUST HALF DOLLARS

FS#	Old FS#	Date/Mint	Brief Description
50-1806-301		1806	6 punched over an inverted 6
50-1806-901		1806	STATES/STATAS; an A is evident under the E of STATES
50-1808-301		1808	1808/7 repunched date
50-1812-101		1812	Doubled LIBERTY
50-1812-901		1812	Reverse die clashed; BER of LIBERTY evident
50-1829-301		1829	Curled base 2 of date over a flat based 2

FS#	Old FS#	Date/Mint	Brief Description
LIBERTY SEATED HALF DOLLARS			
50-1840-301		1840	Repunched Date; 4 and 0 of date repunched south; Reverse of '39
50-1840-302		1840	1 and 8 repunched west, 4 and 0 repunched north; small letters
50-1840-401		1840, Rev. of '39	Die Crack, Open Claw (on branch)
50-1842-301		1842 SD	Repunched Date; 8 42 repunched south
50-1842-801	000.5	1842 SD	UNITED STATES OF AMERICA and eagle doubled
50-18430-301		1843-O	1, 8, and 4 repunched south; 3 repunched north
50-18440-301	001	1844-O	RPD; secondary digits repunched north into rock
50-18450-301	001.5	1845-O	Very strong RPD east; lower secondary 5 very evident
50-18450-302	002	1845-O	Strong RPD; tripled digits, secondary images south
50-18450-303		1845-O	Nice RPD; secondary images west
50-18450-501	002.5	1845-O	RPM O punched over a previously punched horizontal O
50-1846-301	003	1846	6 of date punched correctly over a horizontal 6
50-1847-101		1847	DDO; evident on the shield and LIBERTY
50-1847-301	004	1847	1847/6 overdate
50-1849-301	004.5	1849	RPD; secondary image of lower part of four digits evident west
50-1853-401		1853	Very strong clashed obv die; rays of reverse evident at rock
50-1853-801	004.7	1853	DDR; very strong on UNITED, lighter on HALF
50-1853-802		1853	DDR; best on HALF DOL, AMERICA, and arrows
50-1853-803		1853	DDR; STATES
50-1855-301	005	1855	1855/4 overdate
50-18550-501	006	1855-O	O Over Horizontal O mintmark
50-18560-301		1856-O	RPD; 1 secondary south, 5 and 6 secondary north
50-1858-101		1858	DDO; evident on drapery, skirt, foot, and rock
50-1858-301		1858	RPD; very unusual RPD, right of first 8 and 5
50-1858-302		1858	Misplaced date; 8 protruding from skirt above first 8
50-18580-301		1858-O	MPD; 8 protruding from rock above of second 8
50-18580-901		1858-O	Unusual die clash of reverse; leg of eagle
50-18590-301		1859-O	RPD; 1 secondary image south, and 9 secondary image north
50-19610-401	007	1861-O	Die crack on obverse; Confederate obverse die
50-1865-301		1865	RPD; 1 has secondary image north, 5 has secondary image south

FS#	Old FS#	Date/Mint	Brief Description
50-1866-301		1866	MPD; 6 (possibly two 6's) in rock above last 6
50-1866-302	007.01	1866	MPD; 6 in denticles after last 6
50-1867-801		1867	DDR; evident on motto, beak, eye, and wings
LIBERTY SEATED HALF DOLLARS–ARROWS AT DATE			
50-1873-101	007.1	1873	DDO; evident on shield, gown, foot, scroll, and lower stars
50-1873-301		1873	MPD; digit is evident in denticles below arrows
50-1876-301	007.4	1876	RPD; Large/Small Date; small date is likely that of a 20c punch
50-1876-302		1876	RPD; two secondary digits (likely 6) evident west of 7 and 6
50-1876-303	007.3	1876	MPD; a digit is evident in denticles below 7; not WB 103
50-1876-304		1876	Two digits evident in denticles below 8
50-1876-401		1876 PF	Very unusual variety; top of letter C (matching mintmark style) evident punched in Liberty's neck
50-1877-301	007.5	1877	1877/6; 6 is evident on high surface of 7
BARBER HALF DOLLARS			
50-1892-301	007.7	1892	RPD; very strong with secondary date south
50-1892-801	007.8	1892	DDR; all lettering, arrows, EPU, ribbon, leaves, stars
50-18920-501	007.9	1892	Micro O mintmark; believed to have been a quarter dollar punch
50-1893-801		1893	TDR (lettering on rim, esp. HALF); CONECA DDR-001
50-1909S-501		1909-S	Inverted S mintmark
50-1911S-501		1911-S	RPM; very strong with secondary image west of primary
LIBERTY WALKING HALF DOLLARS			
50-1916D-501	008	1916-D	RPM; D/D strong southwest, C–RPM
50-1936-101	008.4	1936	DDO; very strong at date; tail of 9 and 3 totally separated
50-1936-102		1936	DDO; evident at date, IGWT, shoe, skirt, rays; C-1-O-II
50-1936D-101		1936-D	DDO; evident on date, shoe, skirt, ground; C-1-O-II
50-1936S-101		1936-S	DDO; evident on date, shoe, skirt, ground; C-1-O-II
50-1939D-101	008.45	1939-D	DDO; evident on date, IGWT, shoe, skirt
50-1939D-501		1939-D	RPM; D/D north; CONECA RPM 1
50-1941D-501		1941-D	RPM; D/D northwest; CONECA RPM 1
50-1941S-501		1941-S	RPM; S/S southwest; listed by Fox as S/Horizontal S

FS#	Old FS#	Date/Mint	Brief Description
50-1942-101	009	1942	DDO; evident on breast (master die DDO)
50-1942-801	008.5	1942	DDR; evident on AMERICA, HALF DOLLAR, feathers
50-1942D-101		1942-D	DDO; evident on breast (master die DDO)
50-1942D-501	010	1942-D	Formerly believed to be D/S OMM; it is not!
50-1942S-101		1942-S	DDO; evident on breast (master die DDO)
50-1943-101	010.5	1943	DDO; date, IGWT, LIBERTY, skirt, etc.
50-1943D-101	010.5	1943-D	DDO; date, IGWT, LIBERTY, skirt, etc.
50-1943D-501		1943-D	Reported as a D/S; same die as for the 1942-D; *not* D/S!
50-1943S-101	010.5	1943-S	DDO; date, IGWT, LIBERTY, skirt, etc.
50-1944D-901		1944-D	Hand-engraved designer's initials
50-1944S-501	010.6	1944-S	RPM; S/S north
50-1944S-502	010.7	1944-S	RPM; S/S southwest
50-1944S-511		1944-S	Possible inverted S mintmark
50-1945-901		1945	No designer's initials
50-1946-101		1946	DDO; evident on breast, robe, IGWT
50-1946-801	011.1	1946	DDR; evident on E PLURIBUS UNUM, branches, feathers; C-1-R-III

FRANKLIN HALF DOLLARS

FS#	Old FS#	Date/Mint	Brief Description
50-1948-801		1948	DDR; EPU, HALF DOLLAR, AMERICA, clapper
50-1948D-801		1948-D	DDR; EPU, HALF DOLLAR, AMERICA, clapper
50-1949S-501	011.3	1949-S	S/S south; C-RPM (incorrectly listed in *CPG* #3 as 001.3)
50-1950-101		1950 PF	DDO; date, LIBERTY, IN GOD WE TRUST
50-1950D-501		1950-D	RPM (Possible OMM, secondary S or D); CONECA RPM-001
50-1951-801		1951 PF	DDR (PASS AND STOW, feathers, etc.); CONECA DDR-010
50-1951S-501		1951-S	RPM; CONECA RPM-001
50-1951S-801	011.5	1951-S	DDR; primarily evident on E PLURIBUS UNUM
50-1952-402		1952	Die Cracks, seen on face and lapel
50-1952S-501		1952-S	RPM (very strong); CONECA RPM-001
50-1953S-501		1953-S	S/S, northwest
50-1954-101		1954 PF	DDO; evident on date, IN GOD WE TRUST, LIBERTY
50-1955-401		1955	Clashed obverse die; "Bugs Bunny"
50-1956-101		1956 PF	DDO; most evident on date, IN GOD WE TRUST
50-1956-801		1956 PF	DDR; evident extra thickness all lettering, spread on EPU

FS#	Old FS#	Date/Mint	Brief Description
50-1956-802		1956 PF	TY II/TY I DDR; doubled eagle
50-1956-901		1956 PF	Type 1 Rev. (low-relief eagle); CONECA RDV-001
50-1957-801		1957 PF	DDR; US of A, H D (all), EPU, eagle, right of bell; class II and VI
50-1957D-501		1957-D	D/D; rotated counter-clockwise
50-1959-402		1959	Die Break, seen at throat; "Goiter" variety
50-1959-801		1959	DDR; evident on EPU west (nice separation) and on eagle
50-1960-101	012	1960 PF	DDO; evident on date, TRUST, and LIBERTY
50-1961-801	013	1961 PF	DDR; very strong on EPU, UNITED, and HALF
50-1961-802		1961 PF	DDR; evident on all outer lettering, EPU, eagle's tail feathers
50-1961-803		1961 PF	DDR; evident on all outer lettering, eagle, EPU
50-1962-101		1962 PF	DDO; evident on 2 of date and lightly on lettering
50-1962-901		1962 PF	Possible Misplaced Mintmark, apparent D s'west of STOW
50-1963-801		1963	DDR (on EPU); CONECA DDR-001

KENNEDY HALF DOLLARS

FS#	Old FS#	Date/Mint	Brief Description
50-1964-101	013.2	1964 PF	DDO; evident on WE TRUST, RTY, date
50-1964-102		1964	DDO; strong on WE TRUST, LIBERTY and date
50-1964-103		1964 PF	DDO; medium on IGWT, LIBERTY, date, and hair
50-1964-104		1964 PF, Nml Hair	DDO (on IGWT, date, etc.); CONECA DDO-021
50-1964-105		1964 PF, Nml Hair	QDO (on WE TRUST); CONECA DDO-035
50-1964-401		1964 PF	Accented Hair variety
50-1964-402		1964 PF	Normal Hair variety (normal type; very common)
50-1964-801		1964	DDR; evident on UNITED STATES OF AMERICA, stars, ribbon, EPU
50-1964-802		1964 PF, Acc Hair	QDR (stars, FG); CONECA DDR-003
50-1964D-101	013.4	1964-D	DDO; evident on IGWT, LIBERTY, initials, hair
50-1964D-102			Reserved for future listing
50-1964D-103	013.5	1964-D	TDO; evident on IGWT, RTY, and date, tripled on WE TRUST
50-1964D-104		1964-D	DDO; evident on IN GOD, LI, and 19
50-1964D-105	013.6	1964-D	TDO; evident on IGWT, TY hair, tripled on WE TRUST
50-1964D-106		1964-D	DDO; evident on WE TRUST, TY and hair

FS#	Old FS#	Date/Mint	Brief Description
50-1964D-107			Reserved for future listing
50-1964D-108		1964-D	TDO; evident on IGWT, date, initials, RTY
50-1964D-501		1964-D	RPM; D/D south
50-1964D-502		1964-D	RPM; D/D north
50-1964D-503		1964-D	RPM; D/D northeast
50-1964D-504		1964-D	RPM (D / D / horiz. D); CONECA N/L
50-1965-801		1965 (BS)	DDR; moderate doubling on all outer lettering, stars
50-1965-802		1965	DDR (stars, EPU); CONECA DDR-004
50-1966-101	013.8	1966 (BS)	DDO; evident on IN GOD WE TRUST, profile, date
50-1966-102		1966 SMS	DDO; evident on IN GOD WE TRUST, profile, eye
50-1966-103		1966 SMS	DDO, on IGWT, LIBERTY, profile, tripling on WE TRUST
50-1966-104		1966 SMS	DDO; on IN GOD WE TRUST, LIBERTY, date, profile
50-1966-105		1966, SMS	DDO (profile, ear); CONECA DDO-007
50-1966-106		1966, SMS	TDO (profile, ear); CONECA DDO-020
50-1966-901		1966 SMS	No designer's initials
50-1967-101		1967 SMS	DDO; actually quintupled; evident IGWT, LIBERTY, date
50-1967-102		1967	DDO; evident on IN GOD WE TRUST, LIBERTY, date
50-1967-103		1967	DDO (very strong on GOD, LIB); CONECA DDO-001
50-1967-801		1967	DDR; all reverse lettering, stars, rays; minor DDO
50-1968D-101		1968-D	Tripled-Die Obverse; evident on IGWT, date, and LIBERTY
50-1968S-101	014	1968-S PF	DDO; evident on IN GOD WE TRUST, LIBERTY, date
50-1968S-511		1968-S PF	Inverted S mintmark
50-1968S-801		1968-S PF	Doubled-Die Reverse; all reverse lettering and element
50-1970S-101		1970-S PF	Doubled-Die Obverse; all obverse lettering
50-1970S-102		1970-S PF	DDO (strongest on TRUST); CONECA DDO-002
50-1971D-101	014.3	1971-D	DDO; evident on LIBERTY, 71, GOD WE TRUST
50-1971D-102		1971-D	DDO; all obverse lettering, best on IGWT; very evident on hair
50-1971S-101		1971-S PF	Doubled-Die Obverse; WE TRUST and date
50-1971S-102	014.5	1971-S PF	DDO; all lettering, date, and upper hair
50-1971S-103		1971-S PF	DDO (strongest on TRUST); CONECA DDO-008
50-1971S-801		1971-S PF	Doubled-Die Reverse; all reverse lettering, stars
50-1972-101		1972	DDO; IN GOD WE TRUST, Y of LIBERTY, and date
50-1972D-901		1972-D	Missing designer's initials

FS#	Old FS#	Date/Mint	Brief Description
50-1973D-101	014.8	1973-D	Doubled-Die Obverse; all lettering, date, and hair
50-1974D-101	015	1974-D	DDO; all letters and date, but mostly on WE TRUST
50-1976S-101	016	1976-S	DDO; light spread on WE TRUST; Unc 40% silver
50-1976S-801		1976-S PF Clad	DDR (designer's initials); CONECA DDR-001
50-1977D-101		1977-D	Doubled-Die Obverse; primarily evident on WE TRUST
50-1979S-501		1979-S PF	Type II mintmark
50-1981S-501		1981-S PF	Type II mintmark
50-1988S-101		1988-S PF	Silver Proof; most lettering, best on WE TRUST, date, and mintmark
50-1992S-101		1992-S PF	Silver Proof; most lettering, best on WE TRUST, date, and mintmark

LIBERTY SEATED DOLLARS

FS#	Old FS#	Date/Mint	Brief Description
S1-1865-801		1865	DDR; relatively minor; doubled U of UNITED
S1-1868-301		1868	MPD; top of 6 or 8 evident in denticles below 6
S1-1869-301		1869	RPD; 1 is doubled south of primary 1
S1-1869-302		1869	RPD; base of second 1 is mid-way up between the 1 and 8
S1-1869-303		1869	MPD; top of a 6 or 9 evident in denticles below 6
S1-1871-301		1871	MPD; top of an 8 evident in denticles below the primary 8

TRADE DOLLARS

FS#	Old FS#	Date/Mint	Brief Description
T1-1873CC-301	012.3	1873-CC	MPD; top of digit in denticles below between 8 and 7
T1-1873CC-302		1873-CC	MPD; top of digits (an 8 and 7) in denticles below 8 and 7
T1-1875S-501	012.5	1875-S	OMM S/CC; CC mintmark weak, but visible
T1-1875S-502		1875-S	Similar to above; from NGC, Heritage auction 4-25-02
T1-1876-301		1876	RPD; secondary 6 evident within loop of 6
T1-1876CC-801	014	1876-CC	DDR; all reverse elements, especially branch, talons, wing
T1-1876S-101	013	1876-S	DDO; evident on all obverse elements
T1-1877-101		1877	DDO; evident on LIBERTY and wheat fons
T1-1877S-301		1877-S	RPD; final 7 is repunched with 2nd number south of primary
T1-1877S-801	014.5	1877-S	DDR; E PLURIBUS UNUM, ribbon, US of A and top of eagle
T1-1877S-802		1877-S	DDR; lower reverse elements, TRADE DOLLAR, 420 GRAINS
T1-1878S-801	015	1878-S	DDR; evident on all reverse elements; very strong
T1-1878S-802		1878-S	DDR; evident on UNITED STATES and EPU; not dramatic

FS#	Old FS#	Date/Mint	Brief Description
MORGAN DOLLARS			
S1-1878-005		1878 8TF	VAM 5; DDU
S1-1878-009		1878 8TF	VAM 9; first die pairing
S1-1878-014.11		1878 8TF	VAM 14.11
S1-1878-015		1878 8TF	VAM 15; DDO; doubled LIBERTY
S1-1878-032		1878 7/8	VAM 32; DDR; doubled tail feathers
S1-1878-044	001	1878 7/8	VAM 44; TDO/DDR
S1-1878-115		1878 7TF	VAM 115/199.1; tripled leaves
S1-1878-145		1878 7TF	VAM 145/162; broken M
S1-1878-162		1878 7TF	VAM 162; bottom serifs on N and M of UNUM broken, R of TRUST
S1-1878-166		1878 7TF	VAM 166; spiked P
S1-1878-168		1878 7TF	VAM 168; broken R of TRUST
S1-1878-188		1878 7TF	VAM 188; over-polished L
S1-1878-220		1878 7TF	VAM 220; tripled R of PLURIBUS
S1-1878-901		1878 7TF	Various; Reverse of 1878, flat breast, parallel arrow feathers
S1-1878-902		1878 7TF	Various; Reverse of 1879, round breast, slanted feathers
S1-1878CC-006		1878-CC	DDO; headdress and ear; reverse wide, level CC
S1-1878CC-018		1878-CC	DDO; headdress and ear; reverse close, uneven CC
S1-1878S-050		1878-S	Tripled-Die Obverse; tripled eyelid
S1-18790-004		1879-0	RPM; 0/0/0 (formerly O Over Horizontal O)
S1-18790-028		1879-0	RPM; 0/0/0 (formerly O Over Horizontal O)
S1-1879S-301		1879-S	Reverse of '78; several VAM listings
S1-1880-006		1880	80/79 overdate; "spikes"
S1-1880-007		1880	80/79 overdate; "crossbar"
S1-1880-008		1880	80/79 overdate; "ears"
S1-1880-023		1880	80/79 overdate
S1-1880CC-004		1880-CC	Overdate
S1-1880CC-005		1880-CC	Overdate
S1-1880CC-006		1880-CC	Overdate
S1-1880CC-007		1880-CC	Overdate; Reverse of '78
S1-18800-004		1880-0	Overdate
S1-18800-005		1880-0	Overdate
S1-18800-048		1880-0	"Hangnail" (was VAM 1a)
S1-18800-016		1880-0	Checkmark
S1-18800-017		1880-0	Checkmark
S1-18800-021		1880-0	Checkmark
S1-18810-005		1881-0	0/0; RPM
S1-18810-027		1881-0	DDO
S1-18820-003		1882-0	OMM; O/S; early die state
S1-18820-003		1882-0	OMM; O/S; late die state
		1882-0	OMM; O/S; recused; early die state
S1-18820-004		1882-0	OMM; O/S; recused; late die state

FS#	Old FS#	Date/Mint	Brief Description
		1882-0	OMM; O/S; broken S; early die state
S1-18820-005		1882-0	OMM; O/S; broken S; late die state
S1-1883-010		1883	DDO
S1-1884-003		1884	Dot
S1-1884-004		1884	Dot
S1-1884-005		1884	DDO
S1-1885-008		1885	Dash variety
S1-1885CC-004		1885-CC	Dash variety
S1-1886-001C		1886	Clashed die
S1-1886-020		1886	RPD
S1-18860-001A		1886-0	Clashed E reverse; clashed die
S1-1887-001B		1887	Clashed E reverse
S1-1887-002		1887	Overdate 7/6
S1-1887-012		1887	DDO (front of eye); "Alligator Eye" variety; VAM 12, VAM 12A
S1-18870-002		1887-0	RPD
S1-18870-003		1887-0	Overdate 7/6
S1-18870-030		1887-0	Clashed dies
S1-18880-001A		1888-0	Clashed E reverse
S1-18880-001B		1888-0	Die break
S1-18880-004		1888-0	DDO; "Hot Lips"
S1-18880-015		1888-0	DDR/RPM
S1-18880-301		1888-0	Oval O
S1-1889-019		1889	Die break
S1-1889-022a		1889	Die break
S1-1889-023a		1889	Clashed die
S1-18890-001a		1889-0	Clashed E reverse
S1-18890-002		1889-0	VAM 2 (?); oval O; various VAMs
S1-18890-017		1889-0	Oval O; included above?
S1-1890CC-004		1890-CC	Tailbar
S1-18900-010		1890-0	Die gouges
S1-18900-020		1890-0	DDO
S1-1891CC-003		1891-CC	Die Gouge (near eagle's beak); "Spitting Eagle" variety; VAM 3
S1-18910-001a		1891-0	Clashed E reverse
S1-18910-001b		1891-0	Pitted Die
S1-1895S-003		1895-S	RPM; S/S
S1-1895S-004		1895-S	RPM; S/S
S1-1896-020		1896	RPD; formerly listed as VAM 1a
S1-18960-004		1896-0	Micro O
S1-18960-019		1896-0	RPD
S1-18960		1896-0	Formerly listed as VAM 1A
S1-18980-501		1898-0	RPD
S1-18990-004		1899-0	Small O
S1-1900-011		1900	DDR
S1-1900-016		1900	C4/C3 reverse
S1-19000-005		1900-0	Small O
S1-19000-301		1900-0	O/CC
S1-19000-029a		1900-0	Die break
S1-1901-003		1901	DDR
S1-1902-004		1902	DDO
S1-19020-003		1902-0	Small O

FIVAZ-STANTON NUMBERS CROSS-REFERENCE CHART

FS#	Old FS#	Date/Mint	Brief Description
S1-1903S-002	1903-S	Small S	
S1-1921-301	1921	Wide reeding	
S1-1921D-001a	1921-D	Over-polished	
S1-1921D-001x	1921-D	Double cud	
S1-1921S-001a	1921-S	Die scratch	
S1-1921S-001b	1921-S	Die gouges	
S1-1921S-001b7	1921-S	Die Gouges; "Thornhead" variety; VAM 1B7	

PEACE DOLLARS

FS#	Old FS#	Date/Mint	Brief Description
S1-1921-1003	1921	DDR; line through R	
S1-1922-001f	1922	Field break	
S1-1922-002a	1922	Earring	
S1-1922-002c	1922	Extra hair	
S1-1922-005a	1922	Scarcheek	
S1-1922-012a	1922	Moustache	
S1-1922-401	1922	High Relief; design type of 1921	
S1-1923-001a	1923	Whisker Jaw	
S1-1923-001b1	1923	Extra Hair	
S1-1923-001b2	1923	Extra Hair	
S1-1923-001c	1923	Tail on O	
S1-1923-001d	1923	Whisker Cheek	
S1-1923-002	1923	Double Tiara	
S1-1923S-001c	1923-S	Pitted reverse	
S1-1924-005a	1924	Broken Wing	
S1-1925-005	1925	Missing Ray	
S1-1926S-004	1926-S	Dot Variety	
S1-1927S-101	1927-S	RPM; S/S rotated CCW	
S1-1928S-003	1928-S	DDO	
S1-1934D-003	1934-D	DDO; Medium D	
S1-1934D-004	1934-D	DDO; Small D	

EISENHOWER DOLLARS

FS#	Old FS#	Date/Mint	Brief Description
C1-1971D-901		1971-D	Low-Relief Rev. (above eagle's eye); "Friendly Eagle" variety; CONECA RDV-006
C1-1971S-103	015.8	1971-S PF	Dramatic DDO on all obverse characters; clad Proof
C1-1971S-106		1971-S PF	DDO, 6-0-I; all obverse |letters and date
C1-1971S-501		1971-S PF	RPM; S/S northwest; 40% silver, Uncirc. "Blue Pack"
S1-1971S-801		1971-S PF	DDR (very strong on USA, EPU, 40% Silver denomination); CONECA DDR-005
S1-1972-901		1972, Variety II	B Reverse; CONECA RDV-002; Breen 5749
C1-1972S-101		1972-S PF	Medium tripling on |IN GOD WE TRUST, LIBERTY, date
C1-1973S-101		1973-S PF	DDO; most evident on IN GOD WE TRUST; 40% silver, Proof

SUSAN B. ANTHONY AND GOLDEN DOLLARS

FS#	Old FS#	Date/Mint	Brief Description
C1-1979P-301	016	1979-P	Near Date variety
C1-1979S-501		1979-S PF	Type II mintmark
C1-1980S-501		1980-S PF	RPM; mintmark repunched northeast of primary S
C1-1981S-501		1981-S PF	Type II mintmark

FS#	Old FS#	Date/Mint	Brief Description
C1-2000P-901		2000-P	Spikes through breast of eagle
C1-(2007)-GW-701		(2007), Washington	Missing Edge Inscription
C1-(2007)-TJ-701		(2007), Jefferson	Missing Edge Inscription
C1-(2007)-JA-701		(2007), Adams	Missing Edge Inscription
C1-(2010)-NA-701		(2010), Native Am., Satin	Missing Edge Inscription
C1-2007S-TJ-701		2007-S, Jeff PF	Out-of-Sequence Edge Inscription

GOLD DOLLARS

FS#	Old FS#	Date/Mint	Brief Description
G1-1854-101		1854 Ty 2	DDO/Clashed reverse; strong on obverse lettering, clash
G1-1854-301		1854 Ty 2	RPD on all four digits
G1-1856S-501		1856-S	RPM, S/S; wide northeast; very strong
G1-1862-101	G-001	1862	DDO; evident on UNITED STATES OF AMERICA, top of crown, beads, hair

QUARTER EAGLES

FS#	Old FS#	Date/Mint	Brief Description
G2-1851-301		1851	RPD; evident on 1, 5, and 1
G2-1853-301		1853	RPD; evident on 1 and 8
G2-18540-301		1854-O	MPD; crosslet of 4 in hair curl above 4
G2-1862-301	G-002	1862/1	Overdate, 1862/1
G2-1891-801		1891	DDR; most evident on AMERICA, arrow tips, D of 2-1/2 D

$3 GOLD

FS#	Old FS#	Date/Mint	Brief Description
G3-1882-301		1882	RPD; 1882/2

HALF EAGLES

FS#	Old FS#	Date/Mint	Brief Description
G5-1802-301		1802	1802/1; strong overdate; fairly common
G5-1819-901		1819	On reverse, 5D over 50, possibly 5D/inverted D
G5-1847-301	003	1847	MPD; top of 7 evident in denticles below 4
G5-1847-302	004	1847	MPD; 1 evident in neck of Liberty
G5-1847-303		1847	RPD; 1 and 8 evident south of primary; evident right of 7
G5-1847-304		1847	MPD; base of 1 evident in bust
G5-1848D-501		1848-D	RPM; Breen N/A; CONECA RPM-001
G5-1854-101	004.5	1854	DDO; evident on hair and ear; known as "Earring" variety
G5-1881-301	005	1881	1881/0; overdate 1881/1880
G5-1881-302		1881	Repunched date; 1881/881
G5-1881-303		1881	RPD; 1881/1881; secondary date north of primary
G5-1881-304		1881	RPD; 1881/1881; secondary date west of primary
G5-1881-305		1881	RPD; 1881/1881; secondary slightly north and west
G5-1899-301		1899	RPD; evident on 899

FS#	Old FS#	Date/Mint	Brief Description
G5-1901S-301		1901-S	Overdate; 1901/0-S
G5-1905S-501	006.5	1905-S	S and S; wide east
G5-1906-301		1906	RPD; 6/6
G5-1911S-501		1911-S	Repunched mintmark; S/S, south
G5-1911S-502		1911-S	RPM; VP-001

EAGLES

FS#	Old FS#	Date/Mint	Brief Description
G10-18460-301		1846-O	RPD and RPM; 1846/6 and O/O north
G10-1853-301	007	1853	1853/2 Overdate; evident within opening of 3
G10-1854S-301		1854-S	MPD; base of 1 evident below and between 1 and 8
G10-1883S-301		1883-S	MPD; 3 evident in denticles below primary 3
G10-1889S-501		1889-S	DDR on STATES OF AMERICA, arrows; strong RPM, S/S
G10-1891CC-501		1891-CC	RPM; secondary second C evident far right of primary
G10-1892CC-501		1892-CC	TDR, seen on IGWT; VP-001

DOUBLE EAGLES

FS#	Old FS#	Date/Mint	Brief Description
G20-1852-301		1852	RPD; all digits repunched north
G20-1853-301	G-008	1853	Overdate, 1853/2; evident with 2 inside opening of 3
G20-1857-301		1857	MPD; a digit (likely 1) evident at center right of 5
G20-1859S-101		1859-S	DDO; evident on LIBERTY, hair curl, eye, neck, and profile
G20-1865-301		1865	MPD; digits in denticles; nice
G20-1866-801		1866	DDR; dual hub; small IN over large IN of motto
G20-1866S-301		1866-S	MPD; digit evident left of primary 1 in denticles
G20-1871S-301		1871-S	MPD; digit in denticles (likely a 7); RPD (1 only)
G20-1873-101		1873	Open 3; DDO, LIBERTY
G20-1879-801		1879	DDR; most reverse lettering
G20-1883S-301		1883-S	MPD; digit evident in denticles below second 8
G20-1888-801		1888	DDR; strongest on TWENTY DOLLARS and lower ribbon
G20-1896-301		1896	RPD; all digits doubled with secondary images north
G20-1908-801		1908	DDR; evident on eagle's beak, upper lettering
G20-1909-301		1909	Overdate; 1909 over a 1908 date
G20-1909S-501		1909-S	RPM; S/S, southeast
G20-1911D-501		1911-D	RPM; D/D, east (photo from Camire)

FS#	Old FS#	Date/Mint	Brief Description
G20-1922-801		1922	DDR; evident on motto, lettering, rays, talons
G20-1925-801		1925	DDR; eagle's feathers, rays, IN GOD WE TRUST (NGC)
G20-1926-101		1926	TDO; evident on rays, date, stars, and other elements

CLASSIC COMMEMORATIVES

FS#	Old FS#	Date/Mint	Brief Description
C50-1892-301	C-000.5	1892	Columbian Expo half dollar; RPD, 2/2, north
C50-1892-302		1892	Columbian Expo half dollar; RPD, 2/2, northeast
C50-1892-303		1892	Columbian Expo half dollar; RPD, 89/89, east
C50-1893-301		1893	Columbian Expo half dollar; RPD, 3/3, north
C50-1915S-501		1915-S	Pan-Pac half dollar; RPM, S/S, east; very strong
C50-1915S-502		1915-S	Pan-Pac half dollar; RPM; CONECA RPM-001
C50-1920-901		1920	Pilgrim half dollar; Die Crack/Break, between masts
C50-1925-101	C-001	1925	Stone Mountain half dollar; DDO, 1-O-III
C50-1925-102		1925	Vancouver half dollar; DDO
C50-1933D-101		1933-D	Oregon Trail half dollar; TDO
C50-1935-101		1935	Boone half dollar; DDO (possibly a master die DDO)
C50-1936D-101		1936-D	California Pacific Expo; QDO (LIBERTY), RPM
C50-1936D-501		1936-D	San Diego half dollar; RPM, D/D, south
C50-1951-801		1951	Carver/Washington half dollar; DDR (possibly a master die DDR)
C50-1953S-801		1953-S	Carver/Washington; DDR (possibly a master die DDR)

BULLION COINAGE, 1986 TO DATE

FS#	Old FS#	Date/Mint	Brief Description
SE1-2008W-901		2008-W	Silver Eagle, Burnished; Rev. of '07 (no spur on U of UNITED)
G5-1999W-401		1999-W Unc.	.10-oz.; Proof W-Mintmark Obverse
G10-1999W-401		1999-W Unc.	.25-oz.; Proof W-Mintmark Obverse
P25-2007W-901		2007-W PF	.25-oz.; FREEDOM on Shield Frosted
P50-2007W-901		2007-W PF	.50-oz.; FREEDOM on Shield Frosted
P100-2007W-901		2007-W PF	1-oz.; FREEDOM on Shield Frosted

ABOUT THE AUTHORS AND EDITOR

Bill Fivaz, a coin collector since 1950, has earned recognition as one of the country's most respected authorities on numismatic errors and die varieties. His awards include the highest recognition of the American Numismatic Association, which presented him its top honor, the Farran Zerbe Memorial Award, in 1995. He was elected to the ANA Hall of Fame in 2002.

Bill is widely known as an engaging teacher and a speaker on numismatic topics. He has written hundreds of articles on a wide array of numismatic topics, and has been a consultant to several coin-authentication services. His contributions are noted in many of today's most popular and respected hobby books, including the *Guide Book of United States Coins* (the "Red Book").

Bill Fivaz

Bill has served on the board of governors of the ANA and on the board of directors of CONECA (the Combined Organizations of Numismatic Error Collectors).

To honor his reputation as a teacher and writer, in 2010 the ANA and Whitman Publishing endowed the Bill Fivaz Young Numismatist Literary Award, for YNs aged 8 to 12.

J.T. Stanton has collected coins since 1959 and began specializing in errors and varieties in 1982. Well known as a teacher and lecturer in the die-variety field, he instructed American Numismatic Association Summer Seminar courses for 11 years and started the ANA's annual "Errors and Varieties and Modern Minting Process" class.

The ANA has recognized J.T.'s contributions to the hobby with awards including the Medal of Merit, the Glenn Smedley Memorial Award, the Outstanding Adult Supervisor Award, and two Presidential Awards.

J.T. Stanton

J.T. has taken leadership positions in the hobby community over the years. He served on the board of governors of the ANA from 1995 to 1997. His dedication to CONECA includes terms on the board of directors and as the group's president. He was elected to CONECA's Hall of Fame.

Ken Potter started collecting coins in 1959, and has been an active coin and exonumia dealer since 1973. His focus on errors and die varieties began in earnest in 1979.

Hobbyists know Ken Potter as a prolific researcher and writer whose columns and articles are regularly featured in *Coin World, Numismatic News, World Coin News, Canadian Coin News,* and numerous club publications. His work has won awards from the Numismatic Literary Guild and induction into CONECA's Hall of Fame. He

Ken Potter

is an active member of nearly a dozen hobby organizations, and has served in leadership positions in many of them, including as CONECA's longest-serving doubled-die attributor. He often speaks to coin clubs, schools, and treasure-hunting clubs on the topics of minting varieties and errors.

While Ken is a longtime contributor to the *Cherrypickers' Guide to Rare Die Varieties,* the fifth edition, volume II, marks his first effort as the book's main editor. In this position he has coordinated resources including a network of specialists from around the country, as well as contributing his own original research and photography.

CONECA
New Member Application / Renewal Form

Today's Date: _____/_____/_____

Membership Type: _____ Regular/Annual Member - $25.00
_____ Young Numismatist (under 18) - $7.50

Mailing Options: _____ U.S. bulk rate - No extra charge
_____ First Class or Outside the U.S.A. - $12.50 additional

Total: _____ Amount Due

Name: _____

Address: _____

City: _____ State: _____

Zip +4 Code: _____

Phone: _____ Email: _____

Recommended by: *The Cherrypickers' Guide*

Comments/Interests:
_____

_____

Send application and check/money order (payable to CONECA) to:

CONECA
c/o Mr. Robert Neff, Membership
321 Kingslake Drive
Debary, FL 32713

*Your membership is subject to approval by the Membership Committee and
subject to the rules and regulations set forth in the CONECA Constitution and By-Laws.*